TRUMPET STORY

TRUMPET STORY

by

BILL COLEMAN

NORTHEASTERN UNIVERSITY PRESS
BOSTON

First published in French translation 1981.

English version © 1989 by Lily Coleman

First published 1990 in English in Great Britain by
The Macmillan Press Ltd, London.

Published 1991 in English in the United States of America by
Northeastern University Press, Boston.

Typeset by Rowland Phototypesetting Ltd, England. Printed
and bound in Hong Kong using acid-free paper.

ISBN 1-55553-091-5

MANUFACTURED IN HONG KONG

96 95 94 93 92 91   5 4 3 2 1

CONTENTS

ACKNOWLEDGEMENTS

The only research to be done for this book about my life as a professional musician was to find the correct names of other musicians, many of whom I knew only by their pseudonyms. Without the help of Johnny Simmen who had contact with many of them, their real names would not have been known to readers of this autobiography, myself included. Thank you Mr. Simmen.

And to Richard Dartigues, many thanks for his relentless efforts in finding a publisher interested enough to bring my memoirs to the jazz enthusiasts and others who will read them.

Bill Coleman

DEDICATION

This book is dedicated to Lily Renée Coleman Yersin for her moral assistance when it was needed to continue until the end, and her tireless efforts of typing, translating my memoirs from English to French, and actually managing the process of the publication of this book.

Bill Coleman

PREFACE

Reading about jazz music and its performers can be a fascinating experience when somebody who has been part of the scene happens to be the author. Somebody who lived, loved and played jazz for a life-time. Somebody like Bill Coleman.

Bill, one of the very creators of this music, has been an active performer for over half of a century. Himself a great, original artist, he has worked with and befriended most of the finest jazz-people of several generations. Since Bill Coleman is not an egotistical eccentric but a keen observer and genuinely interested in other people's doings, his biography is a fantastic account of what has happened to Bill himself as well as to his musical associates—and the ever-changing world they are living in.

In my opinion, this is one of those really authentic stories of jazz and the up-and-down life that goes with playing, living and enjoying this music. In addition, the book gives a vivid description of the atmosphere prevailing during the almost six decades while Bill Coleman was so greatly contributing to making and keeping jazz the unique music it is. Any reader with an understanding and love for good music and for good people will go through the pages of this book with an increasing respect and admiration for its author. Because Bill Coleman The Man matches Bill Coleman The Artist. Thank you, Bill, for giving so much!

Johnny Simmen
August 4, 1979

ONE

BORN IN PARIS

I was born in a place called Centerville, Kentucky, USA, on 4 August 1904, but my passport says that I was born in Paris, Kentucky. The reason is that Centerville, Bourbon County, had no courthouse, jail, police, or anyone who represented the law, so the births were recorded in Paris, which was the ruling center of Bourbon County.

I was named William Johnson Coleman. William Johnson was the name of my grandfather on my mother's side. My father's name was Robert Henry Coleman and most people called him Henry. He was a cook. His three brothers were John Coleman, the eldest, Howard Coleman, and Ernest. There was also one sister named Amanda who was married to Sam Sparks. My mother, Roberta Johnson, was a seamstress. She had three brothers, Isaiah, Willie, and Peter, and one sister, Sarah, who was married to John Chenault. Mother was 16 when I was born. Dad was 26. I never knew my father's father or my mother's mother.

Centerville was a village with a population of 450 people, one Baptist church, one Episcopalian church, one barbershop, and a general store that sold food, clothing, farmware, and was also the post office. It had the only public telephone in the village. The population was mostly Negro, but the general store, the blacksmith shop, and the thrasher machine were owned by white people. The village doctor was white. The village was beautiful because part of it was on a hill and the houses were all built of wood, except the Baptist church, which was of brick.

Uncle John Coleman had built many of the houses as he was a jack of many trades and good at all of them. He had built the school and his own house, which was the largest in the village. My grandmother Coleman lived in a four-room log cabin which was the only one in Centerville. I never knew if it had been built by Uncle John.

All around Centerville were farmlands, which ran as far as the eye could see. The two largest farms were owned by the Fergusons and the Haggens. The main crops were wheat, corn, and tobacco. I loved ponies and there were thousands of them on those two farms.

Uncle John had put electricity in his house with some system that he had bought from Sears–Roebuck's mail order house in Chicago. He was the only person in the village who had electricity. He was also the professor of the school, which had students from the first to the eighth grade, all in one room. He was a hard man on children or anyone who crossed him up. If a kid did something wrong in school, he was sent out to get a switch to be whipped with, and if he didn't bring in a good strong one, Uncle John would send him out for another. He whipped his own children just the same as anyone else. No one was teacher's pet with him. But he was also a kind man and would do anything in his power to help someone in trouble.

A few white people lived in Centerville but most of the white men seen around the general store were farmers who lived outside the village. Most of the Negro men worked on the surrounding farms and some worked on the railroad which ran from Paris to Georgetown, a distance of 19 miles. Centerville is seven miles from Paris and 17 miles from Lexington, Kentucky.

Like many towns and cities that I was to know about and visit in later years, Centerville had its music. My father played the snare drum in the hometown band, my Uncle Ernest played tuba and, on rehearsal nights, he would pass by our house blowing with pride on his bass tuba. The "get-together" or rehearsal took place in the summer on the front lawn of my Uncle John Coleman's house. Besides all his various other activities, Uncle John played cornet. Everybody was welcome to listen to the rehearsal, and I am certain that I never missed one, although, at the age of four, I was not yet interested in playing any instrument. There was also a building near Uncle John's house where the band rehearsed in the winter or when the weather was bad. Sometimes there would be a dance in this building with an orchestra from Lexington or Paris. When these dances took place in the summer, we young ones could look in through the windows and listen to the music. That was the most interesting thing that I can remember about Centerville. Then my family moved to Cincinnati, Ohio. I was five years old.

Soon my mother and father separated and we went to live in Crawfordville, Indiana, with my mother, my brothers Robert and Ulysses, and my sister Thelma. I was the oldest. We lived with my mother's sister Sarah Chenault and her family, which included her husband John (another Uncle John) and their four children. I was six and going to school with two young boys who would later become very well-known jazz musicians. They were Wilbur and Sidney De Paris. Wilbur played baritone horn (not saxophone) and Sidney played alto horn. Both horns were the kind used in military or marching bands, but Wilbur and Sidney played compositions. The two of them used to give recitals in the church where my mother was a member and I was obliged to attend services. I was thrilled by Sidney, especially in the years to come.

I remember once, in Crawfordville, a circus came to town and I saw the parade with all the animals and the musicians on top of the circus wagons. One of the bands played *Alexander's Ragtime Band*. I did not know the song at that time, but the melody stayed with me, as well as the sight of my first circus parade. Of course, I went to the circus because when one came to town, in those days, it was a holiday for schoolchildren and for many grown people. The sideshow was the part of the circus that had the freaks, such as a very fat woman, a giant, a sword-swallower, a midget couple, or a person with twelve fingers or toes. The sideshow musicians would come out and play a number on a stage in front of the tent at half-hourly intervals, and that was very exciting to me. I loved to hear music. We used to march in and out of school to the music of a piano played by a girl of about ten.

About two years later, in 1911, my mother decided to come back to Cincinnati and live with my Aunt Mary. Aunt Mary smoked a pipe as did so many women from the South, including whites. Kentucky is not what is called the Deep South, but the racial problems there were the same as those which existed in any of the other Southern states. Aunt Mary was also a great beer drinker. There was a saloon very near her house, and she used to send me to get a bucket of beer for her. She would also eat Limburger cheese and cracker sandwiches which I also enjoyed. I was too young to go into the saloon, so I would stick the bucket under the swinging doors and the barman would see it, come and take it, fill it up for five cents, return it to me under the swinging doors, and also give me a handful of pretzels.

I learned to do many things that have been very helpful to me in later years when we lived with Aunt Mary. Aunt Mary ruled me more than my mother did. A child could not be lazy around her, even at the age of eight years. So I had to sweep the floor and scrub the front and back steps every Saturday, and we lived on the second floor! I also had to scrub and whiten the three front steps that led into the hall; I even remember the product I used to whiten those steps: it was called Bon Ami.

On Sunday afternoons I was allowed to put on my special Sunday clothes and sit out on the nice clean steps, weather permitting, in the summertime. One Sunday, there was a parade passing on 9th Street and the bands interested me to the point where I decided to follow one. I must have been miles away from home when I decided I had better return. I had never been so far away from those front steps alone and I did not know where I was. But I remembered the streets that I had taken and eventually I arrived home, happy to discover that I had not been missed by either my mother or Aunt Mary. That was a beautiful Sunday because I had heard some music, something on the style of what I used to hear on the lawn of Uncle John's in Centerville.

I was going to school on 9th Street, which was near where I lived, and I had a playmate who was blond and Irish. In Kentucky, the white and Negro children never played together, but that was not the case in Cincinnati because the schools were mixed at the time. This boy lived near me on 9th Street and his mother worked in a laundry a few blocks up from the school. She used to give us some pennies now and then to buy candy. We used to fight with two Jewish boys, Ike and Mike Tennenbaum, who were twins. Whenever we caught one of the twins alone, my buddy and I would give him a beating because that's what they did to us whenever they were together and caught one of us alone.

Cincinnati was like New Orleans in many respects because the same boats that sailed up and down the Ohio river from New Orleans to Kansas City all stopped in Cincinnati which had a levee also. The ways and means of making a living in the parts of Cincinnati around the levee up to certain streets were exactly like in New Orleans, because there were saloons, gambling, and prostitutes. The streets where these excitements took place were George Street, from Mound to Central Avenue, 6th Street from Mound to John Street, Carlisle Avenue from Mound to Plum Street, John Street from the levee up to 5th Street, and on a few side streets running from the levee up.

When I was twelve years old, my mother and father had settled their differences and the family was back together again, living on Barr Street. Often my brother Robert and I would go walking on George Street, Carlisle Avenue, or John Street to look at what we called the pretty ladies. The prostitutes on some of the streets would sit in the windows of the house and call the men; they all wore makeup, which other women did not wear. Some stood in doorways and others on the street. George Street was the district of the white prostitutes; Carlisle Avenue, from Central Avenue to Plum Street, and the other streets were where the Negro prostitutes and their pimps held sway.

Another reason I would walk around those districts is that sometimes one of the pretty ladies would want an errand done. They would always give a good tip, as they could not come out. If I happened to be passing at the time, it was almost certain that I would get a quarter for doing an errand. I could do many things with a quarter in those days when a bag of candy for two kids cost five cents.

Every chance I had, which was often, I would go to a movie. I would stay to see the film two or three times. The movie houses were called Nickel Odeons because a five-cent coin was the price of the admission. One could see two or three comedy films and a feature film of five reels. There was an electric piano with a drum attachment in the Nickel Odeons and most of the films were westerns, better known as cowboy films.

Most of the Nickel Odeons were on 5th Street. In one of the theaters in the prominent Negro district on 5th Street they had a woman pianist, Amanda Randolph, who played for the films and vaudeville shows of the TOBA circuit. I learned that the show people said that TOBA (the Theater Owners' Booking Association) stood for "Tough On Black Actors." I supposed it must have been because of the conditions they had to suffer in going from place to place. Most of those shows had their own musicians, and one I remember was quite famous. It was called Drake and Walker. Amanda Randolph was a very capable pianist. Although I did not know music, I knew when it was well played, and Amanda was the first woman I ever heard who played like a man. Drake, of the Drake and Walker show, was a smallish man who had one leg shorter than the other. He played cornet and had one of those long coach horns that had three valves like the cornet and a bell that was about two or three feet long. I did not know anything about jazz or other styles but Drake and his band sounded good to me: it was different from the way the parade bands played. Of course, he did not have as many musicians as a brass band had. Drake came often to the Lincoln Theatre.

Another cornet player came to Cincinnati from New Orleans and he used to advertise for the Lincoln Theatre by playing on a wagon which was pulled around by a horse. He used to play alone. I would follow him for blocks whenever he came on Kenyon Avenue, the street where I lived.

Some other musical events used to happen there. Just across the street from my house lived two brothers whose family name was Johnson. The older must have been 22 and the other was 18 years old. They both played the piano, though they did not read music. Many pianists in those days did not read music but had a natural talent for their instrument. They made their living playing for parties most of the time. During the summer they had their front door open and would play for hours. I used to sit on their steps and listen to them and I was very unhappy when my mother would call me to run an errand.

Another event that used to take place on Kenyon Avenue was a jug band that used to come around often to play in the streets and pass around a hat for people to put money in. There was a harmonica player, a big glass jug that one fellow would blow into and make it sound like a bass, and a violin player named Luther who could make his violin sound like it was saying "Oh Luther." They made good money because everyone enjoyed their music and gave freely whatever they could afford.

A family by the name of James that lived a few doors from me had a player piano. The son was about my age and we used to play together. I would go to his house often and played the different piano rolls for hours. Many people who could not play music had this type of piano.

There was also a neighborhood boy, Willis Ivy, whose mother made him take violin lessons. I was not interested in playing music, and for me the violin was more of an instrument for girls, although I liked the way Luther played it. I never told Willis what I thought of the violin because we were good friends and I did not want to hurt his feelings.

When I was 14 years old we moved to Hathaway Street, which was behind Kenyon Avenue. I never missed a show in the Lincoln Theatre and eventually a trumpet player came to Cincinnati and was engaged to play at the Lincoln with Amanda Randolph. His name was John Nesbitt and he made quite a name for himself later as an arranger. He stayed in Cincinnati for quite some time and he was the best trumpet or cornet player I had heard. When Nesbitt left town, it was to join McKinney's Synco Septet.

One day while I was playing in front of my house with some of the other boys, we saw some young people going down the street with two women who carried trumpet cases. Later we heard some music coming from a house farther down the street. We were curious and we went in front of this house in order to hear the music better. Those sessions happened many times and I was always around to hear them from outside.

I knew a young fellow living on Kenyon Avenue who had started to play saxophone. His name was Clarence Paige, and later he was engaged to play in the summer at an open-air pavilion at Sinton Park. This park took up one block from Kenyon Avenue to Barr Street and from Cutter Street to Mound. There was a tennis court, baseball ground, swings, a small swimming pool for children of two or three years of age, and a sandpile for them to play in. There were also benches for people to sit on to idle away the time. The pavilion was built so that people could stand around outside and listen to the music or watch the dancers. I always managed to have a ringside standing spot.

The saxophone player was the leader and the group was known as Clarence Paige and his Syncopators. There was a girl playing the trumpet, Dolly Jones. I was fascinated by Dolly's playing and she seemed at home with the rest of the musicians. A girl playing in an orchestra with men had never been seen in Cincinnati. I noticed that Dolly was very often putting something liquid on her lips, but I didn't know why she did it. Dolly was one of the women who played at the jam session in my street that I mentioned earlier. (The other one was her mother.)

Clarence Paige played in the Sterling Hotel in the winter. The Sterling was on 6th and Mound Streets and had been a big-time white hotel at one time. But more and more Negro people started to come to Cincinnati from the Southern states, and this part of the city, called Downtown, was where they found homes and places of entertainment. There was a gambling house on 5th Street, between John and Central Avenues, which was run by a man called Ed Gaither. He later opened another on Carlisle Avenue and Mound Street.

My mother used to masquerade in a suit of my father's on Halloween, 31 October, and go into Gaither's gambling house because that day women were allowed in. Almost everybody put on some kind of mask on Halloween and it was just as much fun for grown people as it was for young ones. It was the one time when I could stay out until the wee hours of the morning and not get a whipping for doing so.

The Sterling Hotel held big dances in the winter and I could hear from outside the music coming from the ballroom, but it was not as interesting as in the summer when Clarence would play in Sinton Park.

I was 14 years old when a man by the name of Ernest Moore, who used to play in the band with my father, Uncle Ernest, and Uncle John in Centerville, and was now living in Cincinnati, started a band to teach young boys to play music. I joined the band. I never knew how Mr. Moore managed to do what he was doing. He was not a rich man and did not ask for any money for teaching the boys. I am certain that he could not afford to buy all the instruments that he allowed us to take home. There must have been at least 25 boys in the band, from my age to 17, and the rehearsals were twice a week. After a few months, I was getting along quite well on my instrument, which was the alto horn like the one I had heard Sidney De Paris play in Crawfordville. We gave a concert once on the lawn of a house at 6th and Cutter Streets.

Some of us boys on Hathaway Street started a shooting gallery down in the basement of a house where one of the boys lived. We had saved money running errands for people and bought three BB guns. Those were the kind of guns that fired small ball-bearings. They were single-shooters and repeaters in which you put ten ball-bearings and pumped them into the chamber of the rifle with a handle under the trigger. We used tin cans as targets and lit the basement by candle light.

I started enjoying myself in the shooting gallery to the extent that I stopped going to band rehearsals. My father left Cincinnati to work in another city. If he had not gone away, he would have made me go to the rehearsals. But as my mother never worried about what I did when I was out of the house, I was my own little man. Mr. Moore came to the house one day and took back the horn. I was just not interested in playing music any more.

Another movie and vaudeville house opened on Central Avenue between 4th and 5th Streets. It was there that I saw Mamie Smith, Ma Rainey, and Bessie Smith, the most famous of all the women blues singers. I also worked there for one week. There was a part in the show about a man, his wife, and their many children coming from the South to visit some relatives in the North. There must have been about ten of us from Hathaway Street. We did two shows a day and were very proud to be taking part in a stage show. We had not asked how much we would get but took our job very seriously, always ready ahead of time for the show. But at the end of the week the producer gave us 50 cents each and we were very disappointed.

Negro people could go to the shows uptown but they had to sit in the second balcony which was known as the peanut gallery. There was no segregation in the peanut gallery because white people who didn't have enough money to sit on the first floor or the first balcony sat next to Negroes and conversed with them. I used to go quite often to the Keith Theater on Walnut Street, which was the shopping center of the city. The orchestra in the pit was very good but I was attracted more by the drummer for some reason that I cannot explain. If a Negro was outstanding in show business, he was booked on the Keith circuit which had theaters in most every large city in the United States.

It was at the Keith Theater that I saw Bill "Bojangles" Robinson, who was a great tap-dancer. Bojangles would stand almost perfectly still and his feet would be tapping rhythms that many drummers could not even imitate on their snare drum. Another great showman musician I saw there was a clarinettist named Wilton Crawley. Crawley would put a glass of water on his forehead and do a slow somersault while playing his clarinet, never spilling a drop of water from the glass. I also saw Rudy Wiedoeft who was known as the fastest alto saxophone player of the time.

One of our neighbors, Mr. Thompson, played baritone horn in a band led by a trumpeter named Bert Ferguson who had come to Cincinnati around 1917 and formed a marching and concert band for the Knights of Phythias lodge. I used to clean and polish Mr. Thompson's horn, for which he would pay me.

There were some buildings in Sinton Park that were used as a school for children where Bert Ferguson used to rehearse the band. I went to many of these rehearsals with Mr. Thompson. If anyone played a wrong note in one of the numbers, Mr. Ferguson could tell just who had made the mistake and tell him what note it should be. I just loved the music I heard at those rehearsals.

I had quite a nice voice and I remember a girl who lived in the same building where I lived who was 17 years old. At times she would ask me to sing. If I did not want to, she would say, "I'll give you ten cents if you will sing me a song." And I would sing, because I could go see a movie for five cents and have five cents left to buy some candy or peanuts to eat in the theatre.

I suppose that the reason I had no desire to play music when I was 14 is because I was more interested in becoming a cowboy. Most of the movies I saw were of cowboys. Some of the stars of those films were William S. Hart, Tom Mix, Harry Carey, and a man by the name of Noble Johnson whom I heard was a Negro, but he looked as white as any of the other stars. Douglas Fairbanks Sr. was another star I enjoyed seeing. I don't remember him playing a cowboy role though he did play Zorro in *The Mark of Zorro*. His manner of running over rooftops, jumping over horses, and executing movements that baffled his enemy were fantastic.

My favorite playmate lived on Barr Street but spent most of his time playing on Hathaway Street. His name was Edward Partridge and we remained friends after we grew to be men. Eddie and I used to draw pictures of horses and cowboys. Our dream was to go west and get a job on some ranch.

My mother and father separated again and my father took me and my youngest brother Ulysses to Kentucky for a while. My brother Robert had died when I was 13 years old. My sister was left with my mother. My heart was broken when I had to leave Cincinnati because, apart from drawing pictures of cowboys with my friend Eddie Partridge, we had also started to play with electric trains. Eddie had an after-school job in a shop that sold miniature trains and now and then he would bring something to my house that we could use in the line of railroading. Whether he paid for these things or they were given to him, I didn't know and I didn't care as long as it was something we didn't already have.

Aunt Amanda, her husband, and her children Mattie, Agnes, Frankie Belle, and Thomas Sparks were caretakers on a part of the Haggens' farm and I stayed with them for months. There were cows, hogs, turkeys, and plenty of chickens. Aunt Amanda was saving money from every angle so that she could buy her own home: if her children or I wanted an egg for breakfast we had to pay her two cents for it. I became a real country boy in every respect, except for milking a cow. I just could not get that technique!

Tom Sparks was younger than me and smaller because his father and mother were small people. But Tom was very fast and studious. He must have inherited something in that sense from John Coleman who was his uncle also. None of the children were going to school except Tom, as children living in the country were not obliged to attend in those days. Tom had to walk seven miles to school and seven back home. He and I slept together in a room on the second floor which was like walking into a refrigerator in the winter because it was not heated. We used to get undressed downstairs, run upstairs, and jump in the bed which was also as cold as ice for a few minutes. The mattress was interlined with feathers and didn't take too long to warm up, but we suffered a little time from the coldness of it.

On a farm across from where we lived were two white boys who had a pony and buggy. They drove to and from their school which was on the same road as Tom used to take. When I first came there, Tom told me that these two boys would beat him up at times when they caught him coming home. So I told him that I would meet him on the road one day and straighten the matter out. Eventually, those two boys came along and when they saw Tom with someone larger than he was, they must have figured something was going to happen because they started to whip the pony to make it run as fast as it could. But it couldn't run fast enough and when they came up to us, I grabbed the bridle, stopped the pony, and told them Tom was my cousin and if they ever bothered him again, I would beat their brains out. Tom never had any more trouble from them. I was not afraid of white boys because I had fought them on the streets and at school in Cincinnati. In fact I always had nerve.

Once, when I was twelve years old, I had come to Centerville for the summer and as most of the boys helped with the harvest, I went to work also with a group thrashing wheat. I was what was known as "jumper," the one on the wagon who stacks the wheat when it is thrown up from the ground. One day the thrasher machine broke down and everybody was lying around, waiting until it was repaired. There was a white fellow named Tom McVey who called all the Negro boys "nigger" and he wanted to say something to me. Tom was a man of at least 24. I was sitting on a wagon and he was lying on the ground, chewing on a straw. I heard him when he called me "nigger" but I pretended I hadn't. So he pointed his finger at me and said, "Hey! you, nigger!" I pointed my finger right back at him and told him that my name was William Johnson Coleman and that if he could not call me one of those names, not to say anything to me. His face turned cherry red but he didn't move and I never knew what he had wanted to say to me.

Another time, a pal and I were walking along the pike and we saw some farmers killing hogs, so we went over to see if we could do something and one of the wise guys said, "Yes, can you dance?" When I told him we couldn't, he said, "Well, I'll make you dance!" and he started to shoot at my feet with the rifle he was using to kill hogs. I didn't move and he was so angry that he said, "Get off this farm before I kill you!" We left, but he was the one that lost face.

After some months my father decided to go back to Cincinnati. I was very pleased because Tom had been the only boy around me on the farm and I was happy at the thought of seeing Eddie Partridge, Eddie West, and all the other boys that were in my gang.

We lived on 5th Street, between Mound and Cutter Streets over an undertaker's parlor. The name of the undertaker was Mr. Copeland. When we had lived on Barr Street, the Copelands had lived across the street and I used to make candy-spending money from Mrs. Copeland by watering her lawn in the summer and shoveling coal into her cellar in the winter.

Dolly Jones had left Cincinnati with her mother Dyer Jones. Some medicine shows came to town. They used to put on their shows in any empty lot they could find and no one had to pay to see them. The so-called "doctor" sold bottles of syrup that was supposed to be good for the liver, rheumatism, or heart trouble; his pills were good for blood circulation, aching bones, or any kind of sickness that existed.

There were always some kind of musicians playing those shows and a couple of comedians. Some of the jokes were: "How do you feel Mr. Bones?" and Mr. Bones would answer, "Just like a stove." The other one would ask, "How's that?" and Bones would answer, "Red hot and still a-heating!" Another joke was, "How do you feel tonight Mr. Sampson?" Mr. Sampson would say, "Just like that woman's mouth," pointing at some woman in the crowd. The straight man would again ask, "How's that?" and the answer came: "Wide open!"

A group of these medicine shows would travel from city to city and play in different parts of the town. I heard about one that was playing in a district quite some distance from where we lived, which had a family of musicians working with them. The trumpet player was called Gabriel and I was told he was very good.

One day I was playing in Sinton Park and I heard someone call another boy Gabriel and I was curious to know who this was. He was playing baseball and when I did get a good look at him, I saw that it was Sidney De Paris, with whom I had attended school in Crawfordville, and who played alto horn at church concerts. The medicine shows were always on early in the evening and Sidney started playing with Clarence Paige at the open-air pavilion where Dolly Jones had played. I heard Gabriel blow many times that summer.

Wilbur De Paris played with some orchestra in the Sterling Hotel but as I was only 15 I wasn't allowed in. Sidney didn't remember me going to the same school as he had, but he did remember my cousin Theophilus Chenault and we soon became better acquainted. I never heard the De Paris family playing together, but I was told that the mother, father, and a sister all played music. I don't know if there were more sisters, but there were only two boys, Wilbur and Sidney.

The medicine shows usually stayed in a city one or two months and then moved on to another town. So, when they left Cincinnati, the De Paris family left also and I never saw Sidney in Cincy again.

I was 16 when I decided to leave home. My hangout was in Sinton Park with a group of other boys that had left home or had no parents. Some of them had been in and out of reform school since the age of twelve or younger. When the weather was nice, we slept anywhere we could find a place. I worked a few days at one time in a big hotel as a bus boy and stayed in a room with another boy named Lewis who had lived on Hathaway Street at one time. We were about the same age.

I didn't like the job at this hotel so I quit. I still stayed with Lewis for a few days, but one night I came to his room and he wouldn't open the door for me. So I had to think of a place where I could sleep. Then I remembered that the door leading down in the cellar under Mr. Copeland's undertaking parlor was not locked as there was nothing down there that was worth anything.

I believed in ghosts and would not go near a cemetery at night, so I was a little worried about sleeping in the cellar of an undertaker's parlor, knowing that there must be some dead bodies just over my head. But I was so tired that I could even have slept in a coffin that night. So down in the cellar I went, with dead bodies over my head and my father in his bed, up over the dead bodies. There was an old dusty arm chair there. I knocked some of the dust off, sat in it, and slept like a log.

Among the homeless that hung around Sinton Park at night were three boys who sang barbershop songs. As I had a voice that was not too bad, I eventually started singing with them. The oldest of them, Jesse Seltzer, had lost one eye. Jesse had a voice like a trained singer and he used to give me the voice that I was to sing in the numbers. I had the baritone voice. These three boys had been singing quite a while with another fellow, a pimp and downright hustler who carried a pistol. He was living with a prostitute and didn't hang out with the boys any more. So I had taken his place in the quartet and wasn't doing too bad after some rehearsals.

One night, we got an engagement to sing in a high school on Walnut Hill where there was also a Negro community, but it was a sad night for me because the other fellow, that hustler, showed up and Jesse asked me if it would be alright to let him take my place as he knew the songs better than I did. There was nothing to do except to agree. Since we had accepted to sing at this school for the pleasure I didn't lose any money, but I was disgusted as hell.

Jesse Seltzer had an uncle in Cincinnati and I stayed with them for a while. His uncle had more old papers and junk in his place than you could find on the city dump, but it was a roof over our heads and we had something to eat.

Jesse and I decided to make our way to Detroit one day and, not having enough money to pay for a train ticket, the only way to get there was to hobo. I had never done that before but Jesse knew the ropes and advised me about the correct place to hop a freight train and how to do it. You go along the tracks on a sideroad where a train has to go up-grade and you hide yourself somewhere near until the engine is well past and the train begins to slow down. Freight trains are always very long, and when a freight car is empty the doors are open. So you choose a car and, as the train is not moving at any great speed, it's very easy to hop on. The only worry after that is if the brakeman comes along and makes you get off.

There is no way of knowing exactly where a train is going but we caught one going north of Cincinnati late one afternoon, found a nice box car, and slept until morning. The train was not moving when we awakened and as we looked out, we found ourselves in a freight yard. That's a place never to be caught in because freight cars are sometimes robbed, and if you get caught in a yard and have no business being there, you can be put in jail, even if you haven't stolen anything.

We managed to get out of the freight yard without being seen and found out later that we were near Toledo, Ohio. We hit off on a road going back in the direction of Cincinnati. I don't know if Jesse was disgusted because we were not yet in Detroit or whether he had changed his mind about going there. But he was older than I, the whole idea had been his, and I just went along doing whatever he suggested.

That same afternoon, as we were walking along a road, we met a Negro farmer and he invited us to come home with him to have something to eat and spend the night. It was wonderful because we had only had some apples and pears picked from trees along the road, and a good meal was something we could really appreciate. We slept in a good bed that night and we stayed on the farm for three days helping this man do his farmwork. I chopped him a big supply of wood for the stove as I had learned to chop wood when I stayed on the farm with Aunt Amanda. We left on the fourth day and Jesse told me that the main reason we were leaving was because the man was beginning to suspect that his wife was taking a liking to me. Whether that was true, I didn't know; but I do know that at that time I didn't think of women or girls. I had had some flirts or childhood sweethearts but nothing serious.

We came back to Cincinnati and I stayed with Jesse and his uncle for a while. I was hanging around Sinton Park again and became acquainted with a boy whose only name I can remember was Harry. He may have been a couple of years older than me and he had been in and out of reform school many times. Harry was a born thief and I started going around stealing things with him and another boy.

Harry was the brain of the gang. He was a very nice-looking boy, quite clear, and had very nice hair. I never saw him smile or heard him laugh and he seemed to not have any interest in anything except stealing. We would steal silk shirts off clotheslines and sell them to the pimps in the poolrooms. Cincinnati had plenty of alleys, and women hung their washing in the backyards that had gates and were easy to get into.

We would also wait at a certain place on 8th Street near a viaduct for farmers' trucks that had come into the city to buy provisions. Many of them had to pass over the viaduct going in the direction of Indiana, whose border is not far from Cincinnati. We would hop on those trucks and take cartons of cigarettes and chewing tobacco which we would also sell in the poolrooms.

My next hobo experiment was with Harry. He wanted to go to Lexington, Kentucky, to steal a pistol, so we made our way over one of the bridges spanning the Ohio river and we were in Covington, Kentucky, but we had to go outside town to catch a freight. We caught one coming up-grade and had the nerve to sit in the doorway of an open boxcar and wave to farmers plowing the fields or around the homes that were near the railroad lines.

We arrived in Lexington, and slept in a wagon a little on the outskirts of town. But Harry couldn't find a pistol to steal, and he couldn't think of any scheme to steal one, so we came back to Cincinnati.

One day, I fell when I was jumping off a truck with a carton of chewing tobacco which broke and scattered its contents over the street. There was not much traffic and no one saw this happen except Harry and the other boy who was in our gang of three thieves. We gathered up the scattered packages and sold them the same as we had sold the others.

Another scheme of Harry's was that the three of us would go into a shop which sold stockings, handkerchiefs, and other things for women and children. We had to be certain that there was only one salesperson in the shop, then one of us would ask the price of something in the back of the store while the other two would steal a couple of pairs of stockings, which were usually on display on a line. Or we would take a box of handkerchiefs or anything that could be hidden in our pockets and was not nailed down. These things we also sold to the pimps who would give them to their girls.

The summer had passed and the weather started to get cool at night. That was the toughest part of being away from home and a nice warm place to sleep. But Harry's mind was always working like an eight-day clock and it was not long before he found us a place in a lumber yard, under a shed that was heated to keep the lumber dry. There were no difficulties getting in and out because no one watched the place. So we had a nice warm place to sleep in after the poolroom where we hung out closed.

We had a special restaurant where we could eat a plate of home-fried potatoes for five cents if we didn't have money enough to pay for some meat to go with the potatoes. The poolroom where we hung around was on Mound and George Streets, just in front of Sinton Park, and there was a bakery on 6th Street, not far from the Sterling Hotel that made a cake with apples and raisins which was known as Washington pie. You could get a large piece for five cents and it was very filling. So when I wanted a change from potatoes, it was Washington pie.

Most of the time we could only afford one meal a day. The bread was free in restaurants so we could get our five cents' worth of potatoes, eat as much bread as we could, and drink water. One waitress in the restaurant got to know our habit so well that when she saw us come in the door, and especially if she was alone, she would yell to the cook: "A nickel's worth of spuds!" It was embarrassing but I was hungry and that was the only restaurant where I could get fed for five cents.

One day, we were in a part of the town quite far from the district we usually chose for stealing silk shirts. The police must have learned about our gang or someone may have seen us doing these things and given a description of us to the police. Anyway, a policeman saw us, stopped us and wanted to know what we were doing. We told him we were looking for a job. He said he knew where we could get one and walked us right in the police station where we were locked up immediately.

Later we were taken to the court house and brought to the office of a juvenile court judge who knew Harry. I suppose that he had sent Harry to the reform school a few times. But as we had no stolen goods and no one was there to accuse us or press charges, the judge gave us a lecture and the name of a place where we could get a job.

I went to this place, which was a factory that manufactured ropes. I was hired and worked half a day but never went back for my pay. The place was so dusty with rope dust that it was difficult to breathe.

A few days later, my father found out where I was and came to take me home. He was working in a cleaning and pressing shop, pressing men's suits, women's dresses and coats, and so on. He lived in a two-room apartment in back of the shop. This shop was owned by Mr. Thompson (the man whose horn I used to clean and polish) and Mr. Will Tarleton, a very good friend of my father. He had also played in the Centerville band and was a great collector of Bert Williams's records. The shop was on Walnut Hills, near the school where I was supposed to sing with the Jesse Seltzer quartet. It was a part of the hill where the better-class Negroes lived.

I had been with my father and brother Ulysses about two days when my father noticed a lot of little bugs in the bed. He knew what they were but I didn't, and he knew I was the one who had brought them there. I had been away from home for four or five months and had not taken a bath in all that time so I was full of lice. My father burnt my underclothes and socks and bought me a new suit. Naturally I had to take a bath, as hot as I could stand it.

I liked my surroundings because there was a Ford delivery truck driven by a boy named William Boyd and I went with him on many of his pick-ups and deliveries. I also learned to press clothes and enjoyed operating the pressing machine. I was now 17 years old; so was William Boyd, but he acted much older than I did at the time.

Eventually the cleaning and pressing business went bad and the shop closed. We moved down to a house on West 9th Street and I got a job as bus boy in the dining room of the restaurant in the zoo. (This was not my first job. At eight years of age, I used to light the gas on Saturdays for some Jewish families because it was against their religion to do that. I worked in Kentucky, helping with the harvest of wheat: I planted tobacco and stripped it also. I was the water boy in a rock quarry, I sold papers in Cincinnati, and helped deliver ice. I was very good also at house cleaning.)

As bus boy at the zoo restaurant, I heard many of the summer concerts that took place on the stage of an open-air theater just in front of where the people ate, which was also out in the open. I particularly remember an anvil chorus and a man who played xylophone. He impressed me so much that I started looking at the prices of some in a Sears–Roebuck catalogue.

There was a dance hall behind the restaurant and one night I heard a trumpet sound coming from there. When I had the chance, I walked over there to see who it could be and there was a little Negro boy playing trumpet with his left hand. It was the first time I had seen a Negro musician sitting in with a white orchestra at the zoo or any place else in Cincinnati and I knew that this youngster had to be good to be allowed to play in such a situation. I found out his name was Freddie Jenkins and that he was going to school at Wilberforce University. Freddie was upsetting everybody, but he did not stay in town more than two or three days.

I stopped working at the zoo restaurant after a few months. I never stayed on any job very long and always managed to find an excuse to explain my quitting to my father. Dad had a little round savings bank that would hold only ten cent pieces. It was very small and had a bottom that was supposed to push out only when the bank had $5 in it. There was a screw mechanism on the top but I managed to get into the bottom slot instead and take out the one or two dimes I needed every day for spending money. Since Dad always put his spare dimes in the bank, he soon became suspicious as it didn't seem to be filling up too quickly. He found out what was happening and knew that it was me that was robbing him. Dad had never had to whip me much but this time he tied my hands with a rope and gave me the worst whipping I ever had just to teach me about stealing!

That summer I went to Centerville for a vacation and stayed with Uncle John and his four children. The girls, Matty and Ida, were the oldest, then came my cousin John, and then little Cora. Ida played piano and was the organist at the Baptist church. She was alright for playing hymns but when she played the sheet music of popular songs she would lose time. She read very well but just didn't have the rhythm. Nevertheless, we used to have some swell times with Ida at the piano and me singing.

Uncle John had bought John Jr. a C-melody saxophone and he could play a few songs. John Jr. could get anything he wanted from his father, mostly I suppose because he was the only boy in the family. He also had a Model T Ford, something that many boys in rich white families didn't have.

Uncle John's wife was from a family named Bachelor. Her name was Katharine but everybody called her Kitty. She was a sweet and lovely woman and everyone loved Aunt Kitty.

Before coming back to Cincinnati, I stayed a couple of days in Paris and there was a dance one night with an orchestra called Edgar Hayes and his Collegians. The musicians were going to Wilberforce University and Edgar had persuaded them to spend their summer vacation in Lexington, Kentucky; his home town, and play the summer dance season in Kentucky. The original leader had been Horace Henderson, a pianist, but he was not with the band then because Edgar Hayes was also a pianist and a hell of a good one. Some of the musicians in the band were Joe Beatus and Castor McCord on saxes and Henry Hicks on trombone; but the strong man of the band was trumpeter Freddie Jenkins whom I had heard at the dance hall of the Cincinnati Zoo.

One number that always stayed in my mind was *Maytime*. I shall never forget the way Freddie used to improvise on the melody, or the first words of the song "I found you in Maytime." The musicians were all about my age and it was the first time that I had heard a jazz orchestra that had more than six or seven musicians. This one had ten, but my ears and eyes were closed to every one of them save Freddie. He was the whole orchestra to me.

Dad, my brother, and I moved from 9th Street back to Hathaway Street and I went to work in a fruit sugar-coating factory. There was a family living on the first floor, the Haddins, who were distant cousins of ours. One of the Haddins had married Aunt Mary's daughter. On the second floor were the Hustons. We had two rooms and a kitchen on the third floor and there was a man who lived in a small room next door.

The Hustons were from somewhere way down South and their son came to Cincinnati to live with them. He was older than I and loved to carry a pistol. We both worked at the sugar-coating factory which was at least six miles from where we lived. We rode the streetcar to work and walked home when the day was finished. My sister Thelma stayed with us sometimes, and sometimes with my mother.

My father was offered a job by a rich family near Lexington, Kentucky, as a cook. He accepted, rented our apartment to a Mr. Wade, and took my brother to Kentucky with him. I was allowed to stay with the Wade family which included Mr. Wade's mother and his son. Father had let me stay behind because I was working, but he said that if anything went wrong, I should come to him in Kentucky.

After a short time, Mr. Wade started to make bootleg whisky and there were soon barrels of mash in the small room next door which was now vacant. He had a copper still that fitted on the gas stove. He started doing good business and I remember that a prohibition officer used to come there at times and drink with Mr. Wade. I used to taste the alcohol when it was hot and dripping from the still.

Then Mr. Wade made the acquaintance of a fellow named Charlie and used him to peddle his whisky. This Charlie eventually got to know Mr. Huston's son, and one Sunday, they were out drinking somewhere when Charlie persuaded the boy to sell him his pistol for $12.

When Charlie went out on the street two white men were coming along. Charlie must have recognized them as detectives, pulled out his pistol, and started shooting at them. They kept coming and pulled their guns also. Charlie turned and ran, and the detectives came after him. They finally cornered him in a lumber yard, disarmed him, and took him to jail.

He must have given our address as the place he lived because some detectives came and questioned me. Wade must have got wind of something because the whole family had gone out and left me there alone. The detectives told me that Charlie had been burglarizing stores in the uptown district. They had come with search warrants to look for stolen goods but nothing was there. The door of the small room where Wade had his malt working was locked and they asked me for the key which I didn't have.

They broke the door in and for the first time I saw what was in that room: four or five barrels of yellow liquid, the mash, which had to be left until it came to a certain stage of fermentation. It was then put in the still and cooked. When it came to boiling point, the liquid would drip into a huge jug and you had moonshine whisky. The detectives took all the soap powder they could find, any old dirty rags and garbage, and put all that in those barrels to make certain they could not be used anymore. I never saw or heard anything of the Wades again.

I stayed in the apartment alone for a few days and ate with the Hustons. Their son went back to the South where, he said, he could carry a pistol without trouble and I stayed on with Mrs. Huston, giving her money every week for my room and board.

One day, I was out walking with June, one of my distant cousins who lived downstairs, and two other boys, George Burr and Theodore Means. A nice little woman who must have been about 28 years old stopped us and asked if we could sing. Then she told us she was a social worker and organist at a Presbyterian church and she would like to form a quartet of boys. She offered to give us piano lessons and teach us some religious songs. We accepted her offer and a few nights later we went to the church and started to learn our first church song and take our first piano lesson.

The only one of us who had a piano at home was June, so he and I could practise there, but we could also get into church any time we wanted and George Burr, Theodore Means, and I did most of our practising there. Miss Hargrave lived in a very nice section of Walnut hills and we would go to her home some nights and play our lessons and learn songs.

The main reason we liked to go to Miss Hargrave's was because she had a young sister, Boggs, who was very beautiful and we all had eyes for her. Sometimes, we would go walking and take turns walking with Boggs. Those were delightful moments. Boggs didn't show any special preference for any one of us and I don't know what I would have done if she and I had ever had the chance to be really alone, because girls didn't worry me at the time and I didn't have much conversation for them. I think we all tried to get our piano lessons better than the last one, just to show off in front of Boggs. We began to attend church quite frequently and also sang at special church meetings.

After about four months of training we sang well enough to be invited to sing in some white churches. Those affairs were always for social purposes and our pay and reward were the piano lessons that Miss Hargrave gave us.

But eventually the novelty of singing, rehearsals, and going to church, as well as the attraction to Boggs, began to fade away. It was not too pleasant to practise the piano in June's house because when I felt like doing it, he felt the same way, and, as it was his family's piano, he had the right to practise first. Going to church to practise lost its charm also and we put everything down. Maybe if there had been a piano in my family and my parents had not been separated I might be able to play piano today. Shortly after we broke off relations with Miss Hargrave, George Burr bought a clarinet and tried to get me to buy one, but I didn't have any interest in that or another instrument.

TWO

TRUMPET PLAYING IS NOT EASY

After some months in Kentucky, my father and brother came back to Cincinnati. The year was 1922. I was 18 years old and taller than my father. We lived on lower Carlisle Avenue again.

One day, I was looking in a pawnshop and a cornet trumpet caught my eye. A cornet trumpet is not as short as a cornet and not as long as a trumpet. Every time I passed the pawn shop, I would stop and look at that instrument. I told my father about it and said that I would like to have it. He told me to get to work and pay for it myself. I was not working at the time. My father was never mean to me, but he was not like Uncle John who would buy his son anything he asked for.

I took a job in a printing shop as an errand boy and package wrapper. The price of the horn was $35 and it was a used instrument. That price was quite a lot of money in those days; I earned about $8 a week and paid $5 each week on the horn, but I couldn't even get my hands on it until I had paid it up completely. There was a case that I got with it. The night I brought it home, I suppose I was the proudest boy in town.

I did not sleep too well that night because I was anxious for the next day to come so I could blow my horn. I was still working and did not get the chance to try my instrument until I came home, the day after I bought it.

It must have taken an hour before I could get some sort of sound out of that horn and my lips were sore from trying so hard. Whatever I had learnt when I was 14 years old and played for a while in a kids' band, I had forgotten. But each day, when I came back from work, I would take my horn and in a week's time I was able to play the C scale not too badly.

I was not a kind of genius like Max Kaminsky who was able to play and read a song two days after he got a trumpet though he had never played an instrument before! I began to try and play a number by ear. I didn't know the names of the notes so I would mark on a piece of paper the fingering of the valves such as first and third, first and second, second, open, and so on.

One day I decided to clean the inside of the horn and that's when I found out that I had been cheated by the pawnshop where I bought it. I pulled out a slide and the outside of it came off, leaving the inner part stuck in the stem. All four of the joints were the same. I had to take the horn to a music shop to have it repaired.

After a month of practising and seeming to get nowhere, I put the horn under my bed and forgot about it. My good friend Eddie Partridge was now driving a small bus at a golf club. He had bought a C-melody saxophone quite some time before I bought my horn. He wasn't using it so I asked him to let me take it home and see if I could do something with it. I tried it a few times but never arrived to the point of playing as much on it as I had done on my horn (which was not much). The only successful thing I did with the sax was to take all the keys off one day: I had a hell of a time getting them back in place again.

I had no goal of being a professional musician when I bought my horn but I did want to play for my own amusement. My father didn't push me to continue trying when I lost interest in my instrument, probably because I had bought it with my own money.

I started working at the Cincinnati abattoir, making a better salary than I had ever had before. My first job was opening and cleaning the stomachs of cattle, which gave me such a headache that after four days of working in that stink hole, I told the boss of the department that that kind of work made me sick. He transferred me to the sheep department where my job was chopping out sheep's brains.

After a few days, I became an expert at this job. It was pitiful to hear the sheep bleating as they came around on a large wheel-shaped board with hooks on it, hanging there by one hind leg. When they arrived at a certain place there was a man with a long butcher knife which he would drive through their throats to kill them. The heads were cut off and there was a man who skinned them, then they came along to me. The technique of chopping out the brains was to hit the skull on two sides with a very sharp hatchet. If it was not hit a certain way, the brain would be split. The heads came out to me every five seconds. I could chop out a brain in three.

I worked at the abattoir for about three months. I just could not stay on a job, as some people could, three or four years or more. I was practising my horn again and playing a few numbers by ear not badly.

Next I went to work in a factory that manufactured tin tubs and buckets. I was assistant to a worker who put rivets in tub handles. After a time I took over his place and had an assistant myself. All the machines in that factory were dangerous because sometimes the mechanism would get out of order and the hammer that was in the upper part would slip. Quite a few workers had the tips of their fingers cut or mashed off. My machine slipped at times but I was fortunate enough not to have my fingers in it as it happened. I worked there longer than I had ever worked before but eventually my lazy side caught up with me. One fine Saturday afternoon I collected my pay and that was the last time that I saw the bucket and tub factory.

I didn't hear much music in those days, except for a parade band now and then. The lodges were still burying their members the same way as in New Orleans, though I didn't know anything about New Orleans then. When a lodge member died and his body was being taken to the grave, the band would march slowly, playing some hymns or sad songs. Then they would leave the funeral procession at a certain place and come marching back to their quarters playing a lively march.

Clarence Paige was playing in the Sterling Hotel and there were no more dances in Sinton Park. I was not old enough to go in the hotel to listen to the music but I knew the trombone player in the band, Parker Berry. He had started to play trombone in the kids' band of Mr. Ernest Moore at the same time as I had started to play the oom-pah-pah horn but I had stopped playing and Parker had continued music and become a professional.

Another musician who was playing at the Sterling Hotel was a trumpet player, Harry Martin. Harry had been traveling with his mother in a circus. She was a snake charmer and had come to Cincinnati after quitting a circus. Harry had been born in Ohio and had played with an orchestra from Columbus: the Whispering Serenaders. It was said that the style of this orchestra was to play so soft that the shuffle of the dancers' feet served as part of the rhythm section.

There was a very well-known story in Ohio about the Whispering Serenaders. They were used to working in big exclusive white hotels in different cities in Ohio, but once they were engaged to work in a white hotel somewhere down South. They had been there for a while when they were asked to play for a party one night after their work at the hotel was finished. This party was supposed to be a little outside of the town at a private house. Some men were waiting for them in cars to drive them and their instruments to the party. A few miles out of town, the cars pulled up someplace and there was a gang of white men. This was the party, though not the kind the Whispering Serenaders had expected: it was a head-whipping party.

Being fine musicians and gentlemen didn't mean anything to those jealous Southerners. All that mattered was that the Whispering Serenaders were Negroes. They were all beaten badly and their instruments destroyed. They were told to get out of town as fast as they could. The only reasons for an act of that kind to take place in the South, where anything could happen to a man if his skin was black, were that these musicians were from the North, they played too well for somebody's taste, and they had the nerve to accept an engagement in a white hotel down South.

A pianist by the name of Green came to Cincinnati and I met him along with a young fellow named William who played drums. Green was one of those pianists who played by ear and only in one key. There were, at that time, a couple of other young pianists around town who played by ear and were very popular. One was named Herschel Brown. He could play in any key though he did not read music and was in an orchestra. He really sounded fine.

I started going to different parties with Green and William, and playing the few numbers that I had learned. I was known as Johnson. I don't remember getting any money from these parties, but on Christmas night we went from place to place doing our numbers and drinking eggnog. Many people gave open house parties on Christmas and New Year and eggnog was flowing like water running over Niagara Falls. I was not a drinker of alcohol and still could not stand the taste of beer, but the homemade eggnog is so much like a milk shake with whisky added that it was easy for me to drink it.

My drinking experiences up to that time had been rather odd. My father and mother had told me that when I was too young to know myself, a friend of theirs who had gone to Paris came back to Centerville with some whisky and gave a waterglassful to my parents for a toddy. They placed the glass of whisky on the dining-room table and went to the kitchen to prepare supper. All of a sudden, they heard me saying "Ah!" in a funny tone and came running into the room. I had climbed on a chair, then on to the round table and drunk the whole glass down. They said it hadn't made me sick but I had been so drunk that I fell out of bed during the night and they found me under it in the morning.

I had tasted whisky a few times after that. Once, when I was twelve years old and we were living on Barr Street, Dad had bought a bottle of whisky and hid it in a cupboard. My father was not a drinking man and I had never seen him drunk, but he liked his toddy now and then, and he would also give us one when we had a cold. I was always looking in cupboards and closets to see what I could find, and one day, when Mom and Dad were out, I found this bottle of whisky and took a big swallow of it. It was winter time and the snow was about 15 inches high in the streets. When my parents came home, I said I was dizzy but my father knew I was drunk. He wasn't really angry with me but he told me to get out of the house! I did and sneaked into a large closet we had under the stairs, behind a large trunk where Mother kept the washing to be done. I went to sleep. Later, when Dad didn't see me come home, he got worried and went looking for me. By the time he came back I had awakened and come back in, only to find my mother worried sick that I might have fallen in the snow and frozen to death.

Now I had graduated to eggnog and going to parties! This was my first time to paint the town. I left the last party at about 3 a.m. and went staggering home and slept all day.

My father was not happy with me because I was not working and he eventually told me that I would have to get a job. His buddy Mr. Tarleton, who had been part-owner of the cleaning and pressing shop where we had stayed on Walnut Hills, was now the head porter at the main telegraph office uptown on 4th Street. He told my father I could get a job there, which I did. I started working and stopped hanging around with Green and William. But I still practised my horn. Every other week, I had to go to work early and I would get off early; that was the time that I could practise without disturbing anyone.

I worked at the Western Union place for quite a few months and used to see and hear William Smith, a pianist (no relation of Willie "the Lion" Smith), very often. He was a professional musician and I was a beginner.

Every year in August a portion of the population of Centerville went camping for one week. Those who could not stay the whole week would come for a day or two. These encampments were always on some rich white farmer's land, near a creek that was deep enough to swim and fish in. There was a tent used as a dining room, one where the girls and women slept, and one for the men and boys. After supper, which was usually around six o'clock, the middle of the dining tent was cleared for dancing. Uncle John's piano—or rather Cousin Ida's, since she was the only one in the family who could play—was brought to these get-togethers, and every night, if no other musicians were there, Ida would play and the people would dance to her music, even if she did skip a measure here and there.

Everyone would give some money for the food that was consumed that week and if someone came just for one day and night, they could eat as much as anyone else and not pay a dime.

I was given a week's vacation without pay by the Western Union office and it was just at the time the encampment was taking place. I had spoken about it to William Smith ("Smittie" to everyone) and to a young man named Edgar Courance who was a beginner on clarinet. He was a neighbor and lived on Carlisle Avenue.

Edgar, myself, and an amateur alto player named Alex Baker used to rehearse at Edgar's or Alex's house twice a week. I don't remember how I met Alex but I remember that he lived on Court Street. We got orchestrations from a couple of music publishing stores uptown and one we received was *Three O'Clock in the Morning*, a waltz. There was one place in this number where the trumpet part went as high as A above the staff and that was a note I could not reach. So I made a turn on the note just before the A, which was D for the trumpet as the number was in F, and played the A in the staff.

But getting back to the encampment, Smittie, Edgar, and I arrived in Centerville and were taken to the farm where this get-together was taking place. It happened to be on millionaire Haggen's farm where I had stayed with Aunt Amanda Sparks some years before. We were joined by John Coleman Jr. on C-melody sax and a drummer from Georgetown whose name was James Coleman. (He was not related to my clan.) It was the first time that Smittie and Edgar had been on an encampment and I think it was the first time Edgar had really been in the country, as he had been born in Cincinnati. Smittie had some relatives in Lexington, which was not far from the site of the camp, and quite a few people would come from Lexington and Paris to dance and return home when the dancing stopped. I had a wonderful time. It was the first occasion that most of us making the music had played for an audience.

One night, a fellow came to the camp from Paris and told me that he had an orchestra. He asked me if I would come and work a few nights with him the following week after the encampment was finished. I accepted although I knew that I was supposed to go back to my porter's job at the Western Union after my one-week vacation.

Smittie and Edgar went back to Cincinnati and I went to Paris for a week and played some jobs in that vicinity. I don't remember the name of the fellow who hired me or how much he paid me. The orchestra must have been made up of amateurs like me, but it was the first time I was paid to play music. I went home after the week was over but I had lost the job at the Western Union and my father was not happy.

A trumpet player named Theodore Carpenter had left a carnival and was now playing with Clarence Paige. Carpenter had only one arm, having lost his left one in an accident on a machine that had pulled his arm off up to the shoulder. But that was no handicap for him when it came to playing his horn. He could put a mute in his horn as fast as anyone with two hands and he could wa-wa with a rubber plunger by putting it between his legs and working his body back and forth while sitting.

Carpenter was called "Wingy" by the musicians, because he had only one arm and "wings" is slang for arms. There are not many instruments after a trumpet that a one-armed person can play. Because of the three valves, the trumpet can be held by the little finger and the thumb, whereas a trumpet player with both hands can hold the trumpet with one hand and the other is free to manipulate the valves. Freddie Jenkins fingered the trumpet with his left hand because he had lost the joints in the upper part of the digits on his right hand.

Carpenter started showing me different things concerning phrases on the trumpet and I've always considered him my first teacher, although he was not teaching me to read music. He had traveled with many carnival shows and told me many things about the places he'd been. His mother lived in Cincinnati and at the time I met him, he was living on Richmond Street which was not far from where I had lived with my Aunt Mary. It was on the corner of Richmond and Mound Streets that I used to get beer from the saloon for my aunt.

It was at Carpenter's house that I heard my first Victrola record. The trumpet player on it was Johnny Dunn and the side I remember was a blues called *I've Been Down So Long*. I cannot describe Johnny Dunn's style but I had not heard anyone play the way he did. In fact, I had not heard too many trumpet players except Dolly Jones and her mother, Dyer Jones, Sidney De Paris, John Nesbitt, Freddie Jenkins, and the fellow from New Orleans who played around town on a wagon. There were mostly cornet players in the marching bands but they did not play jazz. I did not care too much about the way Johnny Dunn played but I did copy his style on *I've Been Down So Long* because I was learning the trumpet and it was something to help me learn to play the horn better.

A month or so after I had come home, a drummer called Lee Rainey asked me to play for a dance with him in a small town upstate in Ohio. Lee was an amateur drummer but he had played with Clarence Paige at times. I accepted the engagement and had learned *Tin Roof Blues* well enough to make Lee compliment me on the way I played it. We played it a few times that night.

A few nights later, there was a dance at the Sterling Hotel and the band was a pick-up one that was being led by a trumpeter named Chet. He had played in Chicago for a long time and he was good. I never knew why he came back to Cincinnati. Actually he lived across the river in Covington but worked in Cincinnati most of the time. Lee Rainey was the drummer that night and I came into the dance hall with my horn. When Lee saw me, he asked Chet if I could play *Tin Roof Blues* with the band. Chet looked at me and I suppose he could tell from experience that I was not good enough to play with him, so he told Lee: no, because the music was sounding bad enough already.

I was still rehearsing with Edgar Courance, Alex, a pianist named Trotter, and a drummer named Bill Johnson. John Coleman eventually came to Cincinnati and rehearsed with us also. The group was now composed of trumpet, clarinet, alto sax, C-melody sax, piano, and drums. We had no job in sight but we were amateurs and enjoyed the music we were playing. Trotter, the pianist, was a professional musician who had been put down by most of the other professionals because he was an alcoholic. But he played some fine piano as far as I was concerned. The rest of us did not drink, so we did not care about what Trotter did, and he was older than the rest of us anyway.

Sometime later an amateur trombone player came to Cincinnati and started rehearsing with us. His name was J.C. Higginbotham (Higgy). It was at his sister's house that Dyer and Dolly Jones used to have their sessions when I lived on Hathaway Street. Higginbotham's brother-in-law belonged to a lodge (the Elks I think) and through him we started playing for some of the dances the lodge would give at their meeting hall, over a drugstore at 6th and John Street. 6th Street was a famous market street, especially on Saturday. It was also part of the red-light district where one could hear the latest Bessie Smith records blasted over a loudspeaker from early morning until late in the night.

Higginbotham was ahead of the rest of us as far as style was concerned. I had not heard many trombone players then and the few that I had heard never played the way Higgy did. I never knew who his inspiration could have been. All I can say is that Higgy could blow better than anyone else in the orchestra.

We did quite a few dance jobs for the Elks at their hall and some dance jobs at the only Negro hotel on Walnut Hills. Naturally we all felt very proud to be able to play for dancers. But we were not learning to read very well and John Coleman could not read at all. Nevertheless we had our repertoire and enjoyed playing our solos the best we could.

William Smith, the pianist, was now playing with Clarence Paige but I was at his house quite often. The Chocolate Dandies show came to one of the theaters uptown and with them was a trumpet player, Joe Smith, who was featured in the show. William Smith met Joe Smith and invited him to come to his house for a session one night after the show. I was there with bells on, because Smittie had told me what a great horn player he was and I didn't want to miss hearing one note. I still remember how sweet he played that night. Smittie asked him in which key he wanted to play a certain number, and Joe told him, "Any key!"

One night during the stay of the Chocolate Dandies (shows of that type usually stayed for one month in Cincy) there was a dance at the Sterling Hotel and Clarence Paige's orchestra was playing. I had been to a rehearsal and decided to stop in at the hotel and listen for a while. I put my horn on the bandstand and stood there listening and watching the dancers. Suddenly Joe Smith was blowing that sweet sound that I had never heard anyone play before. After a time I wanted to leave, but I was ashamed to pick up my horn and let Joe Smith see that the instrument was mine. Why I felt that way I'll never know. So I walked away and stood near a door and as a friend of mine came along, I asked him to bring me the case that was on the bandstand, giving him some sort of an excuse for not going to get it myself.

Joe Smith was the greatest trumpet player to play straight melodies with a plunger and although I enjoyed hearing him in those days when I had not heard too many trumpet players, I did not try to play like him. The next time I saw Joe

Smith he was with Fletcher Henderson. But that's another story and I shall speak about it later.

Shortly after the Chocolate Dandies show left Cincinnati, a fellow by the name of Hoskin came to town and contacted Trotter for some musicians to accompany a show that he was going to produce. This show was to play quite a few small towns in Ohio and maybe a few in Indiana. Trotter told Hoskin that he had some musicians. Hoskin had a young violinist with him. We rehearsed the show and opened in a town called Oxford, Ohio. We played there for three days and then moved on to another small town. We did not get any money for the time we played in Oxford. The theaters hadn't been full, but there were a few people every night so we started to wonder where the little money that was taken in had gone.

Hoskin gave us some sort of sad story about the money and just enough change to pay for our room and get something to eat. He promised that the next town would be better as it was larger than the last two. But we had decided that the next town would be the last for us because we did not want to be caught too far from home without enough money to get back. We were also beginning to suspect Hoskin of being a slicker.

There was a young man living in Oxford who became quite friendly with the musicians. His first name was Theodore and he was the first person I had ever known who was a Negro but looked like a white. He came with us when we left Oxford, just to be with the show. We played a theater in Middletown, Ohio, and we told Hoskin that we wanted Theodore to sit in the ticket office with the vendor. We had our first full house that evening and after it was over Theodore came backstage with all the money that had been taken in, except the percentage the theater demanded. We divided the money in equal parts and told Hoskin that we had done our last show for him. It was my first experience in show business as a musician. The violinist must have stayed with Hoskin because I never saw him again, but to my recollection he was very good. I regret that I don't remember his name.

A few days after we came home from that ill-fated tour, Lee Rainey came to my house and asked me if I would like to work at a roadhouse with him. He said the salary would be $35 a week and that almost knocked me over, because my father was not making that much money working hard as a laborer on a construction gang. Neither were many of the musicians and I was still an amateur! I didn't know anyone that was making $35 a week. Back in the early 1920s that was really good loot.

There were many places all over the United States that were called roadhouses because they were situated on a highway outside of a city or town. One could always get a meal or a drink, dance, and listen to music—mostly jazz. This was during prohibition and in roadhouses the sale of alcohol was forbidden. But the clientele could bring their alcoholic drinks and be served ginger ale and ice or home brew, which was a beer made by the bootleggers. Some roadhouses sold bootleg whisky to their well-known and regular customers but not to a stranger because he could be a revenue officer who might close the place down.

I was very elated to be asked to work every night and make the kind of money that Lee offered me. The place was about ten miles outside the Cincinnati city limits on the highway going to Hamilton and Dayton, Ohio. It was called Woodlawn Inn.

The other musicians that Lee had engaged were Edgar Courance, who was now playing tenor sax, and a banjo player named Clay. He lived in Wyoming, Ohio, which is a suburb of Cincinnati. The Woodlawn Inn was in Wyoming also. But the greatest thrill of the job, after the nice salary I was making, was the pianist whom Lee had engaged: the great but unknown Edgar Hayes who had played with Freddie Jenkins and the musicians from Wilberforce College. He was the greatest I had ever heard. We did not rehearse new music during the day but we had at least one new tune to play every week. Lee Rainey would visit the music publishing houses for new songs and we played them on the job. This is the way it was done. Each one of us would take his part and place it on his stand. Edgar Hayes would play the chorus about seven or eight times while we listened and watched the notes. Only Edgar Hayes and Lee Rainey would be playing until we thought we had heard the number enough and knew how to finger it on our instruments, and then we came in.

We worked from 9 p.m. until 2 a.m. and had a big hot meal every night around midnight. None of us did any drinking, so we would have coffee, tea, or milk with our meals.

One night two young fellows and their girl companions came to the Inn after midnight. They looked as though they were coming from a wedding or a college dance because the men were dressed in tuxedos and the girls had on evening gowns. One of the young men came to the bandstand and asked me if he could play my horn. He assured me that he knew what to do with a trumpet and he did!

I had not heard any white jazz musicians because Negroes were not allowed to go to white dances and whites never went to those given by our people, although Negro musicians were engaged to play white dances, private or public, and in many of the white colleges.

This fellow really blew me out, which was not hard to do at that time, because I was still an amateur and he was a professional. I found out later that he was 18 years old, two years younger than me! He blew a couple of numbers and then we talked together during a short rest. He told me that his name was Bill Davison and he was the solo man in the Chub–Steinberg orchestra, playing at Castle Farm which was a big dance hall not far from Woodlawn Inn. Bill Davison was born in a place called Defiance, Ohio, and was known as "Wild Bill" because he was able to drink a large quantity of alcohol at a very young age and I suppose he did some wild things as most young men do, under the influence of alcohol.

One week after the visit of Wild Bill and his friends, they came back to the Woodlawn Inn and Bill wanted to play my horn again, but he was so drunk that he could hardly stand. He really didn't play anything that night and I had my revenge because I blew him out. His friend came to get him and put him in a back room where he immediately went to sleep.

Then this friend of Bill came back to talk with us and I noticed that he was very interested in Edgar's playing. He asked him to play some numbers that we didn't know and after two or three numbers, almost everyone at the Inn was standing around the bandstand listening to the pianist. We in the orchestra were very proud of him. He was just accompanied by Lee Rainey on drums, but Lee was too busy listening to do much drumming.

A few nights later, this fellow came back to the Inn alone. When it was time for us to have our meal, he came into our dining room and sat at our table. He told us that his name was Saughtercamp and that he was considered the best dance pianist in Cincinnati and some other towns in Ohio. He said there was a big record and music shop uptown in Cincinnati on 6th Street called Chub and Steinberg, who had sponsored the orchestra playing at Castle Farm. He gave Edgar a rendezvous to meet him a few days later because he wanted to get him on the list of piano players that were making piano rolls for QRS, the only company I know of that made piano rolls in those days. Edgar Hayes started making piano rolls though I never heard any. Saughtercamp told Hayes that he had forgotten more piano than Saughtercamp would ever be able to play. That was a great compliment for Edgar Hayes coming from a man who was considered the best white dance band pianist in our part of the country.

Lee Rainey had a Model T Ford coupé to go to work in. It was supposed to hold only three people, but four of us used to crowd into it. Edgar was living at Lee Rainey's house with a girl who was supposed to be his wife that he had brought from Kentucky. Her name was Ruby and she was a real fine frame. We finished work around two every morning and it would take us about an hour to get to the Sterling Hotel from the Woodlawn Inn. Edgar Hayes, Lee Rainey, Edgar Courance, and I were the four that crowed into the coupé made for two people.

Every morning as we were coming home Edgar Hayes had a song he would sing in the car. It was "I know where my baby is," and it never had any more words. He meant that he knew Ruby was home and waiting for him. Edgar and I would get out of the car at the Sterling Hotel because we lived on Carlisle Avenue, and it was not far for us to walk from the hotel. Lee and Edgar lived on West 9th Street.

One morning, Hayes had sung his "I know where my baby is" song, and after letting me and Courance out at the Sterling, Lee turned the corner of Mound Street and was going down 9th Street, and what should they see but Ruby and Lee Rainey's wife Alice walking down the street with two men. When Lee and Edgar pulled up beside their wives, the two fellows saw them getting out of the car and ran off as fast as they could. Edgar Hayes never sang that song again.

Freddie Jenkins was still going to Wilberforce University and playing with the orchestra. One night when they had been playing in the neighborhood, they stopped at the Inn to say hello. We were on the bandstand at the time and Hayes asked me to play *I found you in Maytime*. I call it that because those were the words of the first measures. But the real title is just *Maytime*. I had copied the first eight measures the way I'd heard Freddie play it when I had heard him with Edgar Hayes in Kentucky, and I played it that way. Freddie was so pleased that he started calling me brother, and we called each other brother from then on. And the odd part about it, is that we did have a physical resemblance to some degree.

I once heard an orchestra run by a man by the name of Lois Deppe at Elmwood Town Hall, which was another suburb of Cincinnati. Deppe was from Colombus, Ohio, but I think his orchestra had played around Chicago and it was his first time to play in the vicinity of Cincinnati. There was no one in the orchestra that I gave special notice to except Lois, who had such a powerful baritone voice that he stood behind the orchestra and sang without a megaphone which everyone used in those days to bring out their voices. The orchestra did not even have to soften their tone when Deppe sang.

I found out later that the pianist in Deppe's orchestra was a young man by the name of Earl Hines. One night Deppe stopped at the Woodlawn. This roadhouse did not cater to Negroes but the owner would allow them to come in and say hello to the musicians if they were musicians also. A few days after Lois Deppe's visit, Edgar Hayes announced that he was leaving to go with Deppe's orchestra, who was working somewhere in Cleveland, Ohio. We certainly hated to see Edgar leave, but Deppe had offered him more money than he was making at Woodlawn Inn and Edgar wanted to go places, so we said goodbye to him and he left Cincinnati. He still owes me $10.

William Smith was not doing much at that time so Lee hired him to replace Edgar. Although Smittie could play much piano (in fact, to me, he was the best in town after Edgar) we had become accustomed to the way Edgar played and missed him very much. I think the owner of the Inn missed him also because the band was not the same and it was not long after that we lost the job.

The musicians would congregate every afternoon in front of a restaurant on Mound Street between Carlisle Avenue and 6th Street. There was a small shoeshine shop next to the restaurant and the young man that owned the shop had not been in Cincinnati very long. But he was an ambitious fellow, and as the shoeshine shop did not bring him the amount of money he wanted to make, he started selling bootleg whisky.

I started hanging around every day with the musicians, most of whom were older than me. In order to be in good terms with them I used to give them 25 cents every day and sometimes twice a day to help buy a pint of whisky. I was not a drinker so I was always offered the first taste. Usually there would be only four of us for one pint which cost a dollar. If you knew how to drink, all four of you could get a nice taste out of a pint. The reason I was offered the bottle first was because I didn't drink much and when the bottle came back to me—if it did get back to me—there would only be a very small taste left. They usually called it "taking the poison off" if you were the first to drink out of the bottle. We never drank on the street in front of the place where we hung out because that would have been indecent. We would go into some alley or back yard to drink after we bought the bottle. We had to be careful because there was always the chance that a government revenue officer could be passing and would arrest us for illegal possession of moonshine whisky.

After a few weeks of hanging around these hard-drinking musicians and putting in my 25 cents for a pint, I began to have the feeling that I was not getting my share of the deal. So I started to open my eyes and took my first drinking lessons from the others. I soon became one of the best alley-drinking musicians in town.

I began to get some gigs with these musicians who were mostly freelancers and did not care too much to have a regular job. Most of them were 35 years old or more and I was the youngest in the bunch, so they called me the Kid. There was Edgar James, a fat drummer, Wilbur Cocksey, an alto sax player from the West Indies, a pianist named Maycocks, and a few other musicians who came around now and then. But the regulars were Maycocks, Cocksey, Edgar James, and myself.

The first job I did with these new-found friends was a one-week gig in the lobby of the Pekin Theater, which was a movie house owned by a real American Indian. I knew the son of the owner before I started playing music. There was a certain film that was showing for a week, which was a rarity because the movie house usually changed films every other day. We were engaged to play a few numbers, two or three at the end of each showing, and I really enjoyed that week.

The first out-of-town job came not long after we finished at the Pekin Theater. A fellow came from Richmond, Indiana, and engaged the Maycocks group to play a dance there. When the date came this fellow sent a car to bring us to Richmond. There we got as much food as we could eat, plenty of drinks, and we made a big hit with the dancers.

Two weeks later we went back to Richmond and then the organizer told me that he would like me to be the leader of the orchestra the next time they had a dance. There was one about three weeks after that and I took Edgar Courance, who was still playing tenor sax, William Smith (piano), Wilbur Cocksey (alto sax), and Edgar James (drums).

When we arrived in Richmond and I saw the advertising bills and posters for the dance, there was the name of the hall and the date of the dance and in big letters "Professor Johnson Coleman and his Band." I did not like the idea of being called "professor" because my idea of professor was of an older person and for a musician, a professor was someone that knew all about music and was a music teacher. But I had been billed that way and although I played the best I could that night, every time someone called me "Professor" I would tell them that I was not a professor! We played Richmond a few more times and no matter how hard I begged the organizers not to put "Professor" Johnson Coleman on the posters, every time we went there, it was Professor Johnson Coleman. I really never considered myself a leader to the extent of getting more money than the rest of the musicians, so we all had the same pay when the job was finished. Fortunately the other musicians never called me "Professor" in a kidding way or otherwise.

William Smith the pianist rejoined Clarence Paige and I, with Herschel Brown, Edgar Courance, Alex Baker (alto sax), and Bill Johnson (drums). Herschel Brown played piano by ear as did many of the pianists in Cincinnati. Some of them could only play in one or two different keys, but Herschel was one of the few that could play in any key. We could "spell," which is said about a musician when he can't read music very fast. Still that was one advantage that we had over Herschel. But all that Herschel needed was to hear the melody of a number a couple of times and he could play it with the right harmony. In my opinion, Herschel was the second-best pianist after Edgar Hayes and he probably would have become one of the greats of that era if he had known how to read. He was about the age of Edgar Courance and myself.

We never had any job with Herschel, which was a pity because I believe that we would have been more inspired playing for dancers than we were at the rehearsals although with Herschel at the keyboard, even the rehearsals were fine.

Sometime later a fellow called Zack (for Zacharias) White came to Cincinnati from Kentucky. He played banjo. There was also a pianist named Johnny Johnson whom I had heard when I was living on Kenyon Avenue. Johnny Johnson also played piano by ear and he was well known in the higher society Negro class.

One day Zack and Johnny came to my house and told me that a fellow from Michigan who was a drummer wanted some musicians to play weekends at a vacation camp not far from Kalamazoo. They asked me if I would like to be part of the group. I had never been more than a hundred miles from Cincinnati so this proposition sounded great to me. Zack and Johnny did not have to ask me twice if I wanted to go with them.

A few days later we left Cincinnati with the drummer. We were joined by a young alto player from Wyoming, Ohio, named Jimmie Smith. He was the second Negro I had seen who looked like a white. I had gone south from Cincinnati but now I was going north. It was a summer month but the thing that excited me the most was that I was going farther away from Cincinnati that I had ever been, leaving my father for the longest time in my life and getting out in the world by playing music.

Grand Rapids, Michigan, was our headquarters. Every Saturday afternoon we would go to Kalamazoo by bus, and there we had a rendezvous with someone who would bring us to the camp, where we played Saturday night and Sunday afternoon and evening. We came back to Grand Rapids every Monday morning and spent the rest of the week there. We all lived at the same rooming house except for the drummer, whose name I do not remember. He lived in Grand Rapids. We ate in restaurants. It was thrilling for me to be away from home because it gave me the feeling that I was a man looking after myself instead of being home with Dad who went to bed at a fixed time and was very unhappy when I came home late and blew the last puff of a cigarette in the room where we slept. I had no key so my father was obliged to open the door for me at whatever time I came home.

There was a big white dance hall in Grand Rapids, and we used to go and listen to the orchestra that was playing there. We had to listen to them from outside because there were no mixed dances in the USA at that time. It was a twelve-piece orchestra and we could see into the dance hall by standing on a box near the open windows. This band sounded as good to me as the Chub–Steinberg orchestra. I remember that the get-off and hokum man was a stout fellow who had a brass trumpet that he never shined and that gave the horn the look of dark green copper. I didn't know anything about styles at that time, but this fellow could really play and I enjoyed listening to him. As we had nothing to do during the week, we went at least three nights every week to listen to this band.

I had got away from the hard-drinking musicians in Cincinnati and I did not miss drinking. Johnny Johnson met some nice Negro people and soon we were invited to parties. I was very timid with girls but enjoyed playing a few numbers because we were invited to bring our instruments along whenever we went to a party.

One day there was some sort of celebration which must have concerned only the city of Grand Rapids. There were parades with marching bands and floats with flowers and girls. But I was surprised and shocked to hear a group on one of the floats playing jazz songs in unison. All the groups I had ever heard played their numbers in harmony; the groups I had played with also. I thought that those guys must really be amateurs that didn't know anything. I was still an amateur, as were the fellows I was working with, but we would have never thought of playing an ensemble in unison. It was a disgrace to jazz! But it turns out those cats were really ahead of their time. We all know what's been going on for years in jazz since bop came on the scene. Now we play the melody, written choruses, and jive ones in unison, and they sound good.

There was nothing outstanding about our group, but we enjoyed playing together and the public liked us.

At the end of two months we came back to Cincinnati and I decided to stay with my mother. My father and mother had separated for the last time since I was 14 years old. I felt that I was old enough to do what I wanted, and although I had a good father, I knew that I would always be like a young boy to him and not a young man. I was happy living with my mother and sister who was going to high school. Mama let me do as I pleased and I had my own room, which is something I did not have with Dad as he had only two rooms, the bedroom and kitchen-living room combined.

The first thing I did after going to live with my mother was to buy myself a Victrola. The one I bought was the new-style cabinet Victrola which was another piece of furniture for my mother's house. The mechanical part of the Victrola took up half of the cabinet and the other half was for records.

The first record I bought was recorded by a group called the Goofus Five and the title of the numbers on the two sides were *Sadie Green the Vamp of New Orleans* and *Crazy Quilt*. It was an Okeh record which I still possess. I had another by the same group of which one title I remember very well was *In Your Green Hat*. The Goofus Five were white musicians and there were not many race records, which was the name given to records that were recorded by Negroes in those days. Bessie and Mamie Smith, Ma Rainey and some other well-known blues singers of the early 1920s were recording, but no orchestras or small groups of Negro musicians. If they were, I did not know about it. Of course, the blues singers were accompanied by Negro musicians whose names were never on the recording, but neither were the names of the white musicians for that matter.

THREE

THE CLARENCE PAIGE
ORCHESTRA

I joined Clarence Paige's orchestra in the fall of 1923. Clarence augmented his orchestra from the seven- or eight-piece group that he had before to a ten-piece orchestra including himself. The other trumpet player's name was Nassau. No one ever knew his other name or if that was his real name. He was from the West Indies and probably had a name so difficult that it was hard to pronounce or he gave himself that name because he came from Nassau. He was not a very large fellow and he must have traveled a lot and had quite a bit of experience before he hit Cincinnati. He played growl-style trumpet and I wondered where could he have gotten the style, because it was like that of Bubber Miley who was not known in the Middle West at that time. Duke Ellington was unknown also and not recording.

Jimmie Smith, the alto sax player who had been with the group I was with in Michigan, also joined Paige's orchestra. The other members were: William Smith (piano), Wilbur Cocksey (alto sax), Clarence Paige (C-melody sax), Edgar James (drums), and two brothers: Clarence Logan (tuba) and Dan Logan (trombone). But the most outstanding musician in the group was a banjo player named Bob Robinson. Bob came to Cincinnati from West Virginia. Banjos took quite a few solos in the orchestras at that time and Bob was considered one of the best in that part of the country.

We played regularly at a third-floor dance hall named George and Central—it was at George Street and Central Avenue. A show came to Cincinnati featuring a young trumpet player by the name of Cheatham. He came to one of the dances we were playing and sat in with us. I could tell right away that he had quite a bit of experience. After Bob Robinson, it was usually Nassau that had the biggest success because of his growling, which really did not impress me at all. But this night it was Cheatham that showed us all what trumpet playing really was. I talked with him later and he told me that everyone called him "Doc" because one of his uncles was a famous Southern surgeon, the one who had amputated the arm of Wingy Carpenter, my trumpet teacher.

I went to the theater where Doc was playing and to my surprise he was playing alto sax and trumpet in the show. I never knew who the other musicians in the group were because Doc Cheatham was the only one that interested me. The show stayed for two weeks and I went to listen to Doc at least eight times.

The first trip out of Cincinnati that I made with Paige was a catastrophe. We left one morning for Charleston, West Virginia, in a Pierce-Arrow owned by a fellow named Richard Carpenter. A Pierce-Arrow was and still is a wealthy man's car, and how "Rich," as everyone called him, came to own one, I never found out. It was a seven-passenger car but we could get ten musicians in it with Rich driving and we were not uncomfortable. We were all on the slim side except Edgar James. We also had our personal baggage, drums, tuba and the rest of the instruments. All cars had running boards on both sides in those days and a luggage carrier on the left running board. It was surprising how much luggage could be packed on a car. For one thing, the Pierce-Arrow was a long car with the headlights on the fender. When seen coming down a road at night, it resembled two motorcycles, one on the right side of the road and the other on the left. That is, if the road was not too wide.

So off we went in the direction of West Virginia. We arrived in Middletown, Ohio, and were stopped by a motorcycle policeman who claimed that Rich had passed a car going in the same direction as we were at an intersection. I did not know anything about the rules of the road and I could not drive. So I did not understand why we had been stopped. Rich was fined and we all had to pay.

The next trouble was with the tires, which were worn. The weather was quite warm and one blew out in the rear. Rich patched that one and a few miles farther along the road, another blew out. The inner tubes had been patched up so often and the tires were so worn that it was impossible to continue the trip without new tires. Rich could not afford real new tires, so we all had to give from our pockets again in order to buy some used tires that were like new considering the condition of the ones that Rich had on the car when we left Cincinnati.

We eventually reached Charleston, West Virginia, and did not have to play until the next night. The dance was a big success for us and Clarence Paige divided the money in ten parts and then asked us to give a certain amount to Rich for the gas and the time he had put in to drive us. Then we all went out and had a good time.

The next day we left Charleston for Bluefield, West Virginia. To get there, it was necessary to cross the Cotton Top mountains. The road was so narrow that two cars could not pass each other except at certain places where one had to pull in where the road had been widened. One of the curves was so sharp that the Pierce-Arrow had to go forward, then backwards in a certain maneuver in order to take the turn. There was no protection to keep the car from going over the cliff and we were at least 6000 feet above sea level. My heart was in my mouth because, at every curve, I thought we would go off the road. But Rich was a good chauffeur and when we finally arrived on the other side of Cotton Top Mountain, a few miles from Bluefield, it was one of the happiest moments of my young life.

That night, at the dance, the piano was so old, used and out of tune that Smittie was obliged to transpose every number we played. I thought that we would stay in Bluefield after the dance finished, but we packed up and left for Charleston and more trouble!

We had not gone more than one mile from the dance hall when a car with two policemen in plain clothes pulled up besides us and ordered Rich to pull over to the curb. They told him he was speeding. When Rich and some of the others protested these officers declared that he had been speeding when he had come into town *before* the dance and that he would have to pay a fine of so many dollars or all of us would go to jail. So we all had to give from our pockets again. This was the racket that the police pulled on every black orchestra that played in Bluefield. The dance was always a success and those two crooks knew that all the orchestras, including ours, would have some money. They could put a Negro in jail for breathing the same air that they did if they wanted to.

To make matters worse, we had to come back over the Cotton Top Mountains at night! I was frightened enough when we came over them during the day when I could see what was happening. I was sitting in the back seat, and, as the lights of the Pierce-Arrow were on the fenders, every time we went around a curve I could not see the road, so I had the impression that the car was really running off it. I felt like getting out and walking, but it would have taken me some days to get to Charleston. It was one of the worst nights I have known and I still get the shivers when I think about it.

We arrived in Charleston around eight in the morning and although I had quite a bit to drink before we left Bluefield, I was as sober as a teetotaller and so tired that the moment I entered my room in the hotel, I got my clothes off and hit the hay. I was asleep before anyone could say "Jack Rabbit" and it was late afternoon when I awakened.

We only had those two dances in West Virginia and stayed in Charleston after coming from Bluefield to rest before hitting the road for Cincinnati. After having slept most of the day, a few of us met in a house where moonshine whisky was sold. We were having a grand time when suddenly there was a noise in the kitchen and some white men came in, revolvers flashing, and told everyone in the room not to move. We all had glasses in front of us but Edgar James was the only one who had a few drops in his glass. He was arrested because he had enough moonshine in it to prove that he had been drinking. I never understood what kind of law they had in West Virginia concerning bootleg whisky because these were revenue men and although we had all been drinking, Edgar James was the only one arrested.

We went to jail to see Edgar the next day before we left for Cincinnati and we were told that his trial would not be held for a week. So we had to go into our pockets again to leave Edgar some money to pay for his fine and fare back to Cincinnati when he was freed.

The only thing I got from my first trip out of Cincinnati with the Clarence Paige Orchestra was the memory of that hellish ride in the car!

It was not always pleasant traveling through West Virginia because it was necessary to pass through many small towns and villages, where mostly white miners and farmers lived, and as the bass drum and other baggage were carried on the running board of the car, we could be seen coming into a place from a great distance. The white kids seemed to know that it would be a car with Negro musicians and they would throw rocks at us and call us niggers. It was a bitter pill to swallow and we could not do anything about it. This also happened going through places in Kentucky.

The first time I was ever in jail was when I went to Lexington with Clarence Paige. We decided to buy a gallon of moonshine in Covington, Kentucky, because it was cheaper than in Lexington, someone said. We had some other jobs after Lexington and a gallon of juice would last for a time if we took it easy. We were all staying in a big rooming house owned by a woman named Kate and all the rooms were on the ground floor. Dan Logan and I were staying together, but Dan didn't drink.

I always had a good time when I went to Lexington and the dance was a jumping one. When it was finished, we had some food in a late-morning restaurant and came back to Kate's place and brought out the jug. Dan Logan went to bed and we all gathered in one room and started to drink. Then, after a half hour, I decided that I would have one more drink and then hit the hay. Just as I started for the door, a voice hollered, "Don't anybody move!" I looked around and there was a white hand with a gun in it poked through the window. (It was summer and the window was open.) In stepped a white policeman who told us that we were under arrest. Some more police came in after him and they put us in a Black Maria, as patrol wagons were called, and took us to jail.

After we were booked for having bootleg whisky, they put us in a cell. I lay down on one of the benches and forgot everything until I was awakened about 9 a.m. and was told that we were free on bond. Kate had bailed us out. We thankfully paid her back, and never heard anything about the case after that.

Clarence Paige traveled quite a bit in Kentucky but we had more work just in Cincinnati. We played some dates on a riverboat of the type that went from New Orleans to Kansas City. It would cruise down the Ohio River starting about 4 p.m. on a Sunday and return to the pier at 11 p.m. Sometimes there would be a fight—I should say most of the times, there were fights—that would really get out of control for a few minutes. It would be dangerous because everyone that was trying to get away from the fight would run to the farther side and make the boat lean over and could have caused it to overturn. But the fights never lasted a long time and most of the people would come back to the center and start dancing again. We never stopped playing and we even played as loud as possible to distract the attention of the people from the fight.

There was a white dance hall uptown on 6th Street, between Race and Vine Streets, that started renting out for Negro dances. Clarence Paige's was the orchestra that played for the dances there and the bandstand was about four feet high.

I did not pay much attention to girls at that time. Although I had had a few girl-friends, nothing serious ever came from the friendship. Girls didn't bother me the way they did some of the young men of my age and I was quite bashful. One night Edgar James, who noticed everything, told me that a certain girl was watching me all the time we were on the bandstand. I had seen her many times before at most of the dances we had played. During the next intermission, I asked her to have a drink with me and she accepted. We had a conversation but I did not ask her for a date until I had talked to her at a few other dances. Then it started to get serious and we were together quite often. Her name was Madelyn Grant. She was one year older than me. She was a tall brown-skin girl, not fat but strongly built, with large eyes. She had come to Cincinnati from Birmingham, Alabama, with an aunt—both of her parents were dead. I don't believe I was seriously in love with her, but being 21, it was more of a fancy to have a girlfriend or a lover.

Not long after this romance started, a bandleader by the name of Broadus from Lexington, Kentucky, asked me if I would join him for a month. I told Paige that I would like to leave for a change and accepted the offer of Broadus. He had been quite a big name in jazz and had played many fraternity dances at Yale, Harvard, and other colleges. Love did not have such a hold on me that I did not want to travel.

The first night I played with Broadus was for a dance in Dayton, Ohio. Broadus played C-melody sax. The alto player, Henry Jamerson, was known as "Speechless" because he was not a great talker. I had seen him with the orchestra of Lloyd Scott when they had played at Elmwood Town Hall. The other musicians were: Steve Dunn, a trumpet player with a very nice style; Slaughter Campbell, a banjo player as good as Bob Robinson; and William Benton, on drums. I forget the names of the pianist and the tuba player, who was a big fellow who weighed 240 pounds. He could just get a double B flat tuba around his body and you could not get a toothpick between him and the instrument. Broadus had a big secondhand Packard and the tuba player sat in the back on the left side, which made the car sag in such a way that from the back it looked as though it was going to turn over. We left Dayton after the dance and headed for Lexington. My place in the car was next to the tuba player. When I became sleepy, I laid over against him and slept almost as comfortably as if I was in a bed.

My first trip with Broadus almost ended in disaster. Broadus stopped in a small town to have a cup of coffee because he was feeling tired. But he didn't put the brakes on tight enough and the car rolled backwards down a hill. We on the back seat were all asleep. Fortunately, the musicians that sat in front had not gone with Broadus but were standing on the side of the road. They saw the car start to roll and managed to get two big rocks under the wheels to stop it about three feet from a stream that was at least five feet deep in that particular place.

In Lexington I stayed with Henry Jamerson and his mother. Jamerson had been with an organization known as Musical Spiller when he was very young. Spiller had a musical act made of members of his family and other talented young musicians that he discovered. He arranged with the families of these young musicians to let them travel with him. Jamerson traveled quite extensively with Spiller and then joined the orchestra of Lloyd Scott from Springfield, Ohio, which I had heard when they made their first tour after being in New York. Jamerson had left the Scott orchestra because his mother's health was not very good and she was alone. He was the only child and he decided to stay at home with her until she passed away.

With Broadus, we were playing the same kind of swing music that I was playing with Clarence Paige's orchestra. Steve Dunn, the other trumpet player, and I got along well together and worked out some nice duos on certain numbers. When we were not on the road, we practised quite a bit because there were not many distractions in Lexington, except movies.

After one month, I got homesick for Cincinnati, so I left Broadus, came home and rejoined Clarence Paige. Later, Wesley Helvey offered me a job in a roadhouse situated in Newport, Ohio, an every-night affair, and as Paige was not getting much work, I accepted. I may have been lazy about doing other work but once I had got to the point where I could play something on my trumpet, I wanted to play as often as possible. I may have been late going to school at times, or late getting to another kind of job, but I was never late when it came time to go blow my horn.

Helvey also engaged Edgar Courance on tenor sax and a trombone player nicknamed "Pluto." The pianist was Vincent Thomas. He was one of the few band pianists around town who could read music. The drummer was Leslie Towles and later a banjo player named Jimmie was added to the group.

One day the word got around that a famous New Orleans pianist was in town. As it happened to be a night off, most of the musicians turned up at the place where he was playing. He took charge of every pianist that was in the place. It was Jelly Roll Morton. He was a real talker. He had a diamond in one tooth and when he wasn't playing piano, he was talking about what he had done, where he had been and what he was going to do. At that time, there were no books on jazz and the musicians that played it, so I didn't know if this Mr. "Jelly Roll," as he called himself, had done all the things he said he had. I had never heard anyone play the way he did: there he was not bluffing.

Some months after, Jelly Roll came back to Cincy with the orchestra of Fate Marable. Fate played piano also but he directed the band most of the time. I never knew who the musicians were, but I, and everyone that heard them, knew that we had heard one of the best jazz orchestras that had ever come to town.

Other big-name orchestras that I heard in Cincy were those of Speed Webb, Alphonso Trent, and Bellson, an orchestra from West Virginia that Bobby Robinson and John Nesbitt had played with.

Wesley Helvey took a job across the river in Newport, Kentucky, at a roadhouse and a new drummer named John Hargrave joined the orchestra. He was a better drummer than Towles, who went on tour with a TOBA show called the Whitman Sisters. I had seen this show in Cincinnati and one of the sisters, Alice, was a wonderful tap dancer.

It was at that time, in 1925, that Madelyn and I got married. I had said when I was younger that I would not get married until I was 35 years old and here I was, getting married at 21.

But a funny thing happened to me three months after I was married. I was sent a message to go to see the mother of a girl I had been seeing at times before Madelyn and I became real close. When I arrived at their house, the mother told me that her daughter Leah was pregnant. I asked her what that had to do with me and she told me that I was the one her daughter said had done it. I told the mother that I was just three months married and there was nothing I could do about it. The mother was not angry or upset, but only wanted me to know that I was going to be the father of her daughter's baby!

I told Madelyn about it but denied that I was the father. I really did not believe I was responsible for the pregnancy. A few months before the baby was born, I began to get sick to my stomach. My teeth started hurting me and I had a good one pulled out because it seemed to be the one that was giving me hell. As time went on, nothing I ate would stay down, and I was only comfortable when I slept in a chair. I couldn't blow my horn and eventually my weight came down from 145 pounds to 128 and I was looking like a walking skeleton.

My mother thought that perhaps if I changed the climate and went to Crawfordsville, Indiana, it might be good for me. I had seen a couple of doctors and they couldn't find out what was wrong with me. So Madelyn and I went to Crawfordsville and stayed with my Aunt Sarah. After being there for a week, one night my pains stopped suddenly. The next day a message came from my father, saying that Leah had given birth to a girl at a certain time: that time coincided with the time the pains in my stomach stopped bothering me. I came back home the next day and started to get better. I was happy that I could start blowing my horn again. They named the girl Louise but my brother and the rest of the family called her Sis. We were very fond of her but unfortunately Louise died when she was five years old.

We worked quite a long time at the roadhouse in Newport and when we left that job, Helvey decided to enlarge the orchestra because we had started doing dance work in West Virginia, Kentucky, and other cities in Ohio.

Word got around that the Synco Septet was going to play a dance in Dayton. The septet was later to be known as the famous McKinney's Cotton Pickers. That orchestra had a very big name but it had never come to Cincinnati, so Helvey and a few other members of the orchestra, including myself, decided to go to Dayton, which was 50 miles from Cincy. It was a trip well worth taking.

The Synco Septet was a showband and dance orchestra combined. They were the first and only Negro orchestra that I'd ever seen with such high-quality musicianship and showmanship. They did their show numbers in a manner that the public could dance to and at the same time entertain them with songs in which the musicians would be putting on funny hats, mustaches, women's dresses, or masks. The rhythm section was participating in these numbers too, yet the beat was going on at a tempo where none of the dancers would lose a step. We didn't miss a single sound or gesture. It was really an unforgettable night and we talked about it for days. The composition of the band was: John Nesbitt (trumpet), Claude Jones (trombone), Milton Senior and George "Fathead" Thomas (alto saxes), Todd Rhodes (piano), Dave Wilborn (banjo), June Cole (tuba), and Cuba Austin (drums). McKinney, an ex-drummer, was the business manager of the group.

When Jelly Roll Morton came to Cincinnati with Fate Marable, he was telling everyone whose ear he could catch, that he was going to bring an orchestra to town that would wash Fate's away. So a few months later, Jelly came with his own band. To make a long story short, it was the worst-sounding band I had ever heard. Where Jelly got those musicians only the Lord and Jelly knew. I remember that one of the trumpeters was the funniest looking red-head, yellow complexioned person I had ever seen. In a certain way I felt sorry for Jelly because none of the musicians was doing anything outstanding and poor Jelly was working so hard to try and make the piano cover the band that he was wringing wet from perspiration and looking so downhearted that he would probably had given his diamond tooth not to have been in that predicament that night.

Some records of the Fletcher Henderson band of New York reached Cincy. The first one I heard was at Edgar James's house. On one side of the record there was a number called *Money Blues* with a great trumpet solo by a man called Louis Armstrong. This was, without doubt, the greatest trumpet solo I had ever heard and I bought the record as soon as I could find a copy.

I enjoyed Fletcher's band and eventually found out the names of the musicians, especially the soloists, Charlie "Big" Green (trombone), Joe Smith and Louis Armstrong (trumpets), Buster Bailey (clarinet). Coleman Hawkins was the first tenor sax and bass saxophone player: he could swing a band into bad health. You could hear his sax cutting through when the whole band was giving everything they had.

Then there were Henderson records with Louis Armstrong and Joe Smith, who were great as a team. Later there were records of Louis Armstrong and his Hot Five. The first Louis Armstrong I bought was *Heebie Jeebies*. After that I got any record that Armstrong made. The people at the record shop began to know me as an Armstrong fan and would always put one of his records aside for me when they came in.

I began to copy the style of Armstrong for technical reasons and because I admired his style. I learned to play all his solos note for note. If there was a slight mistake, I copied that too because Louis could get over his horn so fast. Besides, his mistakes were so beautiful that they sounded as though they were made purposely.

Most trumpet players that I heard later who had copied Armstrong's style showed it in their playing, but I never played "Armstrong" when I took a solo. I liked everything about Louis's playing: his tone and the way he could phrase a melody. But I started to develop my own style by trying to play my solos the way I figured Louis might play if he were me. I have never lost my admiration for what he meant to me and what he did to make jazz the music it is today.

The next thrill of my life was when Fletcher Henderson came to town. Zack White and his partner were the bookers of the well-known orchestras that came to Cincinnati. Bringing Fletcher Henderson was one of the highlights of their booking career and for us musicians, it was like having heaven sent to us.

The band came a day before they were to play and the first musician I saw, but didn't know, was Russell Smith. My instinct told me that he was from New York because he was dressed so well: no one around town had the class that he had. We spoke and I told him that I would be at the dance. It was on a Sunday, and they were playing that afternoon and night at the Crystal Ballroom.

I was there that afternoon before the band played their first number and I never moved from the place I had in front of the band until the last number. Joe Smith was the only one that had been in Cincinnati before. It was my first time to see the rest of the musicians. They were: Luke Smith, Joe Smith, and Russell "Pops" Smith (trumpets), Don Redman (alto sax), Buster Bailey (alto sax and clarinet), Coleman Hawkins (tenor sax), Big Green (trombone), Fletcher Henderson (piano), Charlie Dixon (banjo), Bobby Escudero (tuba), and Kaiser Marshall (drums).

Fletcher played most of the songs I had heard him play on records and many I had never heard, but the thing that amazed me most was that "Big" Green usually took his solos after Joe Smith, who was the only trumpet soloist for the jumping numbers in the band, and Green played, note for note, everything that Joe Smith played. Joe's solos were played sweet in the Joe Smith style and there were no solos on trumpet the way Louis Armstrong had played *Money Blues*. "Hawk" was amazing and Buster Bailey was great also. I had not heard too much of him on records.

The arrangements were the greatest I had ever heard and I wondered if the day would ever come when I would be good enough to play in a band like that. We had to work that Sunday night and we were pretty much inspired by the lesson we had received from the Fletcher Henderson orchestra. The only thing missing was Louis Armstrong.

A few months later Fletcher came back to Cincinnati for a Sunday night dance. He was such a big attraction that Zack White was having him at the Armory, which was the biggest hall in town. There was also a dance that Sunday afternoon at the Crystal Ballroom with the Horace Henderson (Fletcher's brother) orchestra from Wilberforce College. I was at the Crystal and Horace's boys, with Freddie Jenkins (trumpet), Joe and Castor McCord (alto sax and tenor sax), and Henry "Red" Hicks (trombone), were sounding real great. Fletcher had given Horace quite a few of his arrangements and Horace came close to playing them like Fletcher.

I noticed a little fat brown-skin guy who was standing against the wall near the bandstand and looked like he was mad at the world. He only smiled occasionally when one of the musicians in the band looked his way. I asked at the intermission who he was and was told that it was Rex Stewart, a trumpet player that had taken Joe Smith's place in Fletcher's band.

In the evening I went to the Armory to hear Fletcher for the second time. The sax section had not changed since the last time. Another trombone had been added, a young fellow named Benny Morton. My interest was mostly in the trumpet section and I noticed that Rex Stewart was extra fast in his execution. Although I didn't know much about styles, I knew that his was different from Joe Smith or from what I had heard Armstrong do on records. Rex was amusing to watch but I didn't understand the way he played or care for it. But the band was just as great as it had been the first time I heard it and the Armory was crowded.

A colored orchestra under the direction of Alex Jackson came to Cincinnati from New York during the year 1926. It was mostly a society orchestra. It had ten musicians; with the leader Alex, who sometimes played soprano sax, they were eleven. This orchestra had nothing in common with Fletcher and Horace Henderson, Lloyd Scott, or Speed Webb. They did not play that kind of jazz but they made a big hit with the women, and wherever the women went, the men were sure to be there. So Alex stayed in the vicinity of Cincinnati for months and even worked at a white open-air dancing place on Vine Street in the suburb of Walnut Hills, where no other Negro orchestra had ever worked.

There were some nice musicians in Alex's orchestra and I became acquainted with Leonard Fields, who had a technique like Rudy Wiedoeft on alto sax, Clarence Wheeler, the first trumpet man, and Goldie, whose last name I don't remember, who played a growl style of trumpet like Nassau from the Clarence Paige orchestra.

One day someone brought me a message from Alex saying that he wanted to see me. I never went to see him because I had an idea that he wanted to ask me to join his orchestra. It was not because I did not care for the style of the band, but because I was afraid that I could not read music fast enough. I found out later that Goldie could not read a note either.

FOUR

THE LLOYD SCOTT ORCHESTRA

Early in 1927 I received an offer to join the Lloyd Scott orchestra. I accepted because I had admired the band the first time I heard it and now I could read music better than I could when Alex asked me to come and join him. I had refused an offer to join Speed Webb's orchestra, who had been campaigning upstate in New York and was getting ready to go to California. When I told Helvey that I was going to join the Lloyd Scott orchestra, he threatened to make trouble for me even if he had to come to New York to do it. I had no idea if or when Scott would be going to New York, but I wanted to join the orchestra and told Helvey that I was leaving regardless of what he intended doing.

Lloyd Scott had also engaged Frankie Newton, a young trumpet player from Virginia. He had been playing with Clarence Paige for quite some time. We both joined Scott's band in Lexington, Kentucky, and played a dance without any rehearsals. Scott played dances on a percentage basis, the same as most traveling orchestras did: 60 per cent for the orchestra, 40 per cent for the promoter. That night Lloyd gave each musician $17. That was the most money I had ever made in one night. He must have had twice that for himself and his brother Cecil, who stood in front of the orchestra with a top hat like Ted Lewis. But it was normal because he had the responsibility of transportation and other expenses. I never expected to find another leader as honest with his men as Clarence Paige—and never did. Clarence divided the money in ten parts and gave everyone the same amount. He just asked us to share the expenses for the transportation if we were playing away from Cincinnati.

But I was so happy about the money I received from Lloyd Scott after the first job that I saw myself already with a big bank roll. The next job we did, I received $7, but that was not at all bad for those days. My bankroll did not grow as I thought it would but I was happy because I was with a bunch of musicians who had been places and had musical ideas that I had not experienced before. The musicians other than Frankie Newton that I did not know were Dicky Wells (trombone), Cecil Scott (clarinet, tenor sax, director), his brother, Lloyd Scott (drums and leader), Harold McFerran (alto sax), and Don Frye (piano). The Scott brothers and Don Frye were born in Springfield, Ohio, Dicky Wells, Harold McFerran, and Mack Walker (tuba) came from Louisville, Kentucky. Frankie Newton was from Virginia, and Hubert Mann (banjo) was from West Virginia.

Harold McFerran and Mack Walker were half brothers. The band had no engagements to return to New York when I joined them, so I went to live in Springfield, Ohio, the home town and headquarters for the Scott brothers. Springfield was a very small town and there was not much in the line of excitement. That did not worry me but my wife, Madelyn, who had joined me there, began to miss her friends and relatives. We started to quarrel and she decided to go back to Cincinnati.

Frankie Newton and I roomed together with a family named Jackson. The band was not getting much work and when we did get a job, we would pay the back rent. There was a restaurant and poolroom near where we lived, which was owned by a man named Rick. We ate there on credit and paid him the same as we did Grandma Jackson—when things were going alright. Neither Rick nor Grandma worried about their money if we were three weeks or more behind in our rent or food bills.

We had plenty of time to rehearse and we did so almost every day. When we found a good idea for a number, Don Frye would play it on the piano and then give each instrument the harmonies it should play. We worked on one number at each rehearsal and after a few months we had a fine repertoire though nothing was written down on paper.

We received an offer to go to Canada for one month to play in a dancing place in Hamilton, Ontario. The engagement was during one of the spring months. We did not know anything about Canada except that it was supposed to be a cold country, so we took our overcoats and other winter clothes with us. When we arrived in Hamilton, the weather was as nice and warm as it was when we left Springfield. This was the first time our band had a one month stay at the same place since I had joined. We really enjoyed playing every night for wonderful audiences.

There were not many Negroes living in Hamilton and none ever came to the place where we were working although there was no prejudice in Canada. Some of us stayed with a Negro family, and the man that owned the house was a Negro also. He had a very large cleaning business with at least 25 employees, and they were all white. A person was allowed two quarts of whisky or other alcoholic drinks a month and could only buy it at government stores. One could also have a case of twelve bottles of beer and there was one label called White Horse Ale that I could get a fine feeling from after two bottles, so we had no worries about drinks.

John Williams got homesick for New York and left the band. Another sax player from Louisville, Lester Carr, took his place. The next one to leave was Hubert Mann. He had received an offer to join Speed Webb's orchestra in California, so Rudolph "Bull" Williams who lived in a town not far from Springfield was hired as banjoist. Rudolph was a very stocky young fellow who had played football at Wilberforce University. He was called "Bull" because of his big face, big hands, and broad shoulders. His father was a preacher but Bull was everything except religious. I had met him a few years before when Edgar Courance and I made friends with a couple of amateur musicians from Hamilton, Ohio, and we would go there for a couple of days every week and play in a small cabaret. I even played my first radio program with Bull, who knew somebody at the radio station.

After our return from Hamilton we had a few jobs that did not pay much. One I remember very well was in the town where Ted Lewis was born. Alex Jackson and his orchestra were playing in a place in the vicinity and people from miles around had gone to hear him. It was another percentage deal and when Lloyd paid us, we received 30 cents each. That was a big drop from the first time I had played with the orchestra in Lexington and received $17 for the night.

I never complained because these were the best jazz musicians I had ever worked with. The Scott brothers, Don Frye, and Dicky Wells had New York experience and I was learning more about music and improving my style, which was different from Frankie Newton's. It was a good thing to have two trumpet players in the same orchestra who had different styles and worked well together in the ensemble. We were like brothers that loved one another, and the band was sounding better and better with each rehearsal.

The next offer came for a one-week engagement. We never realized the actual quality of our playing until we were engaged to replace an orchestra run by a fellow called Warmack at the Arcadia Ballroom in Buffalo, New York, and alternated with the house band who were known as the Buffalodians. The only thing I knew about Warmack was that he was from Louisville, Kentucky. But the Buffalodians were a white orchestra of twelve musicians, well known in the eastern states, and were in the same category as the Casa Loma Orchestra which was one of the best orchestras (also white) ever organized. It was the first time we had played in a dance hall that engaged two orchestras at the same time.

The ballroom was very long with tables on the side. The Buffalodians were on a high bandstand at one end of the ballroom and we were on a stand at the other. They had twelve musicians, and we were ten. I enjoyed listening to the Buffalodians and I have never forgotten one number they featured, *She's the Last Word*—"She can't dance, but for real romance, she's the last word." I still remember most of the words, and when I think of the number now and then it takes me back to my first week in Buffalo when we had a lot of fun.

Jazz battles did not exist then like the ones that were to become famous a few years later; still, it was a jazz contest every night. We were not as well known in Buffalo as the Buffalodians who had been playing the ballroom for years, but we blew enough to have a big majority of the public applauding for us after each number. The Buffalodians were throwing their best numbers at us, and we were throwing our best ones back at them.

Buffalo was the first city that I had been in during the prohibition era that was wide open. It was the same as Cincinnati had been when I was a kid: the saloons were open 24 hours a day and there were plenty of whorehouses, especially in the district where we were staying, not far from the center of the city. This was something new to me and it was perhaps a good thing that we only had a one-week engagement because I did not sleep more than 15 hours that week. I was getting my first real taste of nightlife and I didn't want to miss anything.

There was one particular saloon where all the colored musicians came after their jobs in various ballrooms and clubs. There was a back room that had a piano, and jam sessions or cutting contests, as they were called, were the order of the day from three in the morning until eleven or twelve o'clock the next day. I got my first kicks being able to stand at a bar drinking and talking until the cutting contest got hot. Then I would go in the back room, take out my horn, and join in with the rest of the musicians. Each one would take turns in buying a round of drinks and no one paid any attention to how much money he was spending, especially me.

I learned quite a lot from those contests because sometimes there were three or four trumpet players in the room and no one to play the piano. So we would see who knew how to do some difficult exercises that the others could not do. I learned how to jump from C below the staff to the one above from a young trumpet player who had a style like Joe Smith.

It was in Buffalo that I heard the greatest jazz violinist that ever lived. His name was Robert "Juice" Wilson. Juice played in a ballroom not far from the saloon where the musicians congregated and I went to listen to him almost every night after I had finished work at the Arcadia. We finished at 2 a.m. and Juice worked until 4 a.m.

Violins were not played as a jazz instrument although there were orchestras that used violins in a very commercial way in some arrangements. I've heard the best jazz violinists since that first time but to my estimation, there never was one greater than Juice. He also played clarinet and I used to sit in for a couple of numbers with his group. But the violin was the instrument that he would cut everybody on, so he only brought his clarinet along to the saloon after he had finished his job. I suppose he was called "Juice" because of his drinking habit, but I never saw him drinking more than anyone else.

We ended the week in Buffalo and came back to Springfield. After all the spending I did in Buffalo, I just managed to pay Grandma Jackson and Rick the back debts I had made.

Finally we were engaged to play a dance in Cincinnati. I was very happy because I would be able.to show my friends what a big step I had made when I joined the Scotts' orchestra. My father came to the dance that night, but he listened mostly to Lloyd because drums were his favorite instrument. I had never missed Cincinnati or been homesick since the day I left to join Scott, but it was nice to be home playing in a fine group for all my friends and ole buddies to hear me.

I had bought a large handbag in which I carried the few clothes I needed for two or three days. There was enough room in it for me to put my trumpet, which I usually carried in a bag under my arm. The day after we had played in Cincinnati we had a date in Springfield. We were traveling in two cars and had to meet in front of the Sterling Hotel. Some of the luggage was carried on the running board of the car, so I put my bag where I always put it: on the fender near the motor and left front wheel. The bag was supposed to be tied on before we left.

I had promised Madelyn, my estranged wife, to come and see her before we left town, so I told the chauffeur of the car where I was going and that I would not be long. When I returned, the car with my bag on the fender had left because the chauffeur wanted to get some gas. Word was left that he would wait for me at a certain gas station in Elmwood. I was a little upset because I did not know if my bag had been tied as it should have been.

When I arrived at the rendezvous the first thing I heard was that my bag had fallen off the fender, two cars coming in the opposite direction had hit the bag, and a third had run over it. I thought the fellows were kidding me, but when I saw my bag I found out that it was no joke. It was split half open and when I took my horn out, it was as flat as a pancake. I was broken-hearted to the point of almost crying.

I had no idea how I was going to play the job in Springfield that night. I was rescued by a fellow who had a business of delivering ice. At times when I had nothing to do, I used to help him just to be doing something. He was an amateur trumpet player, so I got in touch with him and he was pleased to let me use his horn. It was not as easy to blow as mine had been, but I made the night.

The next day I took a train back to Cincinnati with my smashed-up horn and went to the Wurlitzer's music shop where I had bought it. I picked myself a new gold-plated Martin trumpet with a beautiful design on the bell. It was $150, which was expensive in those days. But my credit was good at Wurlitzer's because I had bought and paid for my other trumpet on credit. They allowed me $25 as trade-in on my flattened horn.

I came back to Springfield the same afternoon feeling happy because I had such a new, beautiful and easy-blowing instrument. A few days later, we played a dance in Dayton, Ohio, and I had the feeling that I had never played as well as I did that night. I had a case for this horn and I never put it on the fender or running board of any car.

In Springfield there was a family named Paterson who were in the undertaking business. Sometimes Lloyd would engage one or two of their cars to take us on jobs around Ohio. They had some beautiful black limousines, but most of the time, if the jobs were not too far away from Springfield, they had a big old high limousine that ten of us, instruments, and the driver could get into without being crowded. Every time we went somewhere in this car, which had been transformed from a hearse into a sort of bus, one of the back tires would blow out. Such a car would be a historic phenomenon today because the wheels with tires included were three feet high which made the car at least seven feet from the ground to the top.

We started going to Pittsburgh, Pennsylvania and playing dances there in Duquesne and mining towns not too far from Pittsburgh. In every large city in the country, there was wide open vice: bootleg whisky, home brew, gambling, and prostitution. Pittsburgh was jumping and Wiley Avenue was the main drag for the pimps, musicians, and hustlers. We stayed at a hotel there and ate in a big restaurant nearby, owned by a fellow named Gus Greenly.

Gus had known the Scott orchestra before I joined it and he was very fond of Lloyd, Cecil, and the whole orchestra. Gus also had a gambling place next door to the restaurant and there was always $1000 in silver dollar pieces stacked on the crapshooting table. Lloyd Scott was the only one in the orchestra who liked to gamble. He very seldom won anything. With Gus in our corner, we had nothing to worry about if we did not make much money working around Pittsburgh. He would lend the orchestra his personal car if we needed transportation and he would bail us out if we could not pay our rent in the hotel.

One night I went to a club and was jamming with the musicians when a young boy came in and took out an old trumpet that had no caps on the tops of the valves. He did not have any experience and had not been playing very long. But what he played had plenty of fire in it and I could tell that he was trying to play Rex Stewart's style. We started talking and he told me that his name was Roy Eldridge. He told me that he was only 17 and he was married. I don't know if it was true, but after I got to know Roy better, I believed that he could have been married because he was wild enough to do many things that most boys his age would not think of doing.

Life was the same routine with very few dull moments. Sometimes we made good money and sometimes we were broke. But whenever we played, our enthusiasm was high even if we had only a few pennies in our pocket. Just before Thanksgiving, we were in the Buffalo area and our luck had not been very good. For Thanksgiving Day, I could only afford one meal in an Italian restaurant and it consisted of two hot dogs and two tablespoons of Boston baked beans. Bread and water were free.

We played one good dance after Thanksgiving and when we came back to our hotel, Lloyd called a meeting in his room. He had not paid us yet and told us that we had enough money either to take us back into Springfield or to New York, where we could try to get a job. The idea appealed to those that had been to New York before: Dicky Wells, Don Frye, Lloyd, and Cecil. The rest of us were against. I was the first one to speak about not wanting to take the chance. I had plenty of nerve and would go most any place without being asked twice, but I was afraid of going to New York City without a fixed job and knowing no one. So we went back to Springfield.

FIVE

THE GREAT SAVOY ERA

Three weeks later Lloyd received an offer for a tryout at the Savoy Ballroom in New York City, which, I had been told, was the largest and best Negro dance hall in the country. A well-known orchestra leader named Fess Williams had been the house band leader since the place had opened. The tryout was to take place the Saturday before Christmas Day (which came on a Sunday) and the Monday following. The deal was the same for New Year's Day. A woman in Springfield by the name of Miss Americus, who seemed to be quite wealthy, was a friend of the Scott brothers' family, and she sponsored our trip to New York.

Many stories have been told about musicians arriving at places with holes in their shoes; this was my case also. I was happy to be going to New York because we would have work for a few days, but Cecil had told me that sometimes in New York the snow was so high that you could not see the other side of the street (which was true after the sweepers had passed when there had been a real heavy snowfall). I was lucky, no snow had yet fallen in Springfield. I had cardboard in my right shoe which had a hole in it the size of a half-dollar and I was really upset about what the weather would be when we arrived in New York.

We left Springfield one afternoon by train and arrived the next day before noon. I recognized the city when the train hit the outskirts and we saw the tall buildings with clothes hanging on the back windows. I was happy because the sun was shining and there was no sign of snow on the ground, so I knew my feet would not get wet. We arrived at Grand Central Station.

Cecil had also told me about the subway trains. He said that the doors closed automatically and that if one got caught between them, they would risk being killed. I had my first ride on a subway. We could not afford a taxi because we had to be careful with the little extra money we had left from what Miss Americus had advanced us for the trip. So I rushed into the subway train as fast as I could: I did not want to be killed or hurt having just arrived in the City of Cities.

We had all our baggage with us in the subway and we must have looked like a bunch of farmers to the regular New Yorkers because none of us was very well dressed except Dicky Wells. But I was quite surprised when we came out of the subway at 135th Street and Lenox Avenue and I saw how dirty the streets were, littered with dirt and papers. Yet here I was in New York, the "Apple", as it was called by New Yorkers.

Rooms had been reserved for us on 135th Street between 7th and 8th Avenues just in front of a police station. That night the Scotts took us to the famous Savoy Ballroom. I had never seen such a beautiful dance hall before, although I had seen some as large. The Savoy was long but not too wide and 2000 people or more could get in the place. I had been told that there were dance hostesses for men who came alone. You had to buy a ticket for each dance and the hostess was paid a percentage for each ticket at the end of the week. There was a bar for soft drinks, sandwiches, tables with waiter service, and a stand that sold cigars, cigarettes, chewing gum, and candy.

There were two bandstands and one of the bands that was playing when I came in was the Fess Williams orchestra. Fess was dressed in a tuxedo with rhinestones on the lapels and a top hat with the same kind of stones around its band. The other musicians were dressed in regular tuxedos. I recognized George Temple, a trumpet player I had seen when I was younger. George and his brother had been in Cooper's Black and White show. The rest of the orchestra included another trumpet, a trombone, three saxes, and a full rhythm section of piano, banjo, tuba, and drums. I did not hear anything from this orchestra that was sensational or excited my feeling. In fact it was a corny band as far as I was concerned, and did not merit the praise it got. Fess was a sad clarinet player and a corny singer who was also known as the black Ted Lewis. George Temple had most of the trumpet solos and all that he did was growl them. But regardless of what I thought, Fess and his musicians were the pride of the Savoy.

I was standing by a railing just in front of the two bandstands where I could see and hear everything that happened. When Fess finished his set, the other orchestra came on. Both orchestras had their names above their stands and this one was under the leadership of Arthur Gibbs. I had never seen or heard about these musicians but when they started their first number, I knew that it was an orchestra that had something to say, and during their set they said plenty. There was one trumpet who played more and better than the two in Fess's orchestra, one trombone, three saxes, and full rhythm section. The tuba player took ad-lib choruses, which I had never heard a tuba player do before. I had heard bass saxophone choruses, and Mack Walker could riff on the tuba, but this fellow was tops.

When Arthur finished his set, they came off and I left my place to go and find the trumpet player. He told me his name was Leonard Davis. Later I got to know the other musicians: Edgar Sampson (alto sax), Eugene Mikell Jr. (alto sax), Happy Caldwell (a little fellow with a big voice and big tone on tenor sax), George Washington (trombonist), Paul Bernet (banjo), Billy Taylor (tuba), Sam Hodges (drums). I did not bother to listen to Fess Williams any more but every time Arthur Gibbs played a set of four numbers, I found a place across from them where I could hear everything they did.

Once while I was listening to the orchestra, I noticed a girl who was dancing with a fellow. She started smiling at me. I decided that I would ask her for a dance. I was not a lover of dancing and very seldom did it. But the music of Arthur Gibbs was so inspiring. I went to the booth where tickets were sold and bought one. I invited the girl and when we got on the floor, I offered her the ticket. She was surprised and must have thought that I was really a dumb one. She told me that tickets were only necessary when a man danced with a girl who was hired for that purpose. I felt so ashamed that after one dance I made an excuse to leave the floor and never saw her again.

Then came the great day of our tryout for the job, 24 December 1927. The matinee started at four in the afternoon. We were replacing the orchestra of Arthur Gibbs at seven o'clock for an hour while they had dinner. We also replaced Fess's orchestra during their dinner.

Before coming to New York we had had uniforms made by a mail-order place. When we received them, none of us had a perfect fit. It was Oxford grey cloth with a black band around the collar and lapel of the coat, and the same band down the side of the pants. We bought green checkered ties to go with the costume.

When our time came to replace Arthur Gibbs, there was no announcement, but the name of Lloyd Scott had been printed on a sign placed over the name of the band we replaced. No one knew us and we knew no one. The music stands were so high that they almost covered our faces when we were sitting down. And we had no music because all our arrangements had been memorized.

Everybody was anxious to hear what we were going to do. The manager, the hostesses, waiters, and some of Gibbs's musicians delayed going to dinner to hear what we were like. The lindy hop was the rave dance at the Savoy, where it had been started by a group of the wildest dancers I ever saw. When we hit our first introduction to one of our many arrangements, these dancers of the lindy hop almost caused a stampede trying to get on the floor. That was enough to show everybody that we could play. We were not nervous about playing in the famous Savoy Ballroom in the great city of New York for the first time. We became very popular with the lindy hop dancers, and after we had finished our two hours of alternating with the other orchestras, I hung around to listen mostly to the Gibbs band. I talked with Leonard Davis, who told me that we looked like a bunch of country boys when we were waiting to play our first set, but that we really had a jumping band.

We brought something new to the Savoy that was later copied by the Fess Williams bunch and became a fad with every orchestra that played the Savoy. Cecil stood in front of the orchestra like Fess Williams and he also wore a top hat; he could do the Charleston while playing the tenor. The rest of the musicians played sitting down. As the music stands were so high at the Savoy, Dicky Wells, Frankie Newton, and I decided that we would stand up when we had a solo. That made a hit with the public. It also gave whatever number we were playing more showiness and attracted the attention of the people who were not dancing. I believe we were the first musicians in the country to start the style of a soloist standing during his solo.

I became acquainted with some of the musicians of Fess Williams's orchestra: Bobby Robinson (alto sax), Jelly James (trombone), Perry Stone (called "Stony", a little fellow who played tenor), Kenneth Roane (first trumpet), George Temple (trumpet), and his brother (called "Red" because of the color of his hair).

After having played three days, we were paid. The first thing I did was to buy myself a pair of shoes. Before that, I was almost ashamed to walk because I thought that people would see the hole in my shoe. I didn't even dare to cross my legs.

Mack Walker and I were roommates and we started getting acquainted with Harlem from 125th Street up to the Savoy and Lenox Avenue over to 8th Avenue, which had an elevated railway, the first I had seen. Although the streets were dirty, the city itself was very exciting and I had great pleasure taking in the sights.

I had been told about a cabaret called Small's Paradise, so Cecil took Mac and me there during the week when we were waiting to play the New Year's holidays at the Savoy. We went quite early as Cecil said the first show was always the best to see.

The band playing there was led by the pianist Charlie Johnson. The show started. Charlie Johnson left the piano and I never saw him any more that night. But what a band! It had been quite some time back when I had heard Fletcher Henderson. Now here I was listening to an orchestra that was in the same class as Fletcher's and I had never heard of it before! There was an outstanding trumpet player who played fast, clean as a whistle, and used a derby, which he waved over the bell of the instrument to get an open horn wa-wa effect. I was told his name was Jabbo Smith. I had not heard Louis Armstrong in person and I couldn't see how he could be better than this man.

Cecil pointed out an alto sax player and told me that it was Benny Carter, one of the best in the business and a fine arranger also. But Benny didn't kill himself blowing that night. He wore a shade on his forehead to keep the bright light from shining in his eyes. The banjo player was very good, as were the rest of the rhythm section. It was surprising how the band swung without the pianist. The drummer, George Stafford, was another outstanding personality, especially during the floor show, when there were fast numbers that the girls danced, and the finale.

It was my first time to see a floor show, which was not much different from shows in theaters. The girls were beautiful and the comedians funny. The finale was really something to see: when the last girl had gone on the floor, the band kept playing the fast number and the waiters came on, twirling their trays, spinning them on their fingers, then on pencils, then tossing them back and forth to each other. These were the regular size trays that were used in big hotels and were quite heavy.

Charlie Johnson came back to the piano only when the band played the last number of the night. I did not know if he was a good pianist or not because he didn't take any solos, but he had the second-best orchestra that I had heard in person.

Saturday, 31 December 1927 finally came around and we were back at the Savoy to alternate with the two regular bands. We would know at the end of the three days if we had been good enough to be engaged at the Savoy as a regular house band. What surprised us this Saturday was to see the trumpets and trombone player in Fess Williams's orchestra stand up when they took their solos. It gave us a good feeling to know that we had been watched as well as listened to, by the musicians as well as the public.

Two of the many tunes that we had in our repertoire that made a big hit with the dancers were *Willie the Weeper*, which the two trumpets and trombone played in three-part harmony, the way Louis Armstrong had recorded it, and *Springfield Stomp*, which was a collective head arrangement of a number composed by Cecil Scott and Don Frye. When we finished our last hour on New Year's Day 1928, we hung around talking with different people until Lloyd called us all together in a corner and told us that we had been accepted to play at the Savoy as a regular orchestra for six months starting in February.

I had been taking it easy on the drinks because my loot was not too long and I did not know how our six-day audition would turn out, but when Lloyd gave us the good news, Mack Walker and I went out and got juiced. New York City was like Buffalo with its bars that never closed and there were always plenty of people on the streets at any hour of the night and morning. I really felt like I was in heaven because I had a new pair of shoes, I was in the Apple, and would have a regular job the following month. What happened in between did not matter just then.

The next few days were real rough for Mack Walker and me because our money was very short. We were real buddies and shared whatever money we had between us. We could manage only one hot meal a day, so, for our breakfast, we ate sweet rolls of which we got ten for 15 cents. Later we ate a hot meal for 25 cents with coffee or milk in a cafeteria.

After one week of eating like that, Lloyd came around and told us that he had a job for us in a cabaret for the rest of the month of January. It was at the Capitol at 140th Street and Lenox Avenue under a big Chinese restaurant. Lloyd had played the Capitol with one of his orchestras, a few years ago, but the cabaret had lost its popularity and the owner–manager, Johnny Powell, was trying to keep the place going. We started working there on a percentage basis because Johnny Powell could not afford to pay a regular salary. We had to play behind a couple of women singers. They went from table to table whenever there were enough people for them to sing to. Depending on how many people were in the place a song could go for as long as 45 minutes, in which time we could each play a solo behind the singer four or five times. If the singer received a tip for singing at a table, she was to divide half of it with the band. There was also the "kitty," which was a box with a slot in the top: whenever someone requested a number, they were obliged, if we knew it, to put some money in the kitty, which we did not have to divide with the singers. We never made much on this job, but it gave us a chance to become well acquainted with the new numbers we rehearsed during the day, and I no longer had to depend on eating sweet rolls for breakfast.

We were at the club every night to start at nine o'clock, but if there was no one in the place we just sat around and talked. There was a doorman upstairs at the entrance and he would always warn us when someone was coming in by shouting "Party" down the steps. We would jump on the bandstand and strike up a number that made whoever was coming in think that the joint was jumping. We would be playing to three or four o'clock in the morning. We also played the two hours' break for the musicians at the Savoy on Sunday.

I met a fellow about my age, Bob Sawyer, who became a good friend of mine, the first I had made in New York. He taught me how to tie a bow tie (I bought them already tied before that), showed me around in Harlem, and took me to parties. Bob became like a brother to me and I never forgot him because he really showed me what New York was made of.

At the Savoy the dancers that were regular customers and top lindy hoppers became our friends also. There were such names as "Shorty," "Twisted Mouth" George, "the Sheik," "Slim Willy," and "Fats" Rolland. They and the girls they danced with were our real supporters.

Now and then, musicians would drop by the Capitol to listen to the band and some would sit in for some jam sessions. One that I had not heard about was a trumpeter named Cuban Bennett. This man was a musician's musician. He had a tone similar to Joe Smith's, mellow and round, but he did more changes (as harmony was called), and he did not use a plunger as Joe did. He played a few numbers with us and then he asked Don Frye if he knew *Fascinating Rhythm*. I had never heard the number but Don knew it. It was a difficult number to play straight and that's what Cuban did on the first chorus. But after that he ad-libbed and I never heard so many changes played on a trumpet before. He was playing more like a saxophone. Cuban was a cousin of Benny Carter but I was told that he was an alcoholic and no one could depend on him. He could have been in some of the best orchestras in the city, but anyone that hired him knew the chances they were taking. He was a swell person to know and more than a wonderful musician. The only harm he ever did was to himself. Of course, he was not the only musician that alcohol prevented from getting anywhere, but it was a pity that this happened to such a talented man.

We composed a number called *Lawd-Lawd* and decided to really break it in one Sunday at the Savoy. Frankie Newton sang the words and we answered him, singing the same words. Frankie scatted the middle part and there were no other words except "Lawd-Lawd." We played it on the second set alternating with Fess Williams and it went over so big with the crowd that it was the only number we played on that set. The people kept shouting "Lawd-Lawd" every time we finished it. And when we came back on the stand again, there was shouting for the same number. The manager of the Savoy, Charles Buchanan, the owner of the place, Moe Gale, and his father, came out of their office to see what all the shouting was about. Everyone was so enthusiastic about *Lawd-Lawd* that it really tied up the contract for our coming engagement at the Savoy.

Playing the numbers was one of the biggest and best-paying rackets in New York City. Gangsters had complete control of it and they also controlled the bootleg alcohol and most of the bars. Most everybody played the numbers, from one penny to dollars. For one cent it paid $5, so that even the poorest of the poor had a chance. The winning number was the last three digits of the total receipts on the stock market that day. Bob Sawyer taught me how to play the numbers, which could be played straight or in combination form. I still had the bag that had fallen off the car with my horn in it but one day I hit the numbers for five cents, which brought me $25, so I bought a new bag.

The band decided to buy tuxedos to open at the Savoy so we went to a store at 125th Street that sold clothing on credit and bought new tuxedos which made us look much better.

Then came the great day of our opening at the Savoy. We had rehearsed hard during our stay at the Capitol and even had some written arrangements so that we would have some music to put on the high music stands. There was a big surprise waiting for us on opening night. Fess Williams's band had left and so had Arthur Gibbs. The new second band was that of Horace Henderson. Fletcher helped his younger brother by hiring Benny Carter (who had left Charlie Johnson) and Rex Stewart, especially for Horace's debut.

We were on the stand that had been occupied by Fess Williams. I sat on the end on the right side of the stand; Rex Stewart was on the left side of the other bandstand. So we were next to one another. From the very first night until Horace finished at the end of February, it was a battle of jazz which ended in a draw. Benny and Rex did a lot for Horace's orchestra. Benny played much more than I had heard him play with Charlie Johnson and Rex was the fastest man I had ever heard on trumpet. He was better than he was when I had first seen him with Fletcher in Cincinnati and I especially liked his execution of *Tiger Rag*, which was faster than many clarinettists could play.

Each band would have what we called a "killer-diller" number to finish every set and, as the dancers and listeners roared their approval, it was difficult for one band to start after the other had played their killer-diller. Both bands had their fans and there were always discussions among the dancers and the connoisseurs of jazz about which orchestra was the better. The dancers heard everything that was happening on the bandstand while they were still flying through the air lindy hopping.

The Savoy was jumping so much every night that Buchanan was afraid that the floor would cave in. One could stand on the floor and feel it bouncing up and down. The music stands on Horace's bandstand would be bouncing like mad when we were playing. The same thing would be happening on our bandstand when Horace was playing.

So Buchanan asked both bands to cool down a little on each set by playing a medium number, then a slow number, then a waltz, and make the last one jump. What happened was that the dance floor would be half empty during the first three numbers. Each bandleader would write on a slate the type of dance coming next and hold it up for the public to see.

When the sign for the last number would be held up and the band hit the introduction, the hoppers would jump out from every corner of the Savoy as if there was a stampede to see who could get to the middle of the dance floor first. I really got my kicks when it was time to play the last number of the set watching those cats come out jumping like bucking broncos.

Rex and I became very good friends and we started going to bars and jam sessions together. A fellow from Chicago came to New York and opened a hangout for musicians called the Rhythm Club in 131st Street near 7th Avenue. There were pool tables and card games, and, like the bars, the club was open 24 hours a day. Bert Hall was the owner. Musicians who were married and had sweethearts who wanted to get in touch with them could have their chicks call them on the phone or receive letters at the club. When musicians were wanted for a gig, there was a board on which a notice could be posted.

The big attraction however would be jam sessions at least twice a week. A sign would be put up on the board announcing a supper for a certain date. Jam sessions were called suppers: saxophone supper, trumpet supper, etc. Occasionally a drummer, banjo, or bass would be there, but most of the time there would only be a few pianists, who would relieve one another as they became tired.

Jam sessions were also known as cutting sessions, meaning that the musicians that played the best had "cut" the others or, in other words, had won the battle. As many as ten or fifteen instrumentalists could be counted on to be at the club whenever their particular instrument was announced for a supper. Rex and I used to attend those sessions together and I would sit in when the feeling hit me. And when it got too hot for me, Rex would come in and then the joint would really get jumping. He was the master and everybody would play their hearts out to make him play more. The tunes would always be something that was popular.

Another favorite place for jam sessions was the back room of a bar known as Greasy's at 129th Street and 7th Avenue. The place was owned by an Italian, like most of the bars in Harlem, and Greasy was a barman well liked by everyone. Cuban Bennett used to make this place his second home and that's where I really became acquainted with his style of trumpet. Most of the time the sessions were strictly trumpet suppers with a saxophone or trombone sitting in at times. The accompanists would be a guitar—which was becoming very popular in orchestras—or a banjo. There was no piano in the back room. I learned many things in those sessions and many of them would be a record collector's dream today, had they been recorded. Many were the mornings when it would be ten or eleven o'clock as I would leave Greasy's, looking dirty (and greasy) after all the juice I had downed, beside blowing my horn for hours.

Mack Walker and I had moved into a room in the apartment of Billy Taylor, the tuba player that had been with Arthur Gibbs's orchestra at the Savoy. We were now living on Manhattan Avenue and 116th Street and I would take the elevated train after the sessions to get off at 115th and 8th Avenue. People used to look at me in the train, dressed in tuxedo at that time of the day, and they must have thought musicians were crazy people.

I would sleep all afternoon and get up in time to go and get something to eat and then get to the Savoy for another night, which was always a pleasure. If ever I did not feel too well from not having enough sleep, that feeling left me as soon as I got on the bandstand. I was lazy about many things, but when it came to blowing my horn I was always on time at the Savoy.

There was a beautiful girl named Margie who worked at the candy and cigarette counter in the Savoy. I used to talk with her sometimes when I was not on the bandstand. Rex saw me with her quite often, and as he was bashful, he asked me to introduce her to him. A few months after Horace had left the Savoy, Rex and Margie got married and later had two or three children.

I hated to see the Horace Henderson group leave the place at the end of February because I had enjoyed the competition between the two orchestras and so had they. We were real friendly enemies, which made the competition greater and the desire to blow stronger. Rex and I were running together and jamming together and we had become buddies, but the best of friends must part.

Fess Williams's Royal Flush orchestra came back under the direction of a musician from Louisville, Kentucky, named Lockwood Lewis, because Fess had been engaged to direct the pit band of the Regal Theater in Chicago. We changed to the bandstand where Horace had been because Fess had always used the one we had been on. Lockwood played alto sax and clarinet and was a very good showman and lovable person. Dicky Wells and quite a number of other Louisville musicians had come up under the guidance of Lockwood.

The Royal Flush orchestra didn't jump like Horace so the signs announcing the different dances were not used anymore. But we continued to play the hard-driving swing we had played against the Henderson boys because it was our style and we made the hoppers really take off when we were on the stand. But Lockwood and the members of Fess's band who had been working there for a long time were well liked by the Savoy clientele and employees.

Harlem was booming and I had been there three months without going farther downtown than 125th Street. I had had all the enjoyments that I sought from there up to the Savoy. But one day I got the feeling to go downtown and see what the center of Manhattan was like. I asked Bob to be my guide and we took the subway from 135th Street and Lenox down to 42nd Street and Broadway. The tall buildings were amazing. Broadway was the busiest street that I had ever seen and suddenly it seemed to me that all the people in the world must be in New York. There seemed to be thousands of movie houses and theaters. We passed the famous Roseland Ballroom where the Fletcher Henderson and Jean Goldkette orchestras were playing. Goldkette had the best white big dance band in the country and I had heard much talk about the band.

The Savoy had something every Sunday afternoon called Opportunity Day, which was for amateur performers to compete for three prizes: the first was $10, the second was $5, and the third was seven admission tickets that the winner could use at his own discretion. There were amateur lindy hoppers and the regulars that we knew. We had composed a number called *Hop Off*, which the regular hoppers who would compete in the opportunity contest would request regularly. They would rehearse in a corner of the Savoy during week-nights and cooked up tricky steps which they would present on Opportunity Day. Two couples would dance together, then three couples that would change partners, and they would all execute the same steps, just like a section of instruments playing the same riff in unison.

In a weekly local paper that covered the activities of entertainers and musicians, a reporter wrote: "Every Sunday afternoon at the Savoy is Opportunity Day and no wise person will pass up an honest-to-goodness opportunity. Let us see you next Sunday, hopping on it as Lloyd Scott's orchestra hops on *Hop-Off*." Another edition read: "And Lloyd Scott's 'too bad' band every Sunday, oh boy! If you have not heard them, don't miss next Sunday. They hop in *Hop-Off* and you'll hop up and hop while they jazz. No way to make your feet behave, you'll have to let them have their way."

The things those amateurs did were worth more than the admission fee to get into the Savoy. But there were other amateur acts, acrobats, contortionists, and musicians. One amateur who became famous especially in New York at Connie's Inn was a young fellow named Earl Tucker. He had come from Baltimore and wore sailor pants and shoes with taps on them. He was a double-jointed fellow and could twist his body like a snake dancer and tap dance at the same time. He could stand back on his legs in a way that one would think they were going to break. He won the first prize the first time he came to Opportunity Day. People started calling him "Snake Hips." Not long after that, he had become one of the stars at Connie's Inn.

Connie's Inn and the Cotton Club were in the heart of Harlem but the only Negroes who got in were the ones that worked there. These two cabarets catered to the wealthy white customers that called going to Harlem "slumming." Both clubs had extravagant floor shows and the artists and orchestras were the best in the business.

I don't remember what orchestra was playing at Connie's at the time but I think it played semi-classical. At the Cotton Club, which was two blocks up from the Savoy, in the direction of 145th Street, an orchestra led by Duke Ellington was playing and I heard that Freddie Jenkins was in the band. I had heard some records of Duke's with a growl trumpeter named Bubber Miley and a growl trombone player named Tricky Sam Nanton.

But I had the opportunity of hearing Duke's band at the Savoy, where he played at different times for jazz battles. Compared to the two other big bands who shared with him the first place on the hit parade, Fletcher Henderson and Charlie Johnson, Duke's band had a more sophisticated, less aggressive and hard-driving style. Its repertoire was composed mostly of "jungle style" numbers. The quality of the Duke's compositions, the perfection of the arrangements, the impressive interpretation, the quality of the soloists . . . what can I say?

Next door to the Cotton Club was the Lenox Club, which was for Negroes but white people were also admitted. The leader of the orchestra was Banjo Bernie and there was a breakfast dance every Monday. It started at five o'clock in the morning and most of the club musicians and entertainers would meet there to enjoy being together after a week's work. I started going there when we were at the Capitol. The thing lasted until the last party left, which was at midday sometimes! Now and then a musician would sit in with the band but it was never a jam session. The guy would sit in because he felt like playing. I never did because I was having a good time otherwise.

At one of those breakfast dances I saw Freddie Jenkins, who was now known as "Posie," for reasons I was to comprehend later. I also met Sidney De Paris that I had known in Crawfordville, Indiana, when I was six years old. I called him "Gabriel" and he called me "Crawfordville." We were happy to meet again and told each other our experiences. He was now playing with Charlie Johnson's band and had come to the Savoy during a break. His brother Wilbur was still in Philly.

Sidney was surprised to see that I was playing trumpet with the Scott brothers, and he was happy about it. He told me about some changes in Charlie Johnson's band: Jabbo Smith had left, Sidney and Leonard Davis had been hired, and Edgar Sampson had taken Benny Carter's place.

When I spoke of hearing Charlie Johnson's orchestra for the first time, I forgot to mention that Jimmy Harrison, the great trombonist, was in the band. But the night I heard him, I don't remember him having any solos. Jimmy was not in good health and I noticed that he held a hand on his stomach when he was not playing. He had now been replaced by George Washington, which made three musicians of the Arthur Gibbs orchestra to join Charlie Johnson after the Scott band went into the Savoy. Jimmy Harrison died in 1931.

Lloyd informed us one night that John Williams would be coming back with the orchestra and gave Lester Carr two weeks' notice. A few of us did not quite agree that was correct although we had nothing against John. But Lloyd was the leader and it was his privilege to hire and fire whom he pleased.

Buchanan had given us the name of "Lloyd Scott and his Bright Boys" because we were always doing something new in the line of entertaining while playing, without making a number real showy. In *Lawd-Lawd* we all had a little washboard on which we scratched the rhythm behind the scat singing of Frankie Newton and the baritone sax of Cecil. Sometimes there would be a sharp whistle at the end of some chorus before a soloist would come in for the next chorus. Once we cooked up a gimmick on *Tiger Rag*. When it came to the part where the words are "Hold that tiger," we had cap pistols and everyone except the rhythm section would jump off the bandstand and run around the floor shooting these pistols and shouting, "Hold that tiger, where that tiger." It made many of the clients wonder if there was a fight and someone had started shooting; some would head for the nearest exit. Buchanan asked us not to do the number like that because it frightened people.

During these months at the "Track," which was the nickname for the Savoy (because it was as exciting for people to come there as it was to go to a race track), we were paying back the money that Miss Americus had advanced us to come to New York. Our salary was $40 a week, which I thought was good at the time, and it was coming in regularly. I had never worked such a long time at such a salary and if I had not been a great spender, I could have had quite a nice bankroll put away in a short while.

The Royal Flush orchestra left for two nights during the summer season and Alex Jackson, who had worked his way back to New York, was engaged to play the two nights. This was when we got our revenge on his band. They had played a town not far from where we were playing, and they had drawn all the people to their dance. So we had made only 35 cents each for our night's work.

It was sweet revenge because we had always been a better swing band than Alex Jackson's and we proved it those two nights. We threw everything at them except the kitchen sink. After every set we went off of our stand with the dancers still applauding, and each time it was ten minutes before Alex could start his set! In a way I felt sorry for them. They had been big shots in Ohio and perhaps other places, but now they received a lesson in how jazz should be played. They were a sad-looking and downhearted bunch of fellows those two nights.

I had been told about a trumpet player named Ward Pinkett who was said to be one of the best in New York. I eventually met Ward and saw him quite often but never heard him play, which I regretted very much. Ward was not in very good health and had been told by a doctor that he had only a few years to live. I think he was born in Virginia and he went home with the thought that maybe some rest would prolong his life, but he soon became lonesome for the gay life in New York and came back. He said that if he didn't have long to live, he was going to enjoy himself and that's what he did until he died a few years after he came back to the Apple.

The Lafayette Theater, next door to Connie's Inn, was the most popular gathering place for Harlem entertainers in New York and the Rhythm Club was just around the corner from the Lafayette. So there was always plenty of activity in the block between 131st and 132nd Street, with all the musicians going in and out of the club and the show people all along the block in front of the Lafayette and Connie's.

The Tree of Hope was just in front of the entrance to Connie's Inn. It was said that when you touched the tree and made a wish, your hopes would come true. That was a superstition mostly among theatrical people, but there was seldom a time when a musician passed the tree without touching it to bring him luck, whether he was superstitious or not. I don't know how long this legendary tree had been there, but I became one of those that touched it every time I passed.

When I came to New York, and long before that, I was known as Johnson Coleman. Some people called me Johnson and others called me Coleman, which made some people think that my name was Coleman Johnson.

August 1928 came and we went on a tour. We had been in the Savoy for six months, the longest run the band ever had in the same place. Our first engagement was at Pittsburgh. We left New York on a Greyhound bus in the early afternoon and stopped in Gettysburg, Pennsylvania, where I got the surprise of my life. This was at a restaurant where the buses made a regular stop during lunch or supper time.

We went into the restaurant as did the other passengers and, after going to the men's room, we came out and sat down at the counter where food was served. A girl gave us plates, knives, forks, and water. After that no one came to take our order. For some time we did not think that it was unusual but eventually, after seeing everyone else being served, we wondered why we were not. After about ten minutes, a man came to us from behind the counter and said that he was sorry, they did not serve colored people, but there was a Greek restaurant around the corner where we could go.

Here we were in Gettysburg, Pennsylvania. I had studied in school the history of Abraham Lincoln and his issue of the Emancipation Proclamation, and we were refused service in a restaurant that was a regular stop for Greyhound bus passengers! We didn't raise any hell because we tried at all times to be as gentlemanly as possible—and anyway it was no use—but it was embarrassing to us. The driver of the bus should have told us because he must have known about the situation: we certainly could not have been the first Negroes to pass through Gettysburg on a Greyhound bus. The girl that had given us the set-up must have been new in the restaurant and she was probably embarrassed also.

After we had eaten in the Greek restaurant, we came back to the bus to continue the journey. I was with some band members sitting in the back of the bus. There was no prejudice pressure put on us to sit there and those that did go to the back went of their own free will.

We played one week in Pittsburgh for a marathon dance, which was the rage all over the country. How long it had been going on, and how long it lasted after we left, I do not know. It was amazing to see some of the couples so tired that they would take turns sleeping on each other's shoulders. We played slow numbers, fast ones, and waltzes, but the dancers never changed their pace, which was the slowest of slow drags.

From Pittsburgh we went to Cincinnati, where we stayed for one week playing the Greystone Ballroom on a Sunday, Wednesday, and Saturday for white dancers only. Then we played one night at Ed Gaither's country club, which was one of the very few country clubs for Negroes in the States, and owned by a Negro. Gaither had become a millionaire from his two gambling places in Cincinnati. The club, which had golf links and a swimming pool, was about six miles outside of Avondale, a suburb of Cincinnati.

We stayed in Cincy two weeks and although I did not live with my parents I went to see them every day. Dicky Wells would always manage to get to my father's place before me because my old man had learned to make home brew and always had some bottles on ice. When I arrived, Dad would tell me that I was too late as Dicky had been and drunk all the cold beer.

From Cincy we went to Lexington, where we played one week for the fair and it really jumped. Back in Cincy, we played the Crystal Ballroom and then went on to Louisville, Kentucky. I had been there a few times with Helvey but this was the first time with Lloyd Scott. We played a big dance and stayed there a few days. There was a bar in Louisville that I had known from the first time I had gone there. It was very popular with musicians and entertainers because for five cents you could buy a big bowl of beans; for the same price you could have a pair of hot dogs or a big mug of beer. I ate in this place many times, even when I had enough money to afford a meal in a good restaurant. I always loved beans and this place cooked them like the real country people did.

One day Dicky's parents invited the gang to have supper at their home. They made home brew the same as my father and so many other people did during prohibition. We were all at the table in the dining room, eating a fine meal that his mother had prepared, when suddenly we heard a noise as if someone was shooting a pistol in the closet. There was the same sound again a few seconds later, and after that it sounded as if a war had begun. Dicky's parents had made a new batch of home brew and there was a little too much yeast in it. So when the stuff started to ferment, the bottle tops blew off. When someone opened the closet, it was covered with foam. Bottle after bottle blew its top and there was nothing to do but let them blow.

A few days later we left Louisville and went to Springfield and played a park near Xenia, Ohio. People came with their lunches and picnicked on the grounds of the park as we played the late afternoon dance. We came back to Springfield but Lloyd stayed to collect the money.

For two days we did not see Lloyd but news got around that he had been seen in a rented car driven by a chauffeur, two girls accompanying him in the back seat, and money all over the floor of the car. The next day we received notice that there would be a meeting. When we got together, it was easy to see that Lloyd was drunk. He announced that he had lost all the money gambling. He said he was sorry and started to cry. Then he become indignant and accused some of us of doing certain things. He told me that I had been afraid at one time of losing my job with the band and being replaced by Rex Stewart, which was something I had never thought of. He was drunk, had lost our money, and he was being aggressive. But we had always been such a brotherly bunch that none of us was really angry with him. However, we were to leave for New York in a few days and I for one did not know how I was going to get there. We had made nice money during the tour, but we had had some lean days and I was a nice spender also.

A few days later, I was almost knocked off my feet when I received the news that Lloyd had gone back to the gambling place, had won a few hundred dollars, bought himself a new top coat and had taken a train to New York, leaving the rest of us to get there the best way we could. I knew a girl in Lexington who was quite friendly and had loot, so I wrote and told her my situation and asked her to send me enough money to get back to New York. She did it immediately.

We started working again at the Savoy in September. On Wednesday, 12 December there was a big battle of jazz with six orchestras from 8.30 in the evening until 3 a.m. the next morning. Duke Ellington, Ike Dixon (a band from Baltimore, Maryland), Charlie Johnson, Arthur Gibbs, Lockwood Lewis and the Royal Flush orchestra, and Lloyd Scott.

When Christmas 1928 came, the Savoy management gave all its employees a gift of gold pieces. It was our first year as regular employees, so each received a $5 gold coin. The other employees, depending on the length of time they had worked, received $10 and $20 in gold.

In January Lloyd and Cecil wanted to bring Hubert Mann back into the orchestra and we all chipped in to send Hubert his fare. The reason for bringing him back was that Bull Williams had had a dispute with Buchanan and taken a poke at him but missed. Some of the bouncers had grabbed Bull to keep him from taking another lick at Buchanan, who told Lloyd to fire Bull.

We took a banjo player named Teddy Bunn until Hubert arrived from California, where it was said that he had been a member of a Holy Roller church. Hubert arrived while we were having a rehearsal. He was dressed in a lightweight suit, summer shoes, straw hat and had no overcoat. Lloyd managed to get him a tuxedo for the night. When he came to work that night he was so drunk that he went to sleep against the lid of the piano, which was up: he sat next to it in a way that made it easy for him to lay his head on and forget everything.

When Buchanan saw Hubert Mann sleeping on the piano top, he was so angry that he could have bitten a nail in two. He told Lloyd to get rid of him right away. There went the money we had chipped in to pay Hubert's train fare to New York. Teddy Bunn came back the next night and stayed with us until we finished on the last of January.

We went on the road again. Lloyd asked Bull Williams to come back and he accepted. Our first stop was in Baltimore, Maryland. We were traveling by Greyhound bus because we did not have enough steady one-nighters to hire a private bus. We had no agent either as most bands booked themselves at the time. Our next stop was a dance in Frostburg, Maryland, and it was really a frosty place, because it was February and below zero.

About ten people came to the dance. There were two big coal stoves on each side of the hall that were red hot but they did not heat up the place. We kept our overcoats and gloves on and our instruments were like blocks of ice. And we almost had a tragic night because there was no hotel and only one Negro family in the town. Whenever there was a dance in Frostburg for colored people, they came from the farms and surrounding towns where they worked. We were without transportation as the bus would not arrive until 8 a.m. the next day. And we could not stay in the dance hall. What saved us was this one Negro family, who offered to let us sit in their living room by a hot fire until it came time to take the bus. I never found out what Frostburg could be in the spring or summer but I know what it was like the night we were there.

We played Philadelphia for the first time, then Pittsburgh, where we were very well liked. We did towns in Ohio such as Youngstown, where I stayed in a hotel that had so many chinches in the bed that it was impossible to sleep. We played Gronton, Middletown, most of the mining towns, Columbus, and Dayton. Then we went to Detroit, where we played in Jean Goldkette's famous Greystone Ballroom. Lloyd must have really cleaned up that night because he gave us $50 each, the most money I had ever made on a percentage job in one night.

We played a battle of jazz in Cincinnati with Zack White's orchestra, which had as director a young alto player named Tremble, better known as "Inky" because he was so black. I had met Inky some years before in Richmond, Kentucky, where he was born. I had gone there with Clarence Paige and Helvey. Inky had seen Cecil Scott work and copied his style of wearing a top hat which Cecil had copied from Ted Lewis. Zack White had a very nice orchestra but we were too much for them. We also washed away the orchestra of Speed Webb in another battle of jazz. Roy Eldridge and Teddy Wilson were in the band—it was my first time to meet and hear Teddy.

Once in Pittsburgh we alternated with the Cotton Pickers, who were under the leadership of Don Redman. Joe Smith was in the band, but now I was not afraid to play at the same dance as him, and someone told me that Don Redman had asked who I was because he liked my way of playing.

The first time I played with three trumpets was when Gus McClung, whom I had first heard with Scott, came back in the orchestra. Gus had had a dispute with Don Redman when Scott was in New York, long before I joined them. After he left Scott, Gus played with Clarence Paige in Cincinnati. He then joined the Cotton Pickers. But when Don was engaged to lead the band, the first thing he did was to fire Gus. So Gus joined our band in Cincinnati, and Lloyd let Frankie Newton go when we returned to the Savoy.

We were in the Savoy when Marion Hardy's Alabamians came with Cab Calloway, who sang through a megaphone three feet long. Eddie Mallory, one of the trumpet players, became one of the husbands of Ethel Waters. The bass player, Charlie "Fat Man" Turner, eventually opened a bar called Fat Man's on 155th Street and St. Nicholas Avenue which became very popular. Cab Calloway took over the leadership of the Missourians, which later became his band.

Another orchestra from Chicago that came to the Savoy when I was there was Sammy Stewart's. He had some men who became famous: George Dixon and Walter Fuller (trumpets), Chu Berry (whom I had met in Wheeling, West Virginia, tenor sax), and Big Sid Catlett (drums). Sammy Stewart played piano.

Fletcher Henderson was engaged for one night and we had played some numbers, I forget which, but the dancers did not want us to stop. We played for a half hour longer before we finally left the stand. When the public saw that we were not coming back, they let Fletcher play. That was one night when I thought the public was very unfair because I knew, as we all did, that although we had a good band we were really not in the class of Fletcher.

When Fletcher did start to play, I came back on our bandstand to listen to them. After that it was hard for us to play for two reasons! One was that Fletcher had scored with the public, which wanted more when they had finished their set. The second was that we had lost the battle and really did not want to play any more; we still tried, but there was not much fight left in us. Without a doubt, Fletcher Henderson had the greatest dance orchestra in the world, before, then, and long after that. It's worse than a shame that a guy like Paul Whiteman, who could hardly hold a violin, was known as the "King of Jazz."

Another thing that was a thrill for me at the Savoy was the masked ball once every year. The first one we played was called "Arabian Nights" and the second "South Sea Islands." There was also a big ball once a year called the "Female Impersonators' Ball." We called it the "fag ball." Some of them actually were beautiful and looked like women. There were black, brown, yellow, and white ones who came from uptown, downtown, and all around town. Some looked like sweet young girls and others looked like prize fighters with their big muscular arms sticking out of short-sleeved evening gowns. Prizes were given for the best dressed, the best hairdo, and the most feminine. This really was the biggest ball of the season and the funniest also. I never cared much for dancing myself and seldom did, but on "faggot" night, if I had danced, it would have been with a girl whom I knew was a girl.

A well-known dance hall at 7th Avenue and 138th Street was the Renaissance. It was not as large as the Savoy but was very nice, with a large balcony around three sides and one big bandstand. Usually private balls were held there. The leader of the regular orchestra or house band was named Vernon Andrade. Practically every musician in New York worked for Vernon at one time or another because Vernon did not have a regular bunch of musicians working with him. As the Renaissance was not open every night, whenever there was a ball, Vernon would hire whoever was available. But the bands usually sounded not bad.

Another place, smaller than the Renaissance, was the Bamboo, which had a band under the leadership of Joe Steele, a fine pianist. And Chick Webb, whom I had not met but had heard much talk about, was leading a band at a white dancing school on 125th Street and 7th Avenue; it included Bobby Stark, who was said to be a terrific trumpet man.

The Lafayette Theater changed shows each week and bands also. We were engaged for a week, which was the first time we ever played a theater and accompanied the entertainers, dancers, and chorus girls. The bands always played in the pit and if there were fewer than ten musicians, they would supplement the band with two or three more. We had preferred to remain as we were but after the first two shows, we realized that our experience in that kind of work was not very deep. We had to play a "curtain call" number before the show, and we could not get ourselves together sitting in a pit below the stage. We thought that if we played on the stage it would be better. The manager of the theater let us try it and we went over big. The public could see Cecil with his high hat dancing in front of the orchestra and we stood up for our solos as we had done at the Savoy. We also played the rest of the show from the stage and it was something new that the manager of the theater decided should also be done by the other bands coming in.

Beginning in 1929, we went on tour and came back to the "Track" on Easter Monday. Three orchestras played that Monday for twelve hours of dancing: Fess Williams, Luis Russell, and Lloyd Scott. Things went fine for us at the Savoy until Lloyd got drunk one night, had an argument with Buchanan, and took a swing at him. But like Bull Williams, Lloyd missed because Buchanan knew it was going to happen. It was not the first time someone had tried to knock his head off so he knew when to duck. One of the bouncers who was always near when Buchanan had words with someone grabbed Lloyd and held him. Buchanan fired the band then and there. This happened in June 1929.

I knew New York well by that time and I was not afraid to be without work. I started to go to the Rhythm Club every day and some gigs soon came up. One night I had nothing to do and as I had been invited by Bobby Stark to come listen to Chick Webb's band whenever I had the chance, I decided to go. The dancing school was for whites only but colored musicians could go in and sit near the bandstand to listen to Chick and talk with the fellows when they had a smoking break.

Chick was a little humpbacked fellow about four feet tall, but that was no handicap for him when it came to playing drums. He was doing things with those drums that I had not heard another drummer do. He was taking breaks and playing the cymbals with a different beat behind each soloist. He had a real swinging group with a bunch of musicians from which a few became famous: Howard Scott and Bobby Stark (trumpets), Russell Procope (alto sax and clarinet), Elmer "Tone" Williams (tenor sax), Johnny Hodges (alto sax), Ed Cuffee (trombone), Don Kirkpatrick (piano), John Trueheart (banjo), Elmer James (bass), and Chick Webb (drums).

When Chick found out who I was, he told me that he had heard about me and some day he was going to have me in his band. I was to hear this statement from Chick many times and would have been very happy if it had ever came true. Chick had a band that any jazz musician would have been happy to be a member of.

After Chick had finished the night Bobby Stark asked me if I would like to go downtown with him to see his uncle who lived in a district called Hell's Kitchen. I agreed, so we took the El at 125th Street and 8th Avenue and got off somewhere downtown in the 50s on the West Side. Bobby's uncle made his home moonshine. He rolled out a five gallon jug and invited us to help ourselves. He was very proud of Bobby, especially because he was such a good musician. Bobby could put away a lot of juice and so could I, but we didn't make a dent in his uncle's jug. We were flying high when we left, and decided to take a cab to go back.

I don't remember who was in Lou Russell's band when they played at the Savoy on Easter Monday 1929 with us and the Royal Flush orchestra, but Russell was advertised to play two nights with Louis Armstrong. Russell's first name was Luis, but the Savoy had him billed as Lou. Armstrong was being called "Satchelmouth" now. This was his first time in New York since he had left Fletcher Henderson. I was filled with joy at the prospect of being able to see and hear my idol for the first time.

That night, I went to the Savoy quite early because I did not want to miss a note coming from the horn of "Satchel." With Russell, there was a trumpet player named Louis Metcalf who sat on a high stool, wore a cardboard gold crown, and called himself "King Louis"! He had on his crown when Louis Armstrong came on the stand after a big announcement by Buchanan. From the moment that he started the first number until the end of it, Russell's band sounded like a twelve-piece orchestra, yet they were only eight, which was the smallest group that had ever played at the Savoy.

When Satchelmouth came on the stand I was pleasantly surprised because he was a much better-looking man than on the few bad photos I had seen. He was not as fat as I had thought, but he was stocky. His trumpet looked like the most beautiful of golden horns that I had ever seen. The more he played, the better he sounded. He was not playing the things he had recorded in the same manner that I had heard them. He was not copying himself but playing the way he felt. And he must have been feeling mighty good. His fingers seemed to be flying over the valves and what was coming out of his horn were things that I had never heard from any trumpet player before. That's when I realized that Armstrong was the king of all kings of jazz. It was one of the greatest thrills of my life to have heard this man who was destined to do so much for jazz.

Metcalf realized it also because when the next set came he did not put on his crown. The following set he did not come back on the stand. I would have loved to have gone back the next night but I had a gig. I was told that Metcalf had not come to work the next night. Metcalf could play and he had a fine style with plenty of technique. But he never wore his crown again after Louis Armstrong left.

One week before the end of June, Dicky Wells came to my house and said that he had a job for us for the summer with a drummer he knew by the name of Dewey Beasley. The job was upstate in a place called Poughkeepsie, Dewey's home town. We had to play in the Woodcliff amusement park. The salary wasn't much but we could live and have a little group of our own.

So Dicky Wells, myself, Mack Walker, Harold McFerran and Don Frye got together again. The rest of the men were Bull Williams, Melvin Scott (from Dayton, Ohio, alto sax), Bobby Sands (tenor sax), and Dewey Beasley (drums). We worked four days a week and played matinees on special occasions and holidays.

I had started writing to my estranged wife, Madelyn, and we decided to get together again. She came from Cincinnati after I had been in Poughkeepsie about three weeks. The job went fine and we got plenty of rest because there were not many activities except for the park, which had a dock on the Hudson River where excursion boats stopped with tourists.

One day near the end of the season, I received a letter from my old buddy Higginbotham. He was playing with Luis Russell at the Roseland Ballroom. Higgy told me that he could get me into Russell's orchestra. So when we finished in Poughkeepsie, I lost no time getting to New York. I rented a room for Madelyn and me in a place where I had stayed before with Mack Walker. We could cook there, which was much better than having to eat in restaurants, and cheaper for two people.

At the beginning of October I joined Russell's orchestra, which was composed mostly of musicians from New Orleans: Henry "Red" Allen (trumpet), J.C. Higginbotham (trombone), Charlie Holmes (alto sax), Albert Nicholas (alto sax, clarinet), Teddy Hill (tenor sax), George "Pops" Foster (bass), Will Johnson (banjo), Paul Barbarin (drums). I never knew how long Higgy had been with Russell or when he came to New York, but we were both happy to see each other again.

Metcalf had left the band, I was told, because when Russell went into the Roseland he had sent for Red Allen, and Red played too much horn to suit Metcalf, so he quit. Red played first trumpet on everything and took all the solos. Of course, Higgy had plenty of solos and so did most everybody except me. Finally I got a one-chorus solo on a number called *Feeling the Spirit*, which was recorded on 9 September 1929 along with *The New Call of the Freaks* and *Jersey Lightning*. This was my first recording date. For the second one, on 13 September, I had an eight-bar solo in the middle of the second chorus of

Broadway Rhythm. This was recorded for the Banner label, and Russell used the name of "Lou and his Ginger-Snaps." Eventually I got a solo on a head arrangement of *Sweet Sue*. But I never played a first part or had any other solo.

I had been working on a transfer union card which was not acceptable to Local 802 any longer, so Russell advanced me the money to get an 802 card from the Union. About that time, Metcalf took Russell to the Union claiming back pay. The Union scales were different for white and Negro dance halls. The scale at the Roseland was supposed to be $65 a week. The whole band had to go before the Union trial board and we all swore that we were getting the correct scale. They tried in every way to break one of us: if that had happened we would have all been fined. But each one of us stuck to our story and when they called Russell and could not break him, they dismissed the case and told Russell that his men were really with him. The truth is that we were not getting the Roseland scale but I did not think it was very kosher of Metcalf to have enjoyed himself playing with Russell and then, after quitting the band because he was displeased about something, trying to make an unpleasant situation for Russell and the rest of the musicians.

At the Roseland the colored musicians had a dressing room down in the basement of the building that housed the ballroom. The boilers for heating the building and hot water were in the basement and it was necessary to walk up three flights of stairs, which were in the back of the building, to come out of a side door and get to the bandstand that we occupied. After we had played each set, if we did not want to walk down three flights of stairs and stay in a room that had nothing in it but the lockers in which we put our overcoats, we could stand in the back stairway, near the electrician's booth, and play cards until the time came to go back and do another set. There was no such thing as socializing with the dancers or having a special booth inside the dance hall with a table where we could sit and play cards or drink as the white orchestra could do. So after each set, we stood on the back stairway and played cards. I got interested in playing blackjack. We only played for ten or twenty cents, but it was possible to win from $3 to $5 a night if one was lucky. One of the luckiest of lucky guys was Teddy Hill, who never lost.

After about six weeks with Russell, I began to feel the effects of not having a first part to play and only two solo spots, because we did not play *Broadway Rhythm*, where I had an eight-bar solo. Cecil Scott had reformed the Bright Boys under his name with a new drummer in place of Lloyd and had started working in the Savoy. I was lonesome for the "Track," where I could socialize with the people, and I was not satisfied with the role I was playing in Russell's band, so I went to see Cecil one night and asked him what were the chances of my coming back to the group. He was very happy about it, so I gave my two weeks' notice to Russell and I joined Cecil.

The band was now almost the same as the original Lloyd Scott Bright Boys, except for the drummer whose name was Arnold "Scrip" Boling and a banjoist named Casper Towie, who was later replaced by James Smith. I felt the results of not having enough to play in Russell's band and it was almost two weeks before my chops began to get set and strong again.

During my stay with Russell, I enjoyed very much hearing Red Allen play. He had so much of Armstrong in his playing and was the first trumpet player after Louis who had the real New Orleans style. He had technique, a pleasant tone, and really knew his instrument. But I think that Russell could have at least let me play some first parts. I suppose he thought that I should be happy because I was playing at the Roseland, but that kind of prestige didn't mean a bag of beans to me, and I love beans!

After a few months at the Savoy, Cecil wanted to bring Lloyd back in the band and one night in the dressing room he told us of his intentions. But things did not go as he had expected because "Higgy," who seldom disagreed with anything, spoke up and said that if Lloyd came back, he was giving his two weeks' notice then and there. Then we, one after the other, gave our notice and Cecil accepted them all with arrogance. I know that blood is thicker than water and Lloyd was Cecil's blood, but we had had enough of Lloyd taking our money, getting drunk, and doing crazy things. I suppose Cecil must have conned Buchanan into forgiving Lloyd for taking a poke at him, but we really didn't want any part of him. Cecil thought the matter over and when we came to work the next night, he announced that Lloyd would not be coming back. Everything was fine again.

On 19 November we recorded four numbers for Victor. The titles were *Bright Boy Blues*, *Lawd-Lawd*, *Springfield Stomp*, and *In a Corner*. These were the numbers that had brought us fame at the Savoy. Cecil Scott took credit as the composer of *Lawd-Lawd* and *In a Corner*, and included Don Frye as co-composer of *Bright Boy Blues* and *Springfield Stomp*, but the fact was that we had all contributed to the numbers and there was no written arrangement on any of them. I've always considered these my first recordings, as I didn't have anything to play on the Luis Russell sessions except for the chorus on *Feeling the Spirit* and the eight measures on *Broadway Rhythm*.

One night when I came off the bandstand, I noticed three fellows sitting at a table. As I passed they stopped me and asked if I wanted some reefer. They told me they were Mexicans. I asked about the effects of reefer. They told me that it made you feel good and laugh. I had no desire to try it and two sets later when I came off and passed them again, they were all three lying on the table fast asleep. I didn't know if they had laughed themselves to sleep or not, but they were not having a good time as far as I was concerned.

But my first experience with reefers came eventually. We were playing a Sunday matinee and I had started drinking gin early in the afternoon and felt fine. This went on until the Savoy closed and I was feeling real groovy but not drunk. There was a bar on the corner of 132nd Street and 7th Avenue called Pete's, and naturally it catered to the theatrical people and musicians as it was near the Lafayette Theater and the different clubs in the neighborhood. I went to Pete's, ordered a half pint of gin and had drunk about half of it when I saw Cecil and a banjo player named Ike "Ikie" Robinson, come out of the back room and go into the toilet. I had an idea that something was up so I followed them. I saw Ikie taking out a cigarette, saying it was a reefer. He asked me if I wanted to try and I did. I took one big puff and held it in my lungs for a few seconds, as I had seen it done, then another which I also held as long as I could, passed it to Cecil and came back to the bar. Two minutes later, I thought the world was caving in on me. My legs got weak, I grabbed the railing on the bar and my mind started to turn as if I had been spun around like a top. A few seconds later I was able to ask the bartender in a very weak voice how much I owed him. I felt as though I was going to faint and knew I had to get out of there very quick. I paid for my drink, left half of it and went outside.

It was a good thing that I had left my horn at the Savoy. I was living on 140th Street between 7th and Lenox and I decided that I had better walk home as the air would do me good and I was afraid of blanking out in a taxi. I was staggering all the way up 7th Avenue and when I arrived at 135th Street I decided that I had better hide my money so that if I did fall out in the street, I would not be robbed as well. I had $7 and wanted to put it in my shoe. I was so weak in the legs that I was obliged to lean against a house so I wouldn't fall on my face. I eventually reached home and when I got into my room I fell across the bed. I asked my wife almost breathlessly to take my clothes off for me. That was the only time anyone ever had to undress me since I had been big enough to dress myself, and it was the first and last time that I was ever out from drinking and smoking.

We moved to a house on 139th Street between 7th and 8th Avenues, which was supposed to be an exclusive block called Strivers Row. We were two houses from where Fletcher Henderson lived. The Bright Boys came out of the Savoy for a few weeks and played in New Jersey at a country club for Negroes called the Shady Rest. Then we came back to the Savoy.

One afternoon when we had a rehearsal I left too early and arrived at the Savoy 45 minutes in advance. I was tempted to go back home because I lived about five minutes' walking distance from the "Track." Then I decided to stay put and sat in a window watching the happenings on Lenox until rehearsal started.

When it was finished and I was on my way home, I met a woman who was from Cincinnati and a friend of my wife and me. She told me to hurry home because something had happened but she would not tell me what.

I arrived and found my wife crying. She told me we had been robbed. Our room was on the third floor of this private house; the kitchen was downstairs on the ground floor. Two fellows had moved into the room next to ours the week before, but I had never seen them. While my wife was washing the dishes downstairs in the kitchen those fellows heard me leave the room. There was no special lock on any of the doors, so they opened my door and took all my clothes, a nice Big Ben alarm clock that my mother had sent me for Christmas, and ten dollars that I had given my wife. She was going to buy a new dress for Easter, which was the coming Sunday. I lost seven suits. The one I had on had been one of the band costumes that I had taken from the cleaning shop the day before.

The landlady offered us two weeks' free rent as compensation but before the end of the first week, she told us that she was going to move. We found another room on 135th Street facing the police station. Higginbotham had lived in the same room that I was now occupying. I had lived in this block between 7th and 8th Avenue when I first came to New York.

In June 1930 we went on our first tour under the leadership of Cecil Scott and played in Pittsburgh, our old stomping ground, and a few mining towns nearby. On every job when the night was finished, Cecil would give us only a part of our salary and tell us that the place owed us $25 which, he said, they had promised to send us to New York. We began to think that it was strange that after every job there was $25 coming to us, so one of the fellows asked the manager of a place why he could not pay the complete salary. The man said that he did not owe us anything because Cecil had asked him to send $25 in advance as guarantee. We decided to put a stop to the situation. We had a valet for the band named Louis, so we put him at the door of every place we played after that to control the admission tickets. When the night was over, we divided the money in equal parts, and gave Cecil the same amount as we had.

When we came back to New York, we were supposed to go back in the Savoy. We had been getting $45 a week since the beginning and, as we were very popular there, we felt we deserved a raise and told Cecil that we wanted $50 to go back there again. Cecil said that he would ask Buchanan but he didn't think that he would accept it. We told him that if we didn't get the raise, we were not going to work there any more. The next day we had a rehearsal and Cecil arrived with the news that Buchanan would not give us a raise, so we refused to work at the Savoy. That was the end of Cecil Scott and his Bright Boys.

The irony of what happened—and we learned it from Buchanan—is that Cecil was getting $50 for each man since we had played in the Savoy under his leadership, and he was getting a leader's fee of $65 a week. So he was taking nine times $5 from us and didn't want to stop the operation.

Sy Oliver, whom I had met not long after I had joined the Scott band, told me that we did not have the best brass section in the business, but that we had the best *young* brass section he had ever heard. Dicky Wells, Frankie Newton and myself knew each other's feeling so well that if any of us wanted to play a riff behind a sax solo, which we often did, one would start the riff and the other two would pick it up and get the feeling of it before one measure had passed. We played them in harmony and not in unison. And a riff was never exactly the same every time even though the number was played often.

It really broke my heart to think that we had such a promising future, and it all went down the drain because of Cecil's greediness. Cecil sacrificed the opportunity of being nationally known. Both Scott brothers were finished as orchestra leaders.

SIX

SIDEMAN, HERE AND THERE

I went into a dancing school for the first time with a band led by a pianist named Johnny Monnegue. Paul Barnes was on alto sax and Jimmy Wright on tenor sax. Paul Bernet, who had played banjo in Arthur Gibbs's orchestra when I first heard him at the Savoy, played guitar. The other trumpet man was Theodore "Ted" Colin, whom I had seen at the Rhythm Club many times. Ted was the loudest-blowing trumpet player I have ever known but he did not blow out of tune, which is blasting when a guy plays loud. Ted was a fellow with a big head and big face and talked almost as loud as he blew. I don't remember who the drummer was and there was no bass.

Working in a dancing school was not as interesting as working at the Savoy, Roseland, or any other ballroom and the work was harder, especially with Monnegue. For one thing the band was smaller. The school was situated on Broadway, just next door to the Roseland. The job started at 8 p.m. and finished at 2 a.m.

All dancing schools had the same regulations, which was ten cents a dance. The orchestras played the introduction and first chorus of a number, which were Tin Pan Alley orchestrations most of the time. The sax section played the melody of the first chorus and the brass section played the countermelody. At the end of the first chorus, the band stopped and that was one dance. Then the brass section played the second chorus with the saxes playing countermelody. Then there was a third chorus, and so on. Each time we stopped the dance ended and a man dancing with a hostess had to give her a ticket before the next dance started. We played 55 minutes continuously and had a five-minute smoking break.

Dancing schools were the joy of music writers because there were so many of them in New York. The way they functioned, it was not necessary for a leader to have special arrangements as in a ballroom. Someone that had composed a number (or stolen it, as it was the case sometimes) and had it published would distribute his song to the leaders of dancing-school bands and he could be 100 per cent certain that the number would be played regardless of whether it was good or bad.

Johnny Monnegue had been a leader of dancing-school bands for years and had a book of 200 numbers or more. Our night would begin with number one and on through the book until we came to the last number. Then we went from there back down the book, until closing time, which meant that we were reading music from the time we started until we finished the night.

The only time we relaxed and played a few popular jam session numbers that we didn't have to read was when Johnny would get on a drinking binge and not come to work. This happened about every two weeks. We played what we wanted and had fun then, because we knew that when he came back to work the next night, it would be back to the mine again.

There was no flirting with the girls because the bouncers were always watching. Ted and I used to have our drinks to make the time pass. Ted could drink like a fish and was never drunk. He would bring a bottle one night and I brought one the next night. And although the job was hard, we were never too tired to go to some bars when we arrived in Harlem, and drink until the wee hours of the morning.

A few weeks after I started with Johnny, he hired a trombone player named Herb Gregory. Herb had come up in the music game with Rex Stewart and was a great admirer of Jimmy Harrison, and I got a good idea how Jimmy had played from listening to Herb. He had the worst-looking teeth of any horn blower I ever saw. They were snagged and looked as though they were going to fall out at any moment, but when he put his horn to his mouth and started to play, the sounds that came from it were unbelievable.

Herb had not been working much before he joined Monnegue, so for his first week with us, Ted and I shared our bottle with him. He promised to bring in a bottle after he had received a week's pay. There were no nights off in ballrooms or dancing schools and at this place we were paid every Sunday night. Neither Ted nor I brought in a bottle Monday night because Herb was supposed to bring his. After we played a few numbers Herb brought out his bottle and passed it to me. I took a taste and almost gave up my supper. This was the worst alcohol I had ever tasted. There was moonshine whisky known as bathtub gin and white lightning, but this stuff was like cigarette smoke blown into a bottle filled with water directly from the gutter and it tasted as if it could be embalming fluid, if embalming fluid has a taste. I passed the bottle to Ted who could drink anything. But when he did get his breath, after a few seconds, he hollered "Goddamn" so loud that the couples on the dance floor stopped and looked up at the bandstand to see what was happening. Herb was surprised that we did not like his stuff. Neither Ted nor I tried any more of whatever it was. The night was really long before the job was finished and we could get to a bar and have a decent drink.

Sometimes at the dancing school, if there were not many men in the place, the manager would open the front windows on Broadway and give Monnegue a sign to tell Ted to blow out for a while. Then Johnny would be kind-hearted enough to call a number that we did not have to read and Ted would blow so loud that he could be heard for five blocks in any direction.

After a few months with Johnny Monnegue I left and went to another dancing school to work with a leader named Bobby Neal. Bobby was a little fellow about four feet tall who played a double B flat tuba, the biggest tuba ever made. It was much easier playing a dancing-school job with Bobby than it had been with

Monnegue because we played many numbers that we did not have to read. Bobby would do a little show by walking through his tuba and twirling it around the floor. In the band were Arthur Bowie (pianist), Burt Clay (drums), John Collins and Stanley Payne (alto saxes), and Joe Garland (tenor sax), who later became well known as the composer of *In the Mood*, which Glenn Miller made popular in the 1940s.

Bobby was working in a small dancing school on the east side of town, but a big school opened on Broadway over the Strand Theater and was called the Strand Ballroom. It was a high place with plenty of space on the stage for two orchestras and they employed 50 hostesses whereas most places had no more than 15. Bobby was engaged to play the Strand, so he hired Frankie Newton and a trombone player named Jonas Walker. That augmented the band to nine pieces. This was the easiest dancing-school job in New York because another band was also engaged. With three brasses and three saxes, we were able to play some special arrangements. These arrangements were numbered C 1 to C 15. One was by Benny Carter on *Rhapsody in Blue* (C 7 in the book), which had been one of the special numbers played by the Scott band when we started playing other than head arrangements. Arthur Bowie, the pianist, called the numbers, and C 7 was the special of specials. Whenever a musician came to the Strand and Bowie recognized him, as soon we had finished whatever we were playing, Bowie would call for C 7. We played that number so often that we started calling Bowie "C 7".

Very often a young fellow came into the Strand, but he never danced and spent most of his time in the dressing room that we had just next to the bandstand. Sometimes he would be high and go to sleep in a chair until he became a little sober. We found out that his name was Charlie Barnet and that he was from a rich family. But it was some years later, when Charlie took a band into one of the big white hotels, that I found out that he was a musician. He talked with us in the Strand but I don't remember him ever mentioning that he played sax. He really must have liked Neal's band because he came so often and spent his time in our dressing room.

I got a proposition from Horace Henderson to join his band. Horace was playing at the Dunbar Palace, formerly the Bamboo Inn, which was a small dance hall on 7th Avenue, between 139th and 140th Streets. He was using two trumpets—Jacques "Jack" Butler and Gus McClung—when he decided to add another one. But Gus left and was replaced by Wendell Culley, a musician from Boston, who was first-chair man; he had a beautiful tone and so much technique that Horace gave him many solos on ballad numbers. The rest of the men were Bob Carroll (tenor sax), Rupert Cole and John Williams (alto saxes), Sandy Williams (trombone), Horace Henderson (leader and pianist), Bob Ysaguirre (bass), Talcott Reeves (guitar), and Manzie Johnson (drums). Sandy Williams, like Herb Gregory, had a style like Jimmy Harrison and they both loved him. Sandy came from Washington, DC, and had not been in the Apple very long when I joined the band.

We did not stay long at the Dunbar after I joined the band because Don Redman had left the Cotton Pickers to form his own orchestra to record some numbers and wanted Horace and some of the others for the session. I was one of them. He must have remembered me from the time that Scott's band had played a dance in Pittsburgh with the Cotton Pickers and he had asked who I was. The composition of the band was: Leonard "Ham" Davis, Red Allen, and Bill Coleman (trumpets), Claude Jones, Fred Robinson, and Benny Morton (trombones), Edward Inge (clarinet and alto sax), Rupert Cole (alto sax), Bob Carroll (tenor sax), Horace Henderson (piano), Talcott Reeves (guitar), Bob Ysaguirre (bass), Manzie Johnson (drums), and Lois Deppe and Don Redman (vocalists).

Don Redman recorded four numbers: the titles were *Chant of the Weed*, *Shakin' the African*, *I Heard*, and *Trouble why Pick on Me*. The only trumpet solos were done by Red Allen and when these records came out with the names of the musicians, Langston Curl's name was on the cover instead of mine. It probably happened because I had never played in Don's band before.

After the recording was made I didn't hear anything from Don. Bobby Neal was working in a small dancing school and asked me to join him, which I did. A couple of weeks later, Bobby Ysaguirre came to see me and said Don Redman was rehearsing at Connie's Inn and wanted me to join the band. I didn't think it was correct on my part to leave Neal so soon after I joined him again and I explained this to Bobby. So Don Redman opened in Connie's with all the musicians that had recorded with him except Red Allen, Leonard Davis, and myself. His three trumpets were Sidney De Paris, Shirley Clay, and Langston Curl.

Dicky Wells was playing with Charlie Johnson, who left Small's Paradise in 1931. Charlie asked Frankie Newton and myself to join his band. I accepted because Charlie was better known than Neal and the salary would be better also. The members of Charlie's band were: Ben Whitted and Harvey Boone (alto saxes), Benny Waters (who did many of the arrangements, tenor sax), Bobby Johnson (guitar), Dell Thomas (bass), George Stafford (drums), Dicky Wells (trombone), and Leonard "Ham" Davis, Frankie Newton, and myself on trumpets. When we went on tour, Sidney De Paris was added, which made four trumpets and gave the brass section an even bigger sound and more punch than it had before. For my money, Charlie Johnson had a band that was second only to Fletcher Henderson's and he had given Fletcher some tough battles before I joined.

We played a few days in Buffalo at the Ann Montgomery club. There I met trumpeter Peanuts Holland, who was a blowing cat with a lot of technique and a big sound. Another young musician I met at this same club was a fellow named Willie Smith who played alto sax. I jammed with Willie and Peanuts almost every night.

A boy that I had played with at one time in Helvey's band, John L. Henderson, was working in a band at the biggest Negro hotel in Buffalo, so I went to listen to him the night before we had to leave. I had a ball and got so drunk that John told me that I could go to sleep in his room, as he was also living in the hotel.

I told him that I would have to get up at ten o'clock the next morning because the band was leaving at 11 a.m. He said that he would have the desk clerk call me, which he did. But I was still under the influence of the kickapoo joy-juice when I answered the phone, and instead of getting up then, I lay in the bed, trying to get myself together. And went back to slumberland. When I woke up it was midday. I jumped sky high because I was an hour late for the bus. Would Charlie wait for me? was the question I kept asking myself as I put on my clothes as fast as I could! The bus was leaving from Ann Montgomery's place as we had rooms upstairs over the club. When I arrived there I was told that the bus had left just 15 minutes before.

I went back to John's hotel and told him what happened. I had spent most of the money I had the night before and I had left New York being owed a week's salary by Bobby Neal: I had not bothered to collect it because I could trust Bobby. I told John L. that I was going to send a telegram to Joe Garland, who took care of Neal's business, and have him send the money, and John L. told me I could sleep in his room with him until the money came. When the employees of Ann's club heard about what had happened to me, someone offered to take up a collection among them and give me a train fare back to New York but I refused the offer, knowing that I would have my money from Neal. I waited three days but had a ball every night at Ann Montgomery's place jamming with Peanuts and Willie Smith, both of whom I became well acquainted with. Luckily Sidney De Paris was with the band and there were still three trumpets for the job they played the day I missed the bus, which was the last job on the tour.

When I arrived back in the Apple, Charlie didn't have much work for a few weeks and Sidney De Paris went back to Philadelphia, where he had been living before he joined Charlie Johnson.

It was summer in 1931 when Charlie landed a job playing at a big swimming pool called the Lido, which was at 146th Street and 7th Avenue. It was a pleasant job, because it was not too hot during the night and, as we played near the pool, which had no roof, we could not play after midnight. So I went to the Savoy at times.

Charlie Johnson had not changed his habit of playing the first number with the band and then disappearing until it was time to play the last number. But he got hooked when the band played a week at the Lafayette Theater. The name of the show for that week was "Chocolate Drops" and we were in a big stage built like a box of candy. We had to enter this set from the basement by climbing up some steps. When the band was seated before the show started, the top of the box was closed and slowly opened when we started to play the opening number. The piano was in the right hand side of the box and Charlie had to go in first. There was no way for him to get out, and it was the joke of the week because it was the first time that he had ever been in a position where he was obliged to stay at the piano until the end of a show or dance.

One of the attraction numbers that we played that week was an arrangement of *Ding Dong Daddy*, which I sang, and the trumpets played in three-part harmony, exactly as Louis Armstrong played it. It made a hit with the audience, stage hands, and chorus girls.

The Harlem Opera House on 125th Street between 7th and 8th Avenues had been a burlesque show place but it was turned into a theater that showed movies and had stage shows. Charlie Johnson and the orchestra were engaged to play a week there. On the bill was a magician who had a trick stool. He would invite someone from the audience to come on stage to sit on it after he had performed some other magic tricks with them. When someone sat on this stool, the legs would flop down leaving the person sitting flat on their fanny. The musicians had a crap game after every show and Charlie Johnson lost most of the time. We had four shows a day. When 15 minutes was called before the next show went on, the band would be backstage with Charlie explaining why he had lost or what he should have done to win. The guys would maneuver him to the collapsible stool of the magician, which was always at a certain place, and Charlie would sit down on it every time because he would be so busy trying to get over a point. This was our backstage attraction.

But the highlight of the show for me that week was that we were accompanying the one and only Queen of the Blues, Bessie Smith. Bessie was not as popular as she had been, but to me she was singing better than she had ever done. I found out that she could sing other types of songs as well as she could sing blues. One of the songs in her repertoire was *Someone Stole Gabriel's Horn*, which she swung out of this world and which the whole band enjoyed hearing her sing more than any of the blues numbers.

Charlie Johnson didn't get much work after the Harlem Opera House date and the band finally broke up. He never had a regular band after that. Later he went into a dancing-school job, which surprised everybody because he had been the laziest piano player in New York and was never known to stay at the piano longer than ten minutes when he had a big band, except for the week in the Lafayette Theater when he was boxed in.

I joined Luis Russell again in 1931, replacing Otis Johnson. Russell had been working at the Saratoga Club, which was the old Capitol, but the band was in the Arcadia Ballroom on Broadway and 53rd Street when I rejoined him.

The Arcadia was the second-best white ballroom after the Roseland, but for Negro bands, it was better than the Roseland because there was a decent band room up over the bandstand and it was not necessary to stand on the back stairway between sets. We could sit down and play cards or write letters the same as the white orchestra did in their band room. As far as socializing with the clientele was concerned, no band, white or colored, was allowed to do that. And everyone—musicians, bartenders and hostesses—came in and went out the front door. We came and left by a back door at the Roseland.

Russell was now employing three trumpets and Higginbotham was not there. This time I had more solos and played some of the first parts also. The band was: Bill Dillard, Red Allen, and Bill Coleman (trumpets), Jimmy Archey (trombone), Henry "Moon" Jones (alto sax), Albert Nicholas (clarinet and alto sax), Greely Walton (tenor sax), Luis Russell (piano), Bill Johnson (guitar), Pops Foster (bass), and Paul Barbarin (drums).

One night the orchestra of Noble Sissle, who was working in a big white hotel, was engaged at the Arcadia to play a battle of jazz between Russell and the other white orchestra, whose name I don't remember. I had seen Sissle on stage when I was in Cincinnati and in my estimation he was pretty much a ham actor. So it was a night that we were looking forward to, and the Uncle Tom in him was really shown when his band came in dressed in red frocktail coats which made them look like a circus monkey band. There were some good musicians in the band, including Wilbur De Paris and Sidney Bechet, who was supposed to be the best jazzman of the band, but I was never a lover of the soprano sax and Bechet didn't impress me at that time. The band as a whole was the most jazzless Negro orchestra I had ever heard. The white band made Sissle's sound like a fifth-grade school band and Russell's orchestra made Sissle's sound like it was the first time they had ever played musical instruments. It's been said that a band is no better than its leader and I felt sorry for the musicians because they had no leader that knew beans about jazz.

We went to Philadelphia to play one week at the Earl Theater. That was the hardest week I ever worked in a theater. Paul Barbarin left Russell and went back to New Orleans. He was replaced by James Smith, who became a good buddy of mine. The Mills Brothers were the stars of the show. They had been very popular radio stars for a long time and the biggest attraction that ever worked at Connie's Inn. As a rule the Earl Theater worked on the same basis as the Lafayette: four shows on Friday, five on Saturdays and Sundays, and a midnight show on Saturday also. But the Mills Brothers were such a big drawing card that we did seven shows a day. When we finished one show, the half hour for the next one would be called as we were coming off the stage. One short film and the newsreel were shown and we were on stage again. I and everyone else ate the fastest meals ever and no one was ever late for a show.

Two young boys of 12 and 14 years were engaged to dance during the week, but after two days they had to stop because the law did not allow kids that young to work in a theater. They were the Nicholas Brothers.

The band played an opening number. Then the chorus girls did a number. After that a comedy sketch. Then one more time, band number, chorus girl number, comedy sketch, and it would be the Mills Brothers' show for a half hour.

There was a line a quarter of a mile long every show, every day, waiting to get into the theater. The Mills Brothers were great to work with and one could easily tell that success never went to their heads. But brother, oh what a week!

A few weeks later we played the Howard Theater in Washington, DC, and the Royal in Baltimore, but not with the Mills Brothers. Then we did a few days in Bridgeton, New Jersey, before coming back to New York. Russell had no regular work after that, just a few gigs now and then.

The Renaissance Ballroom, which I have already mentioned, was a place where most of the Negro clubs held their dances. The leader of the orchestra was Vernon Andrade, a banjo and guitar player. Vernon never had a band of regular musicians although there were some that usually gigged with him as I did. There were many musicians in the 1920s and 30s who gigged at one time with him: Benny Carter, Rex Stewart, Bobby Stark, and others. With Vernon, I met one of the greatest alto sax men in the business, Hilton Jefferson. Jeff was a very quiet man, but he made his horn talk for him. All the musicians loved him.

Another musician who always had the highest-paid gigs was a drummer named

Peek-a-Boo Jimmy. Peek-a-Boo had played with James P. Johnson, Willie "the Lion" Smith, and Luckey Roberts in the days before I even dreamed of going to New York. I gigged with Peek-a-Boo twice and both times it was really enjoyable. The music we played was not very jazzy because Jimmy was a drummer that had lost sight of what the other drummers were doing. Most of the musicians he hired were a certain age and not up-to-date on jazz either.

But Jimmy was in with the rich folks downtown and he played many high society functions. The first one I did with him was a stag party for some business men who had rented a Hudson River cruising boat and invited about 400 men to cruise up the Hudson. We played but there was no dancing as there were no women to dance with. Finally we docked somewhere and everybody went ashore, where a big picnic with all kinds of seafood and kegs of beer was waiting for everyone including the band. The committee of this outing had engaged Primo Carnera, the giant heavyweight boxer, to give an exhibition. I received $25 for that gig and the same for another I did with Peek-a-Boo in the city, which was not a stag party but a dance. We had all the steaks and beer we could eat and drink. That was something that Peek-a-Boo was always asking for his musicians and himself when he had a gig.

Ralph Cooper, who was a dancer turned orchestra leader, was playing at the Lafayette one week and he had a very good show band. Ralph really knew show business. I saw the band during the early part of the week and really enjoyed its presentation. The shows at the Lafayette always started on Friday and finished on Thursdays. I had been out drinking most of the Tuesday night of the week when Ralph was at the Lafayette. I knew I could sleep late Wednesday. Russell had a dance to play that night in a hall up over the Alhambra Theater at 7th Avenue and 126th Street. I was deep in slumberland when someone knocked on my door about 12.30 in the afternoon. It was Gus McClung, Henry Goodwin, and Reidus "Mack" Horton, three members of Cooper's orchestra. They told me that the other trumpeter, Louis Hunt, was having lip trouble and felt so embarrassed because he had a feature number to do and had been missing the ending for a few days. So he had not shown up for the first show and they had come to ask me if I would come to the theater and be on hand to do the next show if Hunt did not appear. I was so beat, and knowing that I had to work with Russell that night, I told them I could not make it. Two and a half hours later, Gus and Henry Goodwin came back, this time with Paul Bernet, the guitarist who had been with Arthur Gibbs. They told me that Hunt had not shown up for the second show and asked me to do the last two. As it was the second time they had come for me, and I was feeling better than I had earlier, I told them yes.

Ralph asked me if I knew *I Can't Give you Anything but Love*, the way Armstrong played it. Of course I knew it after the many times I had played it for myself along with the record. He asked me if I knew the ending and could I go out and play it in front of the band. That was the number Hunt had been featured on. When the time came to do the number, I walked to within three feet of the footlights and played it the way Satchmo did. It was the first time I had ever received so much applause in my career. When I played it for the last show, all the chorus girls and most of the stage hands were standing in the wings of the stage. I suppose they had heard it the show before and had gathered in the wings to see if I would do it again. I did, thank the Lord.

Between the third and last show I had gone to the job that Russell was playing. I told Luis that I had a show to do and explained why. So he gave me time off to do the last show and I came back later to finish the night with him.

Ralph asked me if I would do the show the next day and I accepted. I went straight home after the dance because the first show was at eleven the next morning and I wanted to get as much rest as possible.

The four shows on Thursday went down great and Ralph had some theater dates to do the following week in New Jersey. I did them with him. After those dates he was going on a theater tour and asked me if I would stay with the band. As Russell was not working regularly, I accepted. Russell agreed that I should do it and wished me luck.

Ralph had signed a contract with RKO, which was the biggest theatrical circuit in the country. There were three tap dancers, Blair, Rice, and Berry, known as the Three Sams; Bessie Dudley, who was a snake-hip dancer; and the band. Ralph danced and also did a parody on *Penthouse Serenade*. Ralph was a very handsome light-colored man and sort of stocky for a tap dancer. He had teamed with a dancer named Eddie Rector who was one of the best that ever wore a pair of tap-dancing shoes. He looked good leading a band and that was a big factor in the success of his orchestra.

The band consisted of the following: Gus McClung, Henry Goodwin, and Bill Coleman (trumpets), Booker Pittman and Leroy Hardy (alto saxes), Alfred Pratt (tenor sax), Mack Horton (trombone), Eugene Anderson (piano), Paul Bernet (guitar), and Arnold "Scrip" Boling (drums). The first hop was Chicago and the following appeared in one of the local papers:

> Ralph Cooper brought his famous band into Chicago last week for an engagement at the Palace Theater and scored an instant hit. The opening of the show found the theater packed and they drew well throughout the engagement. Ralph had assembled some of New York's best musicians and whipped them into a selling outfit. Cooper directs the band, sings a number or two, and does a dance number that equals Robinson [Bojangles] or Eddie Rector in their best days.

Duke Ellington was playing some exclusive place in a suburb of Chicago and I saw Freddie Jenkins and Rex Stewart many times. The fattest musician I ever saw was also in Chicago. His name was Tiny Parham and he played piano. He had an orchestra but I never heard it. I did however see his car: he had had the steering wheel put almost in the middle of the front seat in order to be able to drive. He must have weighed about 400 pounds.

From Chicago we went to the RKO Theater at Cleveland for one week and from there to Denver, Colorado, which was the furthest west that I had ever been. We played the RKO vaudeville theater and visited the Rocky Mountains.

Denver is a beautiful city, a mile above sea level. In the summer it is hot as blazes there. One has to look at the snow on top of the distant mountains to convince oneself that there is any cool weather anywhere. The colored people there had more beautiful homes than anywhere we had been, and to protect those homes, they had their own fire department—something I never saw anywhere else in the USA.

As the theater was in the center of the downtown district, once we were there, we did not go back to the colored district where we stayed until the last show. There was a white restaurant on the street behind the theater. An alley ran between the streets. We ordered our meals from this restaurant and ate them in our dressing rooms. The dressing rooms in the RKO theaters were more comfortable than many hotels that I have been in: thick carpets on the floors, showers, and some had kitchens where the actors could cook.

One day the owner of the restaurant came to the theater and said he would like to invite us for supper, but there was one hitch. He had a banquet room on the second floor of the restaurant and as his clientele was white only, we would have to come in through the kitchen from the alley. We accepted his invitation. What happened was that we went in through the kitchen, came out into the main dining room, and went upstairs. It was quite ridiculous because the only way to get upstairs was through the dining room where white customers had dinner. But a black man could not come through the front door. We had a wonderful supper and the owner even entertained us by playing songs on a mandolin. He told us he was from Detroit and resented the racial prejudice in the South, but he had a wonderful business and could not change the ways of narrow-minded people.

There was a photo shop around the corner from the theater. As I was taking many photos I gave my films to this place to be developed. Black people did not have to go in the back of shops, thank the Lord. I had gone to pick up some photos and I was walking on the outside of the sidewalk when suddenly, someone shoved me. I thought it was one of the fellows from the band who was playing a joke, but when I turned to see who it was, I saw a little old white man with grey hair who said, "Get off the sidewalk nigger," and kept walking. I was mad enough to bite a tenpenny nail in two, but there was nothing I could do.

From Denver we went to the RKO Orpheum Theater in Omaha, Nebraska. During the week there was a dance which we went to after the show. The orchestra was the Blue Devils and I had met one of the trumpet players, George Hutchinson, in Buffalo when I was there with the Scotts' band. He told me that some of the members of the orchestra were staying at the same place we were, a very big rooming house called the White House, because it was painted white. There was a room with a piano and one could buy bootleg whisky there. So we went to the White House after the dance, which finished at 2 a.m., and started a jam session. From our band only Booker Pittman, Alfred Pratt, Leroy Hardy, and I participated. The tenor sax in the Blue Devils band was a light-skinned, red-headed fellow. He told me his name was Lester Young. Lester's playing made a strong impression on me. I could sense he was going to be an outstanding musician. We had a lot of fun drinking and jamming together.

After Omaha we played the RKO theaters of Milwaukee, Wisconsin and Minneapolis, Minnesota. In Minneapolis we shared the bill with Hobart

Bosworth, a movie actor whom I had seen many times in films. I also met my good friend and teacher, Theodore "Wingy" Carpenter, who was playing in a club there. We were really happy to meet again, and he was elated with me because I had come a long way since he had shown me some riffs back in Cincinnati.

Everywhere we played, Ralph Cooper and his band headlined the show. Every theater had big pit bands to play the acts that were not musical, and the musicians in the pits gave us very high praise for our musical ability. We came back to Chicago for a repeat performance of one week and from there we jumped to Boston, Massachusetts, for one week at the RKO Keith Boston Theater.

As we had been the main attraction everywhere, someone thought that we deserved to have a little more money and everyone agreed. We spoke to Ralph, who said that he would look into the matter and at the end of the week, we received a raise. We came back to New York and never worked another RKO theater after that!

Here is the reason. Ralph loved his musicians to the point of doing almost anything to please them: it was one of the most brotherly orchestras that I had ever worked with. When we asked for a raise, Ralph phoned the office in New York but they refused to give us more money. So Ralph kept the percentage he was supposed to send them and gave us the raise. Perhaps he thought that he could arrange things when we returned to New York, but that was not the case.

The band did not break up, however, and we continued to play theaters that were not run by RKO. We played the Lafayette, the Mount Morris, and went on a tour of upstate New York. The tour ended in November 1932. So did the Ralph Cooper orchestra because no more bookings were coming in.

Living with Madelyn had become so unbearable that we separated for the third and last time. Grandma Jackson and her family had left Springfield and moved to New York three years before. Dicky Wells was staying with them. I took a room with Grandma also.

I had met a girl in the subway on New Year's Day 1932 when I was playing Loew's Theater with Luis Russell. She told me that she lived in Leonia, New Jersey, and gave me her address. Her name was Beatrice Twiggs and she told me that everyone called her Beezie. I wrote to Beezie during my tour with Ralph Cooper. When we came back to New York, I went to New Jersey to see her. That was the start of a romance that eventually led us to living together after I separated from Madelyn.

I went back into Russell's orchestra. The musicians were now: John Brown, Bobby Cheeks, and Bill Coleman (trumpets), Jimmy Archey (trombone), Glyn Paque and Henry "Moon" Jones (alto saxes), Bingie Madison (tenor sax), Luis Russell (piano), Lee Blair (guitar), Pops Foster (bass), and Paul Barbarin (drums). We played Baltimore at the Royal Theater and some small towns in New York state before being engaged to replace Don Redman in Connie's Inn, but Russell was the last band to play there. Connie still owes us $200 in back pay.

The show at Connie's was great, with Louise Cook, a beautiful shake dancer;

Paul Meers, one of the greatest classical dancers that New York ever knew, who performed with his second wife Barbara; a comic acrobat dancer, "Jazz Lips" Richardson; the one and only "Snake Hips" Tucker; the Lucky Seven Trio; three girls that had a singing act; and twelve beautiful chorus girls. But Connie's was beginning to lose the white clients from downtown because Harlem was turning bad and so many white people were getting robbed when they came uptown. And Negroes, the few that ever went to the place, were treated so bad, getting the tables where it was almost impossible to see the floor show, that they did not come when the place started losing the white customers.

We doubled in some theaters including the Lafayette. It was hard work because we would be in the theaters from 11 a.m. until 11 p.m. and then have to come to the Inn and do two shows. Each week Connie's was getting deeper in debt to the band and the other folks in the show.

Snake Hips Tucker was a tough guy and loved to fight. When he did his number the customers would throw dollar coins on the floor just to see him do a somersault and go into a split to pick it up. One night a fellow heated a half dollar at his table and threw it on the floor. Snake didn't know the coin was hot but he found out when he picked it up. He finished his dance near that table, came back, and hit the guy so hard that he was knocked out of his seat. The three men who were with him jumped to defend their friend, but some of the waiters who had watched the scene were already standing at their table, so they dug and froze. Connie came up and ordered them to pay their bill and get the hell out of there. He was a reasonable man but did not stand for his show people to be abused.

I never cared for gangsters, but one night, one of America's biggest gangsters came to Connie's and we had a conversation. He was Dutch Schultz, a big man with a pleasant voice. I don't remember what we talked about, but I know that I did not ask him how many guns he carried or how many men were in his gang.

Eventually, in 1933, Connie closed the Inn and Russell went back to the Roseland. I had been the featured soloist in the trumpet section and had some fine solos. Beezie and I had not started living together, but we were sweethearts.

Russell had engaged a drummer–singer whose name was Tiny Bradshaw to direct the band when we went into the Roseland. He had been the drummer in the Blue Rhythm band. Tiny was a light-skinned, red-headed fellow who sang in the type of growl voice that was associated with Holy Roller preachers. Today it's the way that most rock-and-roll singers sing. Tiny made a big hit at the Roseland, and the band was jumping.

SEVEN

FALLING IN LOVE WITH PARIS

Lucky Millinder, who had been one of the directors of the Blue Rhythm, had an orchestra at the Harlem Opera House that was the regular house band. In June 1933 Lucky sent one of his musicians to ask me if I would like to join his outfit for a job in France, because Gus Aiken suffered with some kind of sickness that did not allow him to travel overseas. I was tempted to accept it but did not want to leave New York for several reasons, so I refused the offer.

Red Allen came back to Russell's orchestra but I had my solos and everything was fine. But Beezie had the feeling that I was still thinking about that trip to Europe and told me that I should go to see Lucky and accept the offer if it was not too late. I followed her advice and was engaged.

The Lucky Millinder orchestra left New York on 29 June aboard the *Conte Grande*, an Italian ship, destination Monte Carlo. Members of the band were: Bill Coleman, Bill Dillard, and Henry Goodwin (trumpets), Booker Pittman and Leroy Hardy (alto saxes), Alfred Pratt (tenor sax), Mack Horton (trombone), Eugene Anderson (piano), Arnold Adams (guitar), and Arnold "Scrip" Boling (drums).

I was very excited about being on a big ship of 25,000 tons sailing for Europe. I tried to picture what Monte Carlo and France would be like. We stopped in Boston, left there on 30 June, and hit the high seas.

In the dining room we were placed four at a table, where there was a half bottle of white wine and a half bottle of red wine for each person. But the passengers could have as many bottles as they desired. Like most Americans I had never drunk wine with my meals and I drank one white and two red with my first meal. After that, I had four bottles with each meal. I was quite gay but never drunk for the whole trip, which was eleven days.

With our group were two chorus girls, Ethel Moses and Mary Hart; Freddie "Snake Hips" Taylor; and Jimmy Daniels, a singer. The band rehearsed every day. We swam in the pool on the deck and played cards at night. The trip was fine and the weather beautiful.

We arrived at Gibraltar and small boats came out to the ship with souvenirs to sell, and kids dived in the water to retrieve pieces of money the passengers threw to them. Too bad we could not go ashore. Then we sailed into the Mediterranean. The next day I saw schools of dolphins and flying fish which I watched for hours.

The dolphins followed the boat for miles. We stopped at Naples, Italy, on 9 July, and it was possible to visit some of the city. The next day, we disembarked at Villefranche, France, and went by special bus to Monte Carlo. The houses looked different and so many other things made me know that I was really in a foreign country, 4053 miles from New York.

Rehearsals for the show at the Sporting Club d'Été began the day after our arrival and included the orchestras of Enric Madriguera, who featured Latin American music, and Bela de Racz, a Hungarian. There were also 16 dancing and show girls, most of whom had been in the Ziegfield Follies, and several other artists: singers, dancers, acrobats, comedians, some of which we had to accompany, plus the stars, who were Gloria Grafton, Carl Rendall, Tito Coral, the Arnaut Brothers, Reva Reyes, Mohamed Ben Jamai, Vilma and Buddy Ebsen, Dave and Dorothy Fitz-Gibbons, Freddie Taylor, Mary Hart, Ethel Moses, Jimmy Daniels. All were part of the show which Lucky Millinder and Madriguera's orchestras accompanied. Bela de Racz and his orchestra played dinner music before the shows. They played Hungarian gypsy music, which I had never heard before. There was a cymbalom, which looked like a small piano but was played with mallets, three violins, two violas, and a bass. I really enjoyed listening to this orchestra, whose musicians got a big kick listening to us when we played jazzy dance numbers.

After the show was well on its way, we had the chance to do some visiting, which included Nice at least once a week, the Palace of the Prince of Monaco, and Ventimiglia in Italy. There were many cafés open all night which I visited after we finished at the Sporting and I didn't feel like going home.

One day an orchestra that was playing in some resort in the vicinity of Monte Carlo came over to see us. I knew one of the musicians vaguely. He was June Cole, who had played bass with the Cotton Pickers and Fletcher Henderson. I was introduced to Willie Lewis who was the leader, Ted Fields and his wife Evelyn, and Bobby Martin. Willie Lewis played alto sax and clarinet; Ted Fields, drums; and Bobby Martin, trumpet. Willie and Bobby had played with Sam Wooding, who had brought an orchestra to Europe in the 1920s.

Alfred Pratt met a girl in Monte Carlo and married her before we left for Paris on 6 September. We left Monte Carlo on an early evening train. I had a bottle of cognac and one of the other musicians had one also. I was so excited about going to Paris that I could not sleep. I walked the corridors all night. The coaches with compartments were new to me and I did not disturb anyone who wanted to sleep. I drank my bottle and some of the other one before we arrived in Paris in the morning, but the cognac had burned my throat to the point of my being so hoarse that I could hardly talk. We were taken to the Hôtel Lisieux, rue Fontaine, in the heart of the Pigalle district. I had never heard of Pigalle before. The day was beautiful and I was in Paris, not the one in Kentucky, but *the* P-A-R-I-S! I did not feel sleepy although I had, in a way, walked from Monte Carlo to Paris.

There was a bar downstairs in the hotel owned by Madame Lisieux, who was a beautiful Amazon perhaps in her late thirties. I started to drink with some people in the bar and my voice was getting hoarser and hoarser. Finally someone persuaded me to go up to my room and get some rest, but it was eleven o'clock that night before I got to bed. I slept until 6 p.m. the next day, and when I was awakened I had my voice back again.

The following day we started rehearsing the show we had done in Monte Carlo, with a French orchestra instead of Madriguera, at the Théâtre Rex. This was the largest theater I'd ever seen. The two bands were on the stage opposite each other and they still seemed to be a mile apart. In a few days I learned how to walk from my hotel to the Rex. I met a journalist named Edgar Wiggins, who wrote for the *Chicago Defender* (the largest Negro weekly paper in the USA) under the name "The Street Wolf of Paris."

There were quite a few American Negroes in Paris and many of them made the Hôtel Lisieux their meeting place. There was an American Negro girl named Neeka Shaw who had a cabaret where a fine pianist by the name of Freddie Johnson was playing. I had heard some musicians in New York speak about Freddie Johnson and his piano playing was everything I had heard about. Neeka's place was called the Hot Feet and was on rue Pigalle. Freddie had some Armstrong records and a record player. As Satchmo was my man with a horn, I would go to Freddie's room to listen to them.

I went to Neeka's and jammed with Freddie. One morning I met a trumpeter named Arthur Briggs there, whom I had met before in New York when he was with Noble Sissle at the Lafayette in 1931. Sissle also had a fine young first trumpeter named Joe Keyes with him. For a young man Joe could drink more juice than any two drinking men and still play his horn. Briggs and I jammed at the Hot Feet until the wee hours of the morning and Freddie played more piano than I had ever heard. Briggs was a first-chair man but he could play things at a jam session that made everybody know that he could also take hot choruses, a thing very few first trumpeters in a section could do.

Later, during my sojourn in Paris, I met a quiet, handsome young alto sax player from St. Louis, Missouri, named Cle Saddler. We used to drink together at the Lisieux but I never heard him play. Another famous personality who hung around the Lisieux was Spencer Williams, the composer of *Basin Street Blues*. Kid Chocolate, the famous Cuban boxer, was in Paris, and so was Jimmy Monroe, the husband of Nina Mae McKinney, the movie star.

Freddie "Snake Hips" Taylor and I lived in the same hotel and Freddie was hip to gage, as marijuana or reefers were called. I went to Freddie's room and it would be like walking into a London fog. The windows were closed and reefer smoke would be so thick that you could cut it with a knife. Freddie and Jimmy Monroe would be smoking and to my surprise Kid Chocolate was in the room also. I didn't see Kid smoking but I thought that being in a closed room full of marijuana smoke was not good for a prizefighter. But after all it was his business. I didn't smoke the stuff either after what it had done to me back in New York.

Another club where I jammed was the Cabane Cubaine, which was on the rue Fontaine. I had not been acquainted with Cuban music and to my surprise it was swinging like mad with rhythm that was different from what we played in jazz.

But the musicians had a feeling for jazz, and when a jazz musician came to sit in with them, they played jazz tunes not at all badly. We got together well enough to have some fun jamming, and the clientele liked it.

When the show closed at the Rex, we had a few days to stay before we returned to New York. There had been some talk about taking the show to England but it didn't work out. We received a last-minute notice that we were to leave the morning of 4 October. There was a rush to pack and do some shopping for gifts and Leroy Hardy and I arrived at the railroad station two minutes after the departure of the train. A Frenchman named Georges, who had been taking care of the tickets for the band and registered the luggage, gave us information about the time of the next train. We didn't miss that one.

The conductor came for our tickets later. When he saw them, he started telling us something in French which we did not understand. When we arrived in Nice, I saw all the heavy baggage of the orchestra still on the embankment. I thought that it was funny because the luggage had come on the train the others had taken. From Nice, we had to go to Villefranche to board the Italian steamer Rex, which was the largest ship plying the Atlantic and the holder of the Blue Ribbon for being the fastest ocean liner in the world.

The Rex was supposed to sail from Villefranche at the same time our train arrived in Nice, but Georges had called the steamship officials in Villefranche and arranged the difficult task of postponing the sailing time of the crack Italian liner one hour in order for us to get aboard. A launch was waiting to take us out to the Rex, since there was no landing port in Villefranche for large steamers. All the passengers on board knew that the ship was being delayed from sailing because we were arriving late, so the decks were lined with a curious crowd. They really did wave and cheer us when we climbed up the steps to the boarding deck.

But our baggage, trunks, Arnold Boling's drum case and Wilson Myers's bass—which was in a specially made trunk—were not put on the launch. In fact they were still at the station in Nice. We found out why from the baggage commissary. It had been sent from Paris on a group ticket and, as Leroy and I did not arrive with the group and two tickets were missing, the baggage could not be collected. However, everyone did have a few changes in their handbags and we had to pay a supplement to have the baggage sent by a boat that would be sailing in a few days.

Two musicians were also missing. Booker Pittman and Alfred Pratt had decided to stay in France with their wives. Freddie Taylor also stayed. I did not drink as much wine going back as I had on the trip coming to Europe. The weather was fine until after we passed Gibraltar and got to the Gulf Stream, which was a little rough for a couple of days. We arrived in New York on Columbus Day, 12 October.

A few days after my return to New York I was contacted by Benny Carter, who was forming an orchestra. Benny had formed bands before this, one of which had played the Savoy and another at the Arcadia. I was very happy about the opportunity to work for Benny because he was my favorite arranger and alto player.

Benny said that he would let me know when the band would begin rehearsing, so I went to Leonia, New Jersey, to spend a couple of days with Beezie, whom I had not seen for four months. She was working and could not meet me when I returned to New York. When I came back from Leonia, I learned from Dicky Wells, who was also engaged to play with Benny, that the band had made some records for an English arranger named Spike Hughes. No one knew where to contact me in New Jersey so I had missed my first chance to record with Benny Carter.

But I made the rehearsals. Benny had discovered three musicians who were new to New York. The pianist Teddy Wilson; Frederic "Keg" Johnson, a trombonist; and George Johnson (no relation to Keg), an alto player. I had heard any number of Earl Hines records and there was no greater jazz piano player at that time, but when I heard Teddy Wilson I knew that a new star was going to make his footprint in the sands of jazz. Earl was great and Teddy was destined to become great. He had certain Hines ideas but his style was not a strict copy. He had a very personal way to use his left hand in a modern stride manner.

The composition of the orchestra was as follows: Bill Coleman, Bill Dillard, and Lincoln Mills (trumpets), Keg Johnson, Charlie "Big" Green, and Dicky Wells (trombones), Benny Carter, Glyn Paque, and George Johnson (alto saxes), Johnny Russell (tenor sax), Teddy Wilson (piano), Lawrence Lucie (guitar), Ernest "Bass" Hill (bass), and Cozy Cole (drums). Some of these were new to me although they were New York musicians: Johnny Russell, Glyn Paque, George Johnson, Lincoln Mills, and Lawrence Lucie. Benny had brought Teddy Wilson and Keg Johnson from Chicago. Benny was well known to organize musicians that had never worked together as a group and have them sounding as if they had been together for years. The arrangements he made were more difficult for the sax section than they were for the brass, but he had good men because he knew the ones he wanted and the brass section's work was very effective with the passages he wrote for the reeds.

Benny was admired by a very successful Negro bootlegger named George Ricks, whom most of us knew very well. One of Benny's motives for forming this orchestra was that George wanted to open a club with Benny having the band there. The salary was not great, but like myself, the other musicians admired and loved Benny to the point where we would have worked with him for the pleasure of playing his arrangements, if a job actually could not pay.

George Ricks opened the Harlem Club (formerly Connie's). There was a floor show, the same as Connie had, but the entertainers were not big names, although they were known in Harlem. The band was sounding greater every day and I was the main soloist in the trumpet section. Benny was beginning to play trumpet also but he would not bring it out until he had it under control. There was no singer in the band but things were sounding so good that Benny was inspired to make an arrangement on a number called *Ole Pappy* and sing it.

Another theater on 125th Street, the Apollo, started having stage shows, and it was Benny's band that played the grand opening and the first two weeks. But there was a system known as "kick-back" to the Union Local 802 delegate, Mr. Minton, who later opened the famous Minton's Playhouse. He was the Harlem walking delegate and if the kick-back system ever benefited anyone, it must have been him. The Union delegate fixed the price that theater and dance hall owners had to pay for a band; then they would come to see the bandleader and ask for a percentage. These were the days of gangsterism and a leader and his men had to go along with the system if they wanted to work.

We still came back to the Harlem Club every night after the last show and worked until 3 a.m. Big Green was beginning to suffer with stomach ulcers but he had been, and still was, a heavy drinker. He came to the theater and did the first show every day but then he would be feeling so bad that he would lie on an army cot for the other three shows and eat nothing but clam chowder. When we got to the club, he would be feeling better, and when the club closed, he was feeling good enough to go to a cellar joint across from the Rhythm Club and drink until time to make the first show. He did that for two weeks and Benny never said anything because he liked Big Green. So did the rest of the guys.

When Connie's was in its heyday, most of the time it refused Negroes. I suppose that had something to do with them not coming to the club, even after it reopened under a different name and ownership. True, there were some nights when the crowds were very good, but a successful spot must have a good crowd every night.

The band was wonderful, without a doubt. Quite a few white musicians from downtown came to hear us at different times. Benny Goodman, before he became famous, was one that Benny knew and introduced to the band. Charlie Barnet was another downtown bandleader who came to the club quite often.

The Harlem Club was finally forced to close and we opened at the Empire Ballroom on Broadway. The Empire had opened a year or two before we were engaged to play there. Fletcher Henderson had inaugurated it and worked there quite a while. It was also competition for the Roseland as they were opposite to each other.

A white band was on the second bandstand but I don't remember the names of the leader or of any of the musicians. The conditions were better for us at the Empire than at the Roseland, because we had a bandroom right on the same floor as the ballroom. There was no mixing with the public and a bouncer always stood by our bandstand when we were playing to keep girls from flirting with us.

There were five telephone booths next to the bandroom. The door was never closed, so we could always hear a phone when it rang during the intermission. If a chick wanted to get in touch with one of us, she would telephone from one of the booths. One of us would answer. "Are you one of the musicians?" would probably be the first question! Then she would say she wanted to speak to a certain one who sat at a certain place on the bandstand and that was it. The moral of that story is "Love will find a way."

One night we were quite surprised to see a tall blond fellow standing to one side of the bandstand in full dress clothes. No one ever came to the Empire Ballroom dressed in that fashion. I thought perhaps he was a high society cat who had probably been to a wedding and then decided to go out slumming on Broadway instead of Harlem. When we came off the bandstand, he introduced himself to Benny Carter as we all went to the bandroom to play our usual ten cent tonk to pass the time between sets. Benny brought the fellow into the room and introduced him to us as Baron Timothy Rosenkrantz from Denmark. We later found out that he was a jazz fan and knew a lot about some of the big swing bands and the musicians. We were the first Negro band that he had heard in New York. He had only been in the city a couple of days when he learned that Benny had a band at the Empire ballroom. Timme—as he was later to become known—had come to the ballroom in full dress because that was the way a person of his class went out in his country at that time. The next night he was back again dressed like an ordinary human being. When we finished the night Timme wanted to go up to Harlem, so Lincoln Mills, the trumpeter we called "Link," took Timme uptown. Link smoked reefers and he was the one who introduced the stuff to Timme, who became so fascinated with Harlem that he finally moved there.

For some unknown reason, Benny began to lose interest in the band. Bill Dillard left to join Teddy Hill, who had been the tenor man with Luis Russell at one time and now had his own band at the Savoy. Two weeks before the time for us to finish at the Empire, Benny told us that he would be disbanding.

The word got around very quickly and Teddy Hill asked me and Dicky Wells to join his band. Willie Bryant, an MC and showman who had an act with another showman named Leonard Reed, was forming an orchestra, and he engaged Teddy Wilson, Johnny Russell, Glyn Paque, and Cozy Cole. We all hated to see this band of Benny Carter break up. I considered it—and still do—the best band I ever played with.

In January 1934, Dicky Wells and I joined Teddy Hill at the Savoy. I was back home again. The Savoy was jumping as it always had and I was happy to be back in a place where it was not necessary to stand on the back stairway or go to a bandroom when I finished playing a set. The girls didn't have to call me from a telephone booth and I lived five minutes walking distance from the Savoy.

During the months that Teddy was in the Savoy, the Alabama State College orchestra was engaged for a few days. The leader, Erskine Hawkins, was the second trumpet player I ever heard who could play altissimo C (C above the high one in the treble clef). The first one was Tommy "Steve" Stevens with Jimmie Lunceford, whom I heard at the Lafayette Theater shortly after I came back from Europe.

After a few months at the Savoy, Teddy Hill and orchestra were engaged to play at the Ubangi Club, which had been Connie's Inn and the Harlem Club before. In place of having girls in the chorus line, there were six female impersonators and the main attraction was a lesbian named Gladys Bentley. Gladys was quite plump and wore a man's full dress suit for her act. She dressed like a man, except for a skirt, when she had on street clothes. Gladys played piano, sang, and tap-danced a little.

Allen Drew was a cigar-smoking master of ceremonies and comedian. The six female impersonators were not bad as chorus girls and some looked almost like girls. But later the manager added six more sissies and some of them had muscles like prize fighters. They really looked funny in those chorus girl costumes with big muscles showing in their arms and legs.

They had all chosen female names and one called himself Clara Bow, another was Theda Barra, and one quite famous was known as Mother Smothers. One night a few of us were talking very seriously with Clara Bow and we asked him if he had ever had any sexual relations with a female. He said never: he had always felt that he was a female. The band got along well with those female imperson-aters and none of them ever tried to have an affair with any of us, that I know about. I always was and always will be a guy that digs chicks, and the real ones at that.

A girl pianist and singer by the name of Una Mae Carlisle was also engaged at the club. She had been a protégée of Fats Waller when he was playing for the WLW radio station in Cincinnati.

A few weeks after we were in the Ubangi, Roy Eldridge joined the orchestra. He had been barnstorming with McKinney's Cotton Pickers and wanted to stay put in one place for a while. Roy had already acquired the name of "Little Jazz" and it was an exciting pleasure to work with him and to be in a position to hear him night after night. Teddy Hill had let Bernard Flood go in order to make a place for Little Jazz.

Dicky Wells and I were still living with Grandma Jackson but Grandma died before the end of 1934 and her daughters decided to move to Jamaica, Long Island. I found a room with kitchenette on 142nd Street near Lenox Avenue, not far from the Savoy, and my girlfriend Beezie came to live with me. Beezie had a son and daughter born out of wedlock. They were living with their respective father's families.

Everything was fine until my wife, Madelyn, from whom I had been separated for almost two years, found out that I was living with another woman. One night, when she knew I was at work, she came to see what Beezie was like. She must have really got upset because Beezie was a very pretty girl who had blue eyes, wavy dark red hair, and looked like a white girl. Madelyn told her that she was the real Mrs. Coleman because I was not divorced from her. Of course Beezie knew that. Not long after Madelyn's visit, I received a notice to appear in the domestic court on a certain day. Madelyn had never bothered me until she heard that I was living with a girl who was calling herself Mrs. Coleman. I was ordered to pay $5 a week alimony to Madelyn. I had no out because I was the one who had left her. She didn't really need the money because she was working and making a nice salary, but she was getting revenge because I was with someone else.

One day I was contacted by Billy Taylor to do a recording date with Fats Waller. The Victor recording company had their studios in Camden, New Jersey, so the trip was made by train from New York to Philadelphia and Philly to Camden, on 7 November 1934. Fats had two bottles of whisky which we drank between New York and Philadelphia and he bought two more before we took the train to Camden. He did not ask us for a cent to help him buy it. Fats was really the most happy-go-lucky person I ever knew. When he took a drink, he would pass the bottle around and we all had a fine trip to Camden.

The musicians were Al Casey (guitar), Billy Taylor Sr. (bass), Harry Dial (drums), Gene Sedric (clarinet and tenor sax), and myself. The recording got off to a good start. Fats ad-libbed on all the singing numbers as though he had been playing and singing them all his life although the numbers were chosen by the recording company and not by himself, and he had not seen any of them before they were given to him in the studio. Before each number was recorded, Fats would run it down on the piano and then we would go over it a couple of times to set the solos and get the idea about what riff Sedric and I were going to play in certain spots. Then we'd rehearse once. With Fats, we fell into the groove from the start.

Of course drinks were passed around between each number that was recorded and everybody stayed groovy. We recorded six numbers, but when Fats was playing the organ a reed broke on one'of the pipes. It took an hour before someone found out which one it was that needed to be repaired. During that time we had a big meal, offered by the recording company, and more drinks.

Finally we finished the session and took the train for New York. In Philadelphia, Fats bought two more bottles of whisky, which we drank before arriving at Pennsylvania Station in New York. I didn't feel drunk but when I arrived home, where Beezie had prepared a nice dinner for me, I didn't have any appetite and accused her of cooking some mess that nobody could eat. I left for the Ubangi Club.

I took my horn out, started warming up, and took my place on the bandstand. We always played a few sets before the show came on, so Teddy Hill called three numbers. When he gave the starting beat on the first number, which was one that I had to read because I had not memorized it, I couldn't even see the part. The notes started running together and I could not play eight bars of the tune. I didn't feel drunk, but my mind just wouldn't function, my fingers wouldn't move, and I couldn't see the music.

Teddy asked me what was wrong and I told him about the recording session with Fats and how much I had drunk. We called Teddy "Fess," as so many other orchestra leaders were called. So after hearing my story, Fess told me to go out for half an hour and come back later. I went out, came back, but I was not feeling any better as far as being able to play was concerned. So Fess told me to take the night off. I had seen a trumpet played named Ovie Alston going into the bar of Big John's when I was out getting some air. I knew him very well. I went into Big John's, told Ovie my troubles, and asked him to finish the night for me. So Teddy's band was not without a third trumpet. After that I went to sleep. I had learned a lesson that I never forgot, which was never to try and drink as much as Thomas "Fats" Waller. The next session I did with him, on 5 January 1935, I drank, but not every time the bottle was passed to me.

After our run at the Ubangi Club, the band played a week at the Howard Theater in Washington and had an engagement in the Roseland Ballroom. We then came back to the Savoy. During that time I had got behind in my alimony payments and shortly after I had made the second record session with Fats, I received a notice to appear in the domestic court again and was ordered by the judge to pay $10 a week until the back payments were in order. But I decided that I was not going to pay any more alimony and sent a telegram to my father in Cincinnati, telling him to send me one saying "Come home at once." This I showed to Teddy Hill because I did not want to give two weeks' notice and have the word get out that I was leaving the band, which may have got back to my wife.

I figured that I would stay in Cincinnati long enough to get a divorce, which was much easier to do there than in New York. So Beezie and I packed our few belongings and left the Apple by bus one afternoon in June 1935. In Cincinnati we lived with my father who had two rooms on Cutter Street not far from my mother, so I saw her every day. My brother was living with my father also.

I was not in town very long before all the musicians knew I was there. The two best-known orchestras amongst the Negro musicians were Jack Jackson's, which had come on the scene after I had left Cincinnati, and Clarence Paige's, which was the most popular. Clarence contacted me a few days after I arrived and I started working with·him, doing one night stands in Kentucky, West Virginia, and Ohio.

Earl "Inky" Tremble, whom I had known for many years, played alto sax and was director of the band because Clarence preferred to sit and play tenor. Inky was a nice front man with the style of Cecil Scott, and he was always inventing names for people. He was the one that started calling Melvin Oliver "Sy." When Sy joined Zack White's band, Inky was also a member. He told me that whenever Sy came to rehearsals with a new arrangement, he had such a psychological way of explaining how a certain phrase should be played that Inky started calling him "Psychology," which he later changed to "Sy."

Also playing in the band there was a trumpeter by the name of Thomas "Sleepy" Grider, whom I had met years before in West Virginia. Sleepy was the only musician that I can think of, back in those times, who could probably drink as much as Thomas "Fats" Waller and not get drunk enough for anyone to know it. Sleepy played a nice strong first trumpet and could have become well known in that category if he had been more serious about music. I had met the drummer some years before in Colombus, Ohio. His name was Tommy Smith and he was also a nice trombone player. I don't remember the names of the rest of the musicians except the pianist, whose last name was Grant.

The only two musicians other than Paige still around Cincinnati with whom I had played at the beginning of my career were Edgar James and William "Smittie" Smith. Wes Helvey, my second bandleader, had quit the game and moved to Detroit. He was in the insurance business. I was considered a star trumpeter with Paige because I had lived in New York and made a name among the musicians.

Nobody knew the real reason for my coming back home except my parents. I went to see one of the best lawyers in town, who told me that I could get a divorce for $35 but I would have to stay in Cincy for three months before I could apply for it.

I gigged with Clarence Paige and we played the Lexington, Kentucky, fair in July. My father decided to move into a larger apartment because he liked Beezie very much and thought that she and I would stay in Cincy if we had more room.

He had found a nice three-room apartment with kitchen and bath on the second floor of a three-storey house on 9th Street, near the Shermann School. I really did not miss being away from New York very much.

In August I received a letter from Freddie Taylor, to whom I had given a beat-up trumpet when I left Paris, France. Freddie had stayed in France but was now back in New York looking for some musicians to take back to Europe. He had asked for me especially and had gotten my address in Cincinnati. He wrote saying that he had made good in Paris as an orchestra leader, that he had a six-month contract for a famous club and wanted me to join him. I had bigger eyes for going back to Europe than I did for getting a divorce and I figured that I could get a divorce there also.

I sent Freddie a telegram saying that I would accept his offer and later sent him a letter in which I explained why I was in Cincinnati and told him not to say anything about me to anyone, even the other musicians he had engaged. I knew that if the word got around that I was going to Europe, it would get to Madelyn and that would have been the end of that. New York is a big city with millions of people, but if you are known in a certain circle, the grapevine is the same as in any small town. Everybody in the circle knows why you were born, where, and when.

But sometimes there is a possibility of a secret being kept. There is a certain honor among thieves considering what the circumstances may be, so the word did not get around that I was going to France. Beezie and I arrived in New York on 10 September 1935 and went straight to Leonia, New Jersey, and stayed with her stepfather.

I had to come to the big city for my passport. Before going downtown, I was sitting in Freddie's car on 138th Street between Lenox and 5th Avenue, when I saw a musician that I knew coming down the street. I ducked down in the car like a criminal that was being hunted by the law because I could not afford to have my plans go wrong at that stage of the game.

The night before there was a boxing match between Joe Louis and Max Baer. I took the risk to come over to New York that night and celebrate Joe's victory in a bar on 7th Avenue and 143rd Street after hearing the fight on the radio. Harlem was jumping but I didn't run into anyone that I knew. It would not have mattered much that night anyway. If I had been seen by anyone who might have told Madelyn, I knew that I would be out of the USA before she could do anything to stop me.

The sailing time for the *Normandie* was 10 a.m., and I had to see my buddy Dicky Wells before I left. I had not even written him from Cincinnati to let him know that I was going to Europe because I just wasn't taking any chances. So we came from Leonia early the morning of the 25th and I woke Dicky up about eight o'clock and told him what was happening. He was really happy to see me. I told him why I had left New York a few months ago.

When I arrived in New York, Freddie Taylor told me the other two musicians that would come with us were to be George Johnson, the alto sax player, and my long-time friend Edgar Courance, who had acquired the name "Spider" since he had worked in a club of that name. Beezie and I decided that I would send for her after I had been in Paris one month.

The *Normandie* was the second greatest ocean liner that I had the privilege of sailing on. The first had been the *Rex*, and the *Conte Grande* was far from being a row boat. But the *Normandie* was a floating hotel. A few days after leaving New York, we were taken on a tour of the ship.

Two nights before we were to arrive in Le Havre, George Johnson and I arrived in the dining room dressed as we always were every night, but to our surprise, the men were all in tuxedos. It was gala night, which was something that we knew nothing about. The next night George and I decided that we would not be caught with our pants down again, so we came to dinner for the last night on board in our tuxedos; to our surprise, no one was wearing tuxedos except us. That had not happened on the *Conte Grande* nor the *Rex*, so it must have been only on the French lines that they had gala nights. George and myself were two embarrassed fellows the next day when we debarked on the shores of France.

It was a beautiful day, 30 September, when we arrived in Paris. Freddie had rooms for us at the Hôtel Eden, on rue Pigalle. Later, after we had arranged things in our room, Freddie took us to the Café Lisieux, my hangout in 1933, when I lived in the hotel above. We met the drummer who was engaged to play with the group: his name was William Diemer and I think that he came to Europe in 1927 with a group from Buffalo. The pianist, Jean Ferrier, and the bass player, Eugène d'Hellemes, were French. There was also a guitarist, Oscar Alemán, who was from Argentina.

After rehearsing for one week, we opened at the Villa d'Este on rue Arsène-Houssaye near the Arc de Triomphe and the great Avenue des Champs Elysées. At the Villa d'Este we played matinees, which were called "tea-dances," every day from five until seven in the afternoon. Then we played evenings, from 9.30 until two the next morning. We had no nights off. My first visit to Paris had been so short that the city was still new and exciting at this time, so the routine of playing two hours every afternoon and four hours and a half every night was like a happy game.

One of the first young French jazz musicians that I became acquainted with was tenor player Alix Combelle. Exactly how we met, I cannot recall, but I remember that Alix used to come to my room in the Hôtel Eden and ask me about many musicians in the States, especially those known around New York. Alix spoke English quite well. All that I knew to say in French was "bonjour" and "oui-oui." I had a photograph album with photos of different musicians I had worked with and showed them to Alix. He knew about quite a few of them. Besides Armstrong, he had heard about Henry "Red" Allen. He pointed to Red's photo and his comment was, "Hum, funny face." I also had a nice collection of records, mostly Armstrong, and a portable phonograph; Alix enjoyed listening to them.

About two weeks after we had been in the Villa d'Este, I was asked if I would accept a job singing in a club called L'Heure Bleue on rue Fromentin after I had finished my night at the Villa d'Este. I had never done much singing but I knew the words to many songs and my voice was not the worst that could be heard. So I thought it would be kicks to do a little singing and I accepted the proposition. --

The musicians playing at L'Heure Bleue were known as the Quintette du Hot Club de France. I had not met any of them before and had not heard them in action until the first night I went to sing with them. I had to sing four numbers. It was a very easy job, and the musicians knew every song I wanted to sing. The formation was original and consisted of three guitars, a violin, and bass. I had never heard any group like them for the simple reason that none had ever existed. The violin player was the best I had ever heard playing jazz after Robert "Juice" Wilson and one of the guitarists was the greatest I had ever heard, because guitars in those days mostly played rhythm style. But this fellow took solos and had ideas and a technique that was out of this world.

The violinist spoke English and told me his name was Stephane Grappelli. The solo guitarist was Django Reinhardt. The two other guitarists were Django's brother, Joseph, and Pierre Ferret. They both played rhythm guitar. Louis Vola played bass. Grappelli told me that Django and Joseph were "Manouches," a race of Gypsies. Django had had an accident to his left hand when he was younger and could only use three fingers. But he used those three fingers as if they were ten.

An American woman who had been in France quite a long time was singing at L'Heure Bleue. Her name was Ada Smith but she was known as "Bricktop" because she had red hair and was a light-skin Negro woman. She was quite popular as an entertainer. As a jazz singer she was not very hip. I think she was a little jealous of me and that was the reason that I was told after four days that I was not needed any more. But I had enjoyed my new experience for a few days and remained good friends with all the musicians.

The surprise of surprises was meeting Benny Carter at the Lisieux's bar a few nights after I had arrived in Paris. Since I had been in Cincinnati for a few months before coming to France, I had not picked up on the latest events, and I did not know that Benny was in Paris. He was working with Willie Lewis, who had an all-Negro band, the only one in Europe, working at Chez Florence, a high-society club on rue Blanche, not far from the bar and hotel Lisieux where many of the American Negro musicians would congregate when they had finished their night's work. Benny had come to Paris with a talented young pianist, Garnett Clark. I think that Garnett was from Washington, DC. I had seen him once in some club in New York with another young pianist named Ram Ramirez.

Between Boudon's and Lisieux's was a little Harlem in the early morning when all the night spots were closed. The American musicians and entertainers gathered in those bars and the stores with the "tabac" signs. A trumpeter, Jimmy Bell, whom I had known at Wilberforce University, was now in Paris. He was married to an American white girl, Grace Edwards, who was a singer. Other American entertainers in Paris at that time were Opal Cooper, who sang at the Melody Bar; Snow Fisher, a dancer and drummer; Alberta Hunter, a blues singer; Glover Compton, a singer who accompanied himself on piano; Al Brown, the ex-boxing champ; Gene Bullard, who had a gymnasium on rue Mansart; Marino and Norris, singers; Cle Saddler, an ex-alto sax player; Ray Stokes, pianist; and Harry Cooper, a trumpeter who had played with Duke Ellington at one time.

Another musician and song writer whom I had seen in New York and was now living in Paris was Spencer Williams. I had met him and a few members of his orchestra in Monte Carlo. I now made acquaintance with some other members at Lisieux's: Joe Hayman, alto sax, Johnny Mitchell (guitar), and Frank "Big Boy" Goudie (tenor sax and clarinet). Frank really was a big boy: he was seven feet tall and must have weighed about 300 pounds. He had also played cornet but eventually gave it up. I already knew bassman Louis Vola and Ted Fields, the drummer. Billy Burns (trombone) was so light-skinned that he could have passed for an Italian. He had come to Europe with Sam Wooding. Burns had played with Noble Sissle and pianist Freddie Johnson. He told me Paul Whiteman had offered him a job in his brass section but he had refused since he didn't want to be taken for a white man. The pianist, Garnett Clark, had worked a short while with Willie Lewis's orchestra but it did not go too well because Garnett was quite wild and flighty. So Willie had engaged Herman Chittison, whom I had met some years before in Boston accompanying the comedian Stepin Fetchit.

One week after I had started playing at the Villa d'Este, I was able to go from Pigalle to the Champs Elysées on the bus and I had the feeling that I was learning more and more about the great city of Paris. New York had been the first real big city I had ever seen. It was a thrilling, wide open town, but Paris had everything that New York had and then some. The cafés or bars stayed open 24 hours a day. Living was not expensive. The people were friendly and a jazz musician was considered as a human being. There were also interesting brothels: some were so unique that tourist agencies had night tour visits to them. One very famous and well known to tourists was called Aux Belles Poules, rue Blondel. The calling card mentioned that English was spoken. Another was known as the "House of All Nations" because it had rooms furnished in the style of every well-known country in the world. A certain American musician who had his mother in Paris for holidays took her on a tour of some brothels. Most of the girls in these places walked around nude and a few would have on a short dress or a little apron and that was all.

After being in the Villa d'Este for one month, I asked Freddie Taylor to advance me enough money, as he had promised he would do, for me to send for Beezie. I was surprised and very unhappy when Freddie told me that he was unable to do it. But I had a trick up my sleeve, because I knew that Freddie could not play more than three or four trumpet numbers that he featured in his Snake Hip act. So the following afternoon I came to work high as a kite and that night I was so juiced that I could hardly hold my horn. That really broke the ice. Freddie only directed the band and sang a few numbers when we played for dancers, and with me in no condition to play the arrangements the band did not sound at all the way it should have. When the night was finished, Freddie said that he would bring me the money the next day and he did. He must have had the feeling that I would repeat the performance and it was possible that I might have. Two days after the incident, a ticket was on the way to Beezie and everything was going well again at the Villa d'Este.

There was a young couple who came quite often to the Villa d'Este, and eventually became good friends of the band, especially of Spider and myself. They were Maurice and Vonette Cullaz. The father of Vonette was the Siamese consul. She was a very beautiful girl with long dark hair. They invited us to dinner in their home. Vonette cooked wonderful oriental curry dishes. I was surprised at the large collection of records they had. Maurice had the records I had made with Fats Waller. They had a little son of about two years old, named Pierre, who already loved music.

Another fellow who became quite friendly with the band was an Egyptian musician who played drums. His name was Pierre Fouad. He had recorded with Django and had quite a solid beat with brushes. He invited us to dinner at his home. He also had a fine collection of records. It was there that I heard for the first time Billie Holiday's recording of *Miss Brown to you* with Teddy Wilson at the box. Fouad also had a photo of Bunny Berigan, whom I had heard but never seen. Bunny's recording of *I Can't Get Started with you*, was the greatest he ever did to my estimation. It was the only record, other than some of Louis's, that I copied note-for-note and, at times, I still play it the way Bunny did, just for my own pleasure.

Garnett Clark was living in a house that rented furnished apartments and I decided to take one also. It was about 15 minutes' walking distance from Boudon's café, rue Fontaine. (Boudon and the tabac next door were the American musicians' headquarters.) Beezie arrived the third week in November. I went to the St.-Lazare station to meet her. She was pleased and surprised when she saw the apartment.

On 21 November I did a concert at the École Normale de Musique with George Johnson, Jerry Mengo (a drummer who was half Italian, half American), Django Reinhardt, and a French pianist named Leon Detemple. It was the first time I ever played jazz in concert. The French were way ahead of Americans in the line of giving jazz concerts, because I had never heard of any being done in the States. Armstrong had given concerts in Europe long before the Americans ever thought of using the term "concert" for a jazz session.

I don't remember what the style of the pianist was like, but Jerry Mengo played nice swinging drums and Django was great. I couldn't tell him he was great because I could not speak French and he did not understand English. I had never before played for such an enthusiastic crowd of people as those French jazz fans.

On 25 November 1935 I made my first recording in France, with Garnett Clark, George Johnson, Django Reinhardt, and the bass player June Cole. It was the first time I sang a song on a record. The title was *The Object of my Affection*. We had a fast tempo and I almost choked, trying to sing the last four measures of the middle part; but I made it and Garnett played great piano. We recorded two other titles, *Rosetta* and *Stardust*.

Not long after this I met Hugues Panassié and his friend Madeleine Gautier. Hugues was a jazz critic and President of the Hot Club de France. He knew more about many of the American jazz musicians than I did and it was because of him that I was well known in France for my recording with Fats Waller. He had reviewed and written critiques about the records before I knew that I was coming to France again.

I was invited to visit the club, which was on rue Mansart. There I met the secretary of the club, Charles Delaunay, and the treasurer, Pierre Nourry. In the reception room I saw the names of Coleman Hawkins, Louis Armstrong, and all the known jazz men of the time written on the wall. The club was a meeting place for jazz-lovers. French jazz musicians would come there and listen to records and get information about concerts and news about events in the jazz world.

We were playing at the Villa d'Este on New Year's Eve when William Diemer got high. Around 2 a.m. he felt that someone had insulted him, I don't remember who. The place was packed like sardines in a can but Diemer picked up his bass drum and carried it through the crowd, came back for the rest of his material, ordered a taxi, and went home. We finished around 5 a.m. without drums. The next afternoon he was back at the club and didn't remember why he had left the night before.

On 24 January 1936, I recorded for the first time under my own name. The date was supervised by Hugues Panassié. I had Herman Chittison on piano and Eugène d'Hellemes on bass. I believe it was the first jazz trio in the history of recording to be composed of trumpet, piano, and bass. We recorded *What's the Reason* and *Georgia on my Mind*. I had only heard Chittison play one time when I first met him in 1932 in Boston. "Chit" was fast as lightning. He must have heard Art Tatum many times and studied his style, because he was the next thing to Art as far as technique was concerned. He never wanted the bass to accompany him on his solos. He had a good left hand and I suppose he felt that the bass did not play the same pattern as he did with his left hand and it disturbed his ideas. D'Hellemes was a good solid bass player who preferred to play trombone. He was also a very agreeable fellow and we began to be good friends even though I did not speak French and he didn't speak English. The first date with Chit and Eugène was recorded for Ultraphone.

We recorded again on 31 January 1936 for His Master's Voice and we played *I'm in the Mood for Love* (two versions) and *After you've Gone* (two versions). *After you've Gone* is the best interpretation I ever made on records, I think. Those two records contributed more to my European success than those with Fats Waller had. I had more solo space and I was not under the influence of kickapoo joy-juice as I had when I recorded with Fats. The critics could not know that was the cause of me missing some phrases, so they wrote about my mistakes and at the same time praised my ideas.

I also recorded *Coquette* and the first number I ever composed, *Joe Louis Stomp*, with Edgar Courance (tenor sax), Jean Ferrier (piano), Oscar Alemán (guitar), Eugène d'Hellemes (bass), and William Diemer (drums)! This date is registered in the French discography as being done on 31 January also, but I don't remember having two recording dates the same day.

Sometime in February, Freddie Taylor didn't come to work one night. Spider, George Johnson, and I were paid the equivalent of $50 a week, a very good salary for a musician working in France, as living expenses were about half of what they were in the USA. The custom in France was, and still is, that musicians and other artists working in night clubs are paid every night. So when we finished the night, the cashier said that she would pay us and asked each one how much he earned for a night. The three of us who had come over from the States and were considered the stars of the band were getting 150 French francs a night (the equivalent of $50 for seven nights' work). The cashier seemed quite surprised that we were not getting more, but we were even more surprised when we learned that the pianist was getting 165 francs a night. The bass player, guitarist, and drummer were getting a little less than Spider, George, and myself. We never learned how much Freddie was getting but it must have been a big taste.

The next night when Freddie came to work the owner of the club told him that he was fired but the band could continue. Freddie started pleading with us not to accept the deal and stick with him, which meant that we should refuse to work without him. But we thought that Freddie had not been fair with us by giving the pianist, who was very good but not an outstanding artist, more than we were getting. So we turned a deaf ear to Freddie's plea and continued to work. It was a good thing we did, because if we had walked out, we would not have been able to work anywhere else in Paris and might have been expelled from the country, since the owner of the Villa d'Este had the permission for us to work in France, but only at his club. Spider, George, and I got a raise and I was considered the leader of the group although we decided together which numbers we would play.

Georges Carpentier, the ex-heavyweight boxing champion, had a bar next door to the Villa d'Este and he came in the club every night. He always danced at least once a night and spoke to each one of us as he danced by. Oscar Alemán, the guitarist, was a small-built fellow, very full of life. When Georges Carpentier spoke to Oscar, he always called him "little monkey." Georges spoke English as well as I did, whereas Oscar didn't know one word of English. But Georges had called him a little monkey so often that Oscar began to know the word and asked what it meant. Jean Ferrier told him: "un singe!" The next time that Georges came in, he was standing at the bar and Oscar was so impatient to reply that he yelled out while we were playing a number, "Hello Georges Carpentier, you big white monkey!" We were all surprised because we didn't know that Oscar had learned that sentence. Georges started to dance and when he was in front of the bandstand, he asked us what Oscar had said. Maybe he had not caught all the words because we were playing at the time when Oscar yelled to him, or maybe he couldn't believe his ears. Before any of us could say a word, Oscar said again loud, "Hello Georges Carpentier, you big white monkey!" Georges laughed about it, but he never referred to Oscar as a monkey again.

As we played every night and had been working under those conditions for months, I decided to take a night off. But I was to be sorry after. Coleman Hawkins had come to Paris from Holland and he came to the Villa d'Este that evening and sat in with the band.

The people never applauded when we played except when Freddie and Oscar did attraction numbers. Freddie danced his snake-hip routine and played a number on the trumpet. Oscar, who could not read a note as big as the piano, could play classical numbers on the guitar and also did some numbers on a ukulele. Edgar Courance told me that when Hawk first started playing, no-one paid any attention to him. When he played a second number, some people at the bar turned away from their drinks and started to give an ear to what was happening. And by the time they finished a third number, the whole place was digging Hawk. Nobody was ever applauded in the Villa d'Este the way that Coleman Hawkins was. I always regretted taking that night off, but after that, the public paid more attention to what we had to offer, thanks to Hawk.

There was a second orchestra at the club which played tangos. We each played half-hour sets and therefore the job was not too hard. We finished at 2 a.m. and it was seldom that I went straight home. Some mornings it would be between nine and eleven o'clock before I got to bed but I was always on time for the job at 5 p.m. matinée time and I always felt in good condition.

There was a club on rue Fontaine not far from the Boudon's called La Cabane Cubaine (Cuban Cabin), where a fairly nice orchestra, mostly Cuban, was playing. They knew many jazz standards and I went there quite often and jammed. The place didn't close before 6 a.m.

Willie Lewis started broadcasting to England from a station on the Champs Elysées, the Poste Parisien, and asked me to join him for the broadcasts. It was good publicity for me because I started getting letters from jazz fans in England; some told me that they had the recordings I had made with Fats and they were happy to hear me broadcasting to England. Benny Carter had left Willie Lewis for a position as arranger for the British Broadcasting Corporation in England before Willie had started his broadcasts.

On 15 May 1936, I recorded with Willie Lewis. As George Johnson was also engaged for this date, it augmented Willie's orchestra to an eleven-piece band plus two singers: Adelaide Hall, who had been famous in many of the New York Cotton Club revues, and Alice Man, whom I had never heard of before.

Coleman Hawkins had stayed in Paris for a short time only and was living in Holland. But he came back to Paris at times and Willie engaged him for a broadcast on 30 May. I had seen Hawk when I was young in Cincinnati, had heard him at the Roseland (from the electrician's booth), and heard him at the Savoy. I hung out in Big John's, Pete's, and some other bars where Hawk had his private bottle. He knew about me and we had conversations sometimes. But I was going to play on the same program with the Master and that was a great honor for me.

Willie Lewis asked me to join his orchestra in June 1936, at the end of the Villa d'Este contract. He offered me 170 francs a day; I could have got more from him, had I realized the value of money at that time and cashed in on the power of my popularity. I was known as the best American jazz trumpeter in Europe at that time.

I enjoyed working at Chez Florence in Willie's orchestra. We started work at 11 p.m. and played until 1 a.m. and then had an hour and a half off. A French orchestra played during our off time and when we came back, we worked until five or six o'clock in the morning, depending on how many people there were. The good thing about working Chez Florence was that there was no afternoon tea dancing.

On 3 July I had another concert at the École Normale de Musique. The other participants were Alberta Hunter, the blues singer; Garland Wilson, a pianist–singer; and Chittison with the orchestra of Christian Wagner. The place was packed to standing room only. Alberta Hunter had been in Europe for quite some time. Garland Wilson was not a real jazz pianist but played an exciting entertainer's type of piano. I had seen Garland on the stage of the Apollo in Harlem a few times but never met him until this concert. Christian Wagner played alto sax and clarinet. He was considered one of the best French jazz clarinettists.

On 15 July, the Willie Lewis orchestra, with all the orchestra's wives, left Paris for Knokke, a beautiful summer resort in Belgium. This was my first time to go to Belgium: it was always thrilling for me to visit a new country. Willie was engaged for six weeks to work in the Casino Kursaal. The casino was very large and we played in a hall that seated about 1200 people. It was also the hall where concerts were presented by a big symphony orchestra composed of classical music professors of Belgium. Well-known conductors and opera stars were engaged to appear there.

There was a symphony orchestra that played every night and we were on a bandstand next to the stage they occupied. Across from us was a Swiss orchestra of nine musicians whose name was The Lanigiro Syncopating Melody Kings. Later, when I became better acquainted with the musicians, I asked one of them what the word Lanigiro meant. He told me that it was "original" spelled backward. We played for dancing, which did not start until after the classical concerts was finished, around 10 p.m.

One of the trumpet players in the symphony orchestra became interested in the way I played. He would listen to me almost every night. He told me that, for certain numbers in the classics, he changed mouthpieces and was quite surprised that I didn't change mine, but played high notes and low ones on the same mouthpiece.

The band had ordered a white uniform before we left Paris. The first night we wore them it seemed as though those uniforms lifted our spirit sky-high because we played better than we had been, at least that was my feeling. Willie Lewis did most of the singing in the band but I featured in a number called *The Music Goes Round and Round*.

We stayed in a big hotel named the Trianon right on the beach when we arrived in Knokke but later found a *pension* (room and board) named the Derby It was five minutes walk to the casino and the beaches, and cheaper than the hotel.

Most everyone in the orchestra and their wives rented bicycles, and we would ride to Zeebrugge, Bruges, a jewel of a town, and Sluis, Holland. We got plenty of exercise riding to different places and going to the beach.

I was never a heavy beer drinker but I drank less alcohol during our stay in

Knokke. There was a cafe called Berry's under the terrace of the casino that served good German beer called Dortmund. After every set most of us made a bee-line for this cafe. I was actually getting a kick out of beer for the first time of my life. Monsieur Berry looked as though he was Hitler's twin brother; the same little mustache, and he combed his hair in the same manner as Hitler. He was a real nice person and we enjoyed his company.

Louis Vola had played bass with Willie in Chez Florence but Willie had engaged a Cuban bass player named José Riestra for the Knokke engagement. I could understand a little French by now, but Riestra didn't speak English and he spoke French with a strong Cuban accent, which made it very difficult for me to understand him. He was a fine solid bass and wonderful person.

We played two weeks in the big hall, then went downstairs in a smaller club called the Pingouin. Adelaide Hall was an attraction. The band sang some spiritual numbers: Willie always sang the lead. He had a wonderful baritone voice and sang with great power. The Pingouin was more suited for a jazz orchestra than the big hall, but we had success in both places.

Benny Carter had a vacation from his job at the BBC, so he and his wife Inez came to Knokke. Benny was on holiday and never sat in with the band although he came to the club often. Another famous opera singer who had sung in the casino was a Negro woman, Miss Catherine Yarbo. I saw Catherine when she did *Aida* in Knokke and she was a great artist. She had her vacation after playing the casino and stayed in Knokke for two weeks. She did not know how to ride a bicycle so she and another woman friend of hers rented a four-wheeled pedal contraption and rode to Sluis and Zeebrugge with us.

We finished at the Pingouin on 31 August. Willie had a two-week engagement in The Hague, Holland, at a dance hall called the Tabarin. Willie and Chittison had continued to live in the Trianon hotel in Knokke. The day we left for Holland, Willie hired a bus. We were all to meet in front of the Trianon. Everybody was there except Chittison. Willie went back into the hotel to see what happened to Chit and found that the hotel owner would not let Chit leave because he had not paid his rent during the six weeks he had been there. I don't know how this could have happened unless Chittison had arranged to pay at the end of the season, and when the time came to pay it, he pretended he didn't have the money. Chit was not a gambling man, although we would all shoot some craps now and then. Willie paid him every week, the same as he did the rest of us, but anyway he paid the bill for Chittison. I know that Chit never paid one franc back to Willie. I was to find out some other little mean things about Chittison's character later.

We played at the Tabarin from 1 September until the 15th. Holland was very nice and I had never seen so many bicycles before. Couples rode together holding hands, and parents had their children in little seats attached over the rear wheel. There were delivery bicycles, flower peddlers on bicycles, and people even moved their furniture from one place to another on bicycles. At lunch time and evenings when jobs were finished, the traffic was thick as flies in an open garbage can on a hot summer day!

EIGHT

INDIA AND EGYPT

Beezie and I came back to Paris after a week's vacation in Brussels and lived in the same building on rue de la Tour d'Auvergne. I had a lot of trouble with taxi drivers when I lived on this street. I couldn't speak much French and like many of the lazy American musicians in Paris at that time, I didn't try too hard to learn the language. Sometimes when I wanted to take a taxi home, I would have to ask three or four drivers before I could find one who understood me. I would say the name of the street to him the same as I had said it to the others and by luck he would understand.

Willie started working Chez Florence again. Not long after we had opened, a violin player named Leon Abbey contacted me to see if I would like to go to India with him. I had heard about him in New York as the leader of an orchestra that came to Europe a few months before I arrived in the Big Apple. He had taken Fletcher Allen, an alto sax player who had played with Lloyd Scott before I joined the band. The Scott brothers used to talk about him often. Leon Abbey and Fletcher were in India when I came to France in 1935.

This offer to go to India really excited me. The conditions were $50 a week, room, board, and transportation from Paris to Bombay and back. I would have to pay Beezie's transportation and board but that was a small matter. The excitement of going to India was all that mattered to me.

I gave my notice to Willie and naturally he was upset because there was no one in Europe who could replace me. He asked if I wanted more money to stay with him. I told him that it was not a matter of money, but that I wanted to see as much of the world as possible, whenever I had the opportunity to do so. I suggested as my replacement either Frankie Newton or Jacques Butler, with whom I had gigged and knew quite well. The musicians that hung out at the Rhythm Club called Jack "Tonics" because he always talked about the tonics in musical harmony.

Before my departure, we had a recording session with Willie Lewis's band on 15 October 1936.

We left Paris on 21 October for Venice, Italy, where we took a boat for India. Leon Abbey had gone to Chicago and came back with a tenor player named Antonio Cosey. The pianist was Charlie Lewis, who had come to Europe with Leon Abbey. The other musicians were Arthur "Horse" Lanier, alto sax and singer; Ollie Tines, drummer; and Emile Joseph Christian, a white trombone player who had switched to bass—he had played with the Original Dixieland Jazz Band and had lived in England and France a few years.

We passed through Switzerland, which was a beautiful country, and arrived in Venice on 22 October. We went from the railroad station to the pier by taxi-gondolas. It was fascinating to see the way the gondolier guided the gondola through the traffic on the canals. From the pier there was a launch to take us to the ship, the *Victoria*. It was a very nice ship but there was one bringdown. The men had to be in a cabin together and the women in another. The only two couples were Leon Abbey and his Italian wife and Beezie and me. On the boat we met an English singer, Aimée Denton, who was going to India to sing in the Taj Mahal Hotel, Bombay, where we would be working.

The weather was beautiful in Venice and we left the port in the afternoon. The following day we rented deck chairs and I began to get better acquainted with the musicians. This was Leon's second engagement at the Taj. Charlie Lewis was known as "Dizzy". We started calling Cosey "Bags" because he had a ruptured testicle which really showed, but it didn't seem to bother him physically. He in turn called everybody "funny looking," even Beezie and Leon's wife (whose nickname was Boop), and they were both beautiful.

We arrived at night in Port Said, Egypt, and went ashore for a few hours. It was early evening and the ship would not sail until night through the Suez Canal, which took at least twelve hours to traverse. Egypt was the starting point going to the Far East. There were so many sights that we saw for the first time, which convinced us that this part of the world was the land of the pharaohs. To our way of thinking, the men were wearing grandfather nightgowns. The women wore long black robes and covered their faces so that only one eye showed. This was another world.

The shops were beautifully oriental with many tempting things to buy, but I was not looking for souvenirs at that moment. There were sidewalk cafés, the same as in France, and that was the only link between Eastern and Western ways.

One guy really knocked us out. He was about six feet tall, real dark and had on what we called a nightgown that was five inches above his ankles, a wide brim straw hat, and a pair of black shoes that looked long enough to be skis. He really reminded us of an Apollo Theater comedian and we all almost had a chronic spasm from laughing so much at this sight. We decided that we had seen the greatest of all comedy acts and went back to the ship happy as a cow chewing its cud.

We awoke the next morning going through the canal. It was the first time I ever saw a desert, except in films. There were some small villages and cities along the length of the canal. The largest city before reaching Suez, the Eastern gateway of the canal, was Ismailia. There were interesting monuments to see on both sides of the canal and in some places the sands were so hot that heat waves could be seen rising. I saw, for the first time, camel caravans and Egyptians riding on the rear of their little donkeys while their veiled women were walking behind. It was very exciting.

After we left Port Tewfik I noticed quite a number of Arabic people on the lower deck with what must have been the whole of their worldly belongings. Leon, who had made a trip like this before, told me that they were deck passengers. This deck was protected with a canvas cover against the sun. People slept on the floor and ate in the third-class dining room.

We met an American white couple who were dancers, who were also engaged at the Taj Mahal. They were known as Tracey and Hay. We took photographs posing with camels that didn't have an easy life like the ones in the zoo.

The whole trip was marvelous and we arrived at Bombay on 2 November, ten sailing days from Venice. We were met by the manager of the Taj Mahal Hotel, Mr. Faletti, an Italian who was a naturalized British citizen, and by two Negro musicians who were living in India and were going to play with the Abbey band. One was Crickett Smith, a trumpeter, and the other was Rudy Jackson, an alto sax player. Crickett and Rudy had come to Europe in the early 1920s.

We had seen many exciting things in the port towns we visited but Bombay gassed them all. The taxis were open-top five-passenger cars, mostly American-made, and I could see in front, on the sides, and from the back without difficulties. There were so many sights that I almost had a sore neck turning it so much from the time we left the port until we reached the Taj Mahal Hotel. One sees newsreels and movies about India which are very interesting, but when you see these things with your own eyes, it's fantastic.

The Taj Mahal was a very large and beautiful place on a street overlooking the bay. The front faces the city and I learned later that the architect who drew the plans committed suicide after the hotel was completed because the back was built facing the bay and it should have been the other way around. On the left side of the Taj Mahal, facing the bay, was a monument called the Gateway to India.

I had a very large room assigned to me in the hotel until other lodgings could be arranged. The bed was very large also and had mosquito curtains. Mr. Faletti presented us to the assistant manager, an Indian named D.R. Banerjee who was to look after us personally.

I also met a pianist and accordionist named Teddy Weatherford. Teddy was an American Negro who had traveled over most of the Far East and had a big name amongst the early jazz musicians before I came on the scene. Teddy had been in India quite a few years and was very popular with the English dignitaries and others in Bombay high society.

The next day we started rehearsing the show, which had six acts, and included a troupe of English girls and a tap-dancer named Rosalind Wade. A French trombonist, who had been in Bombay for some time, was added to the orchestra, which came to ten musicians. We opened a couple of days later. Arthur Lanier sang ballads and we formed a quartet with Lanier, Leon Abbey, Ollie Tines, and myself to sing variety numbers. The job was not hard because we only worked four nights and two matinees a week.

The management found two apartments for us. Leon and his wife, Cosey, Lanier, Beezie, and I stayed in a six-room apartment called Moby Mansion.

Charlie Lewis and Ollie Tines were in an apartment not far from where we lived with their Anglo-Indian girlfriends whom they had met during their first stay in Bombay. Crickett Smith and Rudy Jackson lived with their Anglo-Indian women. We also had a servant to clean our apartment and run errands.

Some of the acts that we played in the Taj did not have their music arranged to suit the formation of the orchestra and had no parts for trumpets. Cosey wrote my parts in the key they were supposed to be played. Crickett and Rudy had played in Sam Wooding's orchestra and they both were fine musicians. Crickett had always been a first-chair man. I played second part in the brass section and took the jazz solos. Cosey took the hot choruses on tenor and Leon Abbey had some on violin. The trombone player, Leonardi, was a straight man and played only what was written, but he also played violin, which was nice for some of the acts we accompanied.

Although we were in an apartment where there was a kitchen, the only time we used it was when we wanted some real Southern fried chicken or other home style food. Otherwise we ate at the Taj, but the food we were served was never very well seasoned and was not the same as that which was served in the main dining rooms. The Indian employees ate in the same dining room as we did, but they had special food cooked with curry.

The head waiter was named Peter and, like most of the waiters, he was from Goa, a part of India that was governed by Portugal. We told Peter that we liked curried food and, from then on, we were served some quite often.

One thing I had a hard time getting used to was lizards. They were everywhere, even in the best hotels and houses. Our beds had screens to protect us from mosquitoes, but there was no way to keep lizards out of the house. They were about two and a half inches long with tails almost twice as long as the body and were known as wall lizards. Whenever we used the stove in the kitchen we had to light it and leave the oven door open so that the lizards would get out before it got too hot. We did not want any fried lizards in our baked macaroni!

I drank less alcohol in India than I was drinking in Europe. I suppose the desire was lessened by the climate. We had plenty of canned beer that was furnished by the hotel. For a woman, Aimée Denton, the singer, could down a few. Charlie "Dizzy" Lewis liked his juice although he did not drink too much while we were in Bombay.

But one day Dizzy got on a bender and got friendly with an Indian who had a street act for tourists, a battle between a snake and a mongoose. Dizzy bought a python and took it home. No one was there when he arrived and the juice started getting Dizzy down, so he got on a bed with the python and went to sleep. When his girl friend Ivy came home, the sight that she saw sent her out of the house screaming like mad. Dizzy was lying on his back with his mouth wide open. The python was coiled around his body and its head was five inches from his mouth. The alcohol scent from his breath must have paralyzed the python to the point where it could not squeeze the life out of him. Ivy went to get her brother and with the help of some friends they got the python into a cloth bag and gave it to the zoo.

It is not possible to write about all the sights I saw and the things I did beside playing music in India because this is a book about my life with a horn, with a limited account of the places I've been and the musicians I've known and worked with. I wouldn't have missed the opportunity of going to India even if Willie Lewis had offered me five times more money than the salary I had when I left him. I had a horn and would travel, and faraway places were the ones I wanted to see the most.

The Taj Mahal was jumping on Christmas Eve and especially on New Year's Eve. The room was filled with English dignitaries, diplomats, and maharajahs. Some brought their families. I saw two maharajahs that I had seen in Paris at Chez Florence. One was the Maharajah of Cochin, the other was the Maharajah of Kapurthala, who took his European gals with him whenever he went. There were six or eight of them. There were some young princes who stood near the bandstand like the jazz-lovers did at the Savoy. Later in the night, when it came time to push the old year out and welcome in the new one, they started throwing cotton balls at us and we threw them back at them. Everybody let their hair down and started having a ball.

Faletti had allowed us to invite our wives and girlfriends to a bar that was in back of the main dining room. There were Beezie, Boop, Ivy, the girlfriend of Charlie Lewis, and Ined, the sister of Ivy (who was Ollie Tines's girlfriend) and their brother, who was about 17. We finally had a break and went to the bar. The young brother of Charlie Lewis's girlfriend Ivy came to me and pointed out a fellow sitting at the bar, saying that he had insulted Beezie. Then the girls said that they were sitting at the bar when this guy came in and asked the barman, "Who are these bitches? Get them out of here, they stink." Furious, I went to the bar and asked this jerk what was the idea of insulting my wife and the girls that were with her. He started to puff up and asked me who the hell I was. I swung a right to his chin that knocked him off his stool. Cosey was standing near and the blow also caught him on the jaw but it didn't hurt him. This fellow went and got Faletti and told him that I had hit him and he could get rid of me. Faletti told him, "Yes, and now you should come with me because you've had enough to drink." This guy turned out to be the American vice consul, known to raise hell when he started juicing; nobody liked him. Faletti and everyone else who knew about him were glad that I had put him in his place. Later in the season, there was a big diplomatic ball at the hotel and the vice consul came. He stayed sober the whole night but gave me looks as if to say, "That trumpeter must be out of his mind."

Our music was jazz even though quite commercial at times, because we played for a public that was mostly European—a very wealthy and select clientele. I met only two Anglo-Indians that were interested in jazz. I remember one was named Rudy, who played alto sax, but I never heard him play. He and his buddy used to come to the hotel often in the afternoon after we had lunched and ask us questions about jazz music and musicians they had heard about.

Sometimes when I would be taking my afternoon siesta I would hear some Indian music on someone's gramophone and it was great music. They had their type of jazz, which included fine soloists on instruments the names of which I did not know, and favorite singers. I suppose that if I had been an arranger I would have taken more interest in Indian music. But I did listen to those sounds and got my kicks. I'm sorry that I didn't buy any instrumental or vocal records, but I did spend a small fortune on photographic film.

One night we played a big party given for Ali Khan, the son of the Aga Khan. This party was on a boat and was catered by the Taj Mahal Hotel. I think that it was the birthday of Ali. The diplomats, maharajahs, maharanis and Bombay's high society were there. The boat sailed out into the bay and after dinner Ali wanted to undress and dive in the bay from the highest deck to swim around the boat. It was said that that was his delight whenever he went out on a boating party. But he was restrained that night because it was rumored that there were sharks in the bay and they could have been attracted by the lights of the boat.

During one of the intermissions I was sitting on an upholstered bench near the bandstand. A beautiful blond woman was sitting on the same bench and started talking to me. What the conversation was, I don't remember, but this lady was very nice. Later I excused myself and got on the bandstand. Someone told me afterwards that she was the English wife of Ali Khan, who would become the mother of Prince Karim, the present Aga Khan. At that time, they had not been married very long.

The six months in Bombay passed very fast and in April 1937 we left India on the *Conte Rosso*, an Italian boat headed for Venice, where we landed on 8 May. The next day we were in Paris. The trip was great coming back, the same as it had been going. Beezie and I had a cabin to ourselves on the boat this time. Teddy Weatherford had never been in Europe and had decided that he was coming back with us. Charlie Lewis brought his girl Ivy back with him.

In a very short time Leon Abbey landed a job in a night club at Place Pigalle, but I didn't care much for the place and the band seemed to have lost something of its style and gaiety, so I gave my notice to Leon and rejoined Willie Lewis.

Willie had succeeded in getting Jacques Butler in my place when I left for India but he was pleased to have me back in the band again. Willie had added George Johnson to the sax section. Wilson Myers was on bass. With me rejoining the orchestra, we were eleven musicians and the only all-Negro American orchestra in Europe.

Willie's orchestra was working at the Ambassadeurs, across the street from the American Embassy at Place de la Concorde. Shortly after I had rejoined Willie, Teddy Hill and his band came to Paris with a Cotton Club revue and played quite a few weeks at the Moulin Rouge. The revue was staged by Clarence Robinson, who was very well known in Harlem for staging shows at the Cotton Club, the Apollo Theater and other clubs.

Teddy had changed a few musicians since I left the band in 1935. Bob Carroll, a Redman alumnus, was on tenor sax, having replaced Chu Berry. Wilbur De Paris had been added on trombone. There was also an 18-year-old trumpeter named John Birks Gillespie, whom the other fellows in the band called "Dizzy." He had replaced Frankie Newton, who had come in the band after I left. I had never heard Dizzy play but I saw the show a couple of times. There were not many solos because the band accompanied the actors and only played an overture number before the first and second parts of the show.

Hugues Panassié had asked Dicky Wells to form a group for a recording session for 7 July 1936. The group included Bill Dillard, Shad Collins, and myself (trumpets), Dicky Wells (trombone), Django Reinhardt (guitar), Richard Fullbright (bass), and Bill Beason (drums). We recorded *Bugle Call Rag, Between the Devil and the Deep Blue Sea*, and *I Got Rhythm*, which later became collector's items.

The session was supervised by Hugues Panassié. It was another first in jazz: it was the first group of that type to have recorded without piano accompaniment and also the first time that three trumpets and a trombone had been recorded in that manner. Dicky Wells made the arrangements. Dicky and I did three other numbers without the other two trumpets: *Sweet Sue, Hangin' Around Boudon*, and *Japanese Sandman*, of which *Hangin' Around Boudon* became the most popular. With Django playing the kind of rhythm guitar only he could play, we did not miss the piano. Bill Dillard had a soft, mellow tone and could take nice choruses, although he was considered a first-chair man, and one of the finest around New York. Shad Collins was the hard-blowing type who was influenced very much by Roy Eldridge's style. Perhaps the records might even have been better if Dizzy had been included because the sound of four trumpets playing and phrasing the way we did those numbers had not been recorded in those days. But it seems that most of the musicians had something against Dizzy because he was so young and maybe a little wild to their way of thinking. I never heard Dizzy play then and have a solo. Panassié didn't care for him and thought that he hadn't had enough experience compared with the others.

After a few weeks at the Moulin Rouge, the Cotton Club show moved to the Ambassadeurs, next door to where we were playing. Sometimes I would see Dicky Wells coming from around the back of the building and he told me that he had been back there, listening to our band. The Cotton Club show then left for England and Willie Lewis's band left for another season in Knokke but George Johnson did not go with the orchestra. Maybe he was only engaged for the Ambassadeurs job.

We had to play matinees and stayed up most every night but we still found time to ride bicycle, go swimming, etc. One day I was out riding the bicycle with some of the gang and I was going along a very speedy pace. There are special sidewalks along many of the roads in Belgium and Holland for bicycles but in some places these special roads come to an end and you are riding on regular road again. That was the case that day but after a little while I saw that the bicycle road started again. I was going so fast that I missed the entrance. When I realized that I was going to fall the first thing I thought about was to protect my lips. I fell with both hands covering my face, but my upper lip received a small cut on the side near the middle where I placed my mouthpiece. My face was also scratched near my right eye and I could not work for two days.

Ray Ventura was the leader of the biggest French jazz orchestra in France and he was engaged to play upstairs in the large hall of the Casino Kursaal. Ray had an orchestra of about 16 or 17 musicians and an American girl singer, Betty Allen.

Ventura had a real show band and he also had the best musicians in Europe. One outstanding musician was a French trumpeter named Philippe Brun. Philippe had spent a few years in England and was influenced by Armstrong, but with a little of his personal feeling about how jazz trumpet should be played. He was way out in front of many of the other European trumpeters.

After six weeks in Knokke we went to the Ostend Casino for two weeks. Beezie's daughter Joan, who was four years old, was living with her father in New York. Beezie received a letter saying that someone in the family had an incurable illness and they were going to send Joan to us. She was due to arrive a week before we finished at Ostend, so Beezie went back to Paris a week before me. When the band came back we went into Chez Florence for a short stay because Willie was engaged to play at a pavilion for the great Paris Fair of 1937.

On 4 October 1937, I recorded with Alix Combelle, the best French tenor sax player. The pianist was a New Yorker named David Martin, whose family had a music school on 136th Street. Dave accompanied quite a few classical musicians and singers, and was also a jazz pianist. He was in Europe at this time accompanying Eddie South, who was known as the "Dark Angel" of the violin. The session was recorded under the name of Combelle. The other players were Wilson Myers (bass), Roger Chaput (guitar), and Jerry Mengo (drums). We recorded four numbers: *Exactly Like you, Alexander's Ragtime Band, Hangover Blues*, and *Sometimes I'm Happy*. *Hangover Blues* was my composition. That title had no link with my state of feeling. *Sometimes I'm Happy* was never issued. I never found out why.

On 18 October Willie Lewis and orchestra recorded six numbers with the full band. On 12 November I recorded under my own name with Stephane Grappelli, Joseph Reinhardt (guitar), Wilson Myers (bass), and Ted Fields (drums). Whenever Hugues Panassié asked me to record, I seldom asked who the other musicians would be. When I arrived at the studio I recognized all the musicians but noticed that there was no pianist. I asked who was going to play piano and Hugues answered, "Stephane." I didn't know that he played piano but he was as good an accompanist as Dave Martin.

On 19 November I recorded *Bill Coleman Blues*, accompanied only by Django on guitar. This was another first for Hugues Panassié because it was his idea to record just the two of us as a duo. The other five numbers on that date had Christian Wagner (clarinet and alto sax), Big Boy Goudie (tenor sax and clarinet), Emil Stern (piano), Lucien Simoens (bass), and Jerry Mengo (drums).

After the engagement at the Paris Fair, Willie Lewis and orchestra were engaged to go to Alexandria, Egypt. This was as thrilling as the trip to India. I had seen Egypt for a few hours going and coming from India and now it was possible to spend some weeks there. I was now a daddy because Joan was with Beezie and me. The musicians who were married took their wives with them.

We left Paris for Marseille on the morning of 13 December 1937. As our ship the *Champollion*, did not sail until the evening, it was decided that we would spend a few hours seeing Marseille. The wives went sightseeing together and the men did the same. It is not possible to say how many cafés or bars we stopped in, but when we returned to the ship, I was really sailing before we left port. A half hour away from Marseille the sea became very rough. The ship was doing everything except flying and, with all the juice in my stomach, the pitching and lurching became too much for me and I became seasick for the first and only time in my life.

We arrived in Alexandria on 17 December and had rooms reserved in the Hotel Syracuse. Again I was thrilled by the spectacle in the streets; the way the natives dressed, the traffic, hundreds of little donkeys and carts everywhere.

The place where we were to work was called the Monseigneur. The owner was a Greek named Pastraudis. He also owned a big restaurant and a bakery that supplied bread to the English military camp in Alexandria. We played in a hall facing the sea in the afternoon from five to seven, and at night we played in a smaller hall in the back of the building. The clientele was mostly European and aristocratic Egyptians. It was the first time that an all-Negro orchestra had played in Alexandria and we made a big hit with the public.

Farouk, the King of Egypt, was married on 20 January 1938. Three days were declared holidays with celebrations everywhere. Only the young unmarried girls did not cover their faces, wore bright colored dresses, and dyed their hair with henna. Some painted their toenails with it as many never wore shoes. Everybody was in a happy groove for those three days.

A couple of weeks after we were there, Jacques Butler, Wilson Myers, and myself decided to form a singing trio. The first tune we learned was *Once in a While*, which we rehearsed until we had it perfected. As the band always did an entertaining spot of singing popular songs and spirituals once in the afternoon and once at night, we asked Willie to let us do a number. No one in the band knew that we had been rehearsing as a trio except Chit and when we asked Willie if we could do a number, he consented reluctantly. We surprised him and the rest of the fellows and received the most applause of the evening. That encouraged us to rehearse a few more numbers and we were able to do extra ones when the public asked for them. To us we sounded as good as the Mills Brothers! Jacques had a tenor voice, Myers was an alto, and my voice was a light baritone.

We always knew that Willie Lewis got quite a lot of money for the band: that was normal because he did the business. But somehow we learned that he was getting much more than we thought, yet he had not offered us any more than we made in Europe. So one night we had a meeting with Willie and told him that he was taking advantage of us and we wanted a raise. Willie started to cry and deny the fact, but he had forgotten that he had told me, and maybe someone else, that he could cry real tears anytime he wanted to. We told him that if he didn't give us a raise then and there, we would not come to work the next day. He finally gave in.

When we finished at the Monseigneur we had a few days' wait before the ship back to France sailed from Alexandria, so Burns, his wife Louise, Beezie, and I visited Cairo. We made a visit to the Sphinx and the Pyramids of Giza. We visited the most famous mosques of Cairo and rode camels around the Pyramids. We left Egypt and arrived back in Marseille on 30 March 1938. We passed through Paris on our way to The Hague, where Willie had a one-month contract in the Tabarin Club.

Bobby Martin, the ex-Willie Lewis trumpet man, had gone to the States and come back to Europe with an orchestra composed of Glyn Paque and Ernest Purce (alto saxes), Johnny Russell (tenor sax), Ram Ramirez (piano), Kaiser Marshall (drums), and Ernest "Bass" Hill (bass). Jacques Butler, Billy Burns, Johnny Mitchell, and I joined Bobby's band for a recording session in Hilversum. We recorded two numbers, *Crazy Rhythm* and *Make Believe Ballroom*. On 4 May, I recorded again in Hilversum with the Willie Lewis band. We played six numbers.

When we came back to Paris at the end of May, Willie didn't have a job for us until an engagement in Knokke the middle of July. Oscar Alemán was the leader of an orchestra in a dancing hall on rue Fontaine. Spider Courance had left the Villa d'Este, where he had continued to work after I left there, to join Willie Lewis. Oscar asked me if I would care to work with him until it was time for me to go to Belgium. Although I didn't care for the type of music Oscar was playing, as it was mostly Latin-American, I accepted the job because it was something to do to keep my chops up.

Valaida Snow, the third woman that I had heard play trumpet, was in Paris working as an attraction in some club, and the manager of the place I was working with Oscar also hired her to come in and do a 20-minute attraction. When I first heard Valaida, she was wailing, but now it seemed as though she had lost something, although she still blew strong.

On 13 June I recorded with Eddie Brunner, who was a Swiss tenor sax and clarinet player and a damn good swing man. Alix Combelle and Noël Chiboust were the two other tenors. Eddie Brunner blew clarinet on most of the numbers we recorded. Chiboust had played trumpet before switching to tenor sax and he and Combelle were the best French tenor men. The rest of the group were Herman Chittison (piano), Oscar Alemán (guitar), Roger Grasset (bass), and Tommy Benford (drums). I knew Tommy from New York: he was a swinging drummer.

Oscar's orchestra became sadder and sadder to me every day and when Willie's gang finally started in Belgium again it was a couple of weeks before I could get really in the groove. Oscar's band didn't swing and after playing two months with him, I couldn't swing for a long time regardless of how hard I tried. But I kept fighting and finally got myself back in shape.

We finished the season with two weeks at the Casino at Ostend in September, as we had done the year before, and Willie announced that he was disbanding. But when we arrived in Paris, he told me that he would contact me in a few days. Ted Fields decided to go to the States. A few days later, Willie told me that he had a contract to open in a big dance hall in Paris called the Coliseum.

Willie engaged Tommy Benford as drummer. To replace Jacques Butler, with whom he had had a dispute, Willie engaged a trumpeter named Theodore Brock, who had been in France for a long time. He also hired Roscoe Barnett, a tenor man who was said to be the wealthiest American Negro musician in France. I never found out where Brock or Barnett were from in the States or who they had come to Europe with. I should have been a little more nosy than I was, but I never did ask other people any questions about themselves. Big Boy Goudie had left the band also and Fletcher Allen had been hired in his place.

We opened at the Coliseum in October with a French orchestra on another stand. There were about 30 dancing hostesses engaged to dance with men who came alone.

Jimmy Monroe, brother of Clark Monroe who had a famous club in Harlem, was in France because his wife Nina Mae McKinney, who had starred in the first all-Negro movie produced by Hollywood, *Hallelujah*, was working in London. Jimmy could not get permission to stay there and could only visit her for a few days at a time. Jimmy opened a club in a small street called Cité Pigalle. Spider Courance and his wife lived on this street and also Joe Hayman and his wife. Bob Greir—another American Negro who had been in Paris for some time—was Jimmy's partner, and the club, which I was told had never been a success for anyone that had ever tried to run it before, became a big hit and meeting place for most Americans that were in Paris, and there were plenty of them. The club featured the latest jazz records and became a rendezvous for American Negro artists and their French friends.

Beezie and I had our ups and downs. I was very jealous and reproached her for having become too independent. We had disputes about Joan. I thought she was too hard with the kid and she said I was too soft with her. Joan didn't get along too well with her mother. (We had put Joan in a private school a little outside of Paris shortly after we came from Belgium.)

One night I came back from work and Beezie was not home. She didn't come home until about eight o'clock that morning. When I asked her where she had been, she told me she was at Jimmy Monroe's place with Mae and Spider. I didn't raise any hell, but warned her not to let it happen again. Two nights later I came home, and there was no Beezie. This time she came home about 4 a.m. I didn't say a word but the next day I packed all my belongings and took a room in a hotel not far from the Coliseum.

When the news got around that Beezie and I had separated, many of our friends asked me not to leave her stranded in Europe. Every week I gave her an allowance. When she didn't come for it, I took it to her. At times I wanted to go back to her but I felt that we would not get along because I believed that Mae had a bad influence on her.

Meantime, I received a letter from the director of the Taj Mahal Hotel in Bombay asking me if I would come there alone to join an orchestra they had engaged which included Crickett Smith and Rudy Jackson. I really enjoyed my stay in Bombay and I suppose that if I had been offered the opportunity to go back with a group formed in Paris, I might have accepted. But I didn't have any desire to go alone, so I refused the offer.

In December, Mr. Pastraudis, the owner of the Monseigneur in Alexandria, came to Paris and contacted Billy Burns to form an orchestra for his place. Why he did not want to take Willie Lewis again, I never knew, unless Willie could not get out of the contract he had at the Coliseum.

Some of us had begun to get a little fed up with Willie, and Burns knew who we were. So he told us about the Alexandria deal and that the loot was good. We decided to form a group and keep it a secret. There were Joe Hayman and Fletcher Allen (alto saxes), Billy Burns (trombone), Herman Chittison (piano), and me. We contacted Spider Courance, who was again working at the Villa d'Este. Billy Burns knew a drummer from Holland, Arthur Pay, who was a Negro born in the Dutch West Indies. Pastraudis had said that there was an Italian bass player already in Alexandria.

Before leaving Paris, I gave Mae enough money for Beezie and Joan to go back to New York. Mae was coming to Egypt after Spider got settled there. She told me that Beezie was out of town, staying for a few days with a sick friend.

We left Paris by train for Italy on 5 December 1938 without telling anybody and sailed from Genoa the following day, on the Italian liner *Esperia*. On board I met the violinist Bernardo Alemany who was the leader of an Argentinian orchestra that Pastraudis had engaged also. We had a wonderful trip but when we arrived in Alexandria, we could not leave the boat because Pastraudis did not have working permits for us. But he was a big man in Alexandria and he told us that he would arrange everything. We stayed on board, the ship sailed for Haifa and came back to Alexandria the next day. Pastraudis had the permits and everything was in the bag.

We had met a Belgian woman, Mme. Piers, who managed the Pingouin in Knokke. She had come to Egypt when Willie Lewis went there and acted as his secretary. She had fallen in love with some fellow in Egypt and stayed there. She was now working for Pastraudis and became our manager when we started working in the Monseigneur. Our salary was three Egyptian pounds a day each and that was more than we had made with Willie Lewis in that country. Fletcher Allen was a good arranger and after a few days of hard rehearsing, we had a nice repertoire. We incorporated the band and took the name of Harlem Rhythm Makers.

Jazz had not been very popular or well known in Egypt until Willie Lewis went there and his band made a big hit; so when we returned, with a less commercial band than Willie's, we had a great success with the clientele. Many of the young jazz-lovers, who were mostly from rich families, came to hear us at least three times a week. There were many rich Greek families in Egypt and also many rich young Egyptians with whom we became well acquainted.

We wore a grey uniform for the afternoon matinee and tuxedos at night. Every day the band got better, and I became the featured singer. My voice was not bad and I had more nerve to try and sing than the rest of the fellows. In the room where we worked at night the cashier was a young fellow who liked to hear the *Donkey Serenade*, a number we played though we didn't care much for it. This fellow was a talented artist and he would make different drawings of an ass and send it to the bandstand by a waiter. He was such a nice guy who really loved our music that we would play the number to make him feel happy.

Eventually we received news that Willie Lewis and the Coliseum management had put in a complaint against us to the French government for leaving without giving notice and we would not be permitted to enter France for five years. That did not worry us because we had a fine jazz orchestra and everything was going swell for us.

Our biggest honor and the most celebrated occasion we experienced was when our orchestra was engaged to play for the wedding reception of Muhammad Reza Pahlevi, the crown Prince of Iran (who became the Shah of Iran) and Princess Fawzia, the sister of King Farouk. The wedding took place in Cairo on 15 March 1939. Unfortunately the reception was not given in the palace of the king, which would have been very exciting, but in a very large mansion near the center of the city. The orchestra was placed on the landing of a large staircase, just a few steps down from the room where the reception was held.

During the banquet we played softer than usual. Later the atmosphere became gay. Confetti and cotton balls were passed out and we were included in the fun because Farouk and some of the other royalty started throwing cotton balls at us and we threw them back. Later we were asked to come up to the floor where the reception was held to play a special number for the newlyweds and the rest of the royal household. Now I could say that I had played for some crowned heads of Egypt and bald heads of Europe.

On 4 April we were engaged to play in Cairo again for a ball given by the Woman's Health Improvement Association at the Shepherd's Hotel, which was the largest and most expensive hotel in Egypt. The ball was given under the patronage of King Farouk.

Pastraudis closed the Monseigneur in August for the whole month. We went to the beach every day and enjoyed the vacation.

Mae Courance had come to Alexandria a month after we arrived there. She and Edgar were living in the Syracuse Hotel, where I had stayed my first time in Egypt. Eventually there was a three-room apartment free on the top floor of the hotel so Joe Hayman and I moved in with Mae and Spider. Mae did the cooking and we shared the expenses. Burns had bought a white Packard sports car with a rumble seat from Pastraudis and we went to Cairo a few times. During the holidays, Pastraudis decided that he didn't like Arthur Pay and Mme. Piers and had them put out of the country. When we started again in the Monseigneur, we had an Egyptian drummer named François. Though his parents must have been French he was born in Egypt.

As Egypt was a British protectorate it was normal that there were many families of the British Royal Navy. We became friends with four British soldiers who were jazz fans. Three of them played in a military band: Henry Campbell, who played tenor sax; A.J. Henderson, known as "Ginger" because of his red hair, who played trumpet; and Teddy Hill, who was a very talented drummer —we really enjoyed it when he would come around and sit in with us. He was the best drummer in Egypt. There were many bands in Europe and the USA that would have been happy to have him as a drummer. Ginger was not a jazz trumpet player and he called himself our second, no-solo-taking trumpet.

We also made friends with a couple of Egyptian military aviators and some coastguard officers. After we became well acquainted with the coastguard officers, they used to give us big pieces of hashish and told us how they got it. There was plenty of hashish smoking in Egypt. Women were not allowed in Egyptian bars or sidewalk cafes but every cafe had a supply of water pipes, better known as hubbly-bubbly pipes, and they were not for drinking tea with. Hashish was plentiful everywhere but I never found out if there was a law against it or only a law against smuggling. These officers told us that whenever they caught someone trying to smuggle in hashish they would take a big portion for themselves, and turn in a certain amount as evidence against the prisoner. They didn't sell it to us; it was a gift.

We had a band valet whose name was Hassan, but we called him Sam. Whenever we received a big hunk of hashish we would have Sam come to our place to prepare it because there is an artistic touch that must be used to prepare a hubbly-bubbly pipe and Sam knew how to do it. It did not become an every day habit with us to smoke hashish but it was kicks to get high now and then.

The attitude of Pastraudis towards us began to change. We noticed that when he was standing at the bar which faced the bandstand in the room where we played in the afternoon he would be talking with someone with his personality smile on his face, but when he looked at us on the bandstand, he had a look of hatred. We found out later that he detested us.

After having Arthur Pay and Mme. Piers put out of the country, he pulled a dirty trick on Fletcher Allen for no reason that we could see. Fletcher had been living for a long time with Elsie, an Austrian girl whom Fletcher had brought to Egypt. Pastraudis knew that Fletcher and Elsie were not married so he had her deported. That hurt us almost as much as it did Fletcher.

A few months after Elsie left, Burns's wife Louise received a message asking her to come home as quickly as possible. Burns decided to go with her and started making preparations to leave. Naturally he wanted to sell the car he had bought from Pastraudis. Pastraudis knew that this was going to happen, so he arranged things in a way that no garage owner would buy it and Burns was obliged to sell it back to Pastraudis for about a third of the price he had paid for it.

An Armenian trombone player named Gielaby replaced Burns. Of course there was a small difference in the band's punch from when we started at the Monseigneur, because we had an Italian drummer and an Armenian trombonist. But the front line was as strong as ever with the three saxophones, Chittison, and myself, and we still had the favor of the public.

One afternoon Spider got drunk. He always had a bad temper when he drank. He sat at the left end of the bandstand, which was one foot high. A young English officer who came to the place quite often was sitting at a table at the corner of the stand and he had one foot on the stand. For some reason, Spider didn't like it. So he told this officer to take his foot off the bandstand. The rest of us had no idea of what was happening. Suddenly there was a big confusion and I saw this young officer standing up, his face bleeding. He had not moved his foot when Spider told him to and Spider had hit him. The fellow was ready to fight back when someone jumped between them. We were all quite disgusted with Spider because what he did was really uncalled for. The young man left and we continued to play.

When Pastraudis came in, someone told him what had happened. He fired Spider for two weeks and told him that he could not come back to work until he had begged the fellow's pardon in front of his commanding officer and paid his doctor's bill. So for two weeks we played without a tenor. Spider didn't misbehave after that when he got high.

I knew by experience that Spider was temperamental when he was drunk. One night in Paris we had both been drinking. We were having a good time with Beezie and Mae and we were making the rounds of a few bars. In one of them, Beezie and him were playing and Beezie accidently hit Spider on the mouth. He wasn't angry about it, but later we were in a bar called Sans Souci at rue Pigalle and Spider began to get nasty with me and accused me of hitting him on the mouth. I kept telling him that it happened when he and Beezie were playing. We had some more drinks. Later he started accusing me again. The next thing I knew was that I was getting up off the floor!

Spider had hit me on the chin when I was not expecting anything like that from him and I wasn't looking at him at that moment. My head just missed a radiator by the wall and I was stunned for a couple of seconds. I got up and started at him but he grabbed me and started crying, saying he was sorry. A couple of policemen who were standing outside the bar came rushing in and asked what the trouble was. We pretended that we were only playing. I didn't keep any bad feelings against Spider although I was hurt.

Hitler had been causing trouble in Europe for a few years and on 3 September 1939, France and England declared war on Germany. That cooked our goose for coming back to France, even if it had been possible. Pastraudis really jumped on the chance of taking advantage of us by cutting our salary to one pound a day. That didn't kill our spirits and I suppose he was very disappointed by that. At one time he had invited us to his home, but now he was giving us dirty looks!

The end came in December 1939 when Pastraudis said that he would continue our engagement if we accepted another cut in salary. We didn't know what future lay ahead for us but we had taken all that was possible from Pastraudis and that was the last straw. As we could not go back to France and all of Europe was at war except Italy and Switzerland, Pastraudis said that he would pay our transportation back to Italy as he was not obliged to pay it back to the USA.

We were supposed to leave Alexandria at the end of December. Meantime, we were offered a job at the Carlton, a new club that was due to open on 1 January 1940, but Pastraudis had obtained our deportation papers and the club owners did not have the puli with the government to combat Pastraudis's decision to put us out of the country.

From Italy we would have to pay our fare to New York and that would have left me and perhaps some of the others without a penny. So we decided to go see the American ambassador to try arrange a deal to work our way back to New York on one of the many American Export Line ships that came often to Alexandria. We never got to see the ambassador but managed to see the vice consul. When we explained our case to him, he told us that there was nothing they could do for us. They were there for the interest of Ford Motors, Standard Oil, and other big American concerns and said that we boys should have been prepared for the events that were facing us. I believe it would have been different had we been white!

The day before we were to leave Egypt, Spider, without any of us knowing about it, went to the Italian Embassy and explained to someone there that we were being put out of the country and our transportation was paid on the Italian line who would be obliged to support us as long we were stranded on their ship. We would not have been allowed to get off the boat in Italy without passage paid to another port. Spider also explained that there was a place opening that would engage the orchestra and had agreed to pay the rest of our transportation from Italy to New York but they could not get the permission from the government. So the Italian Embassy got busy. We didn't know the result until the next day when we were at the docks getting ready to board an Italian boat for Naples. We were all there except Chittison. Someone came with the news that we were permitted to stay in the country for two months and we had to go immediately to the working permit office.

There were five of us left from the original seven Harlem Rhythm Makers and the Carlton's management had received the permission for the five of us; but Chittison had not come to the docks and we didn't know where he was. So a detective was sent for and told to find Chittison. A half hour later, Chit was in the office. He was in love with an Egyptian girl and had made arrangement with Pastraudis, unbeknownst to us, to stay in Alexandria. I'm not certain he was happy to have to work with us. I imagine that Pastraudis must have turned green when he found out that we had been permitted to remain in Alexandria. I never saw him again and never wanted to.

We engaged Bob Haye, a white drummer, but we had no bass. We had also to play for five acts. Mae Courance had sung with a trio for a while in Paris and she didn't have a bad voice. She was engaged as singer. The clientele at the Carlton was 100 per cent English and at that time the *Lambeth Walk* song and dance was very popular. So for two months we had to play the *Lambeth Walk* at least three times a night.

On 25 February we left Alexandria on a small Italian boat called *Egeo*. We stopped at the island of Rhodes, which we had time to visit. The next stop was Greece and we visited Athens. It was a three-day trip from Alexandria to Naples, and we were obliged to stay in Naples five days before we had a ship to New York. We met an Italian sailor and a civilian who became friendly with us and showed us around the city and took us to some restaurants where we could eat good and not pay too much. The sailor, who was on permission, spent every day with us. We had to report every day to the American Embassy, where our passports were canceled for any further trips in Europe. Some jazz fans got the news that we were in town so they came to see us. One of them invited us to his home, which I remember was on the hill which overlooked the bay and the center of Naples.

We left Naples on 5 March 1940 on the Italian liner *Saturna* and the trip was 11 days. We jammed most every night with the musicians who played in first class and they were really happy because they seldom had a chance to play jazz.

At one time in Paris, some musicians had been on the snow kick. Snow is jive language for heroin. A certain musician that I knew very well was using it. One night he tried to get me to take a sniff, but I wasn't taking any chances on trying any form of dope. I smoked a little gage now and then but I was afraid of anything else except alcohol.

But perhaps it was because my love affair had gone wrong that I had decided to buy a package of snow before I left for Egypt. I was so afraid that the Swiss or Italian customs agents might come on the train and perhaps search me or my luggage, that I hid the package under the mat in the vestibule of our coach. We arrived at the station of Genoa, Italy, and after going inside the station, when everyone was off the train, I pretended that I must have forgotten something on the train and went back to recover my package of snow.

Many months after I had been in Egypt I remembered the stuff, and before we left I looked everywhere for it. I really did not want it to be found amongst my belongings when I arrived in New York, but it was impossible to find it. I had a turtle neck sweater, which I had bought before I left New York, that had a zipper-up collar and two pockets with zippers on them. I had not used this sweater during my stay in Egypt but one day on the *Saturna*, way out in the Atlantic, I decided to put it on. As I was strolling along one of the decks I put a hand in one of the pockets and felt something like a piece of paper. When I pulled it out and looked at it, I realized that it was the package of heroin. With apprehension I took it and felt gay for the rest of the trip. But I never touched any after that.

NINE

THE GREAT COMEBACK

We arrived in New York on 16 March 1940 and after being away four years and six months, it was almost as thrilling to return to the Apple as it had been the first time I came there in 1927. Thanks to the management of the Carlton in Alexandria, who had paid our fare from Naples to New York, I had $100 when I landed. That wasn't much money, but at least I could make it last until I found work. This was not too difficult as I had not been away long enough to be forgotten.

New York was still having winter weather and there was snow (the real thing) on the ground. The only hotel in Harlem that was well known to me (because of the publicity it had received from the Basie recording) was the Woodside on 7th Avenue and that's where I went. I paid a week's rent in advance. After installing myself in my room, which was quite a disappointment, I headed straight for the Rhythm Club. Some of the musicians I had known for years greeted me with joy, and others I had also known for years greeted me as if I had been coming to the club every day for the last four years and six months. But what the hell, that's the Apple.

One of the first things I had to do upon my return to New York was to be reinstalled in the Musicians' Union because I had let it drop in 1936. It cost me $50. There was a syndicate in Paris, France, but hardly any musicians belonged to it.

Beezie had found out by some means that I had returned and where I was staying. She came with Joan to see me. We patched up our differences and I moved to the place where she lived on 154th Street up on Sugar Hill. It had more class than down in Harlem and I was pretty satisfied with the surroundings and very happy that Beezie and I were together again.

I had not got a divorce from my first wife, Madelyn, and my alimony case was still pending in the domestic court. My mother had written me once and told me that Madelyn had come to her in Cincinnati when I was still in Europe and said that she would not press charges against me if I came back to the States. Nevertheless, one day a detective came to my house with a subpoena for me to appear in the domestic court. I went with the detective and was locked in a cell in the courthouse until my case was called. This was the second time I had heard the clink of a jail door close on me. Eventually my case was called but, as Madelyn was not there, the judge dismissed it. It never came up again.

The Golden Gate Ballroom was a new dance hall for me. It was at Lenox Avenue and 143rd Street, just two blocks from the Savoy, which managed it. The first time I went there I heard the big band of Coleman Hawkins, who had returned to the States from Europe in 1939. It was a fine band. The orchestra included Joe Guy and Tommy Lindsay (trumpets), Earl Hardy (trombone), Eustace Moore and Jackie Fields (alto saxes), Ernie Powell (tenor sax), Gene Rodgers (piano), Charles Smith (bass), Arthur Herbert (drums), and Thelma Carpenter (vocalist).

I had not heard the recording the "Bean" had done of *Body and Soul*, but I had heard about it. Naturally it was Hawk's biggest hit and when he played it that night, chills ran up and down my spine. Hawk had come back from Europe and let everybody know that he was still the master of the tenor sax and had lost nothing by being away for a few years, although it was often said that a musician usually lost something if he stayed in Europe too long. Hawk was the great Hawk he had always been and playing better than in his Fletcher Henderson days.

Another night I heard Benny Carter's big band, which was great also. Benny never had a bad band. The musicians were: Joe Thomas, Shad Collins, and Russell Smith (trumpets—Benny also played trumpet), Sandy Williams and Milt Robinson (trombones), Benny Carter, Carl Frye, and George Dorsey (alto saxes), Sammy Davis and Stafford "Pazuza" Simon (tenor saxes), Sonny White (piano), Ulysses Livingston (guitar), Hayes Alvis (bass), Keg Purnell (drums), and Roy Felton (vocalist). Some nights the two bands would be Hawk's and Benny's and that made for a battle of alto and tenor sax with honors being distributed even.

Teddy Wilson was no longer with Benny Goodman and he had also formed a big band, which played certain nights at the Golden Gate. In the band were: Adolphus "Doc" Cheatham, Carl "Bama" Warwick, and Harold "Shorty" Baker (trumpets), Jack Wiley and Floyd "Stumpy" Brady (trombones), Rudy Powell (alto sax and clarinet), Pete Clarke (alto and baritone sax), George Irish and Bob Carroll (tenor saxes), Al Casey (guitar), Al Hall (bass), J.C. Heard (drums), and Jean Eldridge (vocalist). Buster Harding was arranger and second or standby pianist. I found it a very interesting orchestra because all the musicians were new to me except Teddy and Doc Cheatham.

On 4 April I recorded with Joe Marsala and his Delta Four, a session supervised by Leonard Feather. I had met Leonard in Paris. He was a British jazz critic and wrote for the English musical paper *Melody Maker*. He had come to New York shortly after the war started and was later to become one of the contributors to *Down Beat*, which was the best jazz magazine in the States at one time. Leonard also played piano and composed.

With the Delta Four for this recording session there were Pete Brown (alto sax), Joe Marsala (clarinet), Carmen Mastren (guitar), Gene Traxler (bass), and Dell St. John (vocalist). Joe Marsala was well known in the jazz field, as was Traxler, and they both were musicians with plenty of class. I had known Pete Brown for years. He was a big guy playing alto sax. He played very staccato in an abrupt disconnected style, very original. He was the swingingest alto player I had ever heard. Dell St. John was a Negro girl who had a fine voice and could sing the blues in a style that was strictly Dell. Joe Marsala, Carmen Mastren, and Gene Traxler were white and they were the first white musicians that I ever recorded with in the States. We recorded four numbers: *Wandering Man Blues*, *Salty Mama Blues*, *Three O'Clock Jump*, and *Reunion in Harlem*.

Shortly after the recording with Joe Marsala, I joined Benny Carter's orchestra, replacing Joe Thomas. Otherwise the line up remained the same as it was when I heard Benny at the Golden Gate. In fact it was at the Gate that I joined the band and we also played at the Savoy on different nights. On 20 May 1940 the band recorded *Pom-Pom*, *Serenade to a Sarong*, *Night Hop*, and *Okay for Baby*.

When I joined Benny Carter, the only musicians in the band that I knew well were Shad Collins, Russell Smith, Sandy Williams, and Milt Robinson. The rest had come on the scene while I was tooting in Europe. But I soon became well acquainted with the others. Ulysses Livingston lived not far from me at 155th Street and St. Nicholas Avenue, so we became very good friends.

Just under where Ulysses lived was a bar called Fat Man's. Fat Man's name was Charles Turner and he had played bass in Marion Hardy's Alabamians, the band that Cab Calloway had come to New York with. I had played opposite them at the Savoy with Scott. Fat Man and Eddie Mallory, a trumpet player with Hardy's band, had opened the bar together, but Fat Man eventually bought out Eddie's interest and was now the sole owner. It was a very modern bar and became quite a hangout for the musicians who lived in the neighborhood.

The Golden Gate closed and the band worked a few weeks at the Savoy. Benny engaged Vic Dickenson in the trombone section. He had been in Count Basie's band and he told me that Basie had told him to take a rest because he was hitting the bottle too heavy and his playing was getting a little too sluggish. But within two weeks Basie recalled Vic and he left Benny. Benny knew this would happen, but he and the rest of the gang enjoyed listening to Vic for the short while he was with us.

A few months after I had returned to the USA, Louis Armstrong was playing a week at the Roxy Theater downtown on 7th Avenue and 50th Street, and I went to see the show. "Pops," as he was now called, had taken over the Luis Russell orchestra. As I knew all the musicians, I went backstage after the show to say hello to them. I had seen Pops plenty of times and had a photo with him, Irving Randolph, and myself that was taken in Cincinnati in 1935. But I wanted an autographed photo so Higginbotham took me to Louis's dressing room and I asked Pops for a photo. He said, "Sure Gate, I'll give you one. What's your name?" I told him. Then he asked me if I was the Bill Coleman that had spent some time in Europe. I was floored when he asked me, because I didn't think he knew anything about me. It really made me happy to know that the great Louis Armstrong knew about Bill Coleman.

In August, Benny Carter accepted a job in a dance hall at Coney Island, an amusement park in Long Island, and we played a month there.

A very good friend of the orchestra was John Hammond, a rich young man who came quite often to the Savoy. He was the sponsor of Count Basie and responsible for Basie coming to New York. He also had put Charlie Christian in Benny Goodman's orchestra. I had known John for quite some time. One day I received a message from him, saying that Teddy Wilson no longer had a big band but was forming a small group to go into a place called Café Society Downtown in Greenwich Village, a section in lower Manhattan on the West Side. John wanted me to join Teddy because he liked my solo work and probably thought that I'd be happier in a small group where I would have more liberty than in a big band, which was true. I liked working in big orchestras because of the harmonious sounds of the different sections working together, and especially with three trumpets cutting riffs through an arrangement, but I had a desire to work with a small group in a club, which was something I had not done before, so I gave my notice to Benny Carter and joined Teddy Wilson.

The drummer was a fellow named Yank Porter: he had worked a long time at the Harlem Club and I had known him for years. Benny Morton was on trombone, Jimmy Hamilton was a clarinettist whom I didn't know before, and the bass player was Al Hall, whom I had seen in Teddy's big band.

The Café Society Downtown was at Sheridan Square and owned by a man named Barney Josephson. The manager was Harold Johnson and they had a great barman called Lew. There were four acts in the show, three of them discovered and sponsored by John Hammond.

Boogie-woogie was popular and John had put together the three greatest exponents of that style of piano playing. They were Meade "Lux" Lewis, Pete Johnson, and Albert Ammons. Pete Johnson and Albert Ammons were working as a team. There was a great blues singer named Big Joe Turner whom the two boogie-woogie pianists accompanied. The three of them would really rock the joint every night. They could drink plenty of booze too and carry it well.

Another act was the Golden Gate Quartet. Their names were Bill Johnson, Clyde Reddick, Orlandus Wilson, and Henry Owens. They had a style of singing gospel songs but this was more like Holy-Roller singing to me because it had a jazz rhythm and these fellows would slap their thighs with their hands in 4/4 time. Yank accompanied them with wire brushes on the snare drum and the joint kept jumping.

The other act was a young woman named Hazel Scott. Hazel was a classical pianist who would play a classical number and then do the same number in jazz. She was well trained and was also an arranger and jazz singer. Yank also accompanied her with wire brushes. In fact he only played with wire brushes, which sometimes didn't give the band the push it needed. We didn't play loud because it was not necessary. Teddy had a soft touch on piano, Benny Morton was at his best when playing not too loud, and so was I. That was the big difference in playing in a big band and a small combo. In a big band you must blow loud, and my ideas and technique were not so good when I had to play loud. Hamilton had a nice soft sound on clarinet and was really an admirer of Benny Goodman. So Yank's brushing style was nice for the band, except, as I mentioned before, it didn't always give the band a push on certain numbers. Al Hall was a solid bass player.

Yank Porter had worked at the Café Society before. When Teddy went in, he had to use him as Yank was very well liked by Barney Josephson. John Hammond also put pressure on him to hire me, although I had worked with Teddy in Benny Carter's orchestra. I know that he had another trumpet player in mind when I was pushed on him.

Teddy was quite a nice person but I soon found out that he had a funny character. We used to play a certain number in which he would play his solo in a minor key and the rest of the solos were in major. I liked the way Teddy made it sound in minor so one night I asked him if I could play my solo also in minor. He told me yes, but after I had taken my solo, he did not play his, and then I knew that he didn't like it because I had played it in minor. I never asked to do it in minor again.

On the recording side of things, I did a few more sessions in 1940. On 4 October I did four numbers with singer Eddy Howard; on 15 October I did a session with singer Billie Holiday where I didn't play any solos; on the same day I did another recording with Benny Carter and his All-Star Orchestra—we recorded two numbers; I recorded four numbers with singer Chick Bullock and his All-Star Orchestra on 6 December; and on 9 December I played a session with Teddy Wilson and his Orchestra where we did four numbers.

In December 1940 Barney Josephson branched out and opened a Café Society Uptown on East 58th Street. It was a real plushy joint. The Café Society Downtown was not a very large place and there was only one small dressing room for musicians and entertainers. But at the Uptown, the whole building was occupied by the club and there was a big dressing room for the two bands, the Golden Gate Quartet, and the Boogie-Woogies. There were at least four other quite large dressing rooms: they were all on the third floor.

The club featured Teddy Wilson and Eddie South's orchestra, the Gates, the Boogies without Joe Turner, Hazel Scott, and a comedian named Penner. Eddie South was a violinist who had been trained by some of the finest violin professors in Europe and especially in Hungary. He was a classical musician who could play jazz and had recorded some duets with Stephane Grappelli in France.

The club jumped from the opening night on, and the clientele was of a higher class than that at the downtown club. Most every night for the first show, which went on around eleven o'clock, the place was so crowded that there were tables on the dance floor and just enough space to push the two baby grand pianos against the bandstand for Pete Johnson, Albert Ammons, and Hazel Scott. For the second show at two o'clock, there were fewer people but still a good crowd and the show could be put on in the middle of the dance floor. The Golden Gates had to squeeze in between the two pianos when they went on for the first show.

We didn't do too much drinking at the bar because we had spacious rooms upstairs where we could play cards with Pete, Albert, and some of the Gates when we had our rest periods. We formed a club composed of those that liked a few tastes every night and bought our bottles of kickapoo joy-juice at a whisky store near the club. But if a friend came in or a client who admired a certain musician invited one of us at the bar, we accepted.

After a couple of weeks of everything going well, Barney began to be "Mr. Josephson" because of the success of the Uptown Café Society. He put up a sign

With his first band, Wesley Helvey Orchestra, 1924: (left to right) Bill Coleman, Buddy Lee, Louis Thompson, J. C. Higinbotham, John Hargrave, Slaughter Campbell, Vincent Thomas, Wesley Helvey, Edgar Courance, Henri Jamerson

With Cecil Scott's band – second period 1929–30: (back row, left to right) Dickie Wells, James Smith, Don Frye, Mack Walker, John Williams; (front row, left to right) Arnold Boling, Bill Coleman, Frank Newton, Cecil Scott, Harold McFerran

A happy reunion: Richard Clark, Bill Coleman, in his coat, Arnold Adams, Bill Beason

At the Villa d'Este in Paris with Freddy Taylor's orchestra: (left to right) Freddy Taylor, Bill Coleman, Edgar Courance, George Johnson, William Diemer; (behind) Eugène D'Hellemes, Oscar Aleman

With Willy Lewis orchestra: (back row, left to right) Ted Field, Jacques Butler, Frank "Big Boy" Goudie, Bill Coleman, Wilson Meyers, Joe Hayman; (front row, left to right) Billy Burns, Herman Chittison, Willy Lewis, Johnny Mitchell

With Teddy Wilson's orchestra, Café Society, New York, 1940: (left to right) Yank Porter, Al Hall, Teddy Wilson, Benny Morton, Bill Coleman, Jimmy Hamilton

At Café Society: (left to right) Count Basie, Teddy Wilson, Hazel Scott, Duke Ellington, Mel Powell

Louis Armstrong and Big Sid Catlett

1943 – Café Society with trio Ellis Larkins

1947 – Orchestra Billy Kyle: (left to right) Billy Kyle, Freddie Williams, George Duvivier, Bill Coleman, Wallace Bishop, Charlie Holmes

1949 – With Don
Byas on tour of
France and Europe

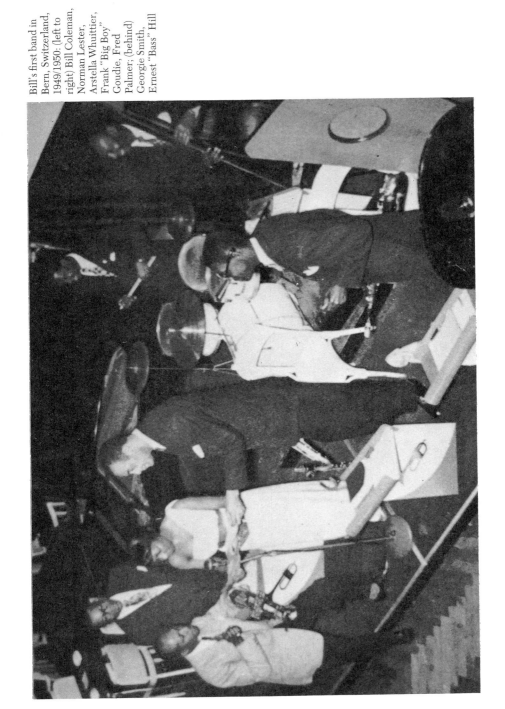

Bill's first band in Bern, Switzerland, 1949/1950: (left to right) Bill Coleman, Norman Lester, Arstella Whuittier, Frank "Big Boy" Goudie, Fred Palmer; (behind) Georgie Smith, Ernest "Bass" Hill

Cocktail party with musicians of Jazz at Philharmonic in Paris, 1952: (back row, left to right) Roy Eldridge, Ray Brown, Jo Benjamin; (middle row, left to right) Jacques Butler, Bill Coleman, Ray Briant (actor); (front row, left to right) Maurice Cullaz (jazz critic and journalist), Lester Young, Max Roach

Wedding picture at the American Church in Paris

In a loge at the Salle Pleyel in Paris: (back row, left to right) Pat Paterson (dancer), Bill Coleman, Mezz Mezzrow; (front row, left to right) Tommy Brookins, Lionel Hampton, June Richmond, unknown people, Lily Coleman

Visit of Louis and Mezz Mezzrow at "the Trois Mailletz" in Paris where Bill was working

With jazz critic and writer Johnny Simmen, violinist Stuff Smith and promotor Arild Videroe – Bern 1965

On tour in Austria with pianist Joe Turner, Albert Nicholas, and Ola Ringström, pianist from Swiss band, the Tremble Kids

London: (left to right) Wally Fawkes, Alan Littlejohn, Bill Coleman, Bruce Turner, John Chilton

Jazz festival of Joinville (Paris) with Ben Webster and Benny Carter 1971

Degustation of Chili con
carne with Milt Buckner at
Bill's home

In Cadeillan 1980, with friend
Guy Lafitte (tenor sax)

One of the very last concerts in Limoges, France, 11 February 1981 with orchestra of Oliver Jackson.

in our dressing room which specified that no sideman in the orchestras would be allowed to sit at a table with a client. The only exceptions were for Hazel, who was the star of the show, Teddy Wilson, Eddie South, and of course the comedian. As a rule, Pete and Albert always went upstairs after their numbers because they preferred to enjoy themselves talking, telling jokes, and drinking with the rest of the cats. But I refused to obey the sign and whenever someone asked me to sit at their table or have a drink at the bar, I did. So did Al Hall. I felt that I was as much a gentleman as Teddy, Eddie South, or Barney himself, and if a rule had been made in the beginning not to allow any of the employees to sit at a table or drink at the bar, and it had applied to everyone, I would have accepted it, but not this way. In any case, Barney never complained about our socializing.

I mentioned before that Eddie South was so well trained on his instrument that I doubt that he ever made a mistake during his long career as a violinist. But one night he was playing a classical number that had a passage of eight bars for violin alone and Eddie made a mistake which those that heard it dismissed as something that could happen but was not supposed to happen to a great performer like Eddie. The next night Eddie did the number again on his attraction set and he missed the passage at the same place again. That did bug him because he had played the number many times before without missing a note. I and the others that witnessed this incident really felt sorry for Eddie. He was very upset and by the third night we all knew that he was fighting with himself and that's what he did for almost a week. When he did at last conquer it, he played the number a couple of nights but I never heard him play it afterwards.

We worked at the Uptown for one month and left for a two-month engagement in Chicago, at the Ambassador East Hotel, which was one of the finest hotels in the city. We were to play in the Pump Room, where only one other Negro orchestra had ever played, and that was John Kirby's Greatest Little Big Band in the World. I had heard many of their broadcasts and had never heard six in-strumentalists that sounded like ten. Kirby's band had played in many places where Negro musicians had never played before and the Pump Room was one of them.

Teddy engaged his favorite drummer, J.C. Heard, who had been a member of Teddy's big band, and added George James on baritone sax. This made the front line four horns, trumpet, trombone, clarinet, and baritone sax. The baritone gave the band a heavier sound and the arrangements that Teddy wrote also made us sound like a bigger band. For this job we had white frocktails made in New York and everything we wore was white from collar and bow tie down to socks and shoes. Only Teddy wore a black full dress suit.

I had never been to Chicago before and enjoyed the idea of going there, particularly since I had heard many nice things about it. It was George James's home, and Teddy Wilson and Benny Morton had been there a few times also. Most of us stayed in a hotel on the South Side, which was the Harlem of Chicago. We were there for a few days before we were to start working in the Pump Room, so we reported to the Musicians' Union to receive our transfer cards. We were told by a secretary that if a transit musician was introduced in a public place, he was not allowed to stand up and bow to the public if he got applause!

At the Ambassador, we had to do a musical show at a certain time every night. The number Teddy had chosen to feature me was Gershwin's *I've Got Plenty o' Nuttin'*. There was also three nights a week when we had to broadcast. We could not blow very loud except during our show and for the radio, so Benny Morton and I played muted except for those two occasions. When I had a solo on an up-tempo number, I used to turn my back at times and blow at J.C., who sat in back of me. It may not have looked very nice but there is a certain amount of push in fast numbers that made it almost impossible for me to play if I had to hold back and use a mute at the same time.

One night we were playing *Sweet Georgia Brown* and on the last chorus J.C. was really pushing and the number was swinging more that night than ever before. I had a feeling that I could never have had if Yank Porter had been on drums. So I turned towards J.C., blew the way I felt, and ended on a high F. When we came off the bandstand for the intermission, Teddy told me that I should not play high notes in that place. I replied that I didn't see anything wrong, and told him that no one ever said anything to him about playing high notes on the piano. He didn't like what I told him, but never said anything about the notes I played after that.

There was a small hotel on the South Side, whose club featured small combos, that was open until the wee hours every morning. There were also musicians playing in most of the bars, and Chicago was jumping. Al Hall and I were drinking buddies and we used to go to this hotel most every night after we finished at the Pump Room, which was at 2 a.m. The club was managed by a dancer called Broadway, whom I knew from New York. Roy Eldridge brought a band in during our stay in the city, and I met his drummer, whose name was Carl "Kansas" Fields. I became better acquainted with Kansas later when he came to New York.

We had Monday nights off. One Monday night the orchestra of Count Basie played a dance at some large hall. When I was in Egypt I had rented a big radio and had heard a broadcast of Basie for the first time. But being able to hear the band and see it on stage was real kicks and I'll never forget the impression I had listening to them. At the time when I heard the Basie broadcast in Egypt, they had played a number called *Blue and Sentimental* which featured a tenor sax who sounded very much like Hawkins. I had long wondered who it was, so when I caught the band in Chicago, I asked Dicky Wells who the tenor was. He told me it had been Herschel Evans and that he was dead now.

J.C. had a radio in his car, and one night as we were coming from work, we caught a broadcast of Duke coming from somewhere in California. They were playing a number called *Flamingo* and a male singer was singing it. This fellow really had a wonderful voice. Duke's band was sounding great as usual but it was the singer that had really captured our attention. At the end of the number the speaker announced that we had just heard a new voice of the great Duke Ellington orchestra, Herb Jeffries.

We finished at the Pump Room on the last day of March and I went back to

New York. It was understood that we were to go back to the Café Society Uptown in six weeks' time, so during the wait I did a few gigs.

Two weeks before we were to go back to the Café Society, Al Hall came to my house and told me that he and I would not be included in Teddy Wilson's orchestra when it opened. He had gone to see Teddy, who had give him his notice, and told him that I would not be in the band either. I promptly went to see Teddy to have the news directly from him and he told me that Barney Josephson did not want Al and me in his club any more. I was very angry about the turn of events because I had not accepted or tried to get another regular job as it had been certain before we left Chicago that I would go back to the Café Society with Teddy.

I told Teddy to tell Barney that I had lived many years before I ever worked in his place and that I would continue to live without working there again. I could have reported the matter to the Musicians' Union after Teddy had started to work at the club. He would have had to pay me two weeks' salary because he had not given me two weeks' notice. I'm happy that I didn't. The only benefit I would have got would have been two weeks' salary and a lost friendship, although Teddy and I never were great friends. I liked and always did admire him from the first time we worked together in Benny Carter's orchestra.

Timme Rosenkrantz, who had come to New York in 1933 and eventually became known as the "Barrelhouse Baron," had married a Negro girl named Inez Cavanaugh. They opened a record shop on St. Nicholas Avenue near 147th Street. I started making the shop my hang-out. Soon after that, Timme suggested I should form an orchestra and he would manage it. Timme was in the know as to what was happening in the jazz world and knew the owners of most of the clubs uptown and downtown. So we talked about the band I should lead for a few days and then started putting the idea into action.

Harry White, an ex-Cab Calloway trombonist known as "Father" White, was also a fine arranger, but he had become an alcoholic and was not in demand at the time. He started hanging out in Timme's record shop, and when we had worked out the details of my orchestra, Harry agreed to be the arranger.

We contacted a pianist named General Morgan—his first name really was General. He was a fine pianist. Also Arthur Herbert (an ex-Coleman Hawkins drummer), Franz Jackson (tenor sax), and Herb Flemming (trombone). Father White was living in a back room of the record shop and Timme was feeding him and also gave him a little drinking money. The shop wasn't doing too well, so not much money was coming in. We musicians weren't working, so we had nothing to offer in the way of money to pay for the arrangements.

But things were going along nicely at the rehearsals and one day I think that Timme or Inez hit the numbers for five cents and decided to have a little party for the band. Timme had been speaking about a famous dish he used to cook called Danish fish balls. They were made with fish and mixed with mashed potatoes, served with a white sauce, and—to my surprise—were very tasty.

After two months of rehearsing, Timme told us that the next week we would have an audition at Kelly's Stable, a well-known jazz spot on 52nd Street, between 6th and 7th Avenues. Kelly's Stable was a jazz club long before the Famous Door and a few other 52nd Street joints became famous.

Franz Jackson did not show up at the next rehearsal or the one after that. We had no idea what had happened to him, so we engaged a clarinettist named Eddie Williams and on the following Tuesday night we went to the Stable to do the audition. The bass player was a young guy named Benny Moten. Generally an audition was done in the afternoon, but the two owners of Kelly's Stable, whom I only knew as George and Nick, wanted us to audition in the evening, in order to obtain the reaction of the public to our playing. There were two other orchestras auditioning that night. One of them was under the name of Franz Jackson. He had pulled a dirty trick on me by saying he would play with me until he found out where and for whom the audition would be and then formed his own group to undermine me for that job.

By the time each orchestra had played four sets it was time for the place to close. I had done auditions with other orchestras, but this was the first time I did one that was similar to a night's work and was not paid. But musicians always had to do things that were not kosher in order to land a job, so the ordeal was sort of normal. As Timme was my manager, I didn't put any questions to George or Nick. When the night was finished, Timme told us that the prospects for landing the job looked good but that the owners would like us to come back the following week and do another audition under the same conditions, which meant nothing for us but something for the place, if you get what I mean, as Fats Waller would say.

Fortunately the musicians were not difficult and although we were all experiencing rather difficult times, we were willing to come back the next week for another try at getting the job. We returned and things were the same as the Tuesday before except that Franz Jackson and the other orchestra were not there and two other groups were making the audition with us. When the night was finished, Timme told us that he was supposed to call the owners in a day or two to get their decision.

A few days later, Timme called and then told us that George wanted us to come back the following week to do another audition and we froze. We had become aware of the jive that George and Nick were putting down. The two groups that played there every night were off on Tuesdays and those guys had worked out a scheme where they would have three groups come in on Tuesday nights under the pretext of auditioning for the job. As the auditions did not pay anything, they were having one night a week of free music and making a nice profit. Nice work if you can get it.

Soon after that, Timme was in no condition to go anywhere else to try and get us a job because his face broke out with some kind of infection. As I was not the go-getter type, the band never got its foot off the ground. That was my only venture in the bandleading business in the States.

On 12 February 1941, I did a recording session with Chick Bullock and his All-Star Orchestra, and we recorded four numbers.

I started hanging around the Rhythm Club again and managed to pick up a few gigs with Kaiser Marshall, the first well-known drummer of the Fletcher Henderson orchestra. There was a little fellow who played alto sax (not very well) named Leon Gross, but all the musicians called him "Bossman," and he got quite a few gigs also. Times were difficult and musicians accepted jobs whatever price they could get.

Kaiser called a dollar a potato, and when he would ask me if I would do a gig with him, he would explain that the job only paid three potatoes. During those lean days, three potatoes was better than no potatoes, and there was a saying amongst musicians that if you did not want the gig, there was a boy around the corner who would accept it. As I was one of the boys around the corner I did quite a few gigs with Kaiser and Bossman. The bands were usually good musicians and there were never any hard arrangements to be played because there were always different musicians for each gig, except for two or three regular fellows that Kaiser and Bossman could depend on being free at any time.

Sometime during the late spring, Sidney Bechet happened to come to live across the street from me. We knew each other casually but eventually got better acquainted and Beezie became quite friendly with the girl Sidney was living with. Gigs were coming in less and less, so in June I decided to apply for my unemployment benefit, which was everyone's prerogative. In order to receive the benefits, it was necessary to report to the office nearest you for five weeks. Eventually I could get a check for $25 every week for a certain length of time.

During this procedure, Bechet had applied for a summer season job at a place called Camp Unity, which was about 70 miles from New York. The camp was run by the Communist Party and was known to be very liberal concerning the social mixing of races. I had been aware of the existence of this camp from other musicians who had done seasons there. Bechet asked me if I would care to go with him: naturally I accepted. The regular season was for six weeks, starting on 15 July until 1 September. But the camp was open on weekends before the season started.

Bechet arranged for us to get $25 for the weekend, with room and board included from Friday evening until Sunday evening. We played Saturday afternoon and night and Sunday afternoon, which gave us the opportunity to be home Sunday night. I've forgotten who was engaged as pianist, but Manzie Johnson was the drummer and Wellman Braud was on the bass. The first weekend passed without any incidents, but on the second one, Bechet was not satisfied because Manzie had met a white girl and was accompanying her around the camp. Bechet gave Manzie hell for no reason, because there were plenty of mixed couples all over the place. But Bechet didn't want any of the musicians congregating with white girls. He thought it would jeopardize the job. Then he got into a big dispute with Braud, who had defended the rights of Manzie. This really spoiled the second weekend.

The next week, my day to report to the Social Security was changed from Thursday morning at eleven o'clock to Friday morning. On Tuesday of the same week, Bechet hit the numbers for a few cents and loaned me a dollar without me asking for it, but it was to chip in on a gallon of wine. We had been taking a bottle with us the last two weekends as there was no bar at the camp and wine was the only alcoholic beverage we could afford.

Thursday afternoon I went over to Sidney's house and told him that the day for me to report to the SS had been changed to Friday. That was the last time I had to report and then I would be receiving my check every week. I would stop reporting when we started working regularly. After explaining the matter to Sidney, I asked him if it would be alright for me to come to the camp a little later in the afternoon as there were buses leaving New York every two hours that passed near the camp. His reply was that we all must leave together. I said, "But Sidney, we don't have to play that night, and anyway I would be there before supper time!" But he would not consent and insisted that I leave with everyone else.

I always had very little patience with someone being illogical so I got angry. I told him that I was going to stay and report to the Social Security. He told me that if I didn't come along with him and the rest of the musicians he would take me to the Union. I told him that he could take it to the Federal Court if he wished and started to walk out of his house when he called me and said, "And another thing: give me my goddam dollar." I gave him his goddam dollar as I had not spent it, and that was the last of Sidney Bechet for me.

I collected my Social Security, and did a few gigs until Leon Abbey, who was now in New York, offered me a job at the Ubangi Club, which was downtown at the corner of 52nd Street and Broadway. This was the hardest job I ever had in New York. The band was small, consisting of piano, drums, trumpet, tenor sax, bass, and violin. There was a relief band led by a wonderful flautist named Alberto Socarras. He was the first flautist I ever heard who could make a flute sound like a pipe organ playing in the lower register.

Abbey's combo was the band that had to accompany a big revue and the violin was no help because the only two instruments that could really play loud were tenor sax and trumpet. We started at nine every night and there were no nights off. We played dance music and two shows a night. The relief band played one hour after every show. We finished at three o'clock.

One of the last acts in the revue to appear before the finale was called "the Beach Combers" and it was really a wild act and one of the best I've ever seen in a night club. They were two people, a man whose make-up and costume made him appear like a fellow who had been shipwrecked on a desert island, and a girl whom he had presumably found there. At the end of their act he was horse whipping her. They wanted their music as loud as possible and the arrangement had been made for an orchestra with no less than three trumpets. This number was so loud that I never heard what Leon Abbey was playing in it. After having played many acts and music for the chorus girls (who were real girls at this Ubangi Club), when it came to the last eight bars of the Beach Combers my lips would be so tired that I just could not bring the number to a close the way it should have been.

And every night I would hear this fellow saying, "That goddam trumpet player!" when he came off the floor. To him I must have been the lousiest trumpeter in the world. But one thing I know, and that is that they had the hardest act

I ever tried to play for in a small band. The revue should have been accompanied by a large orchestra. I was making $40 a week and I really earned my pay.

A very nice trumpet player named Archey Johnson was in the relief band and after a few weeks of fighting the music of the Beach Combers, I told Leon that I couldn't take it any longer, so I arranged for Archey to take my place and I would play in the relief band. I never knew how Archey made out with the Beach Combers because I was never there until the last of the finale was being played. But Archey didn't stay in Leon's band very long. When he left two trumpet players were engaged, two nice young fellows and playboys, Russell Gillon and his buddy Reese. Two new orchestras were hired after a couple of months and I started gigging again.

In August I was contacted to do a two-week tour with Claude Hopkins, the pianist who had been quite a popular bandleader at the Savoy and the Arcadia Ballrooms. Claude had no regular orchestra now and most of the musicians were engaged at the Rhythm Club. The band consisted of Ludwig "Pokey Joe" Jordan, E.V. Perry, and Bill Coleman (trumpets), Joe Hayman and Norman Thornton (alto saxes), Lem Johnson (tenor sax and a very good blues singer), Claude Hopkins (piano), and Ernest "Bass" Hill (bass). I don't remember the name of the drummer.

The most amusing thing about the tour was that Claude had rented a small bus that could carry about 20 people. Every time we came to a hill that was steep for a quarter of a mile or more, the damn bus couldn't make it and we all had to get out and push. Sometimes we had to stop pushing for about 15 minutes to get our breath. "Pokey Joe" always had a pair of dice with him so the guys would take their minds off pushing the bus and shot craps for ten or fifteen minutes. I filmed them in the act because I always had my movie camera on a tour. I had experienced having to push a car on different occasions on a tour but this was the first time I helped push a bus. But everyone took it more as a joke than a drag. We played some dates in Maryland, Delaware, and Washington, DC. We stayed in DC for a couple of days before the tour ended.

Beezie and I had not been getting along very well for quite some time and we finally separated.

In the last week of September I was engaged by Andy Kirk to replace a trumpeter named Clarence Trice. The position was not to be permanent but I stayed with the orchestra four months and enjoyed every moment. The band consisted of Harold "Shorty" Baker, Harry "Big Jim" Lawson, and Bill Coleman (trumpets), Ted Donnelly and Henry Wells (trombones), Johnny Harrington and Buddy Miller (alto saxes), Edward Inge (clarinet and tenor sax), Dick Wilson (tenor sax), Floyd Smith (guitar), Mary Lou Williams (piano), Booker Collins (bass), Ben Thigpen (drums), June Richmond (vocalist), and Andy Kirk (leader). There were only three musicians in the orchestra that I knew slightly: Shorty Baker, Henry Wells, and Edward Inge (who used to be with Don Redman).

I had however seen Andy Kirk and his "Clouds of Joy" quite a few times when he had a male singer named Pha Terrell with him, and had also admired the piano playing of Mary Lou Williams, who played strong, swinging piano like a man. I soon found out that Mary Lou was also fine arranger because there were quite a number of compositions in the Kirk book that were written and arranged by her and they were swinging, stomping arrangements.

Big Jim Lawson was a quiet big fellow who must have weighed at least 250 pounds but he was solid and not fat. He could drink a lot and never show it and was about the loudest-blowing trumpet player I ever heard after Ted Colin. But he had a wonderful tone and although he could blow loud, it was not blasting.

Shorty Baker was about four feet ten and had one of the biggest tones I ever heard from a trumpeter. He could blow quite strong, had a very personal style, and was an all-round trumpet player. I thought that I could blow fairly loud, but I really had to put everything I could into my horn to be heard in the section.

Edward Inge I knew quite well. I had talked with him many times in Big John's bar and made some Redman recordings with him. He was a fine man who was always very conservative and never seemed to get excited or upset about anything. He was really the type of person who has complete control of himself at all times. And he was one of the finest clarinettists in the business. He played second tenor sax in some of the arrangements, but he was featured on clarinet. Floyd Smith was well known for his *Floyd's Guitar Blues*, which he did on a table-type Hawaiian guitar, and he was quite a funky guitar player on many other numbers.

June Richmond had been in the show at the Harlem Club when the Benny Carter band had played there in 1933. I had also seen her later at the Lafayette Theater. June was quite heavy and must have weighed more than Big Jim although she was just a little taller than Shorty Baker. But she didn't need a microphone or loudspeakers to be heard when she sang. June had a voice like an opera singer but she could swing a number like Ella Fitzgerald and the band didn't have to play soft for her. She also did comical numbers and could do most anything with her voice.

Andy Kirk was a gentle leader who had been a baritone sax player in some orchestra around St. Louis or Kansas City, so I was told. He was very patient with the musicians but no one gave him much trouble except Buddy Miller, who would get drunk occasionally and could not do his job correctly.

The first date I did with the band was at the Howard Theater in Washington. We were obliged to rehearse the show as soon as we arrived. I didn't know any of the band numbers but I was playing the third parts and Harold Baker was a big help in directing me as to what would take place in certain places. The arrangements were not really hard but very effective and I did a fairly good job for the first day.

I had heard about Dick Wilson being a great tenor player before I joined the band and he was considered on a par with Herschel Evans. To me, his tone was not as heavy as Herschel's but his musical ideas were great and he was a hard swinger. I soon found out that Dick was a very heavy drinker. We became great friends within a few days. Big Jim would drink and eat, and so did I, but Dick ate almost nothing. His drinking did not show in his playing.

There was a liquor store near the theater which gave credit to the people working there. There was also a joint across the street from the stage entrance that sold juice and stayed open all night. I hung out with Dick in this place after our last shows until I could not keep my eyes open and would leave him there almost every morning. I lived at a boarding house just in front of the theater. When we closed at the Howard, I had a liquor bill of $45 and the salary was $85 for the week, $70 when the taxes were deducted. Because of Dick Wilson I had spent a big part of it drinking.

The next week we opened at the Famous Door on 52nd Street for one month. The Door was not a very large place but it did good business because the customers never stayed very long and the drinks were quite expensive, which was normal for a place that presented first-class orchestras and attractions.

Shortly before we finished at the Door, Dick became ill and was taken to the Harlem hospital. No one thought that this sickness was serious and all agreed that the rest would be good for him. Al Sears was engaged to sub for Dick and he had a style that suited the band.

After the Famous Door gig, the band hit the road, which was the custom for the Kirk band. The first date was at an amusement park for one night in Montreal, Canada. It was considered usual for the band to make a jump of 500 or more miles from one place to another in a bus and play only one night. I had done plenty of one-nighters with Clarence Paige, Wes Helvey, and Scott, but they were seldom over a couple of hundred miles.

Our next date was in some town in Delaware, two nights later. As we were obliged to pass through New York City I decided to stop there to visit Dick Wilson in the hospital and rejoin the band the next day. When I arrived at the hospital after checking into a hotel, it was past the visiting time, but they allowed me to visit him. There must have been at least 50 beds of sick men in the ward where Dick was and one of the nurses led me to his bed. He was really happy to see me because he had no real friend in New York and therefore no one had visited him. He told me in a voice that was just a little above a whisper that his feet had swollen up and been opened to drain out the liquid. His voice was weak but he seemed to be alright otherwise. He also told me that they gave him a shot of whisky every day, but only one, and if he could find someone that would get him a pint, then everything would be alright. He actually wanted me to say that I would bring him a bottle of juice, but that was out of the question.

The next day I rejoined the band and after the gig in Delaware, we went into the Pearl Theater in Baltimore, Maryland, for one week and then hit the road for some dates in the Deep South. It was my first time as far as Nashville and Knoxville, Tennessee, Atlanta, Georgia, and Birmingham, Alabama.

I had heard many true stories about things that had happened to Negro musicians in the South and was being careful that nothing would cause me any trouble. But the night we played in Knoxville, something happened.

Ted Donnelly and I were rooming together and a couple of local musicians he knew came to the dance. When we finished work, we got together with them in our room and started having a beer-drinking party. A girl who worked in the bar of the hotel was serving us in our room and we were getting more and more groovy with every glass. Finally the girl came in with another order of beer and those two guys started playing with her and had her on the bed. Naturally the chick jumped salty and finally the fellows let her go. She took away some empty glasses and later came back accusing someone of having taken $10 from her apron pocket. She wanted it back or else she was going to call the police.

I knew that I had not taken anything from her because I had not put my hands on her. The guys that were wrestling with her claimed that they had not taken her money. Nobody was guilty and 20 minutes later we were looking into the mugs of two red-faced cops. I realized I was in the Deep South when one of them said, "This gal says that one of you niggers took ten dollars from her and we's a-tellin' yah that if the nigger that took it don't give it back, we gon' take y'all to jail."

And that's where we went because no one would admit that they had stolen the $10 from the girl's pocket. Ted and I had about the same amount of money on us because we had not been paid for the week. At the police station we were searched and I had $7 and a small pocket knife. When the policeman behind the desk saw the small knife, he said, "Damn nigger. You ain't got damn near nothing." They were used to taking long switchblade knives from black men when they were arrested. Ted had one.

But there I was in jail again and I had not done anything wrong. For some reason, I did not give any thought to what would happen the next morning. We were not taken to court and I've always thought that something was phony about the deal. About 9.30 we were taken out of our cell, brought to the desk of the police station, and given our belongings except our money. They said our trial would be heard two days later and they were keeping our money as bond, but we never heard any more about the affair.

Floyd Smith got a real kick out of what had happened. He had an 8 mm. camera and caught us coming out of jail.

It was in Raleigh, North Carolina, where we were playing a dance, that we received word that Dick Wilson had died. Suddenly all the spirit went out of the band. I never heard the Clouds of Joy play as bad as they did that night. Then I started to feel a little angry with all of them except Al Sears, because they had known Dick much longer than I did and had not even made an effort to see him before he passed away.

After some dates in a few other Southern cities we played a night at the Golden Gate Ballroom in the Apple. Buddy Miller was not there when we started the night. The second orchestra was a pick-up band under the leadership of Leon "Bossman" Gross. Leon had Ben Smith, an alto man, with him, and Andy asked him if he would play a set with the band until Buddy came. Buddy played most of the first alto parts and this fellow was reading them as though he had been playing them for years. When Buddy did show up he was too drunk to play. Andy fired Buddy then and there and hired Ben Smith.

We left New York that morning after the dance, hit the road, and finally arrived in St. Louis, Missouri, where we had a two-week engagement strictly for whites. I had a feeling I was on pilgrimage when we rolled into town because I had heard so much talk about St. Louis being a swinging musical town and the fine jazz musicians that came from there. The dance hall closed early enough for me to be able to make the round of some of the clubs. But time had caught up with St. Louis and although I heard some swinging cats and jammed with some of them, I didn't notice any difference in a good orchestra there and a good one in Cincinnati, Chicago or New York. I ran into a few musician friends there including the trumpet player George Hudson, whom I knew since my first trip to Buffalo, and Una Mae Carlisle, whom I had met in Harlem and Paris.

I was in St. Louis on Sunday 7 December 1941 when the extra edition of newspapers came out with the news that the Japanese had bombed Pearl Harbor, but I really got the news from Al Sears, who came to my room in the Booker Washington Hotel and told me that he was going to have his family leave New York because he thought that the Japanese might bombard the Apple next.

During the week, Shorty Baker, who was Mary Lou Williams's old man, had a dispute with her, gave Andy his notice, and said that he was going to stay in St. Louis. I think that he had even agreed to work with some orchestra. So Andy contacted his booking agent, Joe Glaser, and asked him to send a trumpet player to replace Harold. Two days before we closed, a trumpeter named Howard McGhee arrived. Andy Kirk called a rehearsal for the next afternoon and when I arrived McGhee was there. But he was not warming up his instrument or his chops; he was playing piano, and he really could play the box.

Then the day arrived for us to leave St. Louis and Shorty Baker had changed his mind and couldn't stand to let his sweet Mary Lou leave him. It seemed as though Mary Lou might have left the band if Andy hadn't agreed to take Shorty back and Andy didn't want to lose Mary Lou, so he was stuck with four trumpeters because McGhee had been sent to him by Glaser, and he was obliged to keep him.

The bus driver stopped a few miles outside of St. Louis to gas up and I wanted to take a leak. So I went inside the station and asked one of the attendants if I could use the toilet. From inside of the station one could see when cars were coming from either direction and this fellow told me I could, but to make it fast. I wasn't supposed to be seen coming out of the toilet by a white customer.

We played a one-nighter in Little Rock, Arkansas, and then went on to Chicago where Kirk had a month's engagement at the Grand Terrace, one of the biggest and best-known clubs in the city. One night Tiny Bradshaw came to the club with a party, sat with his back to the band, and didn't speak to anyone in the orchestra. He certainly knew me because we had worked together in Luis Russell's orchestra at the Roseland, and he must have known Andy Kirk. But Tiny had had success as a bandleader, mostly in the southern states, and success had gone to his head. A few nights later, Duke Ellington came to the club with a party. As he danced and passed in front of the bandstand, he smiled and nodded at each member of the band. What a difference between that great artist and Tiny Bradshaw, who thought that he was God Almighty.

I didn't have the opportunity to visit any other clubs in Chicago because they were closed when we finished. After two weeks in the Grand Terrace, Andy gave me two weeks' notice because he wanted to add a second trombone. I had not been engaged by his agency and the brass section was not balanced with one trombone. Henry Wells had left the band before we came to Chicago and not long after 1 January 1942, I was back in the Apple again.

TEN

JAZZ IN WARTIME

I started getting odd gigs again. Some of them were with the great Fats Waller, who was doing theater dates of one to three days in small towns of New York, Massachusetts, Connecticut, and New Jersey. Dave McRae, an alto player, was the one who engaged the musicians for the big band Fats was using. We were Jacques Butler, Johnny "Bugs" Hamilton (Fats's regular trumpet man), and myself (trumpets), Herb Flemming (trombone), Cedric Wallace (bass), Al Casey (guitar), Arthur Trappier (drums), Bob Carroll (tenor sax), and there was another alto sax whose name I've forgotten.

Fats was a natural hit everywhere we played. As Bugs Hamilton had been with Fats a long time, he was normally the leader of the trumpet section because he had parts that he played when Fats only used a small combo. He would give Jacques Butler and me the solos that he didn't care for. Sometimes when his lips were not feeling too strong, Bugs would ask me or Jacques to take one of the solos he enjoyed. If his lips were in good shape the next day, he would play the solos again. Jacques and I decided to have a discussion with him about that and he agreed that we should have our regular featured solos.

These gigs were on a weekly basis and sometimes there would be periods of two or three weeks when Fats did not use a big band. Whenever he did, the same musicians were usually available. We had a few days once in upstate New York when Fats was suffering with the gout in one foot. His doctor had advised him not to drink any whisky but told him that he could drink a little wine. So Fats had a gallon jug of muscatel wine in his dressing room every day. He would invite the musicians to drink with him, but he drank most of the gallon.

When I was working at the Ubangi Club with Leon Abbey I was approached one day by a fellow named Roger Kramer who had arrived from Egypt. I had met his brother Leon in Alexandria. Roger told me that he had been in France singing with Arthur Briggs. He was intending to change his name from Kramer to Kay and he wanted to form an orchestra with my co-operation.

We were still working on the project while I was gigging with Fats but in July I was contacted to replace a trumpeter in Noble Sissle's orchestra. The first appearance was at the Howard Theater in Washington, DC. The musicians were: Wendell Culley, Clarence Wheeler, George Wingfield, and Bill Coleman (trumpets), Chester "Butch" Burrell and Herb Flemming (trombones), Ben Whitted and Jerome "Don" Pasquall (alto saxes), Harvey Brooks (piano), Teddy

Giles (bass), Olivette Miller (harp), Wilbur Kirk (drums), and Noble Sissle (vocalist).

I had seen Sissle in some shows that he had co-produced with Eubie Blake in which he had a leading role. But although they weren't bad and some had played in theaters downtown, his acting was always corny to me. He had no real jazz feeling and his type of orchestra was commercial, but sad commercial. I must acknowledge that there were some excellent musicians in the band, jazzwise and classical, but Sissle possessed such bad taste to my estimation that the saying, "a band is no better than its leader" was truer in this case than ever.

A few drinkers in the band had told me that Sissle hated drinking and one had to be cool with the bottle. One night at the Howard Theater, time had been called for the show and as I had a small bottle of juice I was going to take a gulp. I was behind a curtain when I saw Sissle coming out of his dressing room and he was watching me. When I came on the bandstand he told me, so that all the musicians could hear him, that if he ever caught me drinking on his bandstand, he would send me back to New York immediately. I didn't care for him even before I was engaged in his band, but that made me dislike him more. But musicians have their tricks and we managed to get some drinks by sending the band's valet to buy a bottle of bootleg whisky and for each of us a bottle of Coca-Cola, which we would half empty first and then fill up again with the whisky. Sissle was suspicious but didn't say anything.

When the week was finished in Washington, we left for the South, my second time to go deep into it. We played some of the places where I had been with Kirk and finally came to Florida. We stayed a couple of days in Miami and played in Orlando, Tampa, and Jacksonville.

In Tampa I was surprised to see Earl "Inky" Tremble. The last time I had seen him was in 1935 when we played together in Paige's orchestra. Inky had joined some unknown orchestra because nothing much was happening in Cincy. He had gone south with this band and was now making Tampa his home. I had time to have a ball with him and some of his musician friends before we left for Jacksonville.

The following date was on an army camp, where we played a benefit performance. When we arrived, we asked for a place to wash up and freshen ourselves. I had my shaving kit with me but Sissle didn't have his razor and wanted to shave, so I let him use my safety razor. I finished washing up and left Sissle in the washroom. We did the show and when it was over, I asked Sissle what had he done with my razor. He said he had left it in the washroom. He didn't even thank me for the use of it. When I went to get it, I found it on the wash stand full of hair. He had not even cleaned it and that caused me to dislike him more than I had before.

We left for Atlanta, Georgia. We did a lot of night traveling and one time, as the bus pulled into a gas station early in the morning, the stopping of the bus woke me and I began to get thirsty for a nice drink of cold water. I mentioned this to one of the musicians, who told me that there was a water fountain inside the gas station. I went in, saw the fountain, and started to drink. Some of the others were drinking Cokes or eating candy. There was only one man serving. I drank and

JAZZ IN WARTIME / 139

drank and the water tasted so good that even when I had enough, I decided to take a few more swallows for good measure. At that moment someone tapped me on the shoulder and when I looked up, it was Sissle. He said, "The man behind the counter is talking to you." I turned to face the fellow and he said with his cracker accent, "Boy, don't drink out of that fountain. That fountain is for white folks, use that dipper up there." I looked up on the top of the fountain and there was a dipper that looked as though it had been on a city dump for ten years before someone found it and put it there for Negroes! I really didn't feel thirsty any more and went back to the bus.

We did a few more dates in Tennessee and North Carolina and then a week in Detroit at the Paradise Theater, where I gave my notice to Sissle because I had had enough of his band. I would maybe have considered staying longer if he had offered me a raise but he would have preferred cutting off his right hand than do that.

In the meantime I had received letters and telegrams from Roger Kay asking me to hurry back to New York because he was going to take a combo into a new club and he wanted me to join him. I played my last date with Sissle in Louisville, and took an early train to Cincinnati, where I stayed a couple of days to visit my parents and the rest of the family, saw a few old friends and returned to the Apple.

Things had meanwhile turned unfortunate for Roger Kay. He had formed an orchestra with a white drummer, Jim Chapin, a Canadian pianist, a well-known white bassist, Sid Weiss, and Lem Davis, an alto man who had a style something like Pete Brown.

The trumpet chair had been left open for me and the band had worked two weeks in a club located at 152 East 55th Street before I returned. But Roger was not in the band when I came because Sid Weiss had pulled a dirty trick on him.

Roger didn't have a voice as good as he thought and didn't get much success. Sid wanted to get rid of him. He knew that Roger didn't belong to the Union and he had reported him. A Union delegate had come to the club and told Roger he could not work as he was not a member of Local 802.

Sid had promised Roger that he would take charge of the band until I arrived and collect the salary. He said he would give Roger his leader's fee as Roger was the one that had found the job and formed the group. But the boss had cut Roger's salary as he wasn't there any more. Business was not good, and within two weeks after I had joined the band the place was closed. We did a radio show but that was the end of Roger Kay's dream of being a singer and bandleader.

I gigged and did many Sunday afternoon jam sessions at Jimmy Ryan's and a few in Boston at the Ken Club. Once in Boston I jammed with Pete Brown and another time with Coleman Hawkins. The sessions at Jimmy Ryan's, which was across the street from the Famous Door and the Three Deuces on 52nd Street, were presented by Milt Gabler, who owned the Commodore Record Shop near Grand Central Station on East 42nd Street. Jack Crystal, who worked in Milt's record shop, was in charge of the sessions, which featured many well-known black and white musicians: Art Hodes, Pee Wee Russell, Bobby Hackett, George

Wettling, Rod Cless, Sid Catlett, Hank Duncan, Sandy Williams, Wild Bill Davison, and Oran "Hot Lips" Page, to name a few. These sessions really jumped; there were always two bottles of whisky furnished by Milt to get them in a swinging mood. The closing number was always *Bugle Call Rag* and I'm certain that there were never so many different bugle calls played in any other club in the world as were played in Jimmy Ryan's.

I was sharing a three-room furnished apartment on 161st Street with my brother, who was a tailor, when Al Hall, whom I had not seen for some time, called by. He told me he was working the Café Society Uptown with Billy Moore (guitar) and Ellis Larkins (piano). He asked me if I would like to replace Billy Moore, who was sick in hospital. I was surprised because Teddy Wilson had told me two years before that Barney Josephson never wanted Al and me in his place again. I accepted the job until Billy came out of hospital. That night I met Ellis Larkins. He was from Baltimore and had been studying at Juilliard School of Music on a scholarship he had won in his home town.

Teddy Wilson was still in the club with Joe Thomas (trumpet), John Williams (bass), and Sid Catlett (drums). I don't remember who was playing sax but Benny Morton was still with the band. The show had Hazel Scott, the Golden Gate Quartet, two dancers, the Craft Sisters, and Pete Johnson and Albert Ammons, the two boogie-woogie pianists. With our trio of piano, bass, and trumpet, we took care of the dancing. It was the first time that I had played with only piano and bass.

After two weeks, Barney was satisfied and we had a big success with the public, so Billy Moore was out and I was in. We had a salary of $80 a week.

A couple of months after I had been working at the Café Society, Hazel Scott went to Hollywood to play in a movie. Barney went also because he was Hazel's manager. His brother Leon was directing the club. Mildred Bailey was engaged to sing while Hazel was away.

One night a young Swedish fellow, whom I drank with in the White Rose, came to the club pretty well pickled. Time came for the last show and as I passed the bar, this fellow was sitting there and invited me to have a drink with him. I ordered something and then I had to go to the men's room, which was on the second floor. I asked my friend to hold my horn. When I came back, Leon Josephson was furious. The Golden Gate Quartet had gone on while I was away. I was told that the only sound in the place was the song the Gates were singing when suddenly there was a blast that gave the public a start. The young Swedish guy had tried to blow my horn. Leon blamed me for leaving my horn with him and told me I was fired. I told him not to yell at me and if I was fired to give me my two weeks' notice. Ellis Larkins was nervous and thought that would be the end of the trio, but I came to work the next night and Leon didn't say a word about what had happened.

Barney came back and Leon told him that we had had a run-in. He asked me what had happened and I told him my side of the story. The only thing that Barney had to say was that he thought that I was a little too continental! He probably meant that I had too much nerve and pride for a black man. But everything went smoothly afterwards.

World War II had been going on for nearly two years for America. The trio was beginning to become popular. We co-starred with Hazel Scott for a benefit to buy watches for the Soviet Army. It took place at Carnegie Hall on 11 April 1943. The trio did a few numbers and for the finale we were joined by trombonist Frank Orchard and trumpeter Jack Butler.

One night at the club, just before we took the stand, Ellis Larkins in the process of lighting a cigarette burned a finger on his left hand and was not able to play. Mary Lou Williams (who had played with Andy Kirk's orchestra) was not working and she agreed to replace Ellis for a few nights. But in the meantime we had to go on because Teddy Wilson had finished his set. So we asked Sid Catlett to play with us until Mary Lou arrived. With Sid on drums and Al Hall being the solid bass player that he was, the piano was hardly missed. Mary Lou arrived during the first show and stayed with us for four days. It was real groovy because Ellis was a nice smooth pianist but Mary Lou had more feeling for jazz, a heavier touch, and could swing more than him.

Quite a number of musicians were in the army or navy and, as salaries were going up in many jobs, we figured that it would be the right time to ask Barney for a raise. Barney told us that he thought we deserved one, but didn't say he would give us one. When we received the next pay check, there was a message in it, telling us that we had two more weeks in the club. Gene Fields's trio replaced us.

On 15 June there was one of the biggest concerts ever given anywhere at that time. It was in Philadelphia and was sponsored by Sammy Price, the boogie and blues pianist, and Dan Burley, a reporter for a Negro newspaper in New York, the *Amsterdam News*, who was also a pianist and exponent of a rhythm called skiffle. They formed the Basin Street Swing Club and for this session, which started at 1.30 p.m. and finished at 6 p.m., it was a jumping afternoon in Philly. The line-up read like the *Who's Who* in jazz: Sidney De Paris, Chelsea Quealey, Jacques Butler, and Bill Coleman (trumpets), Benny Morton, Brad Gowans, Sandy Williams, and Wilbur De Paris (trombones), Pee Wee Russell, Edmond Hall, Milton "Mezz" Mezzrow (clarinets), Eugene Sedric (tenor sax), Al Hall (bass), Jack Bland (guitar), Danny Alvin and Sid Catlett (drums), Art Hodes, Dick Carey, Ellis Larkins, and Sammy Price (piano).

A club in the Village called Tony Pastor's started giving Sunday afternoon jam sessions, which were presented by Frankie Newton. Some well-known jazz names took part in these get-togethers. Sessions were jumping also at the Village Vanguard, Eddie Condon's club, and Nick's, all situated in Greenwich Village.

The owner of the Village Vanguard, Max Gordon, and a naturalized Frenchman, named Herbert Jacoby, opened a swank club at 152 East 55th Street, the same address that Roger Kay had put a band in. It was called the Blue Angel and it clicked with the high society from the first night it opened. Our trio, which was known as the Ellis Larkins trio, was engaged along with a singer, Claude Alphand, whom, I was told, was the wife of the French Ambassador to the USA. She sang in French. The other attractions were the Bernard Brothers, who did pantomime and a colored girl singer from Canada whose name was Gwyn Tines.

This was the easiest job I ever had during my many years as a jazz musician, and the 52nd Street musicians were really jealous because we didn't start working until 10.30 p.m. and finished at 2 a.m. Claude Alphand had her own accompanist and the Bernards didn't need us for their act.

Gwyn was a very nice-looking brown-skin girl who must have weighed about 120 pounds. She could drink like a fish and never was tipsy. She also smoked, but it never bothered her voice, which was fine and jazzy. I don't think she ever made any records. We treated her like a little sister and when the club closed for the Christmas and New Year holidays, which was very rare in the nightclub business, Gwyn cried on our shoulders because she would not be with us when the club opened again.

I had taken part in several recording sessions during the year 1943: 16 November with Sammy Price and his Blusicians; 8 December with the Coleman Hawkins Orchestra; 21 December with the Lester Young Orchestra. On 16 November I also recorded with the orchestra of Roy Eldridge but I didn't have any solos on that set.

After New Year's Day, when we started again at the Blue Angel, the attractions were the same except for a girl singer named Evelyn Knight. Evelyn was white and came from Washington, DC. Her manager was a commander (or had been) in the navy. We soon found out that Evelyn didn't have much experience because she would skip measures in some of the songs. She began to like us very well. We were able to follow her when she missed the timing in a song and after a few weeks of working with us she became more confident and made fewer mistakes.

Eventually Evelyn was engaged to do a radio show where Paul Whiteman presented an artist every week. I was told that Whiteman also owned some stock in the radio station. Evelyn wanted us to accompany her but someone at the station couldn't stand to see three Negro musicians accompanying a pretty white woman on that show because it was a broadcast done in a studio where the public were invited. So the pianist, bassist, and a trumpet player from Whiteman's studio orchestra came to the Blue Angel anonymously for a few nights to listen and try to copy the way we played behind Evelyn. I heard the broadcast because it was before I went to work. Evelyn skipped a measure in one of the songs and the cats accompanying her didn't know how to cover up for her.

Later during our run at the Angel, Evelyn received an offer to do a broadcast once a week for 13 weeks on Station WJZ providing that the program passed the test demanded by the show's sponsor. We never found out who it was but we were accepted and the program went very well. Evelyn was pleased and so were we because the loot we received was not bad and gave us extra money.

But our success didn't last very long. When we appeared at the studio for the second week's broadcast, we were given notice that our services would not be required after one more broadcast. We were told that the reason was because it was a special program that was heard only in the South and it would cause trouble if it was known in the southern states that Evelyn was white and the musicians Negroes. I never believed that story. Someone at the radio station just didn't like the idea that three black musicians were making good money, so a white trio was taken from the studio and they copied the way we accompanied Evelyn and she did ten more broadcasts without us.

After quite a few months at the Angel we began to feel that we were liked and popular enough to ask for a raise in salary. We got exactly the same answer from Jacoby that Barney Josephson had given us when we had asked him for a raise: "You boys deserve a raise." When we received our pay envelope at the end of the week, there was a two-week notice. Herman Chittison took a trio in after we left and had a very nice guitarist with him, Everett Barksdale.

We started getting some jobs from Joe Glaser's booking agency and once we had an afternoon party to play for a very wealthy family who owned the Hotel Astor. The party was in honor of a son who was a medical ensign in the navy and all the young men who were invited were in the navy also. During one of the times when we had stopped playing to have a few drinks, we got into a conversation with an ensign who said that he was from New Orleans. He told us how much he liked our music and talked about the times when he and some of his relatives and friends would go places on Saturday night to watch the "Oxford Greys" sing, dance, and listen to them play. I didn't grasp the meaning of "Oxford Greys" for a long time and then it came to me that he was talking about Negroes.

We later worked in a very large bar in Newark, New Jersey. The place was circular and the bandstand was in the center. New Jersey was full of crackers and as there was a white girl singing with us some of them didn't like it and spoke to the manager about it. So we worked there for one month and quit the job as we didn't care much about working there either.

Then we were engaged to work in quite a nice place a few miles from Philadelphia. Ellis Larkins came to the job an hour late the first day, with his clothes looking as though he had slept in them for a month. The boss was not very satisfied from the beginning and neither was Al or myself. Al's parents lived in Philly and we stayed with them. Ellis would take a train to New York every morning and one to come back to the job. He was drinking like a fish and looking like a bum. We talked to him about his appearance but it went in one ear and out the other. We were given our notice after the first week. That was the end of the trio.

Al and I started rehearsing with Mary Lou Williams, who had enjoyed the way we sounded when she had replaced Ellis at the Café Society Uptown. After a few rehearsals, we recorded for a small company called Asch Records on 10 August 1944. We cut six sides: *Russian Lullaby, Blue Skies, Persian Rug, Night and Day, You Know Baby*, and *I found a New Baby*. One of the best numbers was *Night and Day*. The three of us had put our ideas together and Mary Lou wrote the arrangement. Another one I liked very well was *You Know Baby*, on which composer Frank Lewis co-operated with Mary Lou and gave me a few extra bucks to sing. But my voice was under-recorded because Asch thought that I was singing too loud. His studio was quite small and so was his sound cabin and he almost faded me out completely on the singing chorus. Two versions of this number were recorded.

Later Asch recorded two numbers with singer Josh White. The line-up was

Mary Lou, myself, Eddie Dougherty on drums, and Jimmy Butts on bass. We cut *Minute Man* and *Froggy Bottom*.

September found us rehearsing with a show that was to make propaganda for the re-election of President Franklin D. Roosevelt. Jack "the Bear" Parker was added on drums and the trio became a quartet. The other members of the troupe were: Will Geer, who was famous on the Broadway theater circuit for the role he played for years in *Tobacco Road*; Roland Smith, a singer well known in Europe and high-society clubs in the States; the late Woodie Guthrie, a guitarist and great folksinger; Woodie's partner Cisco Houston; Jack de Merchant, a singer; Laura Duncan, who had sung in many Negro shows in Harlem and on Broadway; Bernie Hern, a comedian; William Korff; Daniel Nagrin; Helen Tamiris, a classical dancer; and Princess Orelia and Pedro, who had a fine Cuban dance act. The name of the show was People's Band Wagon and it was produced and directed by Edward Royce, whose wife was a classical pianist and accompanied most of the acts. The show was composed of jive, satirical skits, dances, songs and political pep talks, strumming the nation for President Roosevelt. That's what one newspaper critic wrote about the show.

When we hit the road and played Boston, the show was picketed by the Republicans and there was an effort made to close the show. There was almost a panic in the theater when someone shot off a bunch of firecrackers, but the show continued.

We were doing one-night stands and played Chicago, Indianapolis, Milwaukee, St. Louis, and some cities that I've forgotten as we were moving around so fast. The last performance was in New York City on 30 October at the Manhattan Center. The show was a big success everywhere and Adam Clayton Powell Jr. made a speech at the Manhattan Center before the show started which put everybody in high gear. Mr. Roosevelt won the re-election, which made all of us feel as though we had had a hand in his victory.

On 15 December 1944, Mary Lou recorded three numbers for Asch with seven musicians who included Coleman Hawkins, Claude Green (clarinet), Joe Evans (alto sax), Eddy Robinson (bass), Denzil Best (drums), and me. We recorded *Song in my Soul*, *This and That*, and *Carcinoma*. Then there was another session, where we cut *Lady be Good*, with Jack "the Bear" Parker replacing Denzil Best and Al Lucas in place of Eddy Robinson on bass.

We had a real fine trio because we rehearsed well and the arrangements that Mary Lou did were in the groove. Meantime, Al Hall was engaged for the radio show of Mildred Bailey's and that was the reason he was not on the last Asch session.

We heard that Mary Lou had been offered a job at Kelly's Stable for the trio at a salary of $500 a week. Al and I were expecting to get $150 a week and Mary Lou would have $200 because she was the leader of the trio and arranger. But nothing happened and we never knew if the rumor was true because we didn't ask Mary Lou about the deal. So we were rehearsing with no work in view and the trio drifted apart. Later I heard that we had been supposed to go into the Downbeat Club on 52nd Street if Mary Lou could get her 802 Union card as she was on transfer and could not take a regular job until she became a full member of Local 802.

Mildred Bailey was featuring one or two known musicians on her weekly show and she asked me to do a number one week. I wanted to do *Russian Lullaby* and asked Mary Lou to make a lead sheet of the arrangement we had recorded for the staff arranger of Mildred's show. When the day came for the rehearsal, Al, who had seen his part, told me that it was not arranged in the key we recorded it in, which was C for the piano, and that this arrangement was in F. The director of the orchestra, Paul Baron, was a well-known conductor and arranger also. He told the musicians what key they should transpose it to and that was all. Those studio musicians are the best. In the orchestra there was Charlie Shavers, Roy Eldridge, and a well-known white studio trumpeter, Jimmy Maxwell. Teddy Wilson was the pianist, Al Hall was on bass, and Specs Powell on drums. The rest of the musicians I didn't know. That night when it came my time to go on, everything went very well. But I have often wondered what Mary Lou had in mind when she made the score for me to play that number.

While I'm talking about recordings, I almost forgot to mention that in March 1944 I did another recording session with Lester Young and his Kansas City Six. I was overwhelmed with joy to play with them, especially Lester Young. We recorded *I got Rhythm, Jo-Jo, Three Little Words*, and *Four O'Clock Drag*.

Came Christmas and the New Year of 1945, and John Kirby contacted me for a concert gig. There were a few changes from the original musicians who had helped make Kirby the Greatest Little Big Band in the World. In place of Russell Procope there was George Johnson, Bill Beason was the drummer, and Ram Ramirez had replaced Billy Kyle on piano. When we arrived at the place we were to play Buster Bailey and I found a quiet corner and he instructed me on how some of the numbers went. Of course everything was written and only a musician with experience in reading music could make it in that band. A few days later, Kirby asked me if I would like to go to California with him. That was another case of "Have horn, will travel." I had never been to California. I wasn't working and had no great love in New York to hold me there, so it was California here I come.

It was not possible to have Pullman service at the time, because they were reserved for military personnel and transportation of wounded soldiers and sailors, so we had to be satisfied with making the five-day trip in reclining seats. We left New York in February and I really enjoyed the trip because I always did get a kick out of traveling and I had never been further west than Denver, Colorado. I got my one and only view of Las Vegas one night when the train stopped there for about 45 minutes.

There was not much we could do on this long trip because there was no lounge car where we could play cards or other games. Some of the stops in different cities would be as long as two or three hours, and there we had a chance to buy some juice, which we would pass around amongst us and pray that we had enough to last until the next long stop. We bought quite a number of paper-bag lunches as it would be hours between stops and there was no restaurant car on the train. There was a war going on and the most comfortable and convenient trains were for government use.

Kirby was engaged to play a month in a place called Burton's Lounge and

Burton's was one of the two night clubs run by Negroes in Oakland. For one week, Buster Bailey and I got together on the Kirby book which, I must admit, was one of the toughest that I ever had to tackle. One of the hardest numbers I ever played was the arrangement of *Whiteman Stomp* by Charlie Dixon, the Fletcher Henderson banjo player. But most of the numbers in Kirby's book were arranged by Charlie Shavers: Charlie was as tough an arranger as Dixon. By the end of the week I could play some of the numbers without looking at the music.

We played a matinee every afternoon, from five to seven and then from 10 p.m. until 2 a.m. every night. There were plenty of sailors in town because there was a naval base near Oakland. So the town and the joints were jumping. The prostitutes were getting rich and uppity. Even those that looked like wolephants were getting difficult. "Wolephant" is the name that Arvell Shaw, the bass player, called ugly chicks: a mixture of wolf and elephant.

Kirby had a contract at Burton's for only one month, and when our time was up he didn't have a job for the band but his agent was working on a deal. Meanwhile we had a gig in a town about 50 miles from Oakland but Bill Beason had gone back to New York without saying anything to anyone or giving Kirby notice. However Kirby found a guy to replace Beason and we left for a gig in two rented cars. Kirby drove one and Burton the other. Burton had arranged the gig.

Burton wore very thick glasses and as we were going to the gig he told us that he had been drafted in the army but was discharged because his eyesight was bad and one night he had driven a truck into one of the barracks on the army post. It was beginning to get dark and we noticed that whenever a car was coming at us from the opposite direction, Burton would slow down from the 45 miles an hour he was doing. I began to believe Burton's story about his discharge from the army and didn't feel too secure.

The gig went well enough because of the drummer being new and not acquainted with the arrangements. We packed up and started back to Oakland following the car Kirby was driving. Kirby could drive and before we had gone one mile we couldn't see his tail lights. Burton was rolling along at the exhausting speed of about 20 miles an hour and it was a good thing that he was not going faster because suddenly we were off the road, leaning to the right at a 20 degree angle. Burton had managed to stop the car and when I looked to the right there was a river about three feet from where we were sitting.

We got out of the car on the left side and Burton got it back on the road. Everybody was really worried now. We were rolling along at a fast 20 miles an hour again and suddenly we felt the car jumping as though all four tyres had gone flat. I sat up to find what was happening and saw that we were on a rail road track. We were actually going along on the track. George Johnson and I looked back at the same time and saw the big headlight of a locomotive. George had opened the door of the car before I could move and was ready to jump, but then we saw that the locomotive was standing still. It was a good thing it wasn't moving because if it had, this story would never had been told. How Burton happened to get on the track is a mystery. This was one of the most miserable nights I ever had in a car.

Jack McVea was a tenor man in San Francisco who was very well known on the West Coast. He had a band in a place called Jack's Tavern. For his first anniversary there, the owner celebrated with a turkey dinner and cocktails starting at 2 p.m. The John Kirby orchestra was invited and it was really a ball. A jam session was the order of the afternoon and McVea started it rolling with Cappy Oliver (trumpet), Chuck Bailey (piano), Rabon Tarrant (drums), and Frank Clarke, the bass-playing brother of Kenny Clarke. Then the Kirby band played some numbers, after which the two bands joined together for a super jam session. I sort of fell in love with San Francisco because of that swinging party.

Our next move came a couple of weeks after we finished at Burton's Lounge We were engaged to play in San Diego at a place called the Silver Slipper. We left San Francisco on a train that carried no heavy luggage and only went to Bakersfield. From there we took a bus to San Diego. The trip was beautiful and we arrived there early in the afternoon. We went to the club, which was in the downtown section of the city. The club was a run-down joint. We had to wait there until our baggage arrived as it was sent on another train.

I got the urge for a drink and the bar in the joint wasn't open. I came out and saw a bar across the street but for some reason I didn't feel like going in there. I decided to walk to the next corner of the street, but there was no bar, so across the street I went. Things were real quiet inside. I stood at the bar for about four minutes and the barman passed me a few times. Finally he came and asked me what could he do for me. I said, "Give me a drink of whisky with a beer chaser." But he told me, "You've had enough to drink." I was surprised and I answered that I had not had anything to drink and that was why I came in there. He looked at me and said, "I don't care what you say, I said you've had enough to drink." And then it hit me. I said, "Oh you mean that you don't serve colored people in here!" "I'm not saying that, I'm only telling you that you've had enough to drink." Then I realized the reason for the silence when I came in. Everybody in the place was eyeing me and listening to what was said between the barman and me. I could do nothing but walked out.

I was surprised because I had been in plenty of bars in downtown Oakland and nothing like that had happened. That caused me to dislike San Diego, and the atmosphere at the Silver Slipper didn't help me to like the town either, because the people in general were not very friendly.

Benny Waters, the tenor sax man I had worked with in Charlie Johnson's Small's Paradise orchestra, was leading a quartet in a cabaret that was strictly for whites. He came to see me one day and told me that I could come to hear him, but I would have to sit on the bandstand. I had not seen Benny for years and was surprised to meet him so far away from the Apple. I went to hear him, between one of our sets one night, as the place where he was working was very near the Silver Slipper. Benny's wife was playing piano but I don't remember how the band sounded although I do remember that Benny was blowing a lot of alto and tenor.

We finally finished in San Diego and came to Los Angeles, where we stayed in a hotel on 1st and San Pedro which, I was told, was the Japanese quarters before World War II began. After a few days, the hotel started jumping because some of the musicians from Eddie Heywood Jr.'s orchestra were staying there. Buster Bailey and I got together every day with Emmett Berry, the trumpeter, and Keg

Purnell, the drummer. Eddie Heywood was at his height and playing in a club near the hotel.

Buster found a place where it was possible to buy one or more sticks of gage and I did the same thing. Keg liked a taste also, so between us we had some gage and juice every day. The government narcotic agents, known as G-men, were very hard on marijuana in California and we were really taking a chance as every door in this hotel had a ventilation opening that could not be blocked or closed in any manner. It was said that an agent was living in the hotel but nothing happened to us.

After a week in Los Angeles we went to work at the Plantation Club, which was a few miles outside of the city limits. Kirby hired a big car to take us to the Plantation, which I remember as being about one and a half hours away. On the bill with Kirby's orchestra was T-Bone Walker and Betty Roche, who used to sing with Duke Ellington. I had heard of T-Bone but had never seen him in action. He was an outstanding blues singer who accompanied himself on electric guitar. Betty was still a great vocalist.

We worked two weeks at the Plantation and then had a layoff. I was beginning to get lonesome for New York and felt as though I was further away from there now than when I was in Egypt, though I ran into four people in Los Angeles whom I had known back East: Herb Flemming, trombone; Inez Cavanaugh, the wife of Timme Rosenkrantz; the drummer Zutty Singleton; and my old boss and friend, Benny Carter.

Kirby got a gig in some town near LA to do a concert which also fetured T-Bone Walker and Red Nichols with his Five Pennies. I used to buy records by Red when I was still an amateur and I picked up a few things from him although I didn't really go for his style.

T-Bone drove me, Buster, and someone else to the gig. I got more of a kick out of hearing Red Nichols for the first time in person than I did from the old records I had of him. Red had been living in California for years and was almost a forgotten legend. T-Bone went on before us and when we closed the show, he had left and gone back to LA. We had to get back the best way we could and I put T-Bone on my s—t list even if he was a good blues musician.

We did at least three live broadcast shows for the armed forces, which were MC'ed by Ernest Whitman, an actor whom I had seen many times at the Lafayette and Apollo Theaters. Those shows were also recorded on V-disc, but although I heard quite a few V-discs later, there was never one that the Kirby band had done.

On 30 March and 2 April 1945 I did a recording that gave me one of the greatest thrills of my life. Coleman Hawkins had come to Los Angeles and was working at Shepp's Playhouse on 1st Street, just around the corner from my hotel. He was engaged for the recording date and the rest of the lineup was Buster Bailey, Benny Carter, John Kirby, Oscar Moore, Nat "King" Cole, Max Roach, and a girl singer named Kay Starr. It was released under the title of *Capitol International Jazzmen*.

Al Hall had introduced me a few years before to Nat Cole and also to Oscar

Moore, who was Nat's guitarist. They were playing at Kelly's Stable then and had not become well known. I had never heard or met Max Roach. His drumming sent me. Kay Starr was a fine singer who had a real jazz feeling that one associates with a Negro girl singer. We recorded four numbers: *You Can Depend On Me, If I could Be with You, Riffmarole,* and *Stormy Weather* (two versions, one with vocal).

A few nights later Kirby was engaged to do a concert along with some other musicians at the Philharmonic Opera House in LA. This must have been at the beginning of Norman Granz's presentation of Jazz at the Philharmonic, which became famous in later years.

Coleman Hawkins asked me if I would work a couple of weeks with him at Shepp's Playhouse. Howard McGhee was supposed to have come to LA with him but did not show up when Hawk started. I don't remember any of the other musicians who were in the group but it was another great moment in my life to be playing a club date with Hawk and I enjoyed every moment.

When the two weeks were finished, he asked me if I would like to stay longer but Kirby had received an offer to play in a white club in Baltimore. I was lonesome for the Eastern part of the country and Baltimore being only a few hours by train from New York City, I was happy to be going away from Los Angeles. So I refused Hawk's offer and a few days later we were on a train bringing us back east. For the first and last time in my life, I saw part of the state of Texas. It was a beautiful sight to see so many of the foothills and mountains. Many of the landscapes reminded me of some I had seen in hundreds of westerns. I had my camera but no film. They were impossible to obtain because the film companies were supplying films for government needs only, so I missed getting some wonderful shots that would have been pleasant souvenirs.

The trip was five days coming to Baltimore, the same as it had been going to California. When we arrived, Kirby had hired a local pianist and drummer for the club job. (Ram Ramirez had left the orchestra after the Plantation dates.)

There was a white girl named Ginger in the floor show and she was the first woman I ever heard play accordion. I had heard Buster Moten, the nephew of Bennie Moten, playing a piano accordion and he could really swing on it. Ginger was not a jazz accordionist but played a nice commercial style. We often played blackjack between sets and she liked to play the game with us. Baltimore was a Southern city and Negroes and Whites had very little to do with each other, socially speaking. Some of the customers and especially many of the men that came to the club would have wanted to hang us if they had known we were playing cards backstage with a white woman.

We stayed in Baltimore two weeks and then Kirby told us that the job was finished. He didn't give us a plausible reason and none of us pushed the matter because we had not been very keen on the job from the first night we had worked there. So it was back to the Apple and that was the end of the John Kirby band for quite a while.

The only interesting musical thing that happened for me during the next few weeks was a concert at Town Hall on 9 June 1945. It was presented by my old friend Timme Rosenkrantz and the lineup was another *Who's Who* in the jazz world. The concert was recorded. I played two numbers with Billy Taylor, but to my knowledge only one, *Stardust*, was issued.

In July I was engaged by George Johnson to play one month in the Savoy in Boston. A nice little fellow named Johnny Hartzfield was the tenor man and Red Richards was the pianist. Both of them had been in New York for quite some time, but it was the first time I had met them.

I had been in Boston a few times before but I never got too much fun in that town. After one week we were there I decided to have a front tooth taken out. It had rotted away until it was only a half tooth and I wanted a new one put in. Someone gave me the address of a Negro dentist who was considered one of the best dentists in the city.

I went to see him. He took the tooth out and told me that the gum should have to heal before he could install a false one. He gave me an appointment, but when I came back the week after, he apologized and said he had forgot to note the appointment and that he couldn't do anything until the next week. I explained that I would be leaving Boston in a few days. So he gave me the address of another dentist in town. Losing no time I went to see him. The man looked about 75 years old and his office and equipment looked about as old and out of fashion as he did himself. I wanted that tooth put in and decided to risk the chance that everything would be alright. He took a fitting of the tooth and crown and I went back next day to have the work finished.

The following night I could hardly play anything and the last night was almost as bad. What the dentist had done was to put the crown on crooked and the right front tooth was sticking out a fraction of an inch farther than my left front tooth. That disarranged the position of my mouthpiece when I blew. It was quite a few months before I became accustomed to play the way I had done before.

When I returned to New York, I stayed with a girlfriend for a while and then found a room with a tenor player named Bobby Sands. I knew Bobby from when he played with one of Benny Carter's first orchestras. Later he had been with Claude Hopkins. Bobby was a bachelor and had a four-room apartment at Amsterdam Avenue and 161st Street. I had lived in that neighborhood before and liked it very much. I did a few gigs with Bobby and some jam sessions around town.

On 23 September I was back at Town Hall for a concert called BIAJ, which was presented by Specs Powell. BIAJ meant Best in American Jazz. The musicians were Buster Bailey, J.C. Heard (drums), Al Haig (piano), Al Hall (bass), Stuff Smith (violin), Pete Glover (bass), Freddie Jefferson (piano), Teddy Wilson (piano), a percussion duet on tom-toms by Coker and Cimber, Frankie Newton (trumpet), George Wettling (drums), Charlie Parker (alto sax), Al Stein (a 16-year-old saxophone virtuoso), and Four Chicks and Chuck (a vocal group who starred on the Kate Smith Show). The Town Hall concert of Timme Rosenkrantz was eventually issued on an album but BIAJ was not. It should have been, because the concert was every bit as interesting.

ELEVEN

DRUM BOOGIE UNIT 789

One night in October 1945 I was coming out of one of the clubs in 52nd Street and met a drummer named Herbie Cowans, who was known to most musicians as "Cat." Herbie asked me if I would like to go to the Philippines and maybe Japan. I didn't think that he was serious, but I told him yes and gave him my address. A few days later I received a message from Cat saying that the first rehearsal and general meeting would be on 12 October. When I arrived I saw my old friend Edgar "Spider" Courance, Ernest "Bass" Hill, Ben Smith the alto man, and a pianist I had never met, Eddie Allen. We were told by the assistant director of USO shows in New York that we would be getting $95 a week, which was the equivalent of the salary of a colonel at that time. We would receive this amount until we left for the road and then we would get only $25 per week and $70 would be put in a bank on an account. This was the best salary that I had ever made and we rehearsed for six weeks.

During the six weeks we rehearsed we had to take a health examination, which Ben Smith did not pass and Herbie had to replace him. I felt sad about it because besides being a fine musician, Ben was a great person with whom I had plenty of fun. Cat engaged an alto player named Curby Alexander. We had to be inoculated against smallpox, typhus, typhoid, paratyphoid, tetanus, cholera, yellow fever, and even plague. Those shots were really heavy loads to carry and we started taking them the first week of rehearsal. The day after any one of the inoculations my arm would feel as though I had a ton of lead tied to my wrist and I could not put it down. And there was no drinking of kickapoo joy-juice for at least two days after each shot.

During the last two weeks of the rehearsals I worked two nights a week at the Three Deuces on 52nd Street with George Johnson, who replaced the two bands playing there on their nights off, which were Monday and Tuesday. Monday was always the day that I was inoculated and my arm would give me hell. I did not have much inspiration but I tried. One night of the last week I blacked out for a few seconds after some choruses and almost fell on my face. I went out to get some fresh air and my strength came back to me and I was able to finish the night.

Willie Bryant, the ex-bandleader and showman, was the Master of Cere-monies for our group. The girl singer engaged, Melrose Colbert, was, I found out later, the first wife of Ray Nance, the Ellington trumpeter and violin virtuoso.

They were separated. I had never heard of her before but she had a fine voice. There was a comedy act with Henry Matthews, known as "Shorty," and Alfred Chester, known as "Slick." He was the straight man and Shorty was the comedian. There was also a dance team known as Millie and Bubbles. They were married and their name was Martin. Martha Cooke, known as Martha Please, was an acrobatic and fast-tumbling artist.

We were given army officer's uniforms with short jackets and garrison caps, and on the night of 23 November we left New York for San Francisco by train. This time I was making the trip in style because this trip was sponsored by Uncle Sam, who had priority for everything. I had a Pullman berth and ate in the dining car. From San Francisco we were to fly to the Philippines. We were booked in a hotel in San Francisco to await the plane flight. Joe Louis, who happened to be in the city, was staying in the same hotel. We had an interview with one of the leading Negro newspapers and made some photos with Joe.

From the day we arrived in San Francisco, we were on alert, which meant that we should be ready to leave at any hour, but we stayed in Frisco for one week. I became quite friendly with Curby Alexander. Eventually we were notified that we would be leaving the next morning for Hamilton Field, an Air Force base near Frisco. The morning that the Air Force bus came to get us, Willie Bryant was missing. He had taken a train back to New York when he learned that we would be flown to the Philippines. We stayed on the base that night and the next day we were briefed on how to use a Mae West life jacket if something went wrong and the plane would have to ditch in the ocean.

That afternoon we boarded a C-54 and this was a flight for our unit only. We were 12 people with a crew of four in a plane that could carry 60. Our first stop would be at Hickam Field in Honolulu, 2091 miles from San Francisco. This was the first time that any of us had flown in a plane and the pilot told us that we would be flying for 14½ hours before landing at Hickam Field. We didn't have anything to drink other than water, as alcohol was not allowed on the air base or military planes, but we played blackjack and visited the pilot's cabin. That night we ran into some stormy weather which had the plane flying in most every position. The only person who became air sick was the hostess.

Every USO unit had a number and name. Our group was known as Drum Boogie Unit 789. We arrived in Honolulu the next day. Bubbles Martin, who was not feeling well, went to see a doctor at the Hickam Field base hospital. He was put in bed and we were told that we could have passes to go into the city. That was alright with me because I had heard so much about Hawaii and wanted to see what it was like. I didn't expect to see the chicks in grass shirts and I didn't see any. We had no idea about how long we would be in Honolulu but the troupe could not leave one of its members behind. So it happened that we stayed on the island for a week.

We were given a pass every day. On the second night we found a dance hall where some jazz musicians played. The next night we had our instruments and jammed until the joint closed. I saw Pearl Harbor and Waikiki Beach and jammed every night until Bubbles was well enough to continue the voyage. The public of the club was made up of natives and they liked jazz very much. They were used to it and we had a ball.

We left Honolulu for the Philippines. There were stops in Kwajalein, an island in the Pacific Ocean, and Guam. On 12 December we arrived at Nichols Field in Manila and were driven to our quarters in an army weapon carrier. I happened to be sitting at the back end of the truck, which had a canvas top, and when we arrived in the city, the sight that hit my eyes was like a nightmare that had become real. In the middle of the city some buildings were standing, but without roofs or windows. Some were leaning against others that were standing but looked as though they would fall any minute. The destruction was horrifying. It was difficult to imagine how such a terrible catastrophe could be possible.

There were not many USO shows in the Philippines when we arrived and the place where we were billeted was quite nice and not too far from the center of the city. We stayed there for five weeks playing camps nearby. The way we were received was wonderful. Those soldiers had not seen many shows from "Stateside," as they called it.

One day while walking downtown, I was surprised to see an ex-bandleader of mine. It was Teddy Hill, whom I had played with in the Savoy Ballroom. Teddy told me that he had done service in Europe and was supposed to have been discharged and sent back to New York from Germany. But he had a run-in with an officer and the officer had arranged to have Teddy sent to the Philippines instead of being discharged when he was supposed to be. But Teddy was on the list to be sent home in a few days when I saw him.

I became acquainted with some Philippine musicians. One, who played trombone, called himself Felix the Cat. He had played in Japan before the war and told me that he had been associated with an American trombone player known as Slick. I had known Slick also because he had been in Cincinnati for a while and he also played trumpet. He was the first trumpet player I ever knew that played trombone or vice versa, but I never knew his real name.

Felix played with an orchestra, all Filipinos, that had 16 musicians. If you closed your eyes and only heard them playing, you would have bet your bottom dollar that it was the Glenn Miller band. The only weakness was in the solos. But the sound was there. We were invited to a few local spots where they would play now and then and I sat in with them a few times. They gave me all the brass solo parts and I gave them everything I could because I was really getting my kicks playing with a big band and hearing good harmony accompanying me. The musicians were getting their kicks listening to me because they had no soloists of any value in the trumpet section and it pleased them to hear something played as it would have been in the States or on records by jazz musicians.

We played some faraway camps on some other islands, which included Clark Field, Bataan, and Subic Bay. When we returned to Manila on 2 January 1946, we were billeted in a large camp which had formerly been occupied by a military service known as Seabees. There seemed to be hundreds of USO shows there and the camp was jumping. We were about five miles from Manila but there were plenty of little shops near the camp where whisky was sold and it was plentiful and cheap. Curby and I became drinking buddies and the hot weather did not affect us despite the two or three fifths that we drank every day.

There was gambling in the upstairs recreation room and jam sessions downstairs. Jesse Stone, the composer of *Idaho*, had a band which included Franz Jackson on tenor and Louis Bacon on trumpet. Otis Johnson, an ex-Luis Russell trumpeter, and Fess Williams's son Rudy were also with the group. The Jeter–Pillars orchestra of St. Louis fame were there and one of the trumpet players, Sam Massenberg, who had been a member of the Savoy Sultans, was a fine soloist. The bass player was Carl Pruitt, who was well known around the Apple. Jeter–Pillars and a white all-girl orchestra from California were the only orchestras composed of 16 or more musicians. Nelson Williams, another trumpet man, was also with a group. He had been discharged from the army some months before we left New York.

There were two Broadway hit shows with lots of girls at the camp One was *Gingham Girl* and the other was *Meet me at the Astor* Many of the actors were show people that had come out of forced retirement and were very happy because the pay was good and the food was not bad except on Sundays. And the only thing bad about the food that day or any Philippine holiday was the chicken.

Cockfighting is a big sport in the Philippines and there was an arena very near our camp I saw many of those contests, which were very cruel but fascinating. The camp had an arrangement with the management of the cockfight arena to buy the loser of a match because a cockfight goes on until one is killed. Cocks are trained for quite some time before they fight and I suppose they become as tough in character as a prize fighter. So the losers of the fights were served to us as the meat we ate on Sundays and holidays. It was so tough that anyone who had false teeth had to eat vegetables on those days.

Otherwise the food was good, the days were hot, and the nights were just right for sleeping. The men and women had different sections and even married couples could not live together. The housing consisted of a wooden floor, the framework of a large room with no walls, and a canvas roof. There were four army cots, one in each corner, and one could get a mattress and clean sheets from the supply commissioner. A mosquito net was a necessity and flit guns were also supplied because the mosquitoes were malaria carriers.

The camp personnel such as commander, guards, chef, and directors of different departments were all white and in military service. The servants were Filipinos and when we came to the camp there was a sign in the men's latrine in one corner that read, "For Filipinos only!" Of course we went anywhere we wanted to and after a few days I noticed that the sign had disappeared. The young Filipinos had gotten enough of being segregated in their own country and they refused those southern US habits, because of us. There were no more signs afterwards.

One afternoon we were jamming in the recreation hall and a soldier I knew came in. It was Stanley Facey, who at one time had been the piano accompanist for Eddie South, the violinist. There was another soldier with Facey who had a trumpet and they had come to the camp because they had heard that it was possible to blow there.

So Facey sat down at the piano, this trumpeter sat on the piano, and they began to play along with the rest of us who were jamming. But the picture started to change real soon because these two cats started playing so much that everyone else just wanted to listen. And the more they played, the better they seemed to get. I knew that Stanley was strong in the classical field but it was the first time I had ever heard him play jazz and he was wailing. His shirt was soaking wet. He looked as though he had been under a shower. The trumpeter had a style that seemed to be a mixture of Charlie Shavers and Howard McGhee but it was not as hard as Charlie's and he had plenty of feeling and ideas galore. After two hours of jamming, I was able to get into a conversation with him and he told me that his name was Thad Jones, the brother of Hank Jones, the piano man. I had heard of Hank but not met him. He had the reputation of being a fine accompanist and a great soloist. I later discovered that Hank's reputation was not a "conjectural narrative" but a "conformity."

Thad told me that he and Facey were in the US army show and that he had made all the arrangements for it. I had the feeling that Thad was going places after he would be discharged from the army and that premonition came true a few years later. That cat played too much horn at that time not to have gotten better known than he was. I've seen Thad quite a few times since those days and he always mentions to someone around whenever we meet that our first meeting was in the Philippines. I will never forget that day when he and Stanley Facey came to our camp and blew everybody out.

One army camp that we played, not far from ours, was where the Japanese general Yamashita, who had led the invasion of the Philippines, was hanged.

Some weeks passed and a big USO show was arranged in the largest stadium in Manila with the participation of all the USO groups that were assembled in the area. 20,000 people were expected. The concert was sponsored by the American government and there was no entrance fee to be paid. (Curby had lost face with Herbie Cowans, who had sent him home. There was no replacement for Curby so there was only Spider and myself in the front line.)

The big night came and two weapon carriers came to pick up our group. I could never understand the reason for this as there were not that many people in our show to make it necessary to have that much transportation. I don't remember who else left before the carrier I was in, but when we arrived at the stadium, the others were not there. The different shows were going on to do their bit and we were waiting, wondering what had happened! After two hours, the others came without Herbie Cowans. We were told that they had had an accident and that Herbie was injured. He had been sitting near the front in the vehicle, which had seats running lengthwise, and had his arms stretched out along the upper part of the bench-like seat. The driver of the vehicle ran into a truck that had some lumber protruding from the rear and a board came through the windshield and almost tore Herbie's arm off. Some of our instruments were also in the carrier. So there was no concert that night for Drum Boogie 789.

Herbie was placed in the best army hospital, where we visited him a few times before he was sent home. He had the best of medical care possible and was told that his arm could be saved and he would be able to play again.

We began to wonder if we would be sent back to the States before our time limit of six months. We were supposed to go to Japan after our tour of the Philippines and I really didn't want to miss out on that. We were saved by Henry "Shorty" Matthews, the comedian, who had a little experience playing drums. All we wanted really was someone that was able to keep time on the drums and we were still in the business.

Eventually the exodus for Japan started and it seemed that every other day a group was leaving the camp and we were staying on to wave good-bye to them. We were almost the first group to come to the Philippines and almost the last to leave. But the time finally came and on 26 April, we left Manila on the USS *Octorosa*, a small military transport steamer, and arrived at Yokohama, Japan, a few days later.

In Tokyo we were lodged in a building called Honcho House in a part of the city that had not been too badly bombed and for the first time since we had arrived in the Philippines we were not living in a camp. We were still sleeping on army cots, which were quite comfortable when one had a mattress to go with it. We were served meals by beautiful Japanese girls in kimonos and the food was like it would have been in a fine hotel.

One large room in Honcho House had been transformed into a movie hall and the first night we were there, a film called *Lost Weekend* was shown. I've seen films and more films that I shall never forget, but there is a special reason why I shall never forget *Lost Weekend* or the featured actor, Ray Milland. When we arrived in Japan, there had been no shops where one could buy a bottle. That night, I watched Ray Milland, who was an alcoholic, drinking in bars and at home, and I knew where he had hidden his bottle, though he could not remember, and he almost tore his place apart looking for it. I almost went crazy for a drink and would have been willing to pay as much as five bucks for a sip but no one had a drop, or if they did, they were not letting it go. I didn't have a drink until we played the first base a couple of nights later.

Shorty Matthews had begun to play drums not badly and our show made a hit with the soldiers and the Japanese personnel who worked at the different camps.

Tokyo, like many other large cities, had its red-light district and it was the most beautiful one I ever saw. There were individual houses that resembled paintings I had seen of Japan and the girls were really something to write home about. It was more like a fairyland than a whorehouse district and it was hard for a guy to make up his mind which beauty he would care to have.

There was no cabaret life in Tokyo for American servicemen. And if there was any night life for the Japanese, it was off limits to Americans. Tokyo had been pretty well bombed in certain districts but there were plenty of day activities around the Ginza, which was in the center of the city and the most famous boulevard in town.

As there was a shortage of cigarettes in Japan and we were allowed to buy a certain number of cartons a week from the PX (post exchange), there was no end to the wonderful Japanese souvenirs we could have in exchange for a few cartons of cigarettes. I bought many nice silk kimonos and other souvenirs for my family and special friends back home. I also acquired quite a few from the Philippines because conditions concerning cigarette trading were the same there.

I met at the Honcho House a very famous Broadway and Harlem comedian named Johnny Huggins, who did a one-man act. I had seen his act many times and had the honor of playing for him one week at the Lafayette Theater. Everyone that knew Johnny called him "Banjo" because he used the word in association with almost any conversation he had on any subject. If he disliked something, he would say: "That banjo is out of tune," "the strings are broken," or "it sounds bad," and many other expressions concerning the instrument. Johnny was a black-face comedian, the kind of act presented by Al Jolson and Eddie Cantor. But Banjo was a light brown-skin Negro and did a pantomime act as a singer in a very original and amusing way. A trumpeter would stand on stage near the wings and use a plunger to get a wa-wa effect, which coincided with the lips movements that Banjo did, imitating a person singing a song. We were together quite often in Tokyo and I was proud to have been one of the trumpet players capable of accompanying such a fine comedian and person as Johnny "Banjo" Huggins.

On 25 May 1946 we received our last overseas pay and on 31 May we boarded the USS *Marine Serpent*, another military transport ship, for home. I had visited Kamakura, not far from Tokyo, and seen the largest statue of Buddha in Japan.

Jesse Stone's group and *The Gingham Girl* and *Meet me at the Astor* troupes were going home on the same boat and every night there was entertainment aboard in the mess hall after the evening meals. We arrived in Seattle, Washington, on 6 June 1946 and left there two days later by train. We arrived in New York on 13 June.

I had been gone seven months and I had no room reserved when I arrived in New York. The trumpeter Louis Bacon came to my rescue. He had a three-room apartment on 147th Street and told me that I could sleep in the front room for a while. For some weeks I roomed with a woman named Mrs. Fips on St. Nicholas Avenue at the corner of 153rd Street. Whenever Illinois Jacquet came to New York he stayed at this place and Mrs. Fips always had a room reserved for him. One day the landlord of the house where I had lived with Beezie on 154th Street came to see me and told me that he had a room to rent. I jumped at the opportunity. His name was Earl Norman and his wife's name was Stella. I really felt at home with these people, who were more like a brother and sister to me than a landlord and landlady.

Sy Oliver, who had been the arranger for the orchestra of Tommy Dorsey after he had split from Jimmie Lunceford, had left Dorsey. It must have been around the middle of November 1946 that I heard through the grapevine that Sy was forming an orchestra and would be auditioning musicians at a rehearsal studio on Broadway. Sy lived not far from me on St. Nicholas Avenue and we had met many times, mostly on the corner of 155th Street and St. Nicholas in front of Fat Man's bar.

The audition had not started when I arrived, but there must have been at least

60 musicians in the studio. Sy picked certain musicians to go on the bandstand and I was among the first group. At the end of a number Sy asked some different musicians to come on the stand, but told me to stay there. This procedure went on for an hour or more and then Sy finally decided on the musicians he wanted. I was one of them. I believe that he knew in advance who he really wanted in his band. These were: Lamar Wright Sr., Lyman Vunk, Skeets Reid, and Bill Coleman (trumpets), Dicky Wells, Henry Wells, Gus Chappell, and Bill Granzow (trombones), Eddie Barefield and George Dorsey (alto saxes), Willard Brown (baritone sax), Freddie Williams and Gale Curtis (tenor saxes), Billy Kyle (piano), Aaron Smith (guitar), George Duvivier (bass), Wallace Bishop (drums), and Sy Oliver (leader).

Our first engagement was at the Zanzibar Club at 48th Street and Broadway. To my knowledge it was the first big band that had mixed Negro and white musicians to play a nightclub in New York. The first parts in the trumpet section were divided between Lyman Vunk and Lamar Wright, who were both fine musicians. I played the fourth part and had all the jazz solos. Lyman and Lamar also blew very loud, but never out of tune, and I had to blow my lungs out to be heard when we were doing section work because I had been playing in small groups for five or six years and got out of the habit of blowing loud. I even developed lip trouble and had to be replaced by Buck Clayton, who enjoyed playing with the band to the extent that he was not happy when I came back after a layoff of ten days.

It was a swinging band because Sy knew how to make a band do that and he knew how to arrange numbers in a swinging tempo. He also bought arrangements. George Duvivier was an arranger in the Sy Oliver medium. Very few big bands used guitars in the rhythm section any more except for Count Basie. But Sy had one, which was a big help to the section and kept it from being jumpy or otherwise unstable.

One night I told Smittie, as most everyone called our guitarist, Aaron Smith, that I had been in Europe and had recorded with Django Reinhardt. I was surprised when he told me that he knew of Django and considered him the greatest improvising guitarist that ever lived, and a real genius. From that night on, Smittie began to call me "Mighty." I suppose it was because he appreciated the fact that I had been fortunate enough and capable of recording with such a great musician as Django.

George Duvivier and Smittie had been friends for many years. Smittie told me that he was the first one to give George lessons in harmony.

We had a show to play twice a night. There were chorus girls, singers and the usual cabaret routine, but one of the stars was Dusty Fletcher, a comedian whom I had seen many times. His act was very funny and sometimes above the heads of some of the clientele because it was typical Negro comedy and the Broadway cabaret clients were mostly well-to-do white people. The highlight of Dusty's act was when he arrives home drunk and has no key. He rooms with a friend named Richard and they are both so poor that they only have one suit of clothes between them: when one goes out, the other has to stay home. When Dusty discovers that he has no key, he calls out, "Open the door Richard!" There is no response and then Dusty says, "I know he hasn't gone out because I've got on the clothes." After that he starts to climb up a ladder singing, "Open the door Richard." Where did he get the ladder? He had it with him when he was thrown out of a bar for not buying any drinks which he said was nonsense because everybody else was buying, so why should he? We all got kicks out of Dusty's act, but it knocked Lyman Vunk out every night.

Django came to the States to do some concerts with Duke Ellington and was to appear in one at Carnegie Hall. We had an hour intermission while a small group led by Claude Hopkins and including Greely Walton played. Greely and I had worked together in Luis Russell's orchestra. I decided to go and see Django for a few minutes as Carnegie Hall was only a few blocks from the Zanzibar. When I arrived there the atmosphere back stage was very gloomy. I was told that Django had not shown up yet for the concert and nobody could find him. I was disappointed because I had envisaged a short but happy reunion in which I could perhaps persuade Django to come to the Zanzibar and meet the musicians I was working with after he had finished his concert.

Later I heard that Django had met the boxer Marcel Cerdan in a bar and they were both so happy to be able to speak French that they started drinking together and Django forgot about the time of the concert. He came to Carnegie Hall when the concert was almost finished and Duke had already made an announcement to say that Django wouldn't play that night. Anyway Django played a few numbers and obtained a great success, I was told.

On 9 January 1947 we recorded for a new record company, MGM. The titles were: *Slow Burn*, *Hey Daddy-O*, *For Dancers Only*, and *If you Believe me*. There were numbers where some vocals were done by Sy, Dicky Wells, Henry Wells, and the whole orchestra. Sy was keen on the glee club style of singing and knew the technique of it. He had done it with the Lunceford orchestra successfully and on a few numbers with the Dorsey band. I never possessed any of those recordings made with Sy Oliver's band. I would love to have them, especially the one in which I have a very nice solo on *Slow Burn*, a composition and arrangement by Billy Moore.

After two months at the Zanzibar, we finished in January 1947 and were a little disappointed about that. Sy and the musicians had hoped to play longer there. As a rule, bands stayed in clubs of that standing for months on end and in some cases for years, as Duke Ellington did at the Cotton Club in Harlem, Charlie Johnson at Small's Paradise, or Fletcher Henderson at the Roseland Ballroom.

There were other recording dates for MGM before the band left the Zanzibar. One was with the comedy team of Buck and Bubbles, whom the orchestra accompanied, then on 1 April 1947 we recorded four numbers: *I Want to be Loved*, *Lamar's Boogie*, *Twenty-five Words or Less*, and *Walking the Dog*.

I don't remember if the last session we had was for MGM, nor do I know if it was ever issued, but I remember a couple of numbers we recorded. One was titled: *You can't tell the depth of the well by the length of the handle on the pump*, a very long title, eh what! The other was *Bingle, Bangle, Bungle*, and the words referred to a monkey who did not want to leave the jungle because modern civilization was too wild for him.

On 24 January 1947, we went into the Apollo Theatre in Harlem, which was headlined by the orchestra, Jackie Mabley (a woman comedian), and the Four Ravens (a popular singing group). The Apollo changed shows every week. The band had taken on some new members and was now without any of the white musicians. Wallace Wilson and Frank Galbraith, trumpeters, had replaced Lyman Vunk and Skeets Reid. Ernie "White Folks" Powell (tenor sax) had replaced Gale Curtis: he was called "White Folks" because he looked like a white man, but like Willie Bryant and Willie Smith, the alto man of Jimmie Lunceford fame, he was proud to be a black man. Fred Robinson replaced Bill Granzow in the trombone section; Billy Kyle had left the band and was replaced by a young pianist named Buddy Weed; and James Crawford did the week in the Apollo in the place of Wallace Bishop, who had left the band also.

In February we played two weeks at the Savoy but the joint didn't send me the way it had when I was there with the band of the Scott brothers. Later in February we went to Boston for a one-nighter and played a battle of music with the Jimmie Lunceford band. This was really a challenge to Sy because he would have the chance of showing his ex-boss what a good band he had built in a few months. But the honors were equally divided and all were satisfied with the results. The members of the Lunceford band at that time were: Joe Wilder, Reunald Jones, and Robert Mitchell (trumpets), Russell Bowles, Albert "Al" Grey, and Alfred Cobb (trombones), Omer Simeon (clarinet), Muschiclata Hasashaion (alto sax), Joe Thomas (tenor sax), Earl Carruthers (baritone sax), Edwin Wilcox (piano), Charles "Truck" Parham (bass), Albert Norris (guitar), Joe Marshall (drums), and Nick Brooks and Kirtland Bradford (vocalists).

In March we hit the road and one of the nighters we did was in Cincinnati. I took Smitty Aaron with me to my father's place and he and my old man became good friends from the beginning of their acquaintance. Dad made us some of his famous Dixie rolls before we left. These were biscuits eaten hot with the butter oozing out of them. They were great with sausage, mashed potatoes, and gravy, and my Dad was really a champ when it came to making them.

From Cincinnati, we went to Dayton for one night and then to Detroit for a one-week engagement at the Paradise Theater. The pit band was led by Buddy Bowen, an alto sax man whom I had met in New York; the trumpeter was George "Buddy" Lee, with whom I had played in Wes Helvey's orchestra in Cincinnati and who had played also with McKinney's Cotton Pickers.

Another act was the Will Mastren trio, whose youngest member was Sammy Davis Jr. Sammy was unknown at that time but he was responsible for the success of the trio because he was a fine singer and tap-dancer. His uncle Will Mastren and his father Sammy Davis Sr. were the other performers. Sammy used to call me "Be-Bop" but I certainly wasn't playing that style. Oscar Moore's brother, also a guitarist, was the leader of a vocal group, the Three Blazers, who were also in the show.

After the week in Detroit, Sy hired a bus to take us to Gary, Indiana, for a one-night stand. Before we arrived in Gary, the windshield of the bus blew out. We were all shattered to hell but we made it to the gig. Then the bus driver went over to Chicago, which is not far from Gary, and had a new windshield put in and returned to Gary about 1 a.m. We were leaving that morning for Indianapolis after the dance. The bus driver, who was a white fellow, was a jazz fan, and instead of getting some rest after driving so long, wanted to listen to the band because he had never heard it.

The dance lasted until 2.30, and by the time we had packed up, loaded the bus and had a snack, it must have been almost 4 a.m. when we hit the road for Indianapolis.

I usually had to have a few shots under my belt before I could go to sleep, and after we got started it was not long before I went to sleep. I can't say how long I had been sleeping when I was woken by a strange quick movement of the bus. I had the intuition that the bus driver was sleepy and decided to watch his reactions. I sat in the middle of the bus; everyone was asleep now except the driver and myself. Suddenly I felt the bus jerk and I immediately got up and went up to the chauffeur and asked him if he was feeling sleepy. He said yes, but he knew a place where he could get some coffee that stayed open all night and was only about seven miles away. So I stayed beside him and talked to him until we reached the all-night restaurant. And we arrived safely in Indianapolis.

We went to Chicago for a week at the Regal Theater, played a dance in Minneapolis with the Three Blazers as an added attraction, and a dance in some town in Ohio.

In Minneapolis I was surprised to see Earl "Inky" Tremble, the alto sax man. Things had not been good with him and he had not played sax for a long time. He was working in a garage.

In Ohio, Frank Galbraith met some friends he had known for years and, as Sy didn't have any more jobs for a while, Frank stayed in this town. He was the first person that I ever knew that called everybody "baby." At that time, it was quite unusual.

On 17 April 1947, I had a recording session with the Webster–Hardwick Wax Quintet on Al Hall's Wax label. Ben Webster was on tenor sax and Otto Hardwick on alto sax, with Jimmy Jones (piano), Al Hall (bass), and Denzil Best (drums). We cut two sides: *As Long as I Live* and *Blue Bells of Harlem*. We recorded also one number without Otto Hardwick: *All Alone*, which was issued under Denzil Best's name.

We played the Apollo again on 27 June. Pearl Bailey was the featured attraction and Cozy Cole had a revue of dancers and tom-tom players. I had been in an Edgar Hayes band that played some theater dates in Atlantic City, New Jersey, and Pennsylvania with Pearl before she became a big star in the early 1940s. Bill "Bojangles" Robinson was the star of that show. Sy's band was breaking a record by being the only band to play a return engagement in the Apollo within a six-month period. Frank Galbraith had come back and Arthur Trappier, the ex-Fats Waller drummer, had replaced Wallace Bishop.

There was not much cooking after the Apollo date but the band rehearsed once a week anyway. One day, we were rehearsing in the hall next door to the Lafayette Theater when, suddenly, Sy stopped the rehearsal and started to make a speech about something. Afterwards, he asked the musicians what they thought of him. Different ones said this and that but none of us said what we thought except Ernie Powell. Sy had been a sergeant in the army and director of an army band in which Ernie was a member. He told Sy that he was suffering with an army sergeant complex! At the next rehearsal, Ernie wasn't there. The band didn't last very long after that. The last date I played with Sy was a small combo gig in the Blue Room of the Radio City building at 49th Street and 6th Avenue.

I had a few gigs now and then, mostly then, and was getting behind in my rent. But the Normans never bothered me about that and sometimes I would borrow a few dollars from them because they knew that when I made a gig I would pay my rent and give back the money I had borrowed. Earl Norman and I had built a large table in his basement on which we were going to realize our dream of having some miniature electric trains. Earl was an automobile mechanic and a damn good one. He also knew a lot about electricity.

One night in the basement we were talking about work, so he asked me if I knew Earle "Nappy" Howard, the pianist. He said that Earle was the head redcap porter at the Pennsylvania railroad station and asked me why didn't I go down there and see Earle and perhaps I could get a job carrying bags. I told him very politely that I didn't like to carry my own bags and had no eyes for carrying those of other people. Many New York musicians had done it, but for the time being I figured I would make it in the music game even if there was not much on the rail for the lizard.

On 21 November I went into the 845 Club in the Bronx with a small combo led by Billie Kyle. We were all ex-Sy Oliver members except Charlie Holmes, the alto sax man. Freddie Williams was on tenor, George Duvivier on bass, and Wallace Bishop on drums. The band sounded great and it's a pity that it wasn't recorded.

The 845 Club was the only Negro nightclub in the Bronx, which was not very famous as a nightclub district, but this club did very good business. The acts featured at different times were: Derby Wilson (a fine tap dancer on the Bojangles side), June Richmond, who had gone back to her singing act after she left Andy Kirk, Willie Bryant, who was the Master of Ceremonies, Jackie Mabley, and George Kirby. A relief trio was led by an organist, Lawrence "88" Keys. There was also a chorus line of six girls.

George Kirby did an imitation of Joe Louis after he had won a fight and a radio announcer would ask Joe to say something to the listeners. Joe had a very Southern accent and George imitated him perfectly. One night Joe Louis came to the club and George refused to do this part of his act for fear of insulting Joe perhaps. But all the show people were around and kept shouting for the Joe Louis bit, and finally George did it and Joe Louis, who seldom laughed at anything, did so that night.

We stayed in the club until the last day of February 1948 and then it was back to gigging for as many potatoes as I could make wherever it was. From the time that I had done my first gig in 1929 with a pick-up band, many strange things had happened.

The most embarrassing gig I had ever gone on was with a pick-up band which played in Atlantic City under the name of Duke Ellington. This must have happened around 1931 or 1932 and I made the trip with Spider Courance, who still had the same Model T Ford he had bought around 1926. Spider had old tires on the car and we must have had ten blowouts on the way. I thought we'd never make it to Atlantic City on time but we did. The dance was on the pier in a place that was usually reserved for the white public, but that night it was for a Negro dance. The band was under the leadership of Benny Carter but I don't remember who the other members were except Spider and Mack Horton on trombone. We got to the bandstand and after a couple of numbers, some cats standing close to the bandstand who knew the personnel of Duke's orchestra started asking very loudly: "Where is Johnny Hodges?" "Where is Freddie Jenkins?" "Where is Barney Bigard?" and so on. At least whenever Fletcher Henderson had a pick-up band playing under his name, he did come to the gig and directed the musicians for a length of time, but Duke was in New York at the Cotton Club and no one in the orchestra resembled Duke. What an embarrassing night it was.

TWELVE

BACK TO EUROPE FOR KEEPS

I had been in touch by correspondence with Charles Delaunay of the Hot Club of France, who told me in a letter that he was trying to arrange something there that would bring me back there. Charles had been in New York shortly after my return from Japan. I had met him and told him my desire to go back to France. He told me that things were not the same then as before the war, and if I wanted to give it a try, he would see what he could do, though he wouldn't promise anything.

One undated letter I received from Charles mentioned that he almost had a contract for me to play with Charlie "Dizzy" Lewis and Big Boy Goudie but he didn't mention where. The next one was dated 7 October 1948: he was on the verge of getting me a contract in a new club that was going to open and asked me if I was still interested. I wrote immediately saying yes!

At the time, I was rehearsing with a group of musicians of whom I can remember only one, Alton "Slim" Moore, a trombonist. He was about six feet four, weighed about 200 pounds, and was a long way from actually being slim. The pianist and leader lived on 135th Street between 7th and Lenox Avenues. We rehearsed at his apartment a couple of times a week and we had done a couple of gigs together. Most of the cats were beginning to dig the modern jive and I remember the first of those numbers I was introduced to was *Billy's Bounce*. Slim was going all out for the style.

I had mentioned to some musicians that I might have a chance to go to Europe. When our leader got the news through the grapevine, I was excluded from the rehearsals. Oran "Hot Lips" Page took an orchestra into the Apollo for one week and asked me to join the band. I refused because I was expecting word from Charles any day telling me that everything was set. I didn't want to be tied up in any circumstances.

In November I had some luck and hit the numbers twice for five cents and again for 25 cents on 1 December.

On 10 December 1948 I received a cable saying that a plane ticket was waiting for me at the Air France office. I was to leave two days later. I did not have time to tell most of my friends that I was leaving. Only my brother, Roger Kay and his girlfriend Nancy, and the Normans knew about it.

I bought a bottle of whisky, my brother came to the house, and I was packing all night. I didn't realize I had so much of this and that until then. I had told the Normans that I was going to Europe for three months, but I had decided that I was going to stay even if I had to drink muddy water and sleep in a hollow log. That's why I was taking everything I owned. But there was a surprise waiting for me when I arrived at the Air France office. I had $100 of excess baggage. I had only traveled by air when I went to the Philippines on a military plane, where there was no limit to the weight of one's baggage. I was unaware of the weight allowed on commercial flights but when I found out what it was and how much it would cost me, I was almost floored because I only had a few dollars over a hundred.

What saved the situation was an announcement that the flight would be delayed an hour because of motor trouble or something. So I grabbed a taxi, went back to the Normans, had the taxi wait for me, made some quick changes and took only the things that would be necessary for a few weeks. I jumped back in the taxi and made it back down to the Air France office in time for the bus to the airport. I said goodbye to New York and thought about the words of a World War I song I had heard when I was about 15: "How you gonna keep 'em down on the farm, after they've seen Paree?"

The flight was 15 hours. There was a stop in the Azores for more than an hour. When we arrived over the French coast, it was Sunday morning and it was raining cats and dogs. A young man was waiting for me at Orly Airport. He presented himself as Serge Greffet. I had expected Charles Delaunay to meet me because we knew each other and he had arranged the contract for me to come. Serge brought me into the city, but with the weather being what it was, nothing looked beautiful. I was told that I had to do a concert that afternoon. I was not disturbed very much about who I would be working with or how it would go. Somehow I was feeling confident, so happy to be able to play in Paris again after twelve years.

It was one o'clock already. We went in a restaurant near the Opéra to have a meal, then Serge took me to the theater where the concert was to take place. It was the Théâtre Edouard VII. The musicians I was going to play with were there. A couple of them spoke English and that was a big help to me because I had forgotten the few words I had known in French.

The musicians were Michel de Villers (alto and baritone sax), Geo Daly (vibraphone), Bernard Peiffer (piano), Jean Bouchety (bass), Roger Paraboschi (drums). What surprised me most of all was that those fellows were all young —not one was over 30—and they knew most of the jazz standards and classics that I knew along with some modern ones I didn't know. So there was no sweat getting a program together. I was surprised how hip these fellows were to the styles being played in the USA! They were not at all behind the times as I had sort of expected the French jazz musicians to be.

I was also surprised at the large following that jazz had. The theater was full. I suppose I was better known to the public here than I realized, because I had never had such a warm and enthusiastic reception. I was happy about the way the musicians had supported me.

After the concert my old friend Maurice Cullaz and his wife Vonette, whom I had known since 1935, came back stage to greet me. Later, Charles Delaunay took me to the Hôtel La Bruyère, where a room had been reserved. It was in the neighborhood of Montmartre, which I was familiar with. Charles left me and I was on my own.

After unpacking my bags I decided to go out to see if I could find any old familiar faces, especially at Boudon's and at the "Tabac", rue Fontaine. The only one I found was the barman of the "Tabac," who could speak a little English. I learned from him that Big Boy Goudie came around to the corner on a certain day. I was happy to be in Paris again but started feeling a little lonesome for some of the old gang that used to hang around there. The corner had lost its gaiety though it had not changed its looks.

A few days later I rehearsed with the musicians. The pianist, Bernard Peiffer, had a very personal style and could do a good imitation of Erroll Garner. But when he got excited his taste was bad and he seemed to be giving instruction on how to break up a piano in public without using an ax. Michel de Villers had learned a lot from Charlie Parker records and played the style well. His only drawback was that he didn't read music. Geo Daly was considered the Lionel Hampton of France. He and Peiffer did a Hamp and Milt Buckner act on the piano with Geo doing the one-finger bit like Hamp and that always pleased the audience. Jean Bouchety was a fine bass fiddle man and arranger. Roger Paraboschi played solid drums, which is all that a good jazz group needs.

Eventually I ran into Big Boy Goudie, who had spent the World War II years in South America. Later I saw Arthur Briggs, who had been in a concentration camp after the Germans occupied Paris. Briggs told me why the few of the old gang that were still in Paris did not hang around in Boudon's anymore. The owner had collaborated with the Germans and had denounced some Jews and Negroes. I had been eating in the place but went somewhere else after hearing that news.

Rex Stewart was in Paris but I didn't see him until two weeks had passed as I didn't know where he was living. I happened to be sitting at the Omnibus café at Place Pigalle when Rex came along. He had come to Europe in 1947 with a group that included Sandy Williams (ex-Chick Webb trombonist), Vernon Story (tenor sax), Don Gais (piano), Johnny Harris (alto and clarinet), Ted Curry (drums), and Honey Johnson (vocalist). He used an unknown French bassist. It seemed like old times with Rex, whom I had not seen for quite a long time. He gave me his address and invited me to dinner. While in Paris, he was going to a cooking school and said that he would let me know when I should come to his place for dinner.

I was being paid by the week but was only working Sunday afternoons because the new club that I had been engaged to play in had not been finished when I arrived.

Thirteen days after my arrival in Paris, Christmas came and then I got the blues because I had not made the acquaintance of anyone that might have invited me to join them in celebrating the holidays: the few people that I knew were spending that time with their families. So I passed the time in a bar at the corner of rue Fontaine and rue Douai owned by an ex-prize fighter named Roger. The same thing went for New Year. I drank 1948 out and 1949 in. Roger's place was my hangout and although I could not speak very much French and he spoke no English, we made ourselves understood.

One night I was in a bar when someone tapped me on the back. I turned to see who it was and had a great surprise when I looked into the face of Joe Turner, the pianist. It certainly was nice seeing a fellow musician from across the Pond that I could talk some trash with and we really dished the dirt that night. Joe told me that he was on his way to Budapest, Hungary. The next time I saw Joe, it was in Switzerland a couple of years later.

When I arrived in Paris, I had exactly $100 but, as Serge had advanced me some francs on my weekly salary, I didn't have to change any dollars and decided to buy some American Express checks. But I kept delaying this procedure and when I went out I would hide the money somewhere in my room so that if something happened when I was out, the money would not be in my pockets. One day I decided to have a blue suit cleaned and gave it to a cleaning place on rue Pigalle. Two days later I was looking for my dollars and realized that I had put them in the watch pocket of the blue pants I had given to be cleaned. I went to the shop and tried to explain the situation but they didn't understand me or pretended they didn't. I went to see Charles Delaunay and asked him to come to the store with me. But it was hopeless because they claimed that they had not found the money. This did not surprise me because I knew that honesty was one thing and money was another.

The club Charles Delaunay had contacted me to play in finally opened in January. The Edward's band, Don Byas, and I were the main attraction. Don Byas had been engaged to play in the Edward's band. He was a superb tenor man. I knew him from New York of course and I should have been included in the Don Redman orchestra with which he had come to Europe. Unfortunately, Timme Rosenkrantz, who had organized the tour, couldn't contact me since I was away from the Apple end on the road when the band was formed.

There was an added attraction, the dance team of Pops and Louie. I had known both of them when they were kids dancing with the Whitman Sisters' show. Pops was the son of Alice Whitman, who was a great tap dancer and had taught both Pops and Louie how to dance. Louie also sang very well.

The club was nice and rather exclusive but didn't stay open long, although it was successful. But the manager had trouble with his liquor licence and finally had to close the place.

Don Byas and I recorded four sides on 4 January 1949 for a label called Jazz Selections. The following day we recorded five numbers for the Swing label using the musicians of the Edward's band except for Michel de Villers. This was my first recording date in France since 1938.

One Sunday afternoon, there was a concert at the Théâtre Edouard VII, which featured Rex Stewart, myself, and a French trumpeter named Aimé Barelli. On the bill, which took place on 13 February, were some other French musicians: Maurice Meunier (clarinet), Alf Masselier, Claude Marty, Jean-Claude Forenbach (a Hawkins-style tenor player), and Eddie Bernard (a pianist who loved Fats Waller, and James P. Johnson a real swinging cat). I was told that Barelli was the best trumpet man in France. I believed it when I heard him play, for he had a big sound, technique, and a touch of Armstrong in his phrasing.

The Hot Club de France was working and we were booked for some concert tours. We played the most important cities in France, playing to packed houses. The reception was great, the applause terrific—"atomic" wrote Louis Fritch, a critic from Strasbourg. Some jazz fans were following the band from town to town. We had little sleep and lots of drinks. I doubt that now such enthusiastic atmosphere could be recreated.

Beside France, we did concerts in Belgium, Switzerland, and Germany. It was in Zurich that I met a man who later became a great friend of mine, Johnny Simmen. He knew more American jazz musicians than I ever knew existed. And there were very few that he didn't have records of.

We were the first foreign musicians to play in Germany after the war and the public had been starving for some jazz music. Jazz had been forbidden in Germany by Hitler. Our first date was for the German radio in Wuppertal and the director of the jazz department, Dr. Dietrich Schulz-Köhn, was a jazz enthusiast I had met in Paris before the war when I was with Willie Lewis. I had seen the ruins of Manila after the bombings it received during the war, but they looked like a flower garden compared to what the allies had done in Germany.

Inez Cavanaugh had been engaged to make the German tour with us as singer. We gave concerts in Dusseldorf, Dortmund, and some other places before landing in Hamburg, where we did five concerts to packed houses of no fewer than 2000 people at each performance. What surprised me was to see many elderly white-haired people, men and women, in the front rows. The management of the Musikhalle vowed never to rent the place again for a jazz concert because the people in the balconies were stomping and applauding so hard after each number that they thought the place would cave in.

After the concerts we usually went to the famous St. Pauli district with its Reeperbahn, which sported the jumpingest nightlife I ever saw. Cabarets, dance clubs, strip clubs, and beer halls seemed to make up the whole district. The atmosphere was very cosmopolitan and we had a ball.

The only bringdown we experienced was the trip from Hamburg to Bremen, where the tour ended. We nearly froze to death on that local train, which took eight hours to cover 70 miles. We would have gotten there sooner on bicycles even if we had left at the same time!

We did a good concert, however, and after we finished some people invited us to a cabaret for some drinks. We were in this place about ten minutes when some American military policemen asked to see our papers. We showed them our passports and they told us we could not stay there because it was off limits for Americans. I knew that in some places where US soldiers were stationed there were certain night club districts that were off limits for military personnel, but I didn't think that the rule applied to civilians. So I told this MP that I was going to see about it. He said, "Alright, you can see about it now," and told Don Byas and me to come along with him. Don said that there was no need for him to come along because he had not said anything but the MP said, "Yes, you come along also." We were taken in a jeep to the military headquarters and after waiting for half an hour we were finally questioned by an officer who told us that when a place was off limits for Americans, it meant soldiers, sailors, and civilians. That was the end of that, but Don was really salty with me.

Back in Paris, my regular hangout became the Omnibus café in the Place Pigalle, which was a one-minute walk from the hotel where I was staying. Many French and musicians from Martinique met on the square at the Place Pigalle every evening around 6 p.m., which is known as the aperitif hour. It was where musicians were engaged for gigs the way it was at the Rhythm Club back home. I met some musicians I had known before: Django Reinhardt, his brother Joseph, Alix Combelle, André Ekyan, and some Cubans. One was Humberto Canto, who played bongos and danced. Humberto could not speak very good English but I could understand him and we became good friends. He was a very jolly fellow.

There were also two Algerian fellows that I became quite friendly with. One was named Mohammed Hamida and the other was called Pépé. He spoke good English. After a few times talking with Pépé, I figured I knew him well enough to ask him if he knew where I could get some gage. I was never an addict but I liked a little taste now and then. Pépé asked me how much I wanted, and as I didn't know how much it was sold for here, I thought that 3000 francs (about $10) would get me a few sticks.

A few days later Pépé came back with a big package wrapped in newspaper. He told me it was the stuff I had asked for. It was still on the branches. I paid him and when I opened the package, I thought that Pépé had brought me a whole tree! I had to go out and buy a sifter and do the job of separating the seeds and other part from the goody. It took me a whole afternoon to do that, and when it was finished I had a mountain of gage. I filled two shoe boxes and still had more to put in a newspaper package.

Then I became scared and started to wonder if Pépé had brought me all that stuff to get me in trouble with the law. Where could I hide it? Finally I put it all on top of a closet because I had noticed that the room was clean except under the bed and on top of the closet. The dust there was thick enough to plant potatoes.

I covered the packets with dust and thought that I would be safe if there was a search! I wouldn't know anything about it! I had regular visits from some of my friends and would give them a few sticks. The stuff lasted me for about two years.

The Edward's band, Don Byas, and I were still doing concerts. In April we went to the Casino at Knokke for three days with a big show which included the orchestra of Bernard Hilda and Maurice Toubas. Other acts engaged were the Nicholas Brothers, a dance team; Rosario and Antonio, a famous Spanish couple; Borrah Minevitch's Harmonica Vagabonds; the well-known Bluebell Girls from the Lido; and the very famous French artist of music hall and films, Fernandel.

The war had not changed anything in Knokke since I was there the summer of 1938. Everything went well until the last night, when Don Byas went into one of his acts after the last show. Don was high and in the process of changing his clothes, he decided to chase one of the Bluebell Girls who passed his dressing room when the door was open. He was chasing her in his shorts only and the director of the casino happened to be in the hallway of the dressing rooms. He gave Don hell and that killed the chance for us and the band to have a contract for the summer season.

The big thing in jazz from 8 to 15 May 1949 was the Panis Jazz Festival that Charles Delaunay organized in collaboration with Frank Bauer, Eddie Barclay, and Jacques Souplet. Sidney Bechet and Charlie Parker were the stars but there were other musicians that were already in the limelight, whose names were to become much better known than they were in 1949. The American musicians presented at this festival were: Bechet, Parker, "Big Chief" Moore, Oran "Hot Lips" Page, Kenny Dorham, Tommy Potter, Al Haig, Max Roach, Miles Davis, Jimmy McPartland, Tadd Dameron, Kenny Clarke, George Johnson, James Moody, Richie Frost, Don Byas, and myself.

This was an international festival with musicians from six European countries including France. England was represented by the orchestra of Vic Lewis and Carlo Krahmer. From Belgium was Toots Thielemans's trio. The National All Stars were from Sweden, Hazy Osterwald with Ernst Höllerhagen were from Switzerland. France was represented by Aimé Barelli, Hubert Rostaing (clarinet), and André Ekyan (tenor sax), Jack Dieval and his trio, Jean-Claude Forenbach (tenor sax), Leo Chauliac, Lucien Simoens, Hubert Fol, and Michel de Villers (alto saxes), Maurice Meunier (clarinet), Bernard Peiffer's trio, Claude Luter (clarinet), Pierre Braslavsky and their orchestras, Jean Bonal (guitar), and Bernard Hullin (trumpet).

Jazz was jumping in Paris that week at the Salle Pleyel and jazz fans from different countries were there to take in the festival. All the jazz clubs were flourishing—the Tabou, the Vieux Colombier, and the Club St-Germain-des-Prés on the left bank—because all the musicians would go jamming after the nightly concerts or on nights when they did not have to appear at the festival.

One day during the week of the festival, Big Boy Goudie came to my hotel with two friends from Switzerland: Felix Debrit and Peter Wydler. Felix and Peter were jazz fans and Felix advised the owner of a place in Berne called the Chikito as to which jazz men should be engaged or contacted for the place. He wanted me to form an orchestra for an engagement in the Chikito and he had an idea about certain American musicians being in the orchestra. I had no great desire of becoming an orchestra leader but Big Boy was helping Felix to push me by telling me how nice it was to work in the Chikito, because he had already played there with the alto sax player Glyn Paque. I told Felix that I would think it over and promised to keep in touch with him.

Don Byas, myself, and the Edward's band were no longer being booked by the Edouard VII theater group, but someone got us a job playing at a Left Bank club called the Vieux Colombier. It didn't last very long. The band broke up after that engagement.

I did some gigs with different musicians and later went into the Rêve, a dance hall in the Rex theater building, with Charlie "Dizzy" Lewis, who had also engaged George Johnson on alto sax.

After a month at the Rêve, I worked a couple of weeks with a fellow known as

Cuban Pete at the Ambassadeurs, where I had worked with Willie Lewis. Pete was an Algerian but most people who knew him thought he was from Cuba. Pete didn't play an instrument but he was a smooth operator and had collaborated with his pianist and had published some music under his own name. The music that Cuban Pete's orchestra played was Cuban style with a touch of jazz, and I had to wear the type of shirts that all Cuban and many Martinican orchestras wore. As a uniform I didn't care for it. I was missing the good old jazz rhythm, so I didn't stay with Pete very long.

I was supposed to have played a concert in the town of Limoges with the Edward's band but I missed the train because I went in the wrong direction in the subway. No one I came in contact with at the station could speak English and, to make a long story short, I missed the gig. A few days later I was contacted by a jazz fan named Jean-Marie Masse from Limoges, who was the president of the Hot Club there. He arranged for me to appear in Limoges, and a few weeks later I went there alone, and played at a place called the Sully. I was accompanied by a guitarist named Bob Aubert, with Jean-Marie Masse (drums), and Jean-Pierre Bruno (piano).

I stayed with Jean-Marie, whose wife's name was Paulette. They had a daughter, Sylvie, who was five years old and one about two years old, Agnes. Jean believed in eating well and his wife was a very good cook. I had some French food unknown to me and that sent me. Little Sylvie I adopted as my little mama: she was with me all the time and would get me a glass of cognac whenever I asked her. I've been a great friend of Jean-Marie Masse and his family ever since then.

I was so happy about being in France that I celebrated every day with a fresh bottle of cognac which I kept in my room, and I was drinking 15 to 20 cognacs in bars. After weeks, my lips began to get dry and I could not play the way I was supposed to. I knew that it was from drinking too much and that I had to slow down. I even stopped completely for one month.

Kenny Clarke, who had been working in the orchestra of Tony Proteau, a French alto sax player, and Lobo Noccho, a singer, formed an orchestra, and I joined it. Lobo had been in the army, was discharged in Europe, and had settled in Paris. In the orchestra there was Don Byas, James Moody, Hubert Fol (alto sax), Nat Peck (a white American trombonist), Jay Cameron (another white American who played baritone sax), Pierre Michelot (a fine French bass player), and a few more French musicians whose names I don't remember. An English girl named Annabelle Ross was the female vocalist. Later she became very well known as Annie Ross of the Dave Lambert, Jon Hendricks, and Annie Ross trio.

We were engaged to work at Frisco's International Bopera House in Montmartre on rue Notre Dame de Lorette. I was not supposed to stay with the orchestra very long because I had been engaged to go to Nice for two weeks to a place called Club St.-Germain-des-Mers, which was to be opened in late July by Serge Greffet and the director of the Théâtre Edouard VII. In August I was to join the orchestra of the pianist Jack Dieval, to play the month in Geneva, Switzerland, at the Grillon dance hall.

In Nice I worked with Bernard Peiffer, Hubert Fol (alto sax), Jack Smaley (bass), and a young white American drummer named Richie Frost. Jimmy

"Lover Man" Davis, so called because he was one of the co-composers of the famous song *Lover Man*, was engaged as an entertainer. Another singer engaged was Monique Davis, the French wife of Bernard Peiffer.

Hubert Fol told me that the Clarke–Lobo orchestra didn't last very long because Frisco wanted the French musicians to continue to play while the Americans, would take a rest. The business was bad, and Kenny and Lobo did not agree with the way Frisco wanted the band to play. That didn't help the situation so the band broke up after a few weeks.

I had been introduced to Jimmy Davis by Beezie because they were both from Leonia, New Jersey. Jimmy sang and accompanied himself on piano. He had been a warrant officer in the army and came to France after his discharge.

In Geneva with Jack Dieval, we had Kenny Clarke on drums; Paul Vernon, a French tenor man in the style of Dexter Gordon with a little mixture of Lester Young; and Emmanuel Soudieux, one of those solid bass players whose interest was not in being a soloist but backing up instrumental solos with the correct chords and big sound. Kenny Clarke, known as "Klook," I've mentioned before. He was one of the greatest of the "new style." The leader, Jack Dieval, was a good businessman. He was a good pianist who had classical training and came into the jazz field because he liked that type of music and especially the blues. He was a very good accompanist. We also had an American singer, Arstella Whittier, from Rochester, New York. She had a fine voice in the style of Ella Fitzgerald when she sang sweet numbers. We made quite a hit with the public.

Felix Debrit, who had asked me in Paris about leading an orchestra in the Club Chikito, came to see me in Geneva with Johnny Simmen. Johnny came along to help Felix persuade me into taking a group into the Chikito and I accepted the offer: not because I wanted to be a leader—I never felt as though I had the qualifications to be one—but because I decided to give it a try.

Felix told me that Johnny Simmen was the one that put him in contact with Ernest "Bass" Hill and Norman Lester, a pianist I knew but never worked with. Felix was also in touch with an American tenor sax man named Fred Palmer, who was in Italy. I didn't know this fellow but was told that he had been a member of Noble Sissle's orchestra at one time. That was no recommendation to me but it was Felix who was really forming the orchestra that I was to lead.

After I finished at the Grillon dance hall with Jack Dieval, we did a radio show in Lausanne and I was invited to spend a few days with Johnny Simmen (whose real name is Hans Georges Simmen) and his wife Lisette (who doesn't like her real name which is Liza). I had met them, Johnny's sister, her husband, and a girl named Bettina Blockinger the first time I did a concert in Zurich with Don Byas and the Edward's band. After the concert I had been invited to Simmen's home and enjoyed their company until the wee hours of the morning. Johnny had a collection of records that was second only to the collection of Hugues Panassié, which ran into thousands and included most everything that I had made. During my visit with Johnny and Lisette after the Dieval deal, every night we had a record session of recordings I had never heard by musicians known and unknown to me. And what's more, Johnny knew the history of all those musicians including mine and could tell me when and where they were born, the different orchestras they had played with, those that were still living, and what most of them were doing at the present time.

We still needed a drummer and when I came back to Paris, near the end of September, I contacted a West Indian drummer named George Smith whom I had met before and asked him about joining the orchestra, and he accepted. I then wrote to Bass Hill and asked him to start collecting some music in New York. He wrote me back not to worry about music because Norman Lester was an arranger and would take care of the repertoire.

Before I left I did three recording sessions: one with Jack Dieval's orchestra, the second with Sidney Bechet and Kenny Clarke, and the third with Buck Clayton. Buck Clayton had come to Paris with an orchestra which included Merrill Stepter, a trumpeter I had known a long time, and Wallace Bishop the drummer.

We left for Berne, Switzerland, on 24 November 1949. Bass Hill and Norman Lester had arrived in Paris a couple of days before and Fred Palmer had come from Italy. We opened at the Chikito on the 26th with nothing but head numbers. Norman Lester had not written any arrangements before leaving New York and I had not picked up any orchestrations in Paris because Bass Hill had told me that Norman would take care of that end. My first mistake as a bandleader had been made: depending on the word of someone else and not preparing for the event myself.

So there we were, with nice-looking stands of light and dark blue with golden sprayed "B.C." that I had bought, and not one sheet of music on them. But we made out alright because Norman Lester knew any number that was ever popular in jazz as well as many that were not. He played a Fats Waller stride style which, I would say, included James P. Johnson, Luckey Roberts, and also a touch of Willie "the Lion" Smith. He also did a good imitation of singing like Fats. Because of their background and experience Bass Hill and Big Boy Goudie were well known by the public. George Smith was an up-to-date drummer. He also liked to do an imitation of Louis Armstrong's singing which didn't sound very good to me. The weakest man in the band was Fred Palmer, who had no style on tenor and no voice for singing but he insisted on doing it all the time. I had also engaged Arstella Whittier as vocalist because it was stylish to have a canary, as girl vocalists were sometimes called.

I took the occasion to ask Buck if he would make me some arrangements but for some reason which I never found out why, he never did any for me.

Although we had no music on the stands, we still made a hit with the public at the Chikito. Later Norman Lester wrote some original tunes which actually had no swing possibilities and although he was a good piano man he was not an arranger. But we played the tunes every night because I was a beggar and had no choices. But Norman was evil-tempered: whenever we had a disagreement, he would pack up all his arrangements only to take them out again when he was in a better mood.

There was a lot of coming and going of well-known American jazz musicians in Switzerland at that time and all of them used to come to the Chikito for a drink.

They often joined us for a jam, as was the case with Willie "the Lion" Smith, Buck Clayton, George Johnson, Merrill Stepter, and Glyn Paque. The public was warm, receptive, and enthusiastic and the club was jumping most of the time.

Six days before the end of our contract, a special event took place which turned out to cause a major change in my life. A young lady came to listen to the band and as I walked by her during one of our breaks, she asked me for my autograph. She was a sweet-looking, very pretty brunette from just outside Berne. I invited her to have coffee with me the next day.

With the passing of time and a few so-so experiences, I was a bit weary of women and didn't really get seriously involved. I had lived through so many changes that I didn't really believe in love any more, I think. And so when I met that young lady the next day in a brasserie, little did I know that my life was taking such a definite turn. In fact my ship had come to port and I was about to drop the anchor—unbeknownst to me.

Her name was Lily, she was Swiss but her family lived in France. She had been married and was not divorced yet. She had a lot of charm and vitality and I found her very attractive. She didn't speak one word of English. As for me I struggled through 30-odd words of French. Our only safe link was jazz music, which she loved.

During the last month at the Chikito I had met an American white fellow who was a civilian worker for the American army in Germany. This man got us an engagement to play for the army's first celebration of their headquarters, 1 March 1950. Felix was with us. We met a colonel who seemed to be a nice person. He invited Felix, myself, and the fellow who got us the engagement for a drink and then asked me if I would be willing to cut our fee because his budget was not what it should have been.

I was not happy about this but after talking with the musicians I accepted a cut of $50. The colonel was satisfied and took us on a tour of the kitchen, where we saw at least ten refrigerators, all packed with food. He promised us a fine meal after we finished playing. We had a snack before we started. We had to play alternately in two big halls.

We were playing our last set of the night around 3 a.m., and as the public was groovy we did some spectacular numbers. The colonel had been juicing it up the whole night. He heard us and asked us to repeat those numbers in the other hall. I refused because we had been playing all night, had taken a cut in our salary and felt we had done our good deed for the day!

So this bastard ordered every refrigerator to be locked up and told the kitchen personnel not to give us anything to eat. I was really salty. That guy had really no consideration for musicians. We slept on empty stomachs that morning. No restaurants were open in the city when we returned to our hotel.

Felix Debrit had become my manager and had contacted the Bernini-Bristol, a big hotel in Rome where he was offered a six-week engagement. Lily and I were sad at the idea of parting. She had started to study English and we had simply begun to be in love with one another. We were making all kinds of plans, but I had no idea what the future would hold for us.

On 11 March 1950, the band left for Rome. That was a thrill for me because I had learned the history of that great city in school and had heard about its beauty with all the ancient ruins from the times of the Caesars. Now I would have the opportunity of seeing those things.

George Smith left the band because he was obliged to respect a contract he had made for the Cigale, a jazz café in Paris. So Felix had asked an American drummer named Benny Bennet to join me in Rome. Benny was a Negro who looked more like a suntanned South American. He had gotten his discharge from the army somewhere in Europe and stayed in Paris. The next day we had to give an audition to the manager of the hotel. He started to make a stink because the drummer was not the same as the one on a photo that had been sent to him. Felix explained the reason for the change in drummers.

The opening was on 16 March 1950. We followed a big radio band of about 25 musicians and singers altogether. This big package was led by the pianist Armando Travaioli who, I was told, was the best arranger of commercial music in Italy. And here I was with my five musicians and one girl singer, trying to please a house that was accustomed to the sound of a big commercial orchestra. It was quite a wealthy and snobbish audience: some women were using lorgnettes to look at the band! The big band didn't have to use amplification but it was a necessity for us, but the loudspeakers were terrible and badly regulated.

Our efforts didn't last very long because we were told the third day that we were fired. It was like my experience in Alexandria all over again. The next day I took Felix and Bass Hill with me to the American Embassy and we told the lawyer of the Embassy about the affair. He said he didn't think there was much we could do and that a contract with anyone in Italy was not worth the paper it was written on. I was very annoyed, mostly for the situation of the musicians who had come from the States.

A Roman jazz magazine called *Musica Jazz* had this to say about my Bernini-Bristol affair:

> The month of March had brought us a very big disappointment. One of the most famous trumpeters in the history of jazz had been engaged to play at the Bernini-Bristol and had brought with him a combo of fine jazz musicians of good reputation. But what happened was that Bill was fired after only three days. And for what reason? The band did not play the Harry Lime theme, tangos, and Italian commercials. What kind of band was that? Were they not there to please the public and play their requests? So all the people who liked jazz and were overjoyed to have, for once, the occasion to listen to a good jazz orchestra, were more than disappointed because many of them did not have the chance to hear the band.

I became acquainted with Sergio Sangiorgi, who, I later found out, was a count and a lover of jazz. I also became acquainted with bassist Carlo Loffredo, who was president of the Hot Club of Rome, and did a concert with the Roman New Orleans Jazz Band of which he was a member. This happened on 10 April 1950 and featured Arstella Whittier, Big Boy Goudie, Armando Travaioli without his big band, Yvan Vandor (a soprano sax man), and a Spanish tenor man, Salvador Font.

Norman Lester went back to the States. The rest of us decided to stay in Rome and play it by ear; we would continue, either separately or together, as a group.

One day, I received a letter from Lily saying that she was coming to Rome. It was written in French and I could not read much of it, but I thought I understood what day and the hour she would arrive and I intended meeting her at the station. A few days later, I was coming from the American Express Company and happened to look into a taxi that had stopped, and who should I see but Lily. I was surprised because I had not been expecting her at that time. So I wasn't at the station when she had arrived and she had been very upset because she didn't have the address of my hotel, only the American Express Company address. But there is a god for lovers, and it was sheer luck that we met in the street. We have not left one another since!

We had rented a room in a place called Pensione Beccari on the via del Tritone. Many artists lived there. I met a West Indian fellow named Stanley Carter. I had heard of him but never seen him. Stanley played piano and sang. His act was one on the style of Norris Rocco, an American Negro who was very popular in the downtown theater circle of many big cities and white night clubs in the States.

Duke Ellington was on his first tour of Europe after World War II, and it was a delightful pleasure to know that he would be coming to Rome during the time I was there. He played a theater for six concerts and we went to five of them. We had a fantastic time.

Some of the musicians I didn't know were Ernie Royal, a trumpeter, Alvin McCain, a tenor man, Butch Ballard, a drummer that Duke had engaged to play ballads and classic numbers, while Sonny Greer featured on certain numbers that called for his showmanship, and there was Wendell Marshall, a bass player. But Lily and I soon became well acquainted with all of them. Don Byas played with Duke, replacing trombonist Ted Kelly who had taken sick and had to go back to the USA.

Benny Goodman came also in May to Rome with a small combo featuring Roy Eldridge, Ed Shaughnessy on drums, and Toots Thielemans on harmonica.

Big Boy Goudie joined the Martinican orchestra of the Fanfan Brothers playing at the Rupe Tarpea. Bass Hill left for Germany and I managed to get a one-month engagement with Fred Palmer and Arstella Whittier in a club called the Florida. We had an Italian pianist and an Italian drummer, Roberto Zappuella, a 16-year-old drumming wonder: Roberto sounded like a 30-year-old pro. His technique was excellent. He played modern but solid and with a whole lot of feeling. We also had an alto sax man, Al Melili, whom I had met in Egypt. He spoke very good English.

During the day Lily and I went sightseeing and I had a ball filming the ruins and also modern monuments. Arstella had moved to a family pension and told us that there were rooms free and that we could cook there. This pleased Lily and me as we were tired of eating in restaurants and having Italian food twice a day, so we moved.

For a while I was without work and the owner of the pension asked Lily one day why I didn't try to get a job, perhaps as a dishwasher in some restaurant! Some people just don't understand that an artist has to go through slow periods and that no security is attached to our profession. Anyway I always paid my rent when it was due so she had no reason to worry whether I worked or not.

Thanks to Count Sangiorgi, I landed a contract to play the summer season at the Casino of Viareggio but somehow the chips must have been down because there too we ran into problems. The director of the casino pretended, when we got there, that he did not know that four members of my orchestra were Italians. He was refusing to honor his contract with us and to pay the same salary to a mixed orchestra as he would have to an all Negro orchestra—which shows that prejudice works in some strange kinds of ways.

The whole thing was weird because he, the director, had come to Rome to the Club Florida to audition us. What Al Melili told him, I don't know, but I could see that he was afraid to speak up for our rights and I figured that if Sangiorgi or Fred Palmer (who spoke Italian) had been there, things would not have happened the way they did. But we were stuck and I accepted the fact that it was better to do the season with a cut in salary than to do nothing at all. One thing is sure, I was getting sick and tired of the Italian way of doing business.

The casino was rather small; it was all white and located in front of via Carducci, on the seafront. There was a beautiful garden full of palm trees and we played outdoors. The heat was almost intolerable during the day but the evenings were cool. It was a joy to be playing with the sky, the moon, and stars above us. The whole region of Viareggio was communist, as was the director of the casino. This was at the time of the Korean War and although I encountered no difficulties with anyone ever, the director seemed to have the happiest time of his life when he could talk about some of the difficulties the Americans were having. If the US lost a battle, he looked so overjoyed that I thought he was going to wet his pants.

Time passed pleasantly, in spite of these difficulties. We went to the beach, went out for long bicycle rides, took sweet afternoon siestas in the pine groves, and went on excursions to pretty towns like Pisa, Lucca, and Forte dei Marmi. I took miles of films of the scenery.

We also went often to the beach, although I was not a great swimmer but I could float! After a lot of sun bathing, our bathing costumes were colorless and I became as dark as a peace of charcoal.

I had met some musicians from Pisa who had proposed that I do some gigs with them in the region. Lily spoke Italian and was beginning to pick up on English. So I decided to stay around that part of Italy for a while. Our headquarters was still Viarregio. We played a few times in Pisa and we were invited to dinner by a number of people who treated us in royal fashion. I worked with that same group in Montecatini, Vechiano, Sarzana, Lucca, Bagni di Lucca, Forte dei Marmi, etc.

One night we were in Pisa and one of the musicians invited us to a chicken party. He had cooked 13 of them. Our landlady had a funny little dog named Fouffy who was crazy about chicken bones, so we asked our host to save the bones for the dog. There was a huge packet of it, and the next day when we showed it to

Fouffy he ran away screaming so that you would have thought he had seen a ghost.

Towards the end of the summer season, Fred Palmer and Arstella went to Germany to join Bass Hill, who was playing in the orchestra of drummer McAllen, in Berlin, at the Neger Bar. Eventually, Big Boy Goudie replaced Fred Palmer and stayed with that same orchestra for years.

The season had ended and I too had some changes coming up. I had a new three-month engagement at the Chikito in Berne and I went back to Paris to assemble the musicians I needed. It was great to be "back home"—that's the way I felt about Paris—and I was getting a kick out of showing the city to Lily, who had never been there before. I was showing her "my city!"

A few days after we arrived I was contacted to make a five-day tour with a small variety show called Radio Cocktail 51. The three Peter Sisters, who were a very popular singing trio in the States, were now a big sensation in Europe. They had two younger sisters named Edith and Joyce who had formed a singing duo and they were part of the show, which included André Salvador, the brother of Henri, who was a very famous singer and comedian in Europe. I first met the Salvador brothers in late 1935 at the Villa d'Este when they were about 17 and 18 years old. They were looking like twin brothers and both played fine guitar and sang. Don Byas was also engaged for the tour, as was singer Francis Linel and Lucienne Marnay, who was famous for impersonating other actors. The other musicians were French.

The two Peter Sisters were billed as the Peter Sisters Junior and their mother, a fine woman, traveled with them. Our last date was in Montpellier, and there Edith and Joyce ran into some racial problem that I had never before experienced in France. They had been booked in a different hotel from the one we were in, and when they arrived and asked for their reservations, they were told that none had been made for them. Miss Lucienne Marnay was booked in the same hotel and when she heard that the Peter Sisters were refused a room, she raised hell in French because Edith and Joyce didn't speak French. When she was through telling whoever it was at the desk what she thought of them and what scandal she would create, they found the reservation and quick.

We were back to Paris on 28 October 1950 and Don Byas and I were engaged to open a new club called the Perroquet. A Hollywood starlet, Marsha Gayle, was running it. It was located at 49 rue de Ponthieu, near the Champs-Elysées. Rudy Castel led an Afro-Cuban orchestra while Don and I took care of the jazz. Katherine Dunham's show was playing a theater in Paris and one of her young dancers was making her debut at the Perroquet as a singer. Her name was Eartha Kitt. The show was excellent. The club was decorated very nicely but it did not go well in spite of all this, and it closed after a week.

I had gotten my own orchestra together for the Chikito engagement and had hired a Martinican pianist, Pierre Jean Louis. His technique was brilliant and his style had a touch of Thelonious Monk. Georgie Smith was back on drums, and I had found a young American bassist, Alvin "Buddy" Banks, who played an excellent style, a little like Oscar Pettiford. He had been stationed for many years with the occupying forces of the American Army in Germany. I had also a Martinican alto saxophonist, Edouard Pajaniandy, and our regular "canary," Arstella Whittier.

Lily was showing a good business sense and had a special talent for maintaining public relations. She had begun to try her hand at finding contracts for us. We went on a series of concerts in Switzerland and Belgium.

We opened at the Chikito on 1 December and ended on 31 March. Then I had concerts with the group in Brussels, Geneva, Bienne, Zurich, Neuchâtel, and Lucerne. I also had a contract to play at the Cinema Rex in Zurich for eleven days starting on 16 April.

A few days before, Georgie Smith said that he was not going unless he saw my contract. I thought he was kidding because I had never heard any musician ask the leader to let him see his contract. I told him so and told him that he could go. I knew that Wallace Bishop was in Basel, Switzerland, and that he was not working. I contacted him and he was free and willing to join me. We opened the Rex and the band sounded better than before because Bish had more experience on drums than Georgie Smith. But one day the manager of the Rex came and told me that Pajaniandy had come to his office and asked to see the contract and that he had let him see it. Here we go again. I was mad as hell and told him that the contract was a personal matter between him and me. At least I was expecting a little respect from my musicians. But I had found that Edouard Pajaniandy was a trouble-maker. I had had several disputes with him.

By the end of April we were in Blankenberge, Belgium, a summer resort on the North Sea, where we were hoping to spend the summer at the Caveau Majestic. We worked there, on and off, from the end of April until mid-June, when we discovered that the manager couldn't get the working permit for the summer season. As I had no other contract I had to disband and we all went back to Paris, except for Buddy Banks who had married a Swiss girl and went back to Switzerland.

Home was wherever I hung my hat and I traveled with all my earthly belongings. Lily had quite a few things also. When we left Blankenberge for Paris we had 14 bags and had to leave most of them in the corner of the train's vestibule. I was watching over them and was worried about having to open all those bags when the custom agents would come through at the border. But to my surprise and relief, all they did ask was for our passports.

Up to that time, I had always lived in Paris's Pigalle but this time I decided to "emigrate" to the Latin Quarter. Lily and I moved in to the Hôtel Crystal, right across from the Club St.-Germain. This was at the time of the fame of St.-Germain-des-Prés, the district where students, artists, and friends met in the large cafés. Boris Vian played trumpet at the Tabou, the Club St.-Germain was jumping, and Sidney Bechet officiated at the Vieux Colombier. Our favorite café was the Royal-St.-Germain and we used to hang out on the terrace until the wee hours of the morning.

Charles Delaunay offered me an engagement at the Vieux Colombier with the orchestra of Claude Bolling because Bechet went to Juan-les-Pins for the summer season. I accepted. Claude was a very talented young pianist. He was strongly influenced by Duke Ellington and was already arranging at the time. The orchestra included bassist Guy de Fatto, who eventually became a priest and chaplain of the artists. He loved Spike Jones's type of jokes. There were Roger Paraboschi (drums), Jacques Hess (guitar), Maxim Saury (clarinet), and Benny Wasseur (trombone). It was a good little combo.

The joint was jumping every night and this was not an image but for real. Young dancers had been digging on how to do the jitterbug. The Africans were the best dancers but there were some French cats that were on the ball and gave the Africans a tight race.

We were supposed to finish at the Vieux Colombier on 23 September and we had to start at the Club St.-Germain on 17 October. Between these two dates, I went on tour in France with the orchestra of the French drummer Gerard Pochonnet and a few well-known entertainers: Canadian singer Felix Leclerc, Jack Gautier and André Claveau, singers, duettists Varel and Bailly, and others. Felix Leclerc was a very quiet and nice person to be with, but André Claveau was very temperamental and playing the big star. The show was often backstage as much as on stage. It was very funny.

Back in Paris I started working at the club St.-Germain-des-Prés. Claude Bolling had made a few changes in the orchestra: Charles Huss replaced Benny Wasseur on trombone, Robert Barnett was on drums. William Boucaya (baritone sax) replaced Jacques Hess and Gille Thibaut was no longer in the band.

One night in November I was surprised to see Josh White, the popular folk singer and guitarist, come into the club. When I had a break I went to his table. He was with some English people. He had come to Paris from London, where he was working on a radio show for the BBC. He engaged me and the band to do his show, which was to be heard at Christmas. We recorded it on 23 November.

Lots of different artists and showbiz personalities used to come by the club, which was very popular then. Film actor John Garfield came often and also Shelley Winters, who seemed to have a crush on Charles Huss, who looked like Robert Mitchum. She was a bright, dynamic, pretty girl who loved to dance. John Garfield was a heavy drinker and he often went to sleep in his chair. I suppose he was in Paris making a film, as was Shelley also.

One night we had a visit from Tommy Dorsey. I had seen and heard him in New York, but I had never met or spoken to him. I told him that I had been in Sy Oliver's band, who had been his arranger for many years. Someone asked Tommy to play. He didn't have his horn with him but he agreed to play on Charles Huss's. We took photos with him and our band. I already had a picture taken with his brother Jimmy at Jimmy Ryan's in New York, so now I had met the two famous brothers.

On 9 November 1951 I recorded for Jacques Canetti, who was artistic director for Phillips and had been once artistic director for Louis Armstrong in Europe. I had Bill Tamper arrange the numbers and also play trombone. The other musicians were Jay Cameron, who played alto on this session but was actually a baritone player, William Boucaya (baritone sax), Art Simmons (piano), Jean-

Pierre Sasson (guitar), Guy de Fatto (bass), and Gerard "Dave" Pochonnet (drums).

We were all on time for the session except Art, who came two hours later. While waiting for Art, Jean-Pierre Sasson and I composed a number and called it *Jumping at the Pleyel* because we were recording on the stage of the Salle Pleyel. We recorded this number with the rhythm section minus Art Simmons.

Art finally arrived about 4 p.m., and naturally Canetti and of the rest of us were unhappy about this. Art claimed that he had another recording date that he thought would be finished in time for him to do the one with me. Canetti said that he would never use Art for another session, and Boucaya, who was doing a lot of studio work, said that something like that only happens with jazz musicians.

I left the Club St.-Germain after a stormy argument with the guy who managed it. We had a misunderstanding and had words. He became excited and coarse and told me I was fired. I felt like punching him but succeeded in controlling myself. I had been hired by the bandleader and not the management, but since Bolling, who was a very shy leader, let it ride, so did I. I did not want to cause him any trouble since he was afraid to lose his job. I stomped out of there and hit the road again.

I received an offer to do two concerts in Berlin and left by train for Hanover on 27 March. The next day I took a train to Berlin. I was met at the airport by some men from the television and two German jazz fans, Hans Blutner and Fritz Krull. They had brought with them Tiger Jones, an American boxer who was touring Germany.

I went for a TV interview and then played a concert with some very good German musicians after only talking over the few numbers I wanted to play. The public was enthusiastic and I had a great reception. After the concert I was invited to the most popular jazz club in Berlin, a very large place where I jammed with the group of Johannes Rediske, a fine guitarist. Tiger Jones could sing pretty well and he also joined in the session.

As this was my first visit, Hans and Fritz took me sightseeing the next day. The effects of the bombings that Berlin received in World War II could be seen everywhere, but the bricks from the ruins were stacked in neat piles and the streets were the cleanest I've ever seen. I saw the gateway to East Berlin, the Russian War Memorial, and the stadium where Hitler had refused to shake hands with the great American Negro athlete Jessie Owens during the 1936 Olympic Games.

My second concert took place in another theater in a different part of the city. There was a German trumpeter on the bill that night who was known as the best in Germany. His name was Macky Kasper and he was good, but his main claim to fame was that he could blow loud. He had iron chops, as we say.

One day in early April, as I was coming back from a tour of concerts in France and Belgium, Lily and Jimmy "Lover Man" Davis met me at the station. He offered me a part in a cabaret scene for the movie *The Respectful Prostitute*, by French playwright Jean-Paul Sartre. We would have to play several numbers but I can remember only one, a composition of Jimmy's, *'Cause I'm Black*. The actors were Walter Bryant, a Negro Shakespearian actor, and Barbara Laage. Besides me, the musicians were Aaron Bridgers (piano), Jo Benjamin (bass), Bill Clark (drums), and of course Jimmy "Lover Man" Davis (vocalist). Jo and Bill were the accompanists of Lena Horne, the famous and beautiful singer, who was working in Paris at the Moulin Rouge.

On 19 May I left Paris by plane for Morocco to join drummer Gerard Pochonet and his group in Casablanca. There was Charlie Blareau (bass), Bob Aubert (guitar), Armand Borgogno (piano), and Roll Elvins (tenor sax). I had done a number of gigs with Pochonet in France and it was he who had arranged for this contract. We toured in a bus. The landscape and all the road sights had me plunged back in biblical times. I was overjoyed with this stay because, throughout the years, I had developed a sentimental attachment for the oriental way of life and these North African countries.

We played Rabat, several concerts in Casablanca, and Meknes. A one-day surprise Air France strike caused me to spend an extra holiday in Casablanca. I flew back to Paris on 28 May.

The months of June and July 1952 found me gigging around France and Belgium. On 16 July Lily and I left for Chamonix, where we intended to spend the summer. It was a beautiful trip going up into the mountains on a special little train, where the track seemed never to stop going around and up. I was engaged to work for six weeks in a club called L'Outa. It was a nice place on the main street of Chamonix and had a beautiful park-like garden in the back.

I hadn't known any of the musicians I was to work with, although they were from Paris. They were not really jazz musicians but they did a very good job. The guitarist, Harry Katz, was very good; later, and for many years, he became an accompanist of Gilbert Becaud. His brother was married to Ann Peter, one of the Peter Sisters.

We were staying in a hotel where a stream from the mountains passed just under our window. The water was as grey as some days that I have seen and the current was so swift that it sounded like the water that goes over the Niagara Falls in a continuous roar. It was beautiful to see this stream coming down from the mountains and going to Lord knows where with such rapidity, but trying to sleep with that continuous roar was impossible. So after a few days Lily went to a real-estate agency and asked if there was a possibility of renting a small chalet somewhere near. They found one for us that had everything that was needed. We were near the same stream but it didn't roar at this spot, and we were about ten yards away from it with the mountain train passing one yard from our side porch. But that never disturbed us because they were electric trains and there were none at night. We named the chalet "Billily." We went on visits to the Sea of Ice and were happy in our little place. It was the first time we felt we had our blue Heaven. And we also found a little cat.

Lily was doing a lot of thinking on ways and means to promote my European career and she had started to try to get me to do a grand tour of France with American jazz musicians. I had been a little reluctant in the beginning but she convinced me that it would be interesting work and that the publicity all over

France and Europe would be very valuable. Some people had advised Lily against the kind of tour she had in mind, particularly Charles Delaunay, who feared we would lose money, but we had met a young fellow from Toulouse named Jean-Gabriel Formisyn, who was an architect and a great jazz fan. He played trumpet also. He gave Lily a lot of valuable informations about theaters she could contact, jazz clubs, publicity, etc. I wrote to some of the New York friends and musicians whom I wanted with me on this tour: my old pal Dicky Wells (trombone), Jimmy "Slim" Rivers (ex-Benny Carter pianist), and Tommy Benford (drums).

I left Lily in Chamonix after the engagement at the Outa ended and went on the road for several gigs in the south of France. When I returned to Chamonix in early September, there was a letter from Tommy Benford saying he couldn't come with me because he was working with Jimmy Archey's band. I had more gigs in Switzerland and Germany so it was decided that Lily would go to Paris and enquire about a drummer there.

Dicky Wells was very happy to join me and I decided to engage Guy Lafitte, a 25-year-old French tenor man who, the previous year, had made a successful tour with Mezz Mezzrow. He was from Toulouse and he was already an excellent musician with a beautiful tone, very strongly influenced by Coleman Hawkins.

On 10 September I had to leave Chamonix for Geneva, where I was to take a train for Hanover, Germany, to begin a 21-day tour of that country. The leader of the orchestra I had to play with was the trumpet man Fred Bunge. I found out very soon that he was a better musician than Macky Kasper: he had more finesse, a good technique, and more ideas about jazz than Macky had. He was one of the best European trumpeters. Teddy Paris, the drummer, was up-to-date and knew how to push a soloist. I'd say that he was a German Sid Catlett. The pianist was fine, sort of Teddy Wilson in style, and was also an arranger.

In Paris, Lily was meeting with great difficulties in finding a drummer. We had a number of long telephone conversations and finally decided to engage Zutty Singleton. I liked Zutty, whom we called "Face," but I was certain that he would be a very disagreable person to get along with when it came to working, but we were stuck and needed a drummer, so that was that. One day we received notice that Jimmy "Slim" Rivers had died suddenly so there we were without a pianist and not much time left to find one.

Lily had heard about a young Canadian Negro pianist, Randy Downs, who played clubs in Paris. She asked Zutty and his wife Marge to go with her and audition Randy to see whether they thought he could make the tour. Zutty agreed and at the end of the evening he declared that he thought Randy would do OK. Lily lost no time in signing him up to a contract the very next day. Alvin "Buddy" Banks (bass) and Arstella Whittier made up the rest of the group.

All seemed settled but there was trouble in store. A few days later, Zutty went back to hear Randy Downs and that night he didn't like Randy's playing. It must have been a case of Zutty's gauge that had convinced him the first time that Randy was alright! But Lily had signed a contract with Randy and we could do nothing about it whether Zutty had changed his mind or not.

Then it was Arstella who didn't come through. On Lily's advice, she had changed her name to Martine Kay. She wrote that she was sick and could not make the tour. The truth is that she had fallen in love with a guy and would not leave him for several months. Someone told us that there was a singer named Miriam Burton in town. She had been the lead singer in Katherine Dunham's troupe and had a beautiful soprano voice. She was not a jazz singer really, but on ballads she was wonderful. So we engaged her also.

The rehearsals started, as well as a series of interviews with the press and television. This tour seemed to attract a lot of attention from the start. We hired a bus which was owned and driven by an ex-wrestler and acrobat, Louis Lamy. He was a great helper for Lily on the tour. He acted as band valet and road manager.

Our first concert was in Le Havre, on 13 October 1952. We were all a little nervous and Dicky Wells didn't seem to be feeling too well. He said he had a cold and needed to drink some "grogs" (toddies). He had come from New York on this winter tour without an overcoat. We had a great reception and good success. In Rouen a few days later, Miriam brought the house down with her interpretation of some of the tunes from *Porgy and Bess*.

But Dicky was definitely not in good shape and I was beginning to think that he drank and didn't hold his liquor too well. I went to see him in his room and told him to get himself straight so that he would be in good shape for the Salle Pleyel concert in Paris on 18 October because Parisian critics would be there and could influence the rest of our tour. The theater was packed that day and we had a tremendous success, except for Miriam Burton whom the young public started booing as soon as she started singing *Summertime*. She had had a big success in other towns we'd played before Paris, but the Paris fans just don't seem to go for singers, except for big names like Ella Fitzgerald, Sarah Vaughan, and so on.

Of course the rhythm section had its problems and eventually Zutty went into his act, which I had been afraid of. He just couldn't stand Randy and every night he was growling about that sh— pianist! He would even slow down the tempo terribly, and if I said something he'd put the blame on Randy.

I knew Zutty had a reputation for being moody and difficult to work with. He would at times be very unpleasant. It was a pity because he and Marge were such jolly people when you didn't have to work with them. They started to be real drags, staying for themselves, refusing friendly advances. They had an old dog named "Bring Down" traveling with them. It came to the point that Zutty was coming in the bus holding Bring Down tight so nobody would pat that dog. Dicky Wells tried to make jokes and bring gaiety in the bus but Zutty told him to shut up.

Zutty was making me feel miserable and nobody was happy about that situation except Randy and Buddy Banks, who didn't care and were close buddies. Those two were always up to some foolishness. One night at 9 p.m. they had not shown up at the theater. The place was packed. Somebody told me that they had been seen in an amusement park nearby. I went there and found them having a ball on a merry-go-round for kids, wearing two long wool caps with tassels, one green, one red.

The first time I ever saw my name in lights was the night we played in Le Mans,

19 October. I was surprised when I arrived at the Rex Theater in that city and saw "Bill Coleman and his Orchestra" in big red lights on the front.

The next time I saw "Bill Coleman and his Orchestra" in big lights was when we did a concert in Barcelona, Spain, on 19 November. It was a coincidence that it was just one month after Le Mans, and it was a pleasant sight for me to see. I was thrilled to have the opportunity to be the first American jazz musician to do a concert in Spain since Benny Carter had done one there in 1936. It was the first time I had set foot in that country and we were treated like kings. The two brothers Papo, who were two young boys then, took us out in the city to go sightseeing. We didn't have much time but what we did see, we enjoyed.

The tour also took us to Belgium for three concerts, and we had eight in Switzerland, which was something very rare for an orchestra to do in that little country, but I had plenty of friends and fans there. And I'm certain that I'm the only American that ever did concerts in 43 cities in France. We played every big city and some that were not so large. We usually had good crowds, but after having paid the band, the bus driver, and all the expenses, there wasn't much money left for us.

The period between 15 December and 15 January is a very difficult one for organizing concerts, so Lily had asked the musicians if they would agree to work at the Chikito in Berne, at cabaret salaries of course. Everyone had agreed. The Chikito was to close on Christmas and New Year's days and those two days would not be paid.

Dicky Wells went back to the States. At that time he still wasn't feeling well. Miriam Burton went back to Paris. To replace her I engaged a beautiful Negro girl, Suzette Aimes. She sang in a very low register and didn't have much experience, but she somehow sang the way girls such as Aretha Franklin are singing today. She had a new approach to jazz.

Benny Waters replaced Dicky Wells. He had come to Europe with the Jimmy Archey Orchestra. (Tommy Benford, whom I wanted as a drummer, had also come to Europe with Archey's band.) But this orchestra had been badly handled by the agent who had booked them and, after a few concerts, most of the musicians had had to go back to the States. Benny played alto sax and clarinet but he had left his alto in the States and could not find one in Europe that would suit him. However, Benny fitted into the band very well and the front line of tenor, clarinet, and trumpet was very nice. Benny transposed all the alto parts and the arrangements went down well.

We had opened at the Chikito on 16 December. Zutty started to grumble every day that he wanted to be paid for those two days of Christmas and New Year. I told him that I wasn't getting paid either and that I was not going to give him any special favors from my pocket.

On 29 December we received our pay, minus the Christmas night. Zutty was salty when he counted his money but he didn't say anything to me. The next morning, someone called me and told me that Zutty had left the country. Since I couldn't stop him as it was too late now, I wrote to the Union Local 802 in New York and brought charges against him. He was ordered to pay me the equivalent of his two weeks' notice, which made $500. He had to do it and he did. Later, I read in an interview that he had been working with me in Europe for "peanuts." But where Mezzrow had paid him $200 a week, I was coming up with $250, which was very good money then.

When I had been in Geneva with Jack Dieval I had met a young Swiss drummer, Pascal Jeanmairet, also called "Caspoil." He was actually an amateur drummer, but he studied the drums and could play very well. As luck would have it, he was free to join me, even though it was 30 December. That night the band sounded better than it had for a long time because Zutty had been a drag to everyone on the tour and it was nice to see a smiling face behind the set of drums at last and have them played correctly too. Eventually Caspoil and Suzette got involved in more things than music—they fell in love and got married.

Everything was going smoothly when Mr. Tripet, the director of the Chikito, called me into his office because there was some trouble with Buddy Banks. I was shocked when he told me Banks was in the country illegally and that the police wanted him expelled within 24 hours. The problem was that he had married a blonde from Zurich who was a prostitute and, since he could not get a work permit, he had been living off her earnings in Zurich for a year. Banks's story had been that he had married a very rich girl who had a big house and a big car, a wealthy family, etc.

Mr. Tripet had been a colonel in the Swiss Army and could pull some strings. He managed to get permission for Banks to stay as long as he worked with me and as long as I stayed in Switzerland. I had five concerts booked after finishing at the Chikito and had a contract for one month in a club in St. Gallen, near the German border.

A few days before we ended at the Chikito, Banks came to tell me that he was going back to Paris with Randy. About two weeks later a fellow came to the boarding house where Lily and I were staying and informed us that he was a lawyer who was co-operating with a colleague in Paris who was filing a suit against me. His client, Buddy Banks, was claiming that I owed him about $2000 for breach of contract. He was claiming that he had done cabaret work instead of concerts at a lower salary. We had worked together for four months, as we had agreed, though with only three months of concert playing and one month of cabaret work. I was really disgusted with that guy to whom I had given a chance to be known in Europe, who had accepted the job in Berne without having the right to set foot in Switzerland and was now asking for compensation! As for Randy Downs, he was a nice guy but easily influenced and had fallen under the influence of an unstable, fickle person.

Lily, being Swiss, knew of the laws of that country and told me that we should give all the things of value that we had with us to the owner of the boarding house to keep for us, because whenever a law suit was filed against someone, the law could confiscate everything except what was necessary for a person to use for working. In any case it was my instrument and clothing. I had a movie camera, a new projector, and a few other things of value and we gave them to the lady who ran the boarding house. And a few days later the lawyer came back with a detective and presented me with a paper which said that anything of value I had would be taken from me and held until my case was settled. They took two rings that were not of any value, but couldn't take anything else. I had to engage a lawyer in Paris who obtained a settlement in my favor.

I had to go to Paris to find replacement musicians, and I came back to Switzerland with a Martinican bass player named Emmanuel Jude and a Martinican pianist I had already worked with, Pierre Jean Louis. After Berne, we started to play at the Palais Trischli in St. Gallen on 1 February and finished on the 28th. We had quite a nice success. There was a lot of snow and it was carnival time, a big affair for weeks in St. Gallen.

The pianist and singer Joe Turner was now living in Switzerland and happened to be playing in St. Gallen during the time I was there and we were able to get together a few times and reminisce about some good old days (and bad ones) back in the Apple.

After St. Gallen I had two weeks engagement in St. Moritz, a very fashionable resort. We were working at the Casino Hotel Rosatsch-Excelsior.

For three nights Benny Waters was high and bugging everybody by talking loud when someone else was taking a solo. He was talking mostly to Suzette Aimes, who was trying to keep him cool but in vain. So after the third night of Benny's foolishness I went to see him in his room and asked him if he was drinking during the day, and he said he was. I had nothing against Benny for drinking, because I drank also, but I wanted to find out why he was getting so excited. So I asked him what he was drinking and he said Pernod, which is an anise-flavored drink that the French drink as an appetizer. Next I wanted to know if he was putting enough water in it. He was very surprised to hear that this drink had to be mixed with water and ice. All day long he was drinking big glasses of it pure: no wonder he was so excitable on the bandstand! Everything was alright after that.

One night a party came to the Rosatsch and a fellow came up to me and said he was a pianist; his name was Joe. He asked me if he could sit in for a couple of numbers, and naturally I didn't refuse him. He was American and a fine pianist. It was Doris Duke's party and I found out later that he was not only with her party but with her. They came back quite a few times.

After St. Moritz we played in a place called the Hungaria-Esquire in Zurich. It was very pleasant for me to play in Zurich and have some time to spend with my good friends Johnny and Lisette Simmen and their little daughter. Also with Bettina Blockinger, now married with a fine saxophonist and arranger, Harry Pfister. As Pierre Jean Louis could not stay longer, I engaged on the recommendation of Charles Delaunay a young talented French pianist, Jean-Claude Pelletier.

We finished at the Hungaria-Esquire on 31 March, and that was the end of that orchestra. But Lily was preparing another tour for the coming autumn and Benny Waters was going to be included in it. We had also landed a return engagement in June for the Esquire and had a contract for the month of August in Blankenberge, where I had been refused a permit to work the summer before.

In 1953, I disbanded and returned to Paris with Lily. There was another picturesque wedding which took place in Montmartre at that time and was televised: the gypsy violinist Roman Jacowlew married a Spanish actress, Pilar Gonsalez. Luis Mariano, the famous singer, was the best man and I led a celebration parade. Dozens of children were following me, dancing. Quite a few famous movie actors and comedians were present. People were dancing in the street with music provided by a group of accordionists and also tzigane music. Later the mayor of Montmartre made me an honorary citizen of "la Butte," as that district is called.

A few days after that, Jazz at the Philharmonic was giving a concert at Salle Pleyel. Lily decided to organize a cocktail reception for them at the House of Ricard, the well-known aperitif, from 5 p.m. to 8 p.m. I left the Hôtel de Seine, situated on the Left Bank, where we lived then, around 3.30 p.m. to go and pick up my friend Lester Young at his hotel on rue Scribe, near the American Express. Prez was not ready and I had to wait for him to get dressed and he didn't rush in doing so. Finally we were able to get out of his hotel but he told me that he had promised his wife a singing bird that they had read about in an advertisement in some American journal. I knew of a place on rue Scribe, so I took him there. When Prez saw that the birds were not live but stuffed and "sang" with a wind-up machine that made sounds of birds singing, he got completely disgusted. But he bought perfumes and other gifts. When we arrived at the party it was after 7.30. Lily was burning angry with me. She really had reason to be as I had been the host of the party and my absence had put her in a difficult position. Everybody was asking about me and Prez. Some people had to leave early; it was the case of my good friend Arthur Briggs, but a lot of people were still there, Richie Frost, an American drummer who played with Jack Dieval's group when we played Vienna, Ernie Royal and his wife, Jacques Butler, a long-time friend of mine, a Shakespearian actor, Walter Bryant, Roy Eldridge, etc. Lily finally forgave me and Lester for arriving so late, but she didn't forget it!

Lily's efforts to keep me busy were successful but it was the end of my carefree time as sideman or soloist. That was rolling them Pete because months of contracts were ahead. I was in need of some musicians for my coming jobs in Zurich and Blankenberge in August.

I met a young trombone player from the West Indies named Herman Wilson and a friend of his who played bongos and conga drums. He told me that he had never played jazz drums in an orchestra but he thought he would catch on to the technique of playing if he was given a chance. His name was Donald Brown and he was from the West Indies also. I agreed to engage him and even signed as his sponsor for a set of drums. I engaged a very good French pianist named Jack Starling (Jacques Sansonet in French, which is the same, a starling and a *sansonnet* being the same bird). I also hired a Martinican bass player called Lude. With Benny Waters, the group was complete.

We played one month in Zurich. I found out that Donald Brown was a wild cat, always ready to scuffle. One night on the street, while he was with Herman Wilson, he got into a fight with someone and pulled a knife out. Fortunately it was a mild incident, but I had to go to the police station and accept to be a guarantor of their good behavior until our departure from Zurich.

The job at the Hungaria-Esquire was a break-up for the orchestra but we needed an engagement for the month of July to keep us going until the month of August.

Lily decided to go to Germany and try to find an engagement. I was not hot about her going there alone but she could speak German and we had the address of a booking agent in Hamburg. I also wrote to my friend Hans Blutner that Lily would be coming at a certain time and asked him to help her in every way he possibly could. A few days after Lily left a telegram came to the hotel where we were staying, announcing the death of Lily's mother. This really upset me. The telegram had been sent first to the American Express in Paris, then to our address in Zurich, and it would be too late for Lily to attend the funeral. I telephoned to Hans in Berlin but Lily had already been in Berlin and left for Hamburg. I didn't know where to get in touch with her. So the only thing I could do was wait until she came back to Zurich to tell her the sad news.

I had never met Lily's parents—only some relatives in Neuchâtel, Switzerland. Her father and mother had been terribly upset about her decision of getting a divorce. Her first husband belonged to a very wealthy family and they were very proud of her situation. Her mother couldn't understand that she wanted to get married with a colored jazz musician. For them it was a downfall—living like gypsies. In a certain way they were not wrong about that. They had nothing against me; it was my profession. They would rather have seen their daughter married to a plumber.

Lily didn't have any success in finding a contract for July but I was contacted by an agent to do July in Cologne, Germany. The money was thin but I accepted it to keep the musicians from having to lay off a month. In fact I was paying Benny Waters two marks more than I was getting for this job.

The place was called the Moulin Rouge, and it was a real sad club. I saw the owner once. We had to start at 8.30 p.m. and finished at 4.30 a.m. Daylight was breaking and the birds started to sing. It was going to be an unforgettable, endless, and unenjoyable month for me. The crowd was sparse and no one ever came to me and told me they were jazz fans.

But there were jazz fans in Cologne because there was a club named the Tabou, where Wallace Bishop was working with a British West Indian tenor player, Sammy Walker. It was not our music that kept the jazz lovers from coming to hear my band, it was just that the Moulin Rouge was a gyp joint and no jazz fans would have gone there, even to hear Satchmo or Dizzy.

But we met a nice young couple, Gunter and Hildsche, who invited us to their home and also introduced us to some of their friends. Cologne had been very heavily bombed and it was quite a sad sight to see.

On 27 July we finished at that drag joint and arrived on the 28th in Blankenberge, Belgium, and started at the Caveau Majestic that night. We were all feeling as though we had just woken from a terrible nightmare. There were plenty of people smiling and dancing to our music, which made us play with more enthusiasm than we had done for a long time. We spent a lovely month there. In September we went back to Germany to Hamburg, and worked in a big club called the Faun, where we got a nice success.

When I had spent some days in Hamburg with the Edward's band, which was in 1949 and the first time I had been in Germany, a big part of the city was in ruins. When I returned this time it was a new city and the only place I remembered was the big concert hall where we gave four concerts, and the director said that he would never let the place again for jazz concerts because people in the balconies were tapping their feet so hard that he thought the building would cave in.

Another place I remembered was the night spots in the district of St. Pauli, better known as the Reeperbahn. I took Lily there a few times. Claude Dunson was playing in a big German band in one of the joints. One of the places featured women wrestlers in a ring filled with mud. That was an attraction but quite an ugly sight too.

There was an English orchestra under the leadership of a trumpet player named Ken Colyer and his brother Bill, who were playing at a club near the Ripperbahn. My band and Ken's were engaged to do a radio show, which also included an Austrian tenor sax player named Hans Kohler, who was very popular in Germany. Ken played the real old-time New Orleans jazz, and most of the numbers he played on the show were things that I had never heard played by some of the New Orleans orchestras back home. I remember that they were reading the Bible and made a prayer before going on stage.

Hans had his trio and his style was a little like Lester Young and Stan Getz.

I closed at the Faun on 30 September and arrived in Paris on 2 October. Lily and I were planning another tour of France and we had engaged Wallace Bishop to make the tour with us. There was an Indonesian bass player working with him named Eddie O'Hare that we had engaged also. I had been in touch with the trombonist and arranger Bill Tamper to replace Herman Wilson, who had stayed with Donald Brown in Germany. The rest of the musicians were Jack Starling (piano), Benny Waters (tenor sax), and a male singer named Tommy Brookins, who played enough piano to accompany himself. Bishop and Tommy were buddies and had been going to school together in Chicago.

I had finally gotten a divorce from Madelyn, and on 8 October, Lily and I got married in Paris. What a busy day that was! As we were both foreigners in France, we had to run here and there to sign all sorts of papers until the last minute. The civil ceremony was to be performed at the town hall of St.-Sulpice, and the religious rites were to take place at the American Church at the Quai d'Orsay as Lily and I were both Protestants. This was going to be a strictly private affair and we hadn't really informed anyone because most people thought we were married anyway. Neither of our families was present; mine were too far away and Lily's didn't approve, though Lily's young sister Suzanne had flowers sent to us.

We had two witnesses, Colette Lacroix and Sacha Dillot. Our friends Maurice and Vonette Cullaz were there too. As we had forgotten to hire a photographer, Maurice kept running in and out of the town hall building to a phone, trying to locate a photographer. Sacha and the assistant mayor had fallen into each other's arms: they had been in the Resistance together and were reminiscing about the good old days. Finally the ceremony began. At one time the mayor said something which I didn't understand because my French was limited. There was a silence. I decided to say "Yes" and I hit the right note. I had played it by ear and come out right at the coda.

Maurice finally managed to find a photographer, Ollie Steward, a news reporter who wrote for the *Chicago Defender*. He used a flash camera which sounded like a small bunch of fire crackers, but his pictures came out wonderful.

The priest, Reverend William, had insisted on giving us a lecture before the ceremony. He asked Lily if she was aware of the problems created by interracial marriage, especially if we had to go back to live in the USA. Yes, said Lily, she was.

After both ceremonies had ended, we went to have dinner at Leroy Haynes's restaurant on rue Manuel. Haynes made wonderful soul food and we had a ball. We decided to finish that happy day at the Ringside, rue d'Artois, which later became the Blue Note. It was run by an American, Dick Edwards. Lionel Hampton came, kissed the bride, and jammed for hours. That was the end of a hectic but beautiful day for Lily and me.

Then we began our tour of France. Tommy Brookins, like Fred Palmer, liked to play the big star. He traveled around with a blonde Swedish girl whom he used to lock up in their hotel room because he was the jealous type. He did the tour in his Cadillac although the bus I had rented was big enough for musicians and wives (or girlfriends). His whole paycheck must have gone to pay his gasoline bill, but I was not going to pay Tommy's transportation in his private car, not that he had ever asked me anything of the sort.

In Paris we gave two concerts at the Cinéma Cluny. The afternoon one was recorded by Pathé-Marconi. After the evening concert some of the musicians were outside on the sidewalk talking with friends. Some people who lived above the cinema came to their window and yelled, "Quiet, shut up, let the people sleep!" As we didn't move off right away, they came back with a bucket of water. Benny Waters, who was just then coming out of the cinema, received the shower and was entirely bewildered, not knowing what was going on. He got disgusted with us for laughing and cracking up.

After Paris, we still had 43 other concerts to play in France. Instead of "Bill Coleman and his Swing Stars," we should have been called the "Jazz Travelers" or something of the kind. But we were reaching our goal and my name was beginning to be known all over the place. We were getting a faithful public and also faithful friends whom we always met again with pleasure.

We had a concert in Marseille on 27 November and were to fly on the 29th to Casablanca. There were two jazz clubs in Marseille that were enemies. The one who had not sponsored our concerts was trying to make a scandal to keep the concert from taking place. They didn't succeed but they cut all four of the tires of our bus with knives.

On the 28th we had a day of rest and we were invited to the house of Simone Mansi, who was a friend to many jazz musicians. Before dinner, Tommy Brookins started to tell me he was afraid to fly and asked if it would be alright if he stayed in Marseille and waited for us to return. I jumped sky high and told him that the

Casablanca engagement was a big affair and that his name was on the contract. He said OK, he would come.

The next morning, everybody was at the airport on time except Tommy. The president of the Hot Club, who was there to see us off, volunteered to go and find him. He called later to say that Tommy had checked out of the hotel. I left his ticket for him at the airport, just in case, but I had a nasty feeling he wouldn't show up.

In Casablanca, we played for the Lion's Club ball, which was a big deal and they had engaged all sorts of attractions, including a group of real American Indians, with all their feathers! Also Arab musical groups and dancers. I told the organizers that Tommy had missed his plane and would come later. They didn't make any comment. I had never played for an occasion of this type and we all had a ball that night. And Tommy Brookins wasn't missed by anyone.

We had five more concerts to give in North Africa: two in Morocco, at Casablanca and Rabat, and three in Algeria, one at Oran and two in Algiers. We had a nice success everywhere. Tommy wasn't asked about and we didn't miss him. It was a good lesson, really. Charles Delaunay had advised us against engaging a singer, male or female, since, he said, I was a good singer. I had lacked self-confidence but from that time on, I sang more and more often.

We had a day off in Algiers. Louis Lamy, our road manager, took us to visit a place a few miles from Algiers, a big park where there were thousands of monkeys in freedom. We flew back to Marseille on 6 December. The president of the Hot Club was there to meet us and gave me a message from Tommy saying that he was back at the hotel, waiting for us. I gave him a message to take back: "Keep waiting."

We had eight more concerts to play, ending in Dijon on 14 December. The tour had been a booking success for Lily, who three years before knew nothing of this kind of business. We left Paris on 20 December for Switzerland, where I was going to work until March with the group (minus Bill Tamper).

THIRTEEN

CHECKING OUT THE USA

Lily and I had made plans to go to the States for the months of April through June 1954. We sailed on 1 April, on the *Liberté*, which was a fine ship. We enjoyed every mile from Le Havre to New York. I played a few numbers for the gala nights which were scheduled on different nights in each class.

Oran "Hot Lips" Page had booked a hotel room in New York for us. When we docked, at 6 a.m. on 7 April, he was there to meet us with some friends. We had planned to spend a week in the Apple before going to Cincinnati. During that time we saw and heard many of my pals and colleagues, such as Dicky Wells, Al Hall, and Herb Flemming. We often went to the Metropole Bar where Red Allen was leading a band with Herb Flemming (trombone), Cozy Cole (drums), Claude Hopkins (piano), and Lemont "Benny" Moten (bass). Charlie Shavers was leading the other group at the Metropole and the joint was jumping every night.

Lily did not like the city of New York very much. She thought that the hotels and the streets were dirty, that people were hung on money and talked about it all the time, that Americans were very rude. She couldn't stand racism and so was biased against white Americans. But she loved my friends and the jazz scene.

Hot Lips Page, who had a son of 15 years old, was remarried to a school teacher, Elizabeth. They invited us for dinner and we enjoyed being with them. Lips was a natural-born joker and terrific company. He sure surprised us with something that time. He had a big new Cadillac but no driving license and he didn't want one either. He said he wanted to be able to drink his liquor the way he wanted and that if he had to drive, that would keep him from drinking. Whenever he wished to use the car, he would go out into the street to look for someone who could drive it or call a friend. That was typical of him.

On 15 April we left New York and arrived in Cincinnati the next morning. My father and brother met us at the station and they both were looking good and happy. Lily made a hit with them, as she had done with all my friends, and I was very proud of her. My mother and stepfather took her to their hearts as soon as they saw her too. My brother Ulysses had married a nice widow, Zola, who had six children. Thelma, my sister, was separated from her husband and was now living with my father.

Lily and I also stayed with Dad. Lily started to call him Dad, which he enjoyed very much. We were in Cincy from 16 April until 23 May. Of course I saw my old friends Clarence Paige and Smittie, who gave parties for us. We had a swell time also with friends of my brother and sister. She knew a very nice white couple, Bob and Phyl Connors, who invited us to their home. Bob was an amateur pianist who dug Dave Brubeck and was also a photographer. He made some very nice photos of Lily and me. I never once touched my horn because at last I was having a vacation that was not due to lack of work.

We still had ten days in New York before going back. I had a contract for a three-month tour in Germany and needed an alto and a tenor who had to be American Negroes. I went to see my old pal Ben Smith but he was leading a combo at the Baby Grand on 125th Street and had no eyes for leaving the job. Then I thought of my old drinking buddy, Curby Alexander, and went to see him. Curby, with whom I'd had such great times in the Philippines, was in bad shape. He had no work and nothing in sight and had separated from the mother of his two children, one of whom was blind. I could see he really needed help and thought that if I could get him away from his misery and help him blow his sax again, he could make a come back. He accepted my offer and I promised to send him a contract and a boat ticket as soon as I returned to France. A few days later, in a Broadway bar where many cats hung out, I ran into Jimmy Wright, whom I had worked with in a dancing school many moons ago. He played tenor. After a few drinks and some chit-chat of days gone by, he started telling me how well he was doing and about his Lincoln Continental car. I got around to telling him I was looking for a tenor man and told him what it was for. He, like Curby, readily accepted.

The rest of my time was spent enjoying the few days left in the Apple. Many of our friends were glad to see us and came by our hotel quite often: Al Hall, George Duvivier, and Oscar Pettiford, who brought Lily big bottles of perfume. Oscar decided to spend the last night with us. It started at the Metropole, then we went to Jimmy Ryan's, as I wanted to hear Wilbur De Paris's band that was loaded with fellows I'd worked with or known for a long time. Sidney De Paris was in the band on trumpet and bass tuba, which I didn't know he played: he was the only musician I ever saw double on those instruments. The others were: Sonny White (piano), Wilbur Kirk (drums and harmonica), Wilbur De Paris (trombone), and Omer Simeon (clarinet). Omer was the only one I'd never worked with. It was really a happy-sounding group.

When Ryan's place closed, Oscar offered to take us to Minton's Playhouse, which was managed by one of my old bosses, Teddy Hill. I'm even sure he was part owner. I had not seen Teddy since 1946, when we had met in a street in Manila, Philippines.

But the surprise of the night was to see Billie Holiday sitting among the clientele at Minton's that night. I'd always dug Lady Day from the first time I'd heard her, so it pleased me to hear her once more, in person. It was a great thrill for Lily too, who liked her records and could now see her in the flesh.

Oscar would not let me pay for anything and Al Hall, who had joined us as we left Minton's around 6 a.m., suggested that we all go to his place for some breakfast. We also had with us Joan Hill, who had been my common-law stepdaughter. She didn't get along too well with Beezie, her mother. Joan was 20 years old, six feet tall, and had a six-month-old baby, Steve.

After a solid breakfast, Oscar and I went to the hotel to collect our luggage, which had been ready and packed, and the rest of the party went with Lily to the pier.

Oscar gave me two of his recordings with his autograph, which are priceless to me. One was a debut LP called *The New Oscar Pettiford Sextet* and features the man himself with Phil Urso (tenor sax), Julius Watkins (french horn), Walter Bishop (piano), Charles Mingus (bass), and Percy Brice (drums); Oscar plays cello. The other record was a 45 r.p.m. on Imperial Records and had Oscar still on cello, Arnold Ross (piano), Harry Babasin (cello), Joe Comfort (bass), and Alvin Stoller (drums).

We were sailing out on the *Flandre*, another ship of the French Line but much smaller than the *Liberté*. It left the pier around 11 a.m. on 3 June, and we waved to our friends until we could no longer see them. Lily went to our cabin to rest her tired body. I stayed up to see the Statue of Liberty because I wanted to film it and then I too hit the hay for the rest of the afternoon.

On the crossing, we had terrible weather. The boat was shaking like hell, and in spite of not getting seasick, we were glad to set foot on earth. At 10 p.m. on 8 June we were back in Paris. We had enjoyed a wonderful 70-day holiday but we were happy to get back to our regular routine of living again.

One month later, on 9 July, I started working as an attraction at the Ringside, rue d'Artois. Martial Solal, the great French pianist, was leading a trio that accompanied me, and there was also a Negro girl singer from the States, named Pat Boone. Martial was from Algeria and at that time his style was something similar to Oscar Peterson's with a technique like the great Art Tatum. He accompanied me beautifully. I really enjoyed playing with Martial, who was full of ideas and very inspiring.

I stayed at the Ringside until 4 August and started at a place called Metro Jazz, which later became the Trois Mailletz (three hammers). The club was situated on the left bank in the Latin Quarter, near the famous Notre Dame Cathedral, and about ten minutes' walk from my hotel. It was a beautiful cellar, very well preserved, from the twelfth century. The famous French poet François Villon had been imprisoned there. One floor below was another cellar that had been a torture chamber and was now a museum. When a prisoner had died after being tortured, the body was thrown into the well and came out into the Seine river.

Jimmy Wright and Curby Alexander arrived around 20 September. They had traveled with a very well-known pianist in the States who had become quite popular in France in the middle 1930s. His name was Garland Wilson, but he was known to his musician friends as "Mother." Garland had been engaged to entertain at a famous night spot called Le Boeuf sur le Toit, where he and the well-known female pianist Una Mae Carlisle had worked together in the 30s until World War II started.

Jimmy and Curby were really not overloaded with baggage and, to my surprise, Jimmy had no instrument with him. I knew that Jimmy was a big bluffer and therefore his story about a big Lincoln car didn't ring true to me. But I did not expect to see him coming all the way from New York to Europe for a two-month musical tour without an instrument. Curby's luck had been bad but he did at least have a horn to blow. There was an instrument company in Paris called Couesnon, and I knew the director, M. Vincent, very well. They were trying to push their horns into the jazz field and I had received a trumpet. M. Vincent didn't agree to give Jimmy a tenor, but as a favor to me, he was willing to let him have a sax for a bargain price. I was responsible for a weekly payment.

The rhythm section for the tour was the same as for the last one: Jack Starling, Eddie de Haas, and Wallace Bishop. I also engaged a girl singer from Trinidad named Cecily Forde. We left for Germany on 1 October and we had to give 70 concerts from 2 October until 15 December with only six days off.

We were in Kassel on 10 November when someone in the orchestra bought a US army paper called *Stars and Stripes*. There was an announcement that Hot Lips Page had died. I had seen him a few months before. He was in good health at that time and we had not heard anything about him being sick. To my estimation the world had lost the greatest blues trumpeter, who could sing them as well as play them. He also had given me an autographed recording of his, titled *There ain't no Flies on me*.

There were very few towns that we did not play in West Germany, large or small. We played some concerts for the German public and many concerts for British military camps. The camps concerts were usually done in the noncommissioned officers' recreation halls and these fellows really showed us a swell time in every camp we played. After the concert we were getting drinks no end and food.

We played the last date on 15 December and went to Belgium for a television show and three concerts. Then we went to Paris and that was the last time I saw Jimmy Wright. He and I had not gotten along the way we had back in the days when we were with Johnny Monnegue. He was wild and undependable and his playing didn't mean much to me. He was putting on a lot of show with very bad taste, almost playing on his back. A few times, he refused to come to rehearsals. As we were going to be off during the Christmas holidays, Jimmy told me that he was going to the States for that period and would be back before the tour started again. I told him that if he went back to New York, he could stay there because I knew that he was not coming back.

To replace him I engaged Guy Lafitte on tenor. I had another contract for more concerts in Germany and then a contract for a dance hall in Hamburg. Curby Alexander also went back to the USA. He had become a complete alcoholic and nothing could be done. He died a few years later.

I continued touring and making my breakthrough in Europe. This time it was Scandinavia for my first time. One month in Odense, then Aalborg in Denmark at the Tivoli Karolinelund. It was an easy job because it featured only attractions. One of them was an American Negro named Freddie Crump who had a drum act. I had seen him with Cooper's Black and White show when I was a teenager. He was the first black musician to be featured with a white orchestra. He was known as "Rastus" at that time, and was featured with Paul Whiteman's orchestra, but didn't play with the band. He'd been living in Denmark for years and had three daughters that played drums in his act. They were cute little girls.

We had invited my sister Thelma to come to Europe for a vacation. Lily left for Paris to meet her and bring her to Copenhagen, where I had decided to stay for 16 days. My engagement at the Tivoli in Aalborg would be finished in a few days but I started to have a bad case of sciatica and could hardly walk or stand. I went to work with a cane, took a taxi, and had to sit down on the bandstand.

We were living in a pension, and when Lily was away the landlady was very nice about preparing my meals and looked after me like a mother. I started wondering what could I give her as a token of appreciation, and it finally hit me that I could give her a box of good cigars, as I had seen her and other women in Denmark smoking cigars even in streetcars and public places. I did that the day before I left and she was very happy about it. She didn't speak English or French but she made me understand that she was saving them for Sunday and special occasions.

But I was getting a little tired of the road and felt a need to stay in one place for a while. We decided to go back to Paris in the month of August 1955. I started working at the Trois Mailletz and remained there until 1960. A British critic, Max Jones, wrote an article in the *Melody Maker*, titled "The Man from the Trois Mailletz." I had the privilege of going out of the club now and then to do dates in different places and from time to time there was a second attraction like Mezz Mezzrow, Guy Lafitte, Mae Mercer, or Brother John Sellers.

In October 1955, I played a two-day jazz festival in Lyons which featured Sidney Bechet, Chet Baker, and myself. Sidney was the main attraction. His popularity had grown immensely since 1950 and he was the biggest crowd-drawing jazz musician in Europe. At one time I didn't dig him, mostly I suppose because I didn't like the sound of soprano saxophone. But I dug him now and I'm happy to say that he was one of the swingingest cats that ever lived. He inspired many younger sax men who are playing that instrument now.

The musicians who accompanied me at the Trois Mailletz were Michel de Villers, with whom I had made my first tour as a member of the Edward's band. He was now playing alto and baritone sax. The pianist was André Persiany, who was known as the French Milt Buckner, Guy Lafitte was on tenor, Michel Attenoux played clarinet. There was a fine young bass player, Gilbert Rovère, and Jappy Gautier was on drums.

Since the club was closed for January and February, we took the opportunity and hit the road again for six weeks. I had the musicians of the Trois Mailletz with me and Cecily Forde, the singer who was on tour with me in Germany when we played the British camps. She was a beautiful girl, had a fine voice, and was singing in the style of Sarah Vaughan.

It was a difficult tour because that February 1956 broke all records for cold in France. Theaters were ice-cold, water pipes were frozen. We could not warm up the instruments. We were traveling by bus and it was a nightmare for our usual driver, Louis, who couldn't see through the frozen windshield, and roads were icy and very dangerous.

We came back in Paris on 2 March and flew to Algiers to play a big ball at the Hotel St. George. We gave a concert at the Salle Borde on the 3rd. On 10 March I played what was called a New Orleans jazz festival at the Palais des Sports in Paris. This featured bands from several European countries. I met the English trumpeter Humphrey Lyttelton for the first time. I had heard of him as he became England's best-known jazz trumpeter after Nat Gonella, who was the English Louis Armstrong in the 1930s. Humphrey played a fine trumpet.

During that year of 1956 I had four recording sessions; one with the musicians of the Trois Mailletz and Cecily Forde. We recorded four tunes. The three others were with my great friend George Duvivier. For me it was a treat as I have a special feeling for bass and George is on top of my list. He was staying in Paris, accompanying Lena Horne, that beautiful artist and woman. She had a long contract at the Moulin Rouge.

We had the opportunity to rent a nice little apartment in the Latin Quarter, rue de Condé. George came to see us often. Lily had bought as present for my birthday a cockatoo named Coco, but George called him Bahzat! as he had a piercing cry sounding a little like that.

The first of the three sessions was in May with Jean-Claude Pelletier (piano), George (bass), and Roger Paraboschi (drums). We recorded 4 tunes and were very pleased with the result, especially with *Blues in my Heart*. I got the prize of *Jazz Hot* magazine for the best interpretation of the year.

On 12 September we recorded with a septet including Guy Lafitte and a bunch of some of the best jazzmen in France. George was on bass and wrote the arrangements. The last session with George was recorded with strings. The jazz and violins mix was beginning to be much talked about and I wanted to try it out. The day we went to record the weather was very cold and so was the studio. I had lip trouble and I had a hell of a time. We succeeded on putting *April in Paris* in the box, but after that I had to give up. George recorded the band and a few days later I came back to do my part on playback.

The album was called *Album of Cities*. The French critic André Francis wrote in his book *Jazz*, "In *Album of Cities*, Bill Coleman is one of the most refined and distinguished trumpeters one can hear," which was a great compliment. However, maybe it was lack of publicity or promotion or whatever, but that record came out without causing any reaction.

I did a few more sessions, one of them in Holland, another in Switzerland with the Tremble Kids orchestra, whose leader, Werner Keller, was quite a good clarinet player. I particularly liked the pianist, Jean-Pierre Bionda, who played in a light style and was a very versatile and sensitive accompanist.

After my sad experiences in Italy in 1950, I had never felt the desire to go back there, but I got an offer from an Italian guy named Burnier and accepted a three-week tour contract for Italy, as the Trois Mailletz was closing for two months in the winter. I thought maybe there had been some change in the way Italians were doing business!

We left Paris on 4 January: Lily, myself, and the band, with Jack Starling (piano), Gilbert Fanfant (bass), a German drummer, Rolf Luderitz (but we called him Rolfie), Benny Waters (tenor sax), and, last but not least, Albert Nicholas. It was a long time since Nick and I had been in Luis Russell's band, almost 30 years. He was very famous with fans of the New Orleans style, and he was still a beautiful clarinettist. He had made Paris his home lately.

We were touring Italy by train with Burnier. We were calling him "the Creep" because he was tall, skinny, wore a black overcoat and hat, and seemed to be always creeping around a corner like Mack the Knife.

During the tour we were engaged to play a big ball in St. Moritz for the millionaire shipping magnate Niarkos, who was the brother-in-law of Onassis. The ball was given in the Palace Hotel. We were on the bandstand, which was about 15 inches high, and I was standing at the left of the bandstand, when one of the male guests came by on crutches. Just when he arrived at my side, one of his crutches slipped and I had the reflexes to catch him to prevent him from falling. I was sorry for this after because the son of a bitch didn't thank me or even look at me. He would have deserved to break his leg or damn neck. Somebody told me after that it was Niarkos!

Everything went well until we arrived in the south. We didn't have the same crowd as we had in the north. You couldn't see a woman in public. In Naples Burnier went into a very hot argument with the director of the theater about a money matter and Burnier forbade us to play the second part of the concert unless he was paid first. So we were feeling foolish on the bandstand, waiting, and the public was getting nervous. Finally Burnier gave us the green light.

We played Bari on 5 March, down on the boot of Italy. We enjoyed the different views of the town. The weather was beautiful. We went into a restaurant at the seaside to eat some seafood but the windows were so dirty that we could hardly see the sea.

We had a nice crowd that evening, which was the end of the tour. The next morning, we were taking a train back to Milan. Burnier had left with an earlier train, leaving a note saying that he would not be responsible for the transportation of Benny Waters and Rolfie because they had gone to a night club after the concert and jammed with the musicians. Our contract mentioned that we were not supposed to play anywhere without the consent of the office. I suppose that Benny and Rolfie thought that, as it was our last date, it would not matter if they had some fun playing after the concert. But Burnier took this matter as a chance to have some extra loot for the office I suppose. I had experienced some rough deals with Italians before and here it was happening again after the tour had been so nice.

We arrived in Milan on 7 March and went to the office the next day to straighten out things and get our last pay. At the agency they didn't want to discuss the affair of Benny and Rolfie. One thing is certain: there is no winning with Italian impresarios and very few others. So we wished those three cats goodbye and went to our hotel. But the next morning very early I received a phone call from Burnier, who asked us to come to the office.

There they proposed that we should play for a big ball in Milan the next night. It must have been a big deal because they promised to pay the transportation of

Benny and Rolfie and offered us a pretty nice taste. We accepted, played the date, and left Milan the morning of 10 March for Paris.

Then I made a tour in Holland with the Dutch Swing College band during the month of September. This was a real happy tour. This was the drinkingest band I ever knew. I've heard stories about how the guys in the old Fletcher Henderson band could drink, but I actually saw how those cats could bend elbows. I couldn't and didn't try to cut drink with them, but I took quite a few solos with the bottle. What was so amazing about their drinking was that they never let that ignorant liquid interfere with their playing, and they had a swinging group. They were all real great fellows, and that was a tour that I shall always remember as one of the most enjoyable of the many tours I've done during my whole musical career.

Lily and I had planned to make another trip to the USA to visit my father, sister and brother in Cincinnati. I had had the great sadness of my mother's passing in 1954, shortly after we had returned to Europe. On 1 March 1958 we sailed from Le Havre on the *Liberté*, the same ship we had gone on before. The trip was very pleasant from start to finish. We arrived in New York on 7 March and to our surprise, our great friend George Duvivier had reserved us a suite of two rooms in the Hotel Schuyler on 44th Street, between 5th Avenue and Avenue of the Americas. When we arrived at the hotel there was a big bouquet of flowers for Lily, beer, soft drinks, whisky, and even a bottle of Pernod for a little French atmosphere. All this was arranged by George to welcome us to New York! He told us in a kidding way that he would shoot us if we tried to pay for anything.

We stayed in New York for six days and heard quite a lot of musicians: Roy Eldridge, Charlie Shavers, Red Allen, Sol Yaged, Coleman Hawkins, and so on. I didn't find much change in New York from the last time I saw it, but friends told us that there were improvements in the racial relations.

Oscar Pettiford opened a club on 3rd Avenue called the Black Pearl, and we were there on opening night. I heard trumpeter Ray Copeland and Jerome Richardson, the reed man, for the first time. They were both fine musicians and Oscar found time now and then to knock out a few tunes on the bass. It was a very nice club but I heard that it did not stay open very long.

We left New York by train on 14 March and arrived in Cincinnati the next morning. The air-conditioning system had been out of order and the heat was unbearable. We couldn't drink because the drinking water tank was empty and nobody came through selling drinks. We were more than happy to get out of that train.

My father and sister had moved from West 9th Street and were now living in Walnut Hills on Rockdale Avenue, a pleasant suburb. My old buddy Eddie Partridge and his wife Mattie, who was a cousin of mine, lived in the same house as my father. Eddie and I had some drinking good times. My brother and his family lived nearby. We gave a party, my brother gave one, and many of his wife's friends gave parties. Clarence Paige and Smittie invited us. Clarence was still playing and Smittie had changed his name from Smith to Smyth. He was a Union delegate and still played piano in clubs.

I had brought with me an EP, the one I had recorded with George Duvivier.

Someone introduced me to a TV announcer who knew of me and was a jazz fan. I gave him the record and he said that he was going to surprise me. One morning I got a phone call and was advised to watch TV, and there was a funny cartoon with me playing and singing behind *I've Got the Right to Sing the Blues*.

As we were a mixed married couple, trouble could be around any corner, and it was one day. We had decided to visit my Uncle Ernest Coleman, who did not live far away. On our way it started to rain lightly. Lily was carrying a very light-colored handbag in box-calf and did not want to get it wet. As I was wearing a raincoat she asked me to hold it under the coat and just as she gave it to me, a police patrol car was passing and one of the two policemen in it saw the action. They stopped the car and one of them jumped out and came beside me and said to me: "Give me that purse, I saw you snatch it!" I answered, "This is my wife and, furthermore, if I had snatched the bag, do you think that I would stand there and talk to the woman?" Lily tried to tell him that it was true but he asked for our identity papers. Lily's passport was Swiss and written in French: this guy couldn't read it and was getting nervous. At that time the other policeman, who was his superior, came to join us and asked for an explanation. He looked at our passports and asked us to excuse them and went on to tell us that there was a lot of handbag snatching going on. It was a dumb story and it would not have happened if I had been white.

We left Cincinnati on the night of 18 April. My father, my brother and his wife, some cousins, and friends came to the station to see us off. I had bought round-trip tickets on the New York Central railroad line. When we decided that we were going to visit a cousin in Sunbury, Pennsylvania, I went to the railroad station in Cincy to have the tickets changed to the Pennsylvania line. I was told that it was not necessary to change the tickets because the two lines had merged and the tickets were valid on either line.

About 20 minutes after the train had left Cincinnati, the conductor came through the coach collecting tickets. When he took ours and looked at them, he said in a very nasty tone that they were not good for that line. I told him what I had been told at the station but he didn't want to hear anything. Then I knew that he was a cracker and could not stand the sight of mixed couples, especially if it was the woman who was white. He threatened to put us off the train at the next stop, which would have been Columbus, Ohio, if I didn't pay the fare, which he said was $50 each, and kept our tickets. He went into another coach and I went in the vestibule to wait for him to come back because I was not going to take his insults lying down. Finally he came back and I stopped him and told him again what I had been told at the station. He listened and said, as if he was doing me a favor, that he would accept the tickets. His attitude was different now that there was nobody around for him to show off to.

When I came back into our coach, there was a young white fellow sitting two seats from us who asked me if he could talk with me for a while. I sat beside him and he told me that he had heard what the conductor had said about putting us off the train at the next stop from Cincinnati. Almost everyone in the coach had heard the same thing because that bastard was talking loud for everyone to hear him. I had had to tell him that he didn't have to yell at me. This fellow introduced himself and told me that he was a pastor in a church in Louisville, Kentucky, and Columbus, Ohio, where he lived. He would invite Lily and me to spend the night with him at his home, if we were obliged to get off the train in Columbus. I told him that everything was straight and thanked him for his kind offer. Some other white folks told us also that they did not agree with the conductor's attitude. One man said that he had a job in the railroad company and offered to stand witness if we had further trouble with that guy.

The deal with the policeman and the run-in with the conductor were the only things that made this visit to the States unpleasant.

We arrived in Harrisburg, Pennsylvania, the next day. Lily's cousin, André Hoffmann, and his wife Denise met us and we drove to Sunbury, where we spent two days visiting the country. We left Sunbury via Harrisburg for New York, which was a three-hour trip, by train. We had the same suite in the Hotel Schluyler that we had occupied before going to Cincinnati. George again didn't want us to pay anything. We met his mother, Ismay, and we invited her to come to Europe for the summer. Lily offered to be her guide in Europe. She took us at our word and came to Paris a few months later.

On Saturday nights there was always a session at Central Plaza on East 3rd Street, which was run by Jack Crystal. Jack at one time managed the sessions for Milt Gabler at Jimmy Ryan's on 52nd Street; he was a real friend to all musicians regardless of race or religion and his sessions were often a big help to many of the fellows that played them. On Saturday night, 26 April, I played there with Dicky Wells, Eddie Barefield, the great Willie "the Lion" Smith who, I was told, was there for every session, and two drummers, Jo Jones and Panama Francis.

I was very happy to play with old buddies and they were pleased to find out that I had not lost anything concerning my style and ideas, as most Americans believed would happen to musicians who stayed in Europe a long time.

We met a nice young man, Doug Hague, who was a great jazz fan and a critic for different jazz reviews in the States and in England. He was married to a charming Italian girl, Luciana. We also met his parents, Albert and Peggy Hague. They had some juice with them in a bag and kept asking us questions about France, telling us how much they loved that country. We became great friends and still are.

I was on vacation and not looking for work. Besides, I hadn't blown my horn for quite a while. But I was really happy to have been engaged for this session, which was the only time I really wanted to play during my visit to the Apple.

We made the rounds of different clubs. We caught Ben Webster on his opening night at the Village Vanguard. Ben had a fine trio backing him, but the only musician I can remember was Philly Joe Jones. Later that night, Tony Scott came in and blew some clarinet, and had a gone jam session with Ben, who was playing his can off that night.

We left New York aboard the *Liberté* again on 1 May and arrived home in Paris on the 7th. I went back to work at the Trois Mailletz.

FOURTEEN

ON THE ROAD AGAIN

There were some rough times in store for me in 1958. Among them was a tour of Italy. Burnier, the Italian organizer of the tour, had engaged Albert Nicholas (clarinet), Don Byas (tenor sax), who was now living in Amsterdam, and the trio of Michel Hausser, which consisted of Ricardo Galleazzi, an Argentinian bass player who was also a fine trombone man; Dante Agostini, an Italian drummer who was born in France and never had been to Italy before; and Gerard Gustin on piano. Michel Hausser was a real gifted vibraphone player and accordionist. He was one of the three best vibraphonists in France. (The others were Geo Daly and Dany Doriz.) Michel's style was formed on that of Milt Jackson. He was a nice fellow, full of fun.

When the tour had started Burnier asked me to do the presentation of the musicians on stage and make an announcement before each solo. But Don Byas, who was the jealous type, refused. He was afraid that people would think I was the band leader. As a result there was no presentation on stage. Each soloist announced his own numbers.

Pope Pius XII had just died when we arrived in Milan and it was a bad beginning for the tour. Our first concert was at the Teatro Nuovo in Milan. We did a matinee and night concert and the crowds were very small for both. Italy was in mourning for the Pope. Burnier, who had booked these theaters on percentage, was behind in paying us from the beginning. It went on like that for a few days. Dante Agostini started threatening to leave for Paris if he did not get his entire salary. One night Michel Hausser knocked on my hotel door just when I was beginning to sleep well and asked me to come and help him talk to Dante, who had checked his drums at the railroad station, bought a ticket for Paris, and was going to leave on an early train. When I arrived in Dante's room, everyone in the group was there and it took a lot of begging from all of us to get him to stick with us a while longer, which he finally decided to do.

Don Byas had been practising body-building and carried two dumbbells with him in an airplane bag. They must have weighed about 45 pounds or more. Whenever we arrived at a hotel that was up-to-date enough to have a porter, Don would tell him to take the small airplane bag and we would all be waiting to watch the shocked expression on the face of the guy when he lifted it.

The third day of the tour we played in Turin and called that day "Don's day." He had told us that he had stopped drinking since he had married a Dutch girl a few years ago. Don happened to come into the same restaurant where Lily and I were having supper and, after we finished eating, he offered us an after-dinner drink and we ordered grappa, a sort of Italian brandy. He had one also. Later, when we came to the theater, we saw that Don had had quite a few grappas: he was worse than an American Indian when he drank. During the intermission, Don went to the bar in the hall of the theater, and when it was time for us to start, Burnier came to me and asked me to go and get Don because he was raising hell at the bar, taking his clothes off and showing everybody his musculature. People were laughing at him. I finally got him away and we started the last part of the concert. Don had a feature number called *Laura*, and drunk as he was, he was able to play until he got to the coda. It was very special and there was a certain phrase he played before the trio made the last chord with him. But this time Don was so high that he could not find the phrase for at least three minutes. He was running exercises all over his tenor and the musicians were waiting and looking at him very anxiously. Dante was sitting with his sticks in the air and Michel Hausser had his mallets ready to hit the last chord. Finally after what seemed like a lifetime, Don found the phrase, the musicians hit the chord with him, and everybody breathed a sigh of relief. But Don didn't take another drink during the rest of the tour.

Among other places, we played in Parma, the birthplace of Arturo Toscanini. The theater we played was exactly like La Scala in Milan but smaller, so I was told. Of course, there were some very fine grand pianos there, but the one they gave us to use was an upright. They were afraid that our pianist would break strings on one of the others. They did not know, or did not want to believe, that most classical pianists can hit the keys much harder than most jazz pianists do.

The last place we played was Livorno. It was not supposed to have been the last date, but the people were not coming to the concerts because of mourning for the Pope, the organizers said. Burnier was getting more and more behind in paying us. We all joined the side of Dante and told Burnier we would not continue to play if he didn't pay what he owed us in back salaries. His answer was that he didn't have the money: so that was the end of that tour in Italy.

Lily and I stayed a few days in Milan until 28 October because I had to play the month of November in Switzerland. Don took a plane to Amsterdam and the next time I saw him, he told me that it had cost him more to take his dumbbells on the plane than his personal ticket. The rest of the fellows went back to France.

I started a 15-day engagement in Zurich at the Mascotte, a well-known jazz club. A few days after we arrived in Zurich, Lily became very ill and we called a doctor, who happened to be a woman. She said that Lily was suffering with meningitis and also had septicemia. She was taken to a clinic by ambulance. After a few days she was out of danger but then suffered with a severe cardiac deficiency caused by a very low rate of potassium. She had to be under oxygen therapy and we had to hire a private nurse to be with her night and day for a while. Visits were forbidden except to me. But after 15 days I had to leave Zurich as I had dates in Belgium and in France. Lily was feeling a little better, and a few days after my departure was allowed to have visits. I knew she would be well taken care of and we had many friends there that would visit her, our good friends the Simmens, Pfisters, and Steiners. Johnny stayed constantly in touch with me concerning Lily's health.

I went back to the Trois Mailletz on 2 December 1958. Lily came out of the clinic on 8 December, and, as the Trois Mailletz closed on Monday, I was able to fly to get her back to Paris.

I was engaged to play a big gala on 10 January 1959 in Gstaad, the most popular and best-known resort in Switzerland. I didn't know with whom I would be working until I arrived at my destination. The surprise was when I found out that I would be accompanied by Fred Bunge and his orchestra. Fred along with Teddy Paris his drummer were the musicians I had made a tour of Germany with in 1952. So it was a pleasant surprise to see those fellows again, and I knew there would be no sweat that night.

On my return to Paris, I met a trumpet player named Mike Wyatt on the train. He was an English subject from the British West Indies and I had known him since 1948. He had been living in Paris for quite a while before I arrived. He was a very good trumpeter and a much younger fellow than myself and we became good friends.

But I never saw Mike Wyatt or Fred Bunge again after that day: they were both killed in automobile accidents, Mike in France and Fred somewhere in Germany.

Since 1956 Lily and I had been living in a small but nice rented apartment on the Left Bank. In 1959 we decided to buy a little place of our own. We found a flat at 54 rue Monsieur le Prince (a very pretty name to my estimation) in the house where a famous writer, philosopher, and mathematician, Blaise Pascal, had lived. A commemorative tablet is still on the front of the building. We had this place decorated to our taste and it became a beautiful little two-room apartment with kitchen and bath. It was the first home that I ever owned.

I was still working at the Trois Mailletz and playing various galas. Not long after we moved into the new apartment, I was engaged by a piano company in Zurich to do a tour of Switzerland, Austria, and Germany. Albert Nicholas and the pianist Joe Turner were also engaged for this tour. It was a real happy swinging deal thanks to Joe Turner, who was the life of the party with his jokes and the crazy things he did.

The leader of the group, clarinettist Werner Keller, was a good and lively musician. The trumpet man was Oscar Klein, an Austrian; he also played guitar. Oscar was a real solid Dixieland trumpeter and his style reminded me very much of Wild Bill Davison. On piano there was Ola Ringstrom, a young Swede who really could swing. Rolf Eimek was on bass and Charlie Antolini on drums. They were all Swiss except Oscar and Ola.

I went back to the Trois Mailletz for six weeks. Then on 15 May 1959 I flew to Portugal for one week with some French musicians to play a ball for the University of Coimbra and also a concert for the students. Each year there was a week of festivity at the university: the students wore a very original costume, black with a lot of colorful ribbons, topped by capes. They were lively and noisy and we had great fun.

But that time had its share of sadness with the passing of Sidney Bechet in Paris. He died of cancer. Lily, who stood in my place at his funeral, told me how mournful it had been. It was raining by the bucket, some young people had come to Garches, where the funeral took place, with their instruments, hoping they could participate in a New Orleans-style funeral. Some sort of riot had taken place at the cemetery and several tombs had been trampled.

Madame Calvé, the owner of the Trois Mailletz, gave me two weeks' notice on 15 June 1960. She always resented it when I left the club to do a gig, although I was always careful not to leave too often. Actually I think that the French musicians working there were jealous of me and convinced her to take another attraction. I had been working there, on and off, for five years.

I was naturally upset for a good reason. It was summer already and much too late to get an engagement anywhere for the rest of the summer. I had been refusing different propositions because of the Trois Mailletz. We had taken a mortgage when we bought our apartment and were still paying for it. We had no money in advance and were terribly worried. Suddenly we had to face some important changes since the security of a regular salary and a stable job was gone. But, all things considered, Madame Calvé had really done me a big favor. I had settled too comfortably in a routine that had lost its musical excitement, and it was time to move on.

Now that I was free of all obligations, it was becoming possible to look for more interesting things. I could accept all the galas offered to me, some of them paying for one night twice as much as I had been getting for one week at the club.

First, my good friend Jean-Marie Masse from Limoges, who played drums with the Pierre Guyot orchestra, came to my rescue. He offered me the summer season with them in Royan on the Atlantic coast. I was happy to accept, even though the money was not great.

I had to leave on 2 and 3 August to open the first Festival of Comblain-la-Tour in Belgium, sponsored by Joe Napoli. Petula Clark and Charles Aznavour were also on the bill. Lily remained in Royan. She told me that I had been missed and that a crowd had been shouting my name in front of the terrace where the band was playing.

In September I started doing concerts and balls here, there, and everywhere in Europe.

In April 1961 I was engaged for the month to appear in Barcelona, Spain, in a club known as the Jamboree Cava. It was the first jazz club ever opened in Barcelona, and I was the first American jazz musician to be engaged there. The musicians I had to play with were Spanish and they were not too bad at playing jazz, considering that there were very few places where jazz had ever been played in the country at that time. There were two tenor men in the group. One was known as Pocholo, who also played clarinet, and was very popular with the jazz fans. The other was Salvador Font, with whom I had jammed in Rome way back in 1950.

The jazz fans in Barcelona were mostly rich people. There was quite a large number of them, but there was also a crowd of young people, students, writers, and painters. The owner of the place, Juan Rossello, had asked a group of those young painters to decorate the Jamboree to their own taste, and he had given them, for salary, 600 Cuba Libres (rum and Coke). So the cave was decorated in an amusing and colorful way with paintings on the walls and footprints on the ceiling! Of course the group was coming every night to hear jazz and drink their salary and we gave them a big help. The maître d'hôtel, a swell guy named Angelo, was keeping account. The atmosphere was very gay. We made quite a lot of good friends: Ruis, a young leftist poet and painter, François Ferrer, chemist and painter, his young wife Neus, and many others.

I played in that club for several years, on and off. Once the pianist was Tete Montoliu, a blind Catalan with an excellent technique. I also played there with a good modern tenor man from Madrid, Pedro Itturalde. But with time passing, Rossello started engaging artists whose style was getting more and more modern and "free." The clientele stopped coming to the club and eventually the Jamboree Cava closed.

In June 1961 I was contacted to play for the summer season at the Vieux Colombier in Juan-les-Pins on the Côte d'Azur, the club that Sidney Bechet made famous some years before. Badel, the owner, who also owned the Vieux Colombier club in Paris, wanted me to play with a bunch of young French amateurs. He wanted me to try to repeat the same experiment that Sidney Bechet had made with Claude Luter and his Lorientais. Coming back from Belgium and going to another place, I just had a short time to audition the group. It didn't sound too bad but I wasn't very enthusiastic.

We had decided to buy a second-hand car. Albert Nicholas had a Volkswagen Ladybug which had once belonged to Kenny Clarke, and he wanted to sell it. Neither of us could drive, but we decided to take lessons in Juan-les-Pins and asked Nick if he would agree to drive us there. We would pay his expenses and his fare back to Paris. So on 29 June we left Paris with a big load of luggage, our cockatoo, Coco, and our Persian cat, Princess. Both animals were scared to death in that car, and Coco was repeating nonstop, "Bonjour Coco, ça va Coco!" Princess was meowing. Albert was driving at the speed of 50 miles an hour. We tried to find a hotel room in different places but all the hotels were packed, so we had to make the trip without a break except for meals. When we arrived on the Côte d'Azur the next day, Albert was so tired that he was falling asleep at the wheel.

We had a very good friend, Leopold de Lima e Silva, a doctor, who was the son of Mistinguett, the famous music hall star. Leopold had inherited from his mother a very nice little house with a big garden. It was called The Bungalow and was situated between Antibes and Juan-les-Pins, a ten-minute walk to the Vieux Colombier. We were paying a very low rent.

The day after our arrival, I had a rehearsal with the band. It was terrible. We tried for two hours to rehearse two numbers. Most of those kids couldn't read and they had no experience at all. I went to see Badel and told him he had to hire another band. He wanted to put the blame on me because I had agreed to play with them in Paris. I wanted to put the blame on him because I had told him many times that it was a mistake to engage amateurs just to save money, and that I had accepted against my better judgment.

Finally I had the luck to find some nice French musicians who were already in Juan-les-Pins: Raymond Ruer (piano), Nino Ferrer (bass), Stephane Guérault (sax and clarinet), and a very good Swiss drummer, Peter Giger. Nino Ferrer later became a famous singer.

Every night before my first set, a group of young rock-and-rollers were playing for half an hour. It was the beginning in France of the rock-and-roll era. This group was called Les Chaussettes Noires (the Black Socks) and featured a young singer called Eddy Mitchell. Every day we were going through the same routine. A crowd of about a hundred teenagers was waiting outside the Vieux Colombier. At 9.30 p.m. the waiters let them in without entrance fee. (I was even told that they were paid a small fee.) They would stand against the walls and start to shout hysterically, "We want Les Chaussettes Noires!" The group began to play, encouraged by frantic shouts from their supporters. After 30 minutes and many loud requests to come back, the band would leave and the waiters would rush the crowd of youngsters out. I then had to come on with my quartet and play for the paying guests. Fortunately there were some jazz lovers there too and we had our success also, though it was quieter.

Juan-les-Pins had become very well known for its annual jazz festival. It was the second year now and the orchestras of Ray Charles and Count Basie were the big attractions. It was Ray's first time to play in Europe and the first time I ever heard and saw him. He had a small group with two trumpets, three saxes, bass, drums, and the Raylettes. He sent me with his style of playing and singing, and the arrangements were swinging like mad.

As I was already in Juan-les-Pins, one of the organizers of the festival, Jacques Souplet, whom I had known for a long time, wanted me to play one evening at the festival. He told me that there was going to be a very good trio performing that week, the trio of pianist Les McCann, and he thought that it would be an ideal group to accompany me. Eventually I met Les and mentioned to him that Souplet wanted us to play a set together on the last night of the festival. He seemed pleased and I asked him when could we get together to have a little rehearsal. He said he would let me know in a couple of days.

But the days passed and I didn't hear from him. I began to get the feeling that this monkey didn't want to accompany me but wouldn't say so. I even told Souplet about my suspicion but he told me not to worry, that McCann had a stipulation in his contract to accompany a guest artist. Everything would be OK. But every time I saw Les, he would give me an excuse. On the last day, he gave me a rendezvous for that night at ten, saying that we could talk over some numbers before intermission time. I only had three or four numbers to do.

At ten o'clock that night there was no Les McCann. He didn't show until the intermission. He was supposed to play before Basie and I was to do my bit after him and his trio. He offered no excuse for not being there at ten. I asked him if he played *Tea for Two*, *Sweet Georgia Brown*, *Satin Doll*, or *Caravan*: he said that he didn't know any of those numbers. I knew he was a liar so I told him so and to forget it. I walked away. I wouldn't be playing at the festival that night.

I started talking with Budd Johnson, tenor man with Basie, and told him the story. Budd suggested that I ask Basie if he would allow his rhythm section to play with me and said that Frank Wess, the other tenor man, could accompany me on piano. Budd put the proposition to Basie, who was very understanding and thought that McCann had played a dirty trick on me. He agreed to let me use his rhythm section and then had another idea. He said that the band would go on and play a few numbers, then he would present me doing a couple of numbers with the band.

When Basie introduced me, the reception I received was overwhelming. Basie asked me who I wanted to come out front with me to assist in the rounds of solos. I was so excited that I couldn't think of anybody. I didn't speak up quick enough, so Basie motioned for Frank Wess and Frank Foster to come forward. Wess played flute and Foster played tenor on the two numbers I did, which were *Perdido* and *Sweet Georgia Brown*. It was a fantastic feeling to play with that band, being so well accompanied and pushed. Thad Jones, Snooky Young, Sonny Cohn, and Lenny Johnson were in the trumpet section and they were making up riffs behind me that had me blowing my buns off.

When Basie had introduced me I was so thrilled that when I spoke into the mike, I told the public that it was one of the greatest nights of my life, and that I was offering to buy a drink for everyone there. If the public had really taken me at my word, I would have been in debt for years because there were at least 3000 people there.

The two numbers I did with Basie had more effect on the public and meant more to my prestige than any amount of numbers that I could have done with McCann. A photographer, Jean-Pierre Leloir, took a series of shots and gave me an album titled "William meets William," as Basie and I were two Williams born in August 1904.

For the next few years to come, my life was set in a routine: gigs, jazz festivals, concerts, TV programs. There were some very good jazz musicians in Paris with whom I was playing: pianists Claude Bolling and Marc Hemmeler, trombonist François Guin (who led two bands, the Swingers and the Four Bones), Dany Doriz, an excellent vibraphonist, Michel Attenoux, alto and soprano sax, Claude Gousset and Raymond Fonsèque, both nice trombonists and arrangers, and Armand Conrad, a solid tenor man who could swing. Armand had recorded with me and Buck Clayton in 1949 in Paris. Of course I was playing quite often with Guy Lafitte, who is in my estimation the best tenor sax in France and maybe in Europe.

For some time I had a nice little quintet with Gabriel Garvanoff (piano), Jean-Pierre Mulot (bass), and Teddy Martin (drums); Charles Barrié, a good tenor man, rounded up the group. From 1969 the band was composed of Alain Fougeret (piano), Pierre Sim (bass), Michel Denis (drums), and Stephane Guérault (clarinet and tenor sax)—all nice musicians. I was also working, whenever I went to Lyon, with the Happy Cookies and in the South of France with the combo led by René and Pierre Julien from Sète.

In Belgium, where I played often, there were interesting musicians: Albert Langue, Alex Scorier, Sidney Fall (tenor sax), Jean Pol Vanderborght (piano), and Roger Vanhaverbeke, who was considered the best Belgian bassist. I enjoyed playing a cabaret in Brussels which belonged to my friend Pol—a great friend of jazz and jazzmen. Many of the American jazz musicians who had come to Europe had played there also.

In Switzerland there were also very gifted musicians. Henri Chaix was certainly the most popular pianist in the country. Jean Bionda was a very good pianist also. Tenor man Michel Pilet, of French origin; Roland Hugues, a trumpeter who had played with Claude Luter's band; Francis Bonjour, another very good trumpeter with the Wild Cats orchestra; drummer Pierre Bouru; Daniel Humair, drums, who has now a world reputation; clarinettist Jacky Milliet, who played a fine and sensitive style with his New Ragtime band. These are only a few.

On 1 October 1962, I lost my father, who had been ill for quite a while. It was as painful for Lily as it was for me. He was a great man. He died at the age of 83.

In 1963 we decided that our flat was too small. We sold it and took a larger one in the 12th *arrondissement* in Paris. We had been living in the Latin Quarter for twelve years but the traffic was becoming so bad and it was becoming so difficult to find parking space that we had decided to move to a less crowded area. Of course we missed the atmosphere of the Left Bank, the sidewalk cafés, the lively markets, the tourists. It was a big change for us but time doesn't stand still.

I went back at different times to the Chikito in Switzerland, the cabaret where I had met Lily in 1950. I had been nominated honorary president of the Jazz Club of Zurich and also Yverdon, and would often have visitors at the Chikito who were members of those jazz clubs.

In May 1965, I played there for a month and the boss asked me if I would agree to play 15 days with the violinist Stuff Smith as an added attraction with me and my group. Of course I agreed. I knew Stuff from way back and liked his hard swinging and groovy style. That man could swing like nobody else. Unfortunately, he was in a bad state of health, suffering with stomach ulcers. He was not supposed to drink at all, but couldn't help having whisky, which he would dilute with plenty of water. Sometimes he would feel good, and the next day be very moody. The poor fellow died in September 1967 in Munich. He was buried in Denmark.

My next thrill came in 1966 when I went to England for the first time to do a concert tour. I had met an English fellow at the Trois Mailletz, Ronald Sweetman, who was working in Paris. He was a great jazz fan and record collector who wrote articles for different jazz magazines. When Ron eventually returned to England he told me that he was going to try and get me over there.

The problem was a regulation between the American Federation of Musicians and the British Musicians' Union. An American musician could play in England only if an exchange was possible with a British musician in the States. It didn't work for an American musician living in France. At one time I had wanted to hire an English musician to work two weeks with my band in exchange for me going there but I had been told that it was not possible.

So Ron kept knocking on doors and speaking about me until he finally caught the ear of someone. I was contacted by a booking agent, Jim Godbolt, and we got together on the loot, which was no big deal but I wanted to get my foot in there at least one time, so we came to an agreement. Jim Godbolt was working with the Harold Davison Agency, which is the biggest booking agency in England, and with their help he was able to solve the problem of the working permit.

I arrived in London with Lily on 6 April 1966. I must say that Lily and I liked the looks of everything from the moment we landed in Heathrow Airport and we became more and more excited as we approached the great city of London. A kitchenette apartment had been reserved for us in a residential hotel known as the White House.

That afternoon we had a rehearsal at the Six Bells in Chelsea with Bruce Turner and the band. I met Bruce and the boys: Ray Crane (trumpet), Pete Strange (trombone), Ron Rubin (piano), Tony Baylis (bass), Doug Higgins (drums). Jack Higgins (not related to Doug) was in charge of the jazz department of the Harold Davison Agency, but Jim was going to take care of the band during the tour.

I knew of Bruce, who had the reputation of being one of England's greatest alto sax players. I found this to be true. He played clarinet also. The guys and I liked one other from the beginning, and we worked out some pretty arrangements. The band did swing. Bruce's playing was fine and sensitive. He always seemed to be lost in a dream and he called everyone "Dad." He was vegetarian, didn't drink, didn't smoke, but he was crazy about sweet stuff.

Ron Rubin was a fine pianist. For the tour, Lily, Bruce, and I traveled in Ron's car. One day, I was amazed when he told me that his real instrument was bass. He played piano so well that I thought it was his instrument. I never had the opportunity to hear him play bass, but if he played more of that thing than he did piano or even as much, then he was hell on wheels. I even heard he played drums.

The tour took us to Birmingham. The name made me think of the Birmingham in Alabama but the difference between the two places was like night and day, with the one in England being the day! We played 14 other towns. Many of them were small towns but we always had a swinging full house. Bruce and the boys really pushed me and I found out that Bruce was very popular everywhere we went.

We had heard so many bad comments in France about English cooking that we were pleasantly surprised. We ate some superb meals at Jeff and Kathy Aldam's home, and also with Pat and Jack Armitage, Doug and Gladys Dobell, Mike Collier, and Jim Godbolt. John Kendall, Ray Bolden and Doug Dobell took us to a restaurant on the Strand, the Carvery House, where the meats were delicious. You could help yourself to as much as you liked of pink lamb, roast pork with a crispy crust, rare or medium beef, and so on. Our friends the Dartigues, who had come to visit from Paris, took us to Wheeler's, a fish speciality house, with fantastic dishes and a nice decor. And I love to remember all the Indian and

Pakistani foods we sampled with our dear friends Assia and Leslie Parr.

We gave a party at Max and Betty Jones's home for the Bruce Turner gang and a few intimate friends. Max was a well-known critic and reporter for *Melody Maker* magazine for many years. Bruce and the boys had a surprise gift for me, a tin beer mug engraved: "To Bill 'the Guv'nor,' from Bruce, Pete, Tony, Ray, Ron and Doug." Being called "Guv'nor" in England is like being called Boss in an admiring way. That gift was a real sender for me.

Then we went to visit for a few days our friends Ronald Sweetman and his wife Jennifer in the beautiful Sussex village of Steyning, where they lived. Their house was called "Ellington House." Jennifer is a very well-known painter and printer who signed her work with her maiden name, Jennifer Dixon. I am the godfather of their son, William David. We had a swell time and Jennifer and Ronald gave a party in our honor with 60 guests.

During my stay in England I met many English musicians that I had heard about or listened to on record or had already met in Europe: Lennie Felix, a very good pianist; Nat Gonella and Kenny Ball, fine trumpet men; Danny Moss, tenor sax; Ronnie Scott, owner of the famous club under his name in London; Acker Bilk, who had a private-membership club in Soho on Greek Street, which was directed by his brother Dave. I also met the famous singer George Melly in Manchester, and John Chilton, who had written several books on jazz, including *Who's Who of Jazz*, a well-written work that lists all the American jazzmen born before 1920.

Back in France, bad news was awaiting us. We had met, two years previously, a woman who was in the real-estate business. She seemed to be a smart business woman and we had confidence in her ability. We had invested our savings in her housing construction company. But she went bankrupt and we lost every penny that we had saved for years. We had sold our apartment on rue Monsieur le Prince and we were renting the flat where we were living now. There was no use in crying over spilt milk, but it was a bitter pill to swallow. I was 62 years old and stone broke again.

I had met a French musician named Jef Gilson, a pianist. He was quite talented as an arranger and we were going to work quite a bit together. First he had formed a big band and we gave concerts. We also gave two concerts of sacred music in two big churches in Paris, St.-Etienne-du-Mont and St.-Jean-de-Belleville, both times with the participation of Father de Fatto, an ex-jazz musician I had worked with in Claude Bolling's band. The concert in St.-Etienne-du-Mont was televised. I played and sang Negro spirituals. We also gave concerts with a smaller group at Radio-France House and the Cultural Centers. Jef asked me to record an album called *Jazz For God*. I played two numbers, *Jericho* and *Sometimes I Feel like a Motherless Child*, as soloist, and I also played in two other numbers, *Pax* and *Agnus Dei*.

I was offered an engagement with a fashion show for four weeks with a group of four dishy girls who were models. The show played casinos all over France. We even went to Tunisia for three days and gave a show in front of the son of President Bourgiba. The fashion show went on for an hour, then I played half an hour with my trio. There was also a comedian named Jean Raymond with us. We did 10,000 kilometers with our car in four weeks, not counting the trip to Tunisia. It was tiresome but we had a lot of fun anyway as the atmosphere was very friendly. And it was a gastronomic tour also.

My second tour of England was in April 1967. Lily and I arrived in London on the 18th. I was to play with an orchestra I had never heard of. It was their first tour with an American musician. It was the Tony Milliner–Alan Littlejohn Sextet. Tony played trombone and Alan, trumpet and flugelhorn, but on this tour, he played only flugelhorn. The rest of the musicians were Lew Hooper (tenor sax), Matt Mattieson (piano), Mel Cutlan (drums), and Dave Holland (bass). Dave went to the USA a year later and worked with Miles Davis. The sextet was known as a semi-professional orchestra because Tony and Alan had other jobs and did not depend on music for a living. But they played better than some professionals that I had come across in my travels and the group as a whole was real tight and could swing like mad.

After three rehearsals at a club called the Tally-Ho, the first concert took place on 21 April. The tour took in Birmingham again and Manchester.

Buck Clayton was in London during this time and Ben Webster was playing at Ronnie Scott's club. We were engaged to do a recording for a producer named Alan Bates on the Black Lion label. Buck was to write the arrangements. We would be accompanied by the rhythm section of Alex Welsh's orchestra. Jack Higgins, from the Harold Davison Agency, was in charge of the date.

I arrived at the studio at nine that morning and learned that Buck had been taken to a hospital the previous night, suffering from a nose hemorrhage. Ben wasn't there. He was supposed to have arrived with Buck. Jack Higgins called him at his hotel and told him to take a taxi. I started with the rhythm section and got three tunes in the bag. One of the numbers was *Satin Doll*, but I was not very satisfied with the version I recorded. I wanted to do it again, but Higgins said I could do that later. Ben had arrived and we did some original numbers. I composed one in the studio and called it *Pound Horn*. I had heard that studio trumpeters who doubled on flugelhorn were paid an extra pound when it was used at a session, so English musicians called it a "pound horn." Ben also did some numbers alone with the rhythm section. After that I wanted to record *Satin Doll* again but Higgins insisted that some unknown girl he had brought with him could record one number with the rhythm section, and therefore there was no time left for me. We had had to do this album in three hours.

The next day I played the 100 Club and Nottingham on the 29th. I replaced Buck with the John Chilton Swing Kings at a place called the Dog and Fox in Wimbledon on the 30th. Here was another surprise for me when I learned that John Chilton was a musician, and a trumpet player to boot. When I did my first tour in England, John was collaborating with Jim Godbolt in the booking agency business. We had quite a few get togethers but he never spoke of being a musician, and no one else ever mentioned it to me. So naturally it was a surprise when I learned this about John. It was a bigger surprise when I heard him play because he has a real funky style, which is seldom heard these days.

On 1 May the Milliner–Littlejohn sextet and myself became the first jazz group to do a concert in the Purcell Room, which adjoins the Royal Festival Hall. This was a swell place. I could sing without a mike and I do not have a very strong voice as far as singing is concerned. It was a very successful concert.

At the end of the tour the sextet surprised me with a different tin beermug from the one the Bruce Turner boys had given me. This one was inscribed, "To Bill, with admiration and affection from the boys," and their names. They also gave Lily a small one inscribed, "To Lily with love."

Before going back to Paris, we decided to visit some friends in Scotland and we had a lot of fun with those whisky lovers. We were staying in Elgin with Johnny and Mary Thomson, two beautiful people, and we went sightseeing in their marvelous country with them.

On 29 May I was back in England to play a big festival in Birmingham with the Milliner–Littlejohn sextet and Ben Webster. I came back also to London to play a festival at the Hammersmith theater and blew this one with Alex Welsh's band, which was a great deal.

Ben Webster was there also, and it was my first time to become acquainted with a fine trumpet player whom I had heard on records but never met him. His name was Ruby Braff and when we met, the feeling between us was like we had known each other for years. Ruby was with George Wein's Newport All Stars. He played more horn in person that I had heard him do on records and he had a beautiful style.

On 1 July 1967 we moved to Fontenay-sous-Bois, a suburb of Paris, because the rent of our other flat was too high for our deflated purse. We found a very nice four-room apartment on the sixth floor of a modern building and we had a gorgeous view over the woods of Vincennes and Paris.

I had met the famous French singer Michel Polnareff during a tour in France. He liked my way of playing and he asked me if I would be willing to do a duet with him at the Olympia music hall for three weeks in October. We would play *Summertime* together, me having a few choruses on trumpet, then him, imitating the sound of a trumpet with a wa-wa. I accepted as it was good publicity to work at the Olympia, and Polnareff had a big name. The number had big success. Polnareff had a big voice for such a little fellow and he was using a powerful mike also!

In February 1968 I was elected a member of the French Academy of Jazz. The function of the Academy is to pick the best jazz records issued during the year and give awards. There were distinctions for different categories: blues, New Orleans, modern jazz, singers, etc. We would also elect the best French musician of the year. Two other members of the Academy who were not French were trumpeter Arthur Briggs, who has been on the European scene for years, and an American named Sim Coppans, who had a jazz program on radio.

In May Jef Gilson asked me if I would accept to record an album of Negro spirituals for a guy named Pou-Dubois who owned a recording studio, Europa Sonor. I was interested and we recorded some well-known spirituals and some which were completely unknown. Jef made the arrangements. We had some nice

French musicians such as Eddy Louiss (organ), Gilbert Rovère, and Guy Petersen (bass); some of the arrangements were made for a big band.

I had a contract with Pou-Dubois stipulating that I would get royalties when the records were issued. I didn't get a fee in advance. But Pou-Dubois didn't sell the tape to a record company but to the International Record Guild in Geneva. He didn't stipulate that I was supposed to get royalties. In fact he signed a statement declaring that all the musicians and artists had been paid and had no right to claim any payment or royalties. So I couldn't get any royalties from the Guild and it was not worthwhile suing Pou-Dubois, who according to some people was not solvent.

Later I discovered that Gilson had in his possession the master record and had issued the record as he had a small company called Palm. Through the musicians' syndicate in Paris, I tried to claim my rights, and even took a lawyer, but that guy was such a slicker and liar that he was always finding some way to spread confusion. That record is still on sale and I never succeeded in getting more than $40 for it! Good deal . . .

May and June 1968 were bad times for work. Paris was having a revolution and there was a general strike. The Latin Quarter was on fire. Police, attacked by students with paving stones, were using tear gas. All the clubs were closed. Every gig, concert, and job was canceled. There was no gas for cars; metro and buses were not running. When peace was restored, we still suffered the consequences and hardly worked all summer.

Fortunately I had some good concerts coming during the fall. First Antwerp with Ben Webster, Buddy Tate, Jimmy Woode, Wallace Bishop, Milt Buckner, and Joe Turner. Nice to blow with all those friends, and what a happy reunion!

Next a tour in Copenhagen with a Danish trombone player, John Darville, a fine cat, and his group. They were nice musicians and pals. Later that year I went to Oslo, my first taste of Norway, and played with a Dixieland band, the Big Chief Jazz Band. All nice fellows. We had a ball and drank quite a bit. I really liked the country, at least what I saw of it. From there I went back to Copenhagen, where I saw my old friend Timme Rosenkrantz and his wife, Inez Cavanaugh. They had opened a club, and Mary Lou Williams was playing there. I also saw May Mezzrow, the wife of Mezz Mezzrow. She was a cook in a restaurant in town. Another happy reunion.

Buddy Tate had been in Paris and in Europe for a concert tour sponsored by Jean Marie Monestier, the owner of the little record company Black and Blue in Paris. Pathé-Marconi had proposed that I should record an LP with another American soloist, and as I liked Buddy very much, I asked him if he was interested. He liked the idea very much but was obliged to have a word with Monestier about it. We had a few talks about the project. I was obliged to give an answer to Pathé-Marconi, and Buddy was telling me each time that he couldn't get a straight answer from Monestier, but that he was going to make that record. The date was set for 5 December, but until the last day I really didn't know if Buddy would be there for the recording.

The studio had been hired, and so were the musicians. Buddy's last concert was in Barcelona, Spain, and Buddy had called me from there, saying that

Monestier had threatened him not to pay his fare back to New York if he was making the record. In the morning at eight o'clock I went with Lily to the airport to see if he was there! Was I glad to see him! He had a bad cold, and was dead tired, as he had not slept a wink. He told me that at 3 a.m. he was still arguing with Monestier and finally got his way. We went to have breakfast, then to the studio, and we made a nice album entitled *Together at Last*. The other musicians were Georges Arvanitas (piano and organ), Pierre Sim (bass), and Charles Bellonzi (drums). The record got an award from the Academy of Jazz. I did another recording for a British fellow who was trying to push a young British pianist, Mike Garrett. We had Art Taylor on drums, Jean-François Catoire on bass, and François Guin on trombone. I was told that Mike had been doing a lot of classical piano, was very talented, and wanted to play jazz. But we found out that he had never before played with an ensemble and didn't know the art of accompanying a soloist. We did our best and called the album *Three Generations Jam*. It was released in England by my friend Doug Dobell.

Two years had passed since I had been in London but the occasion came for the Expo, a week-long festival sponsored by the Harold Davison Agency and George Wein. It featured many American musicians as well as English groups. Once again I was to meet and work with a famous musician I had heard and read plenty about but never seen. This was the pianist Jay McShann. His personality sent me as soon as we were introduced. Charlie Shavers, Buddy Tate, Albert Nicholas, and I did a public audience TV show for the BBC at Ronnie Scott's club. Jay played and sang some real gone blues which knocked everybody out. He was a wonderful accompanist and really sent me when I did my solos. I had not been playing with a pianist of that class in many moons. I have a tape of that session, thanks to an English jazz-lover and friend of mine, Leslie Parr.

For the second time, I went, just after New Year, to a ski resort in France called Super-Besse. A young friend of mine, the clarinettist Marc Lafferière, was organizing a jazz festival, the concept of which was unusual and very sympathetic. He invited about a hundred musicians, professionals and amateurs. We were all living in the same building, which was usually used as a hotel for holidays by people and students of modest background. I only gave one concert, but Lily and I stayed for the whole week. Many guest artists played there also: Albert Nicholas, Benny Waters, Memphis Slim, the Golden Gate Quartet, Guy Lafitte, and others. Not only were there musicians and their families but also people who came from everywhere as paying guests and would stay for the length of the festival. There would always be somebody to talk with, drink with, make music with. In the daytime, we would go out for a walk, the majority would go skiing, then we would take a nap, go downstairs, and play cards or dice. Bands would rehearse, then aperitif time would come. After supper we all would go to the concert hall. Two or three bands were playing each night. After the concert, at about one o'clock, a lot of people would go four floors below to a club called Le Terrier (the Burrow) and jam there for hours, often until four or five in the morning.

After Super-Besse, we went to Nice, where we got a taste of spring. Then in

April we went to Morocco, to Meknes, Rabat, and Casablanca. It had been a very long time since my last trip there. This time I was playing with a band directed by Jacques Largeaud, who played organ and piano. We had a swell time.

A few weeks later, I went back to Copenhagen to do a TV show with Teddy Wilson. The funny thing is that we flew in the same plane and did not see each other. He must have been in first class. Ben Webster was living in Copenhagen and also did the TV show with us.

I went back to play at the Trois Mailletz. I had been angry for some time with Madame Calvé but decided to forget our differences. Past was past and it's nice sometimes to play in a club. Another club where I started to play was the Caveau de l'Huchette, also situated in the Latin Quarter. The owner was the vibraphonist Dany Doriz. The atmosphere was more easy going than at the Trois Mailletz. People came to dance and musicians were coming and going all the time. The only trouble was that it was a hot and smoky place.

I was contacted by a well-known French composer and singer, Guy Béart, who had a TV program called *Welcome to. . . .* Each time it would be to a different personality, dancer, writer, singer, etc. The program ran for one hour. Guy Béart told me that he wanted to do a *Welcome to Americans*, and asked me if I was willing to contact all the American jazz musicians available in Paris. I accepted and rang Mickey Baker (guitar), Kenny Clarke (drums), Art Simmons (piano), Benny Waters (tenor sax), Cecily Forde, and some others. Guy Béart also asked for Mezz Mezzrow. The show was very successful.

About one month later, Guy Béart called me again and said he wanted to do another show with Duke Ellington, who was in town. Again I was in charge of forming a band. This time I rang the pianist Aaron Bridgers; Michel Gaudry, a fine French bass player; Daniel Humair, one of the best drummers in town; my friend the tenor saxophonist Guy Lafitte; and Mickey Baker on guitar. Guy Béart wanted Cecily Forde again. Cecily was not American but from Trinidad, but she was a very nice singer in the style of Sarah Vaughan. Guy Béart had been very impressed with her performance for the first show.

We were all excited to be with Duke. He came on the set at 5 p.m. dressed in a light blue costume. Guy Béart introduced him to the audience, since the show was semi-public. There were showbiz personalities, artist guests, journalists, and a lot of beautiful girls who were engaged especially to add more glamor to the show. We played two numbers for Duke, *Satin Doll* and *Take the A Train*. Then Béart asked him a lot of questions about his career and about jazz: "What is jazz? What is the future of jazz? What do you think of free jazz? Do you sing? Please sing a song." Duke had a superb sense of humor and he knew how to wangle his way out of the most tricky situations. It was a pleasure to hear him talk. Then he sat at the piano and played some of his compositions. Later he played two numbers with us and at the end we had a jam session. Nothing had been prepared or rehearsed in advance. The atmosphere was terrific. I was amazed at the patience of Duke. It was 1 a.m. when the show was finished.

I had started playing quite often with a very good French trombonist, Raymond

Fonsèque. He was a versatile musician and had already been leading several bands of different styles. The last one was playing ragtime and traditional jazz. We recorded together ten original compositions of his and mine and we were very pleased with the album, which was different from other things that I have recorded. We named the album *Bill and the Boys*. Hugues Panassié wrote that "This record swings so much that it's hard to listen to it while sitting down!"

In June I participated in another French festival located in Normandy, in a village called Luneray, of about 1800 inhabitants. It was taking place in a potato-storage barn and there was an attendance of about 15,000 people in two days! Plenty of amateur bands were there and four or five professional ones. There were also three or four well-known artists as attractions.

The festival started on Saturday night at 8 p.m. and closed at 4 a.m.; on Sunday it ran from 11 a.m. to 8 p.m. The music was nonstop. People could eat and drink there at a very moderate price. The organization was super and all the people of the village, young and old, led by Jean Suplice, were participating at the festival. I never saw a public more enthusiastic and disciplined. Nobody was drunk; everybody, from children to old people, was listening. The entrance fee was small but all the benefit of the festival went to social welfare and charities.

On 21 June I played a concert in Joinville, a suburb of Paris, with Benny Carter, Ben Webster, Kenny Drew, Art Taylor, Michel Sarbady, Johnny Griffin, the Golden Gate Quartet, the Delta Rhythm Boys, Claude Bolling, Memphis Slim, and Slide Hampton. There were going to be three concerts in the same theater but I could only make one as I had to leave for North Africa. Unfortunately the festival was a disaster, with an attendance of only about 150 people at each concert. What a pity, with a program of such talented artists. But the organization had been terrible. It was organized and sponsored by a woman singer, Lallie Patrick, who also owned a restaurant.

Ben Webster didn't show up for the last concert. He had had dinner at Lallie's place, which was situated in front of the Marne river in Joinville. Ben, who was high probably, wanted to wee-wee in the river and fell in the water. He was rescued by the cook of the restaurant, who heard his calls for help.

I gave several concerts in Morocco and went to Tangiers. The band leader was Jacques Largeaud and he had an amateur drummer, whose name was Slim, from one of the oldest tribes in Morocco. He had a very shabby set of drums. During the intermission I was surprised to see Max Roach come into my dressing room. He was having a vacation in Tangiers with his wife, and was staying with pianist Randy Weston, who had a jazz club in town. It was nice to see him, and during the second part of the show I introduced him to the public and asked him to join me for a few numbers, which he did. It was a thrill. Slim couldn't believe his eyes seeing Max Roach playing his old drums as if they were a new set just arrived from the factory.

After Tangiers, I went to Corsica in July. It was my first time there and I found the island very picturesque. From there I went to Palermo for another festival.

FIFTEEN

TRUMPET JUBILEE

The death of Louis Armstrong on 6 July 1971, two days after his 71st birthday, was a great shock to me. He had been ill for a while, but I'd heard he was getting better. It filled me with sadness. I had been an admirer of Pops since I had heard his first record when he played with Fletcher Henderson, and as time had passed, my admiration for him had grown. Like all the trumpeters of my generation, and many of those of generations to come, I had been influenced by his style, his wonderful phrasing, and his musical ideas. He had contributed so much to my own development. I had learned to know and love him and we were very happy, Lily and I, to meet Pops and his wife Lucille whenever they were in Paris. Sometimes we met at our friends Maurice and Vonette Cullaz's home. He loved Vonette's cooking because he loved oriental, food of which he was a connoisseur.

Satchmo was a genius. He amazed crowds and gave a lot of pleasure to the whole world with his original style of trumpet playing and jazz singing. Of course, there have been other geniuses in the world of jazz, but many of them died young. Pops was shining bright for many long years.

Charlie Shavers died two days after Louis. It was another shock for us, particularly since we did not even know he was sick. He died of throat cancer, and the development of his sickness had been very rapid. He was a great trumpeter and a very good arranger. I had known him well when he started to play with John Kirby. Rightfully, I would say that Charlie was the backbone of the Greatest Little Big Band in the World because the numbers they recorded and played on radio were arranged by him, and many were his compositions. They were very exciting to play, as I had experienced while I worked with Kirby.

The last time we saw Charlie was 14 February 1970, in a suburb of Paris called Drancy. He was making a tour with Budd Johnson and Oliver Jackson. I played a part of the concert with my own group and Charlie played the other part. He was only 52 years old. I was told that he asked that his trumpet be placed in the coffin of Louis Armstrong. Thank God, we have their recordings left to keep alive the great musicality of both Charlie and Pops.

The next exciting thing in the travels of my horn and me happened on 21 November 1971, when I was engaged to go to West Africa. It came through the

US Cultural Center's African programming office. Lily and I left Paris on the night of 21 November at 10.35 on an African airline plane and arrived at Abidjan airport on the Ivory Coast at five o'clock on the morning of the 22nd. I had been in North Africa quite a number of times but never in other parts of Africa, so naturally I was excited about being in a part of the world I had seen in movies and heard so much about.

The assistant director of the US Cultural Center (a young man from Boston named Robert La Gamma), his wife, and the director of the National Orchestra of the Ivory Coast met us at the airport and gave us the feeling that we were going to enjoy our stay in Abidjan. We had had no idea of what to expect in a part of the world we had never visited before, but when the time came for us to leave, we knew that we would never forget that country and the wonderful people we met.

The director of the US Cultural Center, who was away in Kenya, had put his villa at our disposal, as well as his boy, Benson, a native of Biafra. We also had a car and chauffeur at our disposal. The house was in Cocody, the residential part of Abidjan. On our way there, we did not know which way to look as everything we saw appeared so beautiful. The daylight itself was something to wonder about. There were giant trees and huge flower bushes everywhere. The natives moved about, men and women, at a slow pace. The women carried huge loads on their heads, walking with ease and grace. When we arrived at the villa, it was more wonderful still. The gardens were full of bougainvilleas of every color and there were big colorful lizards on the walls of the garden.

The aim of the cultural mission for which I had been engaged was to familiarize the National Orchestra with jazz. The director, Jean-Joseph Pango, had many activities to his credit. He was a member of the Social and Economic Council, member of the Athletic and Football League and helped run a youth center. One of his brothers, Father Pierre Michel Pango, was a great musician. He had composed *L'Abidjanaise*, which is the national anthem. He was running a school in Bingerville and had formed a wonderful children's choir. He used all sorts of African instruments for the accompaniment.

I had been engaged to give three concerts in eight days with the National Orchestra and we had a lot of work to do. The band had already rehearsed a few standards: *Perdido, Basin Street Blues,* and *St. Louis Blues.* I had brought with me some of the big-band arrangements I wanted to play with them. The lineup of the orchestra was three trumpets, one alto sax, one tenor sax, two clarinets, two electric guitars, one electric bass guitar, a drummer, and a tom-tom player. There was also a male singing quartet and a female choir of eight. The girls were dressed in their native costumes and some were beautiful. Jean-Joseph Pango played alto sax, accordion, and organ, but he didn't take part in the numbers I rehearsed for the concerts. The musicians were mostly young students and were not very much in the know about jazz, but they loved it and were very co-operative. We rehearsed also a couple of Negro spirituals with the male quartet and the female choir harmonizing the background. The only thing wrong was that they could not play fast: everything we did was in the same tempo.

The first concert was given at the University of Abidjan. It was the rainy season, and that day about 4 p.m. a big storm started. Usually, people told me, it was over in an hour or two, but that day we couldn't see the end of it. The concert was in the open air, and we really thought that we wouldn't be able to play. Fortunately the rain almost stopped and we left for the university. But we had to play under a covered part in the garden and not too many students could see us. We had a big success anyway.

On one of our evenings off we were taken to a restaurant on the lagoon and ate such exotic delicacies as monkey, agouti, antelope, and even bat.

On 26 November we were invited to the residence of the American ambassador for a luncheon in our honor. This was a different reception from the kick in the ass we got when I was in Egypt and couldn't even get a look at the ambassador when we needed help. There were various African and American dignitaries at that luncheon. The director of Abidjan television was there: he told me that the theme of *Afro Motif in Blue*, that I had recorded in 1960 with Budd Johnson and musicians of Quincy Jones, had been used as the signature tune for a program on TV for two years.

We gave a concert in Treichville. There was no air-conditioning and it was so hot that the perspiration ran down my lips so my mouthpiece kept slipping. My last concert was in Bingerville on Sunday, 28 November. The concert had been arranged in the afternoon so that the kids of the town could attend, and it was the largest crowd of the three concerts. It was in the open air and the weather was fair. There were hundreds of kids and thousands of adults, black and white, and they seemed like one big happy family. We really had a big success and I was very happy that the band got such great applause.

I would have liked to have met more musicians and well-known artists that time but the occasion didn't present itself, except for two famous male singers, François Lougah and Ernesto Djedje. On the 29th we went to the US Cultural Center to say goodbye to the staff, Mr. Pango, and the members of the band. We received numerous gifts and we were sad to depart.

From there we went on to Dakar, Senegal, to give a concert for the US Cultural Center also. We stayed in Dakar only three days. Concerning my only concert in the country, it could have made a good Mack Senett comedy film. I had a contract with the American Cultural Center. We were met by the assistant of the director of the center at the airport. He brought us to our hotel and said that I had a rehearsal in the afternoon with an African band. I could sense right away that this guy knew nothing about jazz and had never heard of me.

A group of musicians of lead and bass guitars, a tenor sax man, drums and piano player were to accompany me. We met at the place where they were working. I asked the fellows if they knew the American standards such as *Perdido*, *Tea for Two*, *St. Louis Blues*, etc. They didn't. I asked them what the numbers were they knew. They couldn't name one tune. What made matters worse was that neither the pianist nor any of the others could read chords. I always carry two chord books with me: one in English, the other in French.

Finally they pretended to know *Moanin'*, but when I started to play it with them, it was not the composition of B. Timmons that I knew. So I was obliged to mark them off and tell the director of the Cultural Center that it was impossible for me to work with those men.

He started to ask me if I could play alone for the concert. I explained to him that I needed at least a rhythm section and he said that he would see what he could do, but that band was supposed to be the best in town!

Colette Lacroix, a friend of Lily and me, had given Lily the phone number of one of her friends who was the director of the most important newspaper in Dakar, the *Sun*. When we had met the director of the Cultural Center, Lily had asked him if any report had been printed in the papers about my arrival and about the concert. He said that nothing had been printed concerning the matter. So Lily phoned the director of the *Sun*, who seemed to be a nice person to talk with. He said that he had heard me play several times in France when he was a student there, that he would not be able to attend the concert because he had to leave Dakar, but he would be able to come to the rehearsal with a reporter and a photographer. He was quite upset when he saw that I couldn't play with that band.

He said that if the American Cultural Center really wanted to do something cultural for the people of his country, they should send a couple of American music professors to teach the young students and musicians about the different arts of America and the right approach to the form of jazz.

The director of the *Sun* had come also with a young man in his early thirties who was a trumpet player from Ghana named Mackenzie. He knew a lot about jazz, and was a quiet and nice person. He told me that he had seen the director of the Center the previous week and had told him that this band would be incapable of accompanying me. He had offered to form a little group and make them rehearse but they had declined his offer.

We asked him if he could contact some better musicians. Unfortunately, he said, two were out of town, but he knew a lead guitar, another guitarist, and a drummer. The assistant, who by then was getting worried, said he was going with him. We went to our hotel and waited and waited.

About eleven that night they came back and said they had not been able to find the musicians, who were not in. There was nothing we could do that day and we went to bed disgusted.

The next day we had an appointment at 9 a.m. at the Center, but nobody showed up before 10.30. It was Africa I was told. Then the director's assistant said they were expecting a trio from a military band who were supposed to play jazz, and that the commander had given his agreement. A friend of the director had agreed to lend his piano for the concert. They also rang a fellow who played classical music but knew a few jazz tunes on piano.

Nothing got started until 11.30. The army trio arrived with first-class new material, drums, bass, guitar. I started to audition them. Alas! They really couldn't play jazz, and the drummer was incapable of keeping tempo.

Next came Mackenzie's group. The lead guitarist knew a little about reading chords and was able to help the bass guitarist. We had the drummer of the group I had rehearsed the day before. Mackenzie also played flute and was willing to help as much as possible.

There was one more problem. Their sound equipment was not good. The director of the Center called the army commander, who agreed to let us use their equipment. I rehearsed until 7 p.m., except for a break at lunchtime. The pianist didn't show up. Except Mackenzie, the musicians were not even what one would call second-class amateurs. But I managed to get enough numbers together to make a decent concert.

After the rehearsal we went to our hotel to get dressed and have supper. I had asked the director's assistant to bring me some whisky because I knew that I would need a stimulant.

Just before the concert started, the guy came to my dressing room with a thermos bottle that was able to hold a good cup of coffee. I could have been knocked over with a feather when I poured a drink in a glass and found out that it was half water. I came out of the dressing room and asked a young fellow who had not entered the concert hall if he would go to the nearest bar and bring me a double whisky, and he did.

The hall could only hold about 130 people, and it was full to capacity with important guests, notables, students, and a few Europeans. The first half of the concert was not too bad, with the two guitars and Mackenzie playing flute, and trumpet in the style of Art Farmer. I went to a bar near the hall when intermission time came and the two guitar players must have done the same, because they did not remember much of any of the numbers we had rehearsed. Mackenzie was trying to keep them straight without showing the audience that things were not going right. Lily was also in the audience, and I kept looking at her and smiling whenever it was possible for me to do so. That was the only way I could keep from crying. I can't remember having such a miserable night as that one, and I have had some. If I am ever asked to go to that country again, it will be with my own group.

A week after our return to Fontenay-sous-Bois, I received a letter from the Public Affairs Officer for the American Embassy in Dakar, who apologized to us about what he called "those trying circumstances," and added: "I'm sure you have never spent two more frantic days than the two you recently spent in Dakar!"

I celebrated my trumpet jubilee in 1972. Jean Suplice, the organizer of the yearly Jam Potatoes festival of Luneray in Normandy, found out that 50 years had passed from the time I had bought my first horn, and he decided to make a big thing of it at the festival that year. He arranged for me to become an honorary citizen of Luneray. The ceremony took place the first day of the festival, 11 June.

We arrived at the city hall and were greeted by a group of hunting horn players in their traditional costumes. The mayor of Luneray and the deputy of the county of Seine-Maritime made me an honorary citizen, and I received a diploma stating that I had been a big help to the festival and also to the reputation of Luneray. I had to make a little speech in French and it didn't come out too bad.

After the ceremony, we went to the big potato-storage plant where the festival always takes place. It was eleven in the morning and we heard the choir of Luneray directed by Françoise Suplice (who plays organ and piano also), which was composed of 50 members, male and female. They sang spirituals and many religious songs of the type one can hear in a Negro Baptist church. I played a number with them.

That day I played with five different groups including a group from England, the Tomasso family, directed by the father, Ernie Tomasso, a very fine clarinet player. The youngest son, who was 9 years old, played trumpet: I have a photo of him being introduced to Louis Armstrong. He did a very good interpretation of Louis doing *Sleepy Time Down South*.

I had not been a professional for 50 years: it had taken me almost three years of learning the instrument and two more before I joined an orchestra of any importance. But the word of 50 years of trumpet playing spread, and there were quite a number of celebrations, articles in jazz magazines, TV shows, etc.

.I was at the country home of my friend Felix Debrit in Lugnorre, Switzerland, when I had my birthday that year. Felix was the fellow who assisted me in getting to play in Switzerland in 1949–50. He decided to give a big party to celebrate it and invited Swiss friends and all the Swiss musicians I knew or worked with. We were about one hundred people. The party took place in the garden and the weather was beautiful. Felix had 68 balloons blown up, that corresponded with my age, and which I sent up to the sky at a certain time. It was beautiful to see all those different colored balloons going up to the blue sky and over the lake of Morat until they were out of sight. Felix's piano was taken out in the garden and we had a terrific jam session from early afternoon until 3 a.m. the next day.

That same day I discovered that I had a cyst under an eyelid. I had to have an operation in Paris on 30 October. Everything went alright, but the doctor told me that I should take it easier and that my heart was beginning to get a bit tired.

During one of my tours of Italy, I recorded with the band of Lino Patruno, a very good bassist and guitarist. The album is entitled *Bill Coleman in Milan*.

I started the year 1973 by playing the old one out and ringing the new one in at the Casino in Chamonix. (That was where Lily had started to organize my first tour of France with my own band in 1952.) And that year rolled by with its usual quota of festivals, concerts, and tours.

I went back again to Algeria for a tour with my group, which was quite international for that occasion. I had Vany Hinder, a Swiss tenor saxophonist and clarinettist, a talented musician with some solid experience; Alain Fougeret, the pianist, who was influenced by Bill Evans and a good accompanist; and our good, dependable bassist was Pierre Sim. Pierre and Alain were French but Pierre was of Armenian descent. Michael Silva, an American, was an ex-drummer of Sammy Davis Jr.

I had not been back to Algeria since 1956 and Independence Day and I was curious to see whether there had been any changes. We were to play in Oran, Blida, and Algiers. It was hard, in just a few days, to come up with an opinion. The style of dress for most of the natives had not changed much, except that most of the women no longer covered their faces as they had before. Life seemed very expensive except for necessity products. The streets were less animated and dirty, but it was raining and the wind was blowing, and that could account for the greyness that seemed present.

The Algerians hadn't heard any jazz for a long time. The concerts were very successful, with a large attendance, mostly Algerian and a few Europeans. The public was very enthusiastic and the concert in Algiers was broadcast.

My friend Guy Lafitte had left Paris to go and live in the province of Le Gers in the south-west of France, where he had started raising sheep. Guy always had great affinities with the country and nature, and he wasn't too fond of big cities. Of course he still played a lot of galas and festivals, and that's how we came together again for the jazz festival of Montreux, Switzerland, on 4 July 1973. I was happy to play again with pianist Marc Hemmeler and drummer Daniel Humair. We had a very good bass player with us named Jack Sewing. The concert was recorded for Black Lion, the label of Alan Bates, and was called *Bill Coleman –Guy Lafitte—Mainstream at Montreux*. It was televised also and one can find video-cassettes of it.

I had made two other recordings that same year. One was a session with my friend Stephane Grappelli, our first recording together since the 1937 era, although we have played together on many occasions. We recorded mostly standard ballads. Our only problem was that since each tune had to be only three minutes long, the development of our musical ideas was quite limited.

My second recording was quite different from what I had recorded before. Serge Greffet, whom I knew since 1948 at the time of the Théâtre Edouard VII, had a music publishing company and he wanted me to record for him. My old-time friend the ex-drummer Jerry Mengo did the arrangements for ten original compositions by him and me, and wrote for 17 violins and brass. The record sounds somewhat like the dance bands of the 1930s and 40s and we both liked it very much. But Greffet went bankrupt and the record was not issued until 1981.

"Have horn, will travel" was always my motto. My next thrill was a trip to the island of Réunion in the Indian Ocean. A long journey, full of fun, with Lily and the orchestra of Marc Lafferière (tenor and soprano sax), a swinging little fellow that I knew for a long time. He had a nice little band.

My ex-bass player Pierre Sim was now living in St. Denis and was waiting for us at the airport with some members of the Cultural Center, called the CRAC. We had five concerts to play: one in a theater in St. Denis, two in an open-air theater in St. Gilles, one at the Plaine des Palmistes, and the last one was open-air in the garden of a high school, plus radio and TV shows.

We were fascinated by the picturesque scenery in the streets; the mix of races—black people, white, Indian, Chinese; the markets; the animals like buffaloes; very old giant tortoises; etc.

When we went to St. Gilles, we saw on the side of the road natives who were selling fruits, and we discovered the real taste of some fruits, especially pineapple. Nothing to compare with what we eat back home.

The people of the island were not spoiled by too many shows, and the theater was packed. It was near the ocean and built like a circle with stepped rows of seats. The scenery was beautiful, and it was nice and inspiring to blow under the stars. It was frog-spawning season, and when we came out after the concert, thousands of small frogs were in the field. You didn't know how to walk. Lots of them were crushed by car tires and shoes.

We received invitations, honors, and big medals. The prefect organized for us a tour of the island with a small plane. We were living a dream.

In July George Wein started a long run of jazz festivals in Nice. I was engaged for the first one, and it was a treat to play with my old pals. A statue of Louis Armstrong was inaugurated at the Arènes de Cimiez, where the festival was held in the presence of Princess Grace of Monaco and Lucille Armstrong.

Hugues Panassié passed away on 8 December 1974 in Montauban, in the south-west of France. Anyone who has followed the evolution of jazz since the 1930s knows what an important role Hugues played in its recognition in France and the rest of the world. He made jazz known and respected when it was still considered "jungle music." He fought all his life to help Negro musicians, and when the avant-garde or free jazz wave threatened to sweep away musicians of the older generation, he tried to make sure they would not be forgotten and their music would not be devalued. He was responsible for many of the early jazz recordings of pre-war times in France. Most of those have become collectors' items. I am personally indebted to him for helping me become known in Europe in the years 1930–40, and for many of the recordings he had me do, of which I am proud. I know that many of my American musician friends have for him the same respect and the same admiration as I have.

On 18 December 1974 I received a very high distinction for recognition of my merits and work in France. I was made a knight of the Order of Merit, the second highest distinction in France, created by General de Gaulle. I chose Luneray for the ceremony and I received by the hand of the prefect of the Seine-Maritime district a diploma signed by the President of France, Valéry Giscard d'Estaing, and a big medal.

People were often raving about my strength, my shape, my resistance. It's true that I felt good, that I had stamina, but sometimes you can be careless about signs. I was often out of breath, not when I was playing but when I was walking. Doctors spoke of emphysema. I was supposed to be on a salt-free diet, but I hated it. I should have cut smoking but I was working in smoky places and I was cheating now and then. With the years passing, I had slowed down a lot with drinking.

In September 1975 I made another three-week tour in England. We were staying in London with our good friends, Jeff and Kathy Aldam, who are a swell couple. We traveled mostly by train and I played with local groups. Most of them were semi-professional.

In London I played the Hundred Club with Pete Strange (trombone), Dave Jones (clarinet and baritone sax), Colin Smith (trumpet), Pete Chapman (bass), Johnnie Richardson (drums), and Keith Ingham (piano). Keith was a sort of newcomer on the English scene, and the cats in the know were giving him much credit as a jazz pianist. I thought he was very good.

The leader of the group who played with me in Bracknell was the vibes player Lennie Best. Ron Rubin was on bass. Colin Purbrook was the pianist, and he had quite a name there. A nice band.

At the Seven Dials in London, I worked with Danny Moss, a fine musician, Lennie Hastings, a good drummer, and Eddie Thompson, a blind pianist who had just arrived from a long stay in the USA. The jazz scene was raving about him. He was very good but sometimes he did a little showing off that doesn't really fit in with jazz.

In Newcastle I played with Alex Welsh, so I was very pleased with the group I was working with. There we had the pleasure to visit our dear friends Johnny and Mary Thompson and Mike and Cynthia Lane. After the tour we stayed a few more days to visit other friends. Ginger Henderson, whom I knew in Alexandria in 1938 where he was soldier and played trumpet, and his wife Henrietta we saw in Richmond. We went also to Oxford to visit our good friend John Wain and his family. John is a very talented and eminent writer and poet, and it's always a pleasure to see him. We had some good times also with a swinging lady, Beryl Bryden, also with Valerie Wilmer, who had become a very talented photographer and journalist in the jazz field.

We left London on 7 October. Our faithful friend Ron "Chips" Chipperfield traveled with us to Gatwick. We had a lot of fast walking to do from the airport to the plane, and I was really puffing and tired.

We didn't stay home a long time as I had a gig in Brussels on the 9th, two days after. On 11 October I had to get up at 9 a.m. as I had to participate with Raymond Fonsèque's band at some kind of a session for workers at midday in the suburbs of Paris. I wasn't feeling well and Lily was worried. I took some medicine and decided to go anyway. But 15 kilometers outside of Paris I felt so bad that I had to pull the car to the side of the road. I couldn't breathe any more. I was saved by miracle by an ambulance who took me to the nearest hospital. I was having an edema of the lungs and later had a heart stoppage. I woke up in an intensive care unit, hands tied up and tubes all over, especially a big one in the mouth.

My regular cardiologist named Farid was a Tunisian and he considered me like his father. He came to see me in the evening and told me that I was going to be alright, but advised me to be patient. He assured me that they would take the big tube (for respiratory assistance) away in the morning if I was feeling well.

In the morning I was impatient to see somebody but nobody came around. I just couldn't stand that damn tube. I succeeded to untie my hands and pull the tube out of my mouth, had a good look at it and put it back, but just between my lips. Soon a doctor came, had a look at me, a look at the board, and suddenly realized what I had done. He screamed for help, and in no time three or four persons were in my room. I tried patiently to tell them that I could breathe normally and that the tube was hurting my tongue and teeth.

I stayed ten days in that hospital—enough time to realize that I had to slow down my pace, to stop smoking, to watch my salt diet, etc. Lily went to see the chief doctor and asked him if I would be able to blow again without endangering my life, and he said with a look of commiseration that it would be better if I played violin.

I took it easy for a while but couldn't stay away from life and started to play again in December.

Guy Lafitte, who was living in Gascony, in south-west France, asked me to come and play a concert in Simorre. Lily and I were very impressed by the beauty of the landscape. My friend the doctor said that the climate would be better for my lungs, and we decided to move to the foothills of the Pyrenees, where life is sweet. We have a nice house with a garden. I have become a member of the Bean-Tasters of Gascony and a Knight of Armagnac, which is a brandy like Cognac. The beans are white and taste exactly like the beans cooked in the USA with pork meat, the real soul food style.

We had thought that being away from Paris and living in the country I would semi-retire. But I still got plenty of offers, and was still feeling to blow my horn, meet people, and didn't want to lose all that good loot coming my way.

I came back to London to the Pizza Express in 1977. I had another of those nice trips I was so fond of. This time it was Martinique and Guadeloupe here I come. I had my band with me: Alain Fougeret (piano), Pierre Sim (bass), Michel Denis (drums), and Stephane Guérault. I consider Stephane to be a very good, talented tenor saxophonist, and a very sensitive clarinettist with a style of his own. He is a nice and lively cat, and I like him very much, his young wife also.

I was approached one day at home by a fellow that I knew from Paris, who had been the organizer of the New Orleans jazz festival of St. Leu, a suburb of Paris, for 16 years. He had retired to a small town named Marciac, also situated in the Gers.

He told me that the previous year he and the president of the youth center of Marciac had organized a jazz concert with the orchestra of Claude Luter and it was successful. Now they wanted to organize a jazz festival, and would I agree to help them, give them advice, put them in contact with American musicians, and be the guest star of the coming festival: all for a moderate fee. I was willing to do it, and met the president of the FJEP (Foyer des Jeunes et Education Populaire) and the city mayor.

For the first festival we had the blues singer Memphis Slim, Benny Waters, the Golden Gate Quartet, and me and my band. It was a great success, and afterwards the festival became a regular, gaining reputation each year. I was made honorary president of the Foyer des Jeunes. The year after, Guy Lafitte was made president also.

What had prevented me from getting bored with the routine of playing for so long, is, I believe, the variety of the propositions that I been offered. I played behind comedians and poets, I played often in churches, and had done Negro spirituals and gospel. I played in school for children of all ages, for workers in a factory, on the sea, in the mountains, under all climates. I never knew how to take it easy. If I can't blow the way I feel, I'll quit.

I have developed some of my long-time hobbies such as stamp collecting and miniature trains, for which my passion goes back to my freight-hopping days in Cincy.

I am Uncle Bill to six nieces, and a great-uncle also. Lots of our many friends come to visit, and if my horn isn't sitting in the car on the way to a concert somewhere, it's there on the way to a jam session in the surrounding mountain homes of musical friends. Good for the chops and the spirit!

Sometimes, young people come to ask me how to become a jazz musician. I tell them to study solfège, harmony, work on their horn regularly without tiring; to listen to records; not to get stuck on one style only, because jazz has plenty of expressions; and lastly, to try and bring out their own personality: tone, style, and phrasing. I tell them not to imitate such-and-such a musician, but to try and make their music their own language, their own means of communication.

Now at the age of 77, I am thinking of retiring. I have a new record coming out that I did with the rhythm section of Panama Francis and Guy Lafitte, titled *Really I do*. These memoirs were first issued in French because my dear Lily translated them. I like very much the village of Cadeillan where we live. People are friendly, birds are singing, and the food is great.

My friend Jean-Marie Masse from Limoges used to introduce me to the public as "the Gentleman of the trumpet." I am honored by this title and personally I've always tried to be a modern-time minstrel. He said also that I was the most Parisian of all the American musicians that have ever been in Paris or lived there, because I was born in Paris, Kentucky, and have lived for 30 years in Paris, France.

I've had my share of changes, both musically and otherwise. And so, this is the story of a voyage. From Paris to Paris with a horn . . . and, as the French say, "Vive le jazz."

Discography
Compiled by Evert (Ted) Kaleveld
and Lily Coleman

Abbreviations

arr	arranger
as	alto saxophone
bars	baritone saxophone
bs	bass saxophone
bj	banjo
cel	celesta
cl	clarinet
d	drums
db	double bass
fl	flute
flh	flugel horn
g	guitar
ldr	leader
org	organ
p	piano
ss	soprano saxophone
t	trumpet
tb	trombone
ts	tenor saxophone
v	vocal
vib	vibraphone
vn	violin
wb	washboard

Country of record origin
(Where no country of origin is given, USA is understood.)

E	England
F	France
I	Italy
N	Netherlands
Sz	Switzerland

Record types

EP	45 rpm extended play

(Issue numbers of 78 rpm records are shown in roman type; those of long-playing records are shown in italic.)

1929
Sep 6   New York
Luis Russell and his Orchestra
Bill Coleman, Henry "Red" Allen (t); J.C. Higginbotham (tb, v); Albert Nicholas (cl, as); Charlie Holmes (as, ss); Teddy Hill (ts); Luis Russell (p, ldr); Walter Johnson (bj); Pops Foster (db); Paul Barbarin (d, vib)

402938-c	The New Call of the Freaks	Okeh 8734
402939-c	Feeling the Spirit (JCH:v)	Okeh 8766
402940-b	Jersey Lightning	Okeh 8734

1929
Sep 13   New York
Lou and his Ginger Snaps [= Luis Russell and his Orchestra]
same personnel as session of 6 September 1929

9006-1	Broadway Rhythm	Banner 6536
9007-1	The way he loves is just too bad	Banner 6540
9007-2	The way he loves is just too bad	

1929
Nov 19   New York
Cecil Scott and his Bright Boys
Bill Coleman, Frankie Newton (t); Dicky Wells (tb); Cecil Scott (cl, ts, bars, bs, ldr); John Williams, Harold McFerran (as); Don Frye (p); Rudolph Williams (bj, g); Mack Walker (tuba); Lloyd Scott (d)

57709-1	Lawd, Lawd (band:v)	Victor V 38098
57710-1	In a Corner	
57711-1	Bright Boy Blues	Victor V 38117

57712-1	Springfield Stomp	Victor V 38117

1931
Sep 23   New York
Don Redman and his Orchestra
Bill Coleman, Henry "Red" Allen, Leonard Davis (t); Claude Jones, Fred Robinson, Benny Morton (tb); Edward Inge, Rupert Cole (cl, as); Don Redman (as, v, ldr, arr); Robert Carroll (ts); Horace Henderson (p, arr); Talcott Reeves (bj, g); Bob Ysaguirre (db, tuba); Manzie Johnson (d, vib); Lois Deppe (v)

E 37222-A	I Heard	Unissued
E 37223-A	Trouble, why pick on me? (LD:v)	Brunswick 6233
E 37224-A	Shakin' the African (DR:v)	Brunswick A 9250
E 37224-B	Shakin' the African (DR:v)	Brunswick E 01244
E 37225-A	Chant of the Weed	Brunswick 6211
E 37225-B	Chant of the Weed	Brunswick A 500160

1934
Nov 7   Camden, NJ
Fats Waller and his Rhythm
Bill Coleman (t); Gene Sedric (cl, as); Fats Waller (p, cel, org, v); Albert Casey (g); Billy Taylor (db); Harry Dial (d, vib)

84921-1	Honeysuckle Rose	Victor 24826
84922-1	Believe it Beloved	Victor 24808

84923-1	Dream Man	Victor 24801
84924-1	I'm growing fonder of you	
84925-1	If it isn't love	Victor 24808
84926-1	Breakin' the Ice	Victor 24826

1935
Jan 5   Camden, NJ
Fats Waller and his Rhythm
same personnel as session of 7 November 1934, except Charlie Turner (db) replaces Billy Taylor

87082-1	I'm a hundred percent for you	Victor 24863
87082-3	I'm a hundred percent for you (no v)	Victor 24867
87083-1	Baby Brown	Victor 24846
87083-3	Baby Brown (no v)	Victor 24867
87084-1	Night Wind	Victor 24853
87085-1	Because of once upon a time	Victor 24846
87086-1	I believe in miracles	Victor 24853
87087-1	You fit into the picture	Victor 24863

1935
Feb 26   New York
Teddy Hill and his Orchestra
Bill Coleman, Roy Eldridge (t); Bill Dillard (t, v); Dicky Wells (tb); Russell Procope (cl, as); Howard Johnson (as); Teddy Hill (ts, ldr); Chu Berry (ts); Sam Allen (p); John Smith (g); Richard Fullbright (db); Bill Beason (d)

16923-1	Here comes Cookie	Perfect 16093
16924-1	Got me doin' things (BD:v)	
16925-1	When the robin sings his song again	Perfect 16101
16926-1	When love knocks at your heart (BD:v)	

1935
Nov 25   Paris
Garnett Clark and his Hot Club's Four
Bill Coleman (t, v); George Johnson (as, cl); Garnett Clark (p); Django Reinhardt (g); June Cole (db)

OLA 730-1	Rosetta	Gramophone (F) K 7618
OLA 731-1	Stardust	Gramophone (F) K 7645
OLA 732-1	The Object of my Affection (BC:v)	Gramophone (F) K 7618

1936
Jan 24   Paris
Bill Coleman Trio
Bill Coleman (t); Herman Chittison (p); Eugène d'Hellemmes (db)

| 77624 | What's the Reason? | Ultraphone (F) AP 1235 |
| 77625 | Georgia on my Mind | |

1936
Jan 31   Paris
Bill Coleman Trio
same personnel as session of 24 January 1936

OLA 849-1	I'm in the mood for love*	Gramophone (F) 7764
OLA 849-2	I'm in the mood for love*	
OLA 850-1	After you've gone	
OLA 850-2	After you've gone	
	*omit Eugène d'Hellemmes	

1936
Jan 31   Paris
Bill Coleman et son Orchestre
Bill Coleman (t); Edgar Courance (cl, ts); Jean Ferrier (p); Oscar Alemán (g); Eugène d'Hellemmes (db); William Diemer (d)

OLA 851-1	Joe Louis Stomp	Gramophone (F) 7705
OLA 851-2	Joe Louis Stomp	
OLA 852-1	Coquette	
OLA 852-2	Coquette	

1936
Apr 17   Paris
Joan Warner (v) with Willie Lewis and his Orchestra
Bill Coleman, Bobby Martin (t); Billy Burns (tb); Willie Lewis (as, v, ldr); George Johnson (as); Joe Hayman (as, ts, bars); Frank "Big Boy" Goudie (ts); Herman Chittison (p); John Mitchell (g); Louis Vola (db); Ted Fields (d)

| CPT 2612-1 | Le Coo-coo-coo | Pathé (F) 888 |
| CPT 2613-1 | Magie de la danse | |

1936
Apr 28   Paris
Willie Lewis and his Orchestra
same personnel as 17 April 1936, except omit Joan Warner

| CPT 2630-1 | Stompin' at the Savoy | Pathé (F) 898 |
| CPT 2631-1 | Christopher Columbus | |

1936
May 15   Paris
Willie Lewis and his Orchestra
same personnel as 28 April 1936, except add Adelaide Hall, Alice Mann (v)

CPT 2649-1	I'm shooting high (AH:v)	Pathé (F) 914
CPT 2650-1	Lost (WL:v)	
CPT 2651-1	Alone (AM:v)	Pathé (F) 915
CPT 2652-1	Say you're mine (AH:v)	

1936
Oct 15   Paris
Willie Lewis and his Orchestra
same personnel as session of 28 April 1936, except Arthur Briggs (t) replaces Bobby Martin

CPT 2900-1	Au rythme du jazz, Part 1	Pathé (F) 1027
CPT 2901-1	Au rythme du jazz, Part 2	
CPT 2602-1	Sing, sing, sing	Pathé (F) 1029
CPT 2603-1	Knock, knock, who's there?	
CPT 2604-1	Sweet Sue	Pathé (F) 1030
CPT 2605-1	Organ Grinder's Song	

1937
Jul 7   Paris
Dicky Wells and his Orchestra
Bill Coleman, Bill Dillard, Shad Collins (t); Dicky Wells (tb, ldr); Django Reinhardt (g); Richard Fullbright (db); Bill Beason (d)

OLA 1884-1	Bugle Call Rag	Swing (F) 6
OLA 1885-1	Between the Devil and the Deep Blue Sea	
OLA 1886-1	I got rhythm	Swing (F) 27
OLA 1887-1	Sweet Sue*	Swing (F) 16
OLA 1888-1	Hangin' around Boudon (BC:v)*	
OLA 1889-1	Japanese Sandman*	Swing (F) 27
	*omit Bill Dillard and Shad Collins	

1937
Oct 4   Paris
Alix Combelle et son Orchestre
Bill Coleman (t, v); Alix Combelle (ts, cl, ldr); David Martin (p); Roger Chaput (g); Wilson Myers (db); Jerry Mengo (d)

OLA 1955-1	Exactly Like You	Swing (F) 52
OLA 1956-1	Alexander's Ragtime Band	Swing (F) 11
OLA 1957-1	Hangover Blues (BC:v)	
OLA 1958-1	Sometimes I'm happy	HMV (E) N-4451

1937
Oct 18   Paris
Willie Lewis and his Entertainers
Bill Coleman, Jacques Butler (t); Billy Burns (tb); Willie Lewis (as, cl, v, ldr); Joe Hayman (as, bars); Frank "Big Boy" Goudie (ts, p); John Mitchell (g); Wilson Myers (db); Ted Fields (d)

CPT 3474-1	Ol' Man River	Pathé (F) 1297
CPT 3475-1	Swing, brother, swing	Pathé (F) 1295
CPT 3476-1	Swing Time	
CPT 3477-1	Doin' the New Low Down	Pathé (F) 1296
CPT 3478-1	Swinging for a Swiss Miss	
CPT 3479-1	Basin Street Blues	Pathé (F) 1297

1937
Nov 12   Paris
Bill Coleman et son Orchestre
Bill Coleman (t); Stephane Grappelli (vn, p); Joseph Reinhardt (g); Wilson Myers (db); Ted Fields (d)

OLA 1974-1	Back home again in Indiana	Swing (F) 42
OLA 1975-1	Rose Room	Swing (F) 9
OLA 1976-1	Bill Street Blues	Swing (F) 22
OLA 1977-1	After you've gone	
OLA 1978-1	The merry-go-round broke down	Swing (F) 9

1937
Nov 19   Paris
Bill Coleman et son Orchestre
Bill Coleman (t, v); Christian Wagner (cl, as); Frank "Big Boy" Goudie (cl, ts); Emile Stern (p); Django Reinhardt (g); Lucien Simoens (db); Jerry Mengo (d)

OLA 1979-1	I ain't got nobody	Swing (F) 14
OLA 1980-1	Baby, won't you please come home	
OLA 1980-2	Baby, won't you please come home	Unissued
OLA 1981-1	Big Boy Blues	Swing (F) 32
OLA 1982-1	Swing Guitars	

1937
Nov 19   Paris
Bill Coleman with Django Reinhardt (g)

OLA 1983-1	Bill Coleman Blues	Swing (F) 42

1938
Jan 12   Paris
Alix Combelle et son Orchestre
[personnel uncertain:] Bill Coleman (t, v); Pierre Allier, Alix Rewail (t); unknown (tb); Alix Combelle (ts, ldr); Christian Wagner (cl, as); Frank "Big Boy" Goudie (ts, cl); unknown (p); Oscar Alemán (g); unknown (db); Tommy Benford (d)

Acetate	Daphné	TDF (I) 5010
Acetate	My Melancholy Baby	
Acetate	Alexander's Ragtime Band (BC:v)	
Acetate	Don't be that way	

1938
Apr 29   Hilversum
Bobby Martin's Orchestra
Bill Coleman, Jacques Butler (t); Bobby Martin (t, ldr); Billy Burns (tb); Glyn Paque (as); Ernest Purce (as, bars, arr); Johnny Russell (ts, cl); Ram Ramirez (p); Bobby McRae (g); Ernest "Bass" Hill (db); Kaiser Marshall (d)

Crazy Rhythm	Brunswick A 81578
Let's dance at the Make Believe Ballroom (band:v)	

1938
May 4   Hilversum
Willie Lewis and his Orchestra
same personnel as session of 18 October 1937

AM 482-1	The Maid's Night Off	Panachord (N) H 1037
AM 483-1	Who's sorry now?	
AM 484-1	Swinging at Chez Florence	Panachord (N) H 1038
AM 484-2	Swinging at Chez Florence	Panachord (N) H 2008
AM 485-3	Coquette (WL,BC,TF:v)	Panachord (N) H 1038
AM 486-2	Memphis Blues (WL,BC,TF:v)	Panachord (N) H 1036
AM 487-1	A Shanty in Old Shanty Town (BC:v)	
AM 487-2	A Shanty in Old Shanty Town (BC:v)	Panachord (N) H 2008

1938
June 13   Paris
Eddie Brunner and his Orchestra
Bill Coleman (t); Eddie Brunner (cl, ts, ldr); Alix Combelle, Noël Chiboust (ts); Herman Chittison (p); Oscar Alemán (g); Roger Grasset (db); Tommy Benford (d)

OSW 27-1	In a Little Spanish Town	Swing (F) 55
OSW 28-1	I double dare you	Swing (F) 30
OSW 29-1	Bagatelle	Swing (F) 41
OSW 30-1	Montmartre Blues	Swing (F) 30
OSW 31-1	Margie	Swing (F) 41

1938
June 13   Paris
Greta Keller (v)
Bill Coleman (t); Joe Hayman (cl); Herman Chittison (p); John Mitchell (g); Wilson Myers (db); Tommy Benford (d)

4453	Goodby to Summer (GK:v)	Brunswick A 81859
4454	I'm gonna lock my heart (GK, band:v)	

1938
Sep 28   Paris
Bill Coleman et son Orchestre
Bill Coleman (t); Edgar Courance (ts); John Mitchell (g); Wilson Myers (db, v); Tommy Benford (d)

OSW 43	Way Down in New Orleans	Swing (F) 214
OSW 44	Sister Kate (VM:v)	

1940
Apr 4   New York
Joe Marsala and his Delta Four
Bill Coleman (t, v); Joe Marsala (cl, ldr); Pete Brown (as); Carmen Mastren (g); Gene Traxler (db); Dell St John (v)

R 2796-2	Wandering Man Blues (DSJ:v)	General 1717
R 2797-3	Salty Mama Blues (BC:v)	
R 2798-2	Three O'Clock Jump (DSJ:v)	General 3001
R 2799-2	Reunion in Harlem	

1940
May 20   New York
Benny Carter and his Orchestra
Bill Coleman, Shad Collins, Russell Smith (t); Sandy Williams, Milton Robinson (tb); Benny Carter (as, cl, ldr, arr); Carl Frye, George Dorsey (as); Sammy Davis, Stafford Simon (ts); Sonny White (p); Ulysses Livingston (g); Hayes Alvis (db); Keg Purnell (d)

67781-A	Night Hop	Decca 3294
67782-A	Pom-pom	Decca 3262
67783-A	OK for Baby	Decca 3294
67784-A	Serenade to a Sarong	Decca 3262

1940
Oct 4   1940
Eddy Howard (v)
Bill Coleman (t); Benny Morton (tb); Edmond Hall (cl); Bud Freeman (ts); Teddy Wilson (p); Charlie Christian (g); Billy Taylor (db); Yank Porter (d)

28794-1	Old Fashioned Love	Columbia 35771
28795-1	Stardust	
28796-1	Exactly Like You	Columbia 35915
28797-1	Wrap your troubles in dreams	

1940
Oct 15   New York
Billie Holiday (v) and her Orchestra
Bill Coleman (t); Benny Morton (tb); Benny Carter (cl, as); George Auld (ts); Sonny White (p); Ulysses Livingston (g); Wilson Myers (db); Yank Porter (d)

28874-1	St Louis Blues	Okeh 6064
28874-2	St Louis Blues	
28875-1	Loveless Love	
28875-2	Loveless Love	*CBS KG 30782*

1940
Oct 15   New York
Benny Carter and his All-Star Orchestra
Bill Coleman (t); Benny Morton (tb); Benny Carter (cl, ldr); Sonny White (p); Ulysses Livingston (g); Wilson Myers (db); Yank Porter (d)

28876-1	Joe Turner Blues	Okeh 6001
28876-2	Joe Turner Blues	*Meritt 10*
28877-1	Beale Street Blues	Okeh 6001
28877-2	Beale Street Blues	*Meritt 10*

1940
Dec 6   New York
Chick Bullock (v) and his All-Star Orchestra
Bill Coleman (t); Benny Morton (tb); Edmond Hall (cl); Bud Freeman (ts); Teddy Wilson (p); Eddie Gibbs (g); Billy Taylor (db); Yank Porter (d)

29221-1	Smiles	Okeh 6013
29222-1	It had to be you	
29222-2	It had to be you	*Meritt 8*
29223-1	My Melancholy Baby	Okey 6261
29223-3	My Melancholy Baby	*Meritt 10*
29224-1	Back Home Again in Indiana	Okeh 6261

1940
Dec 9   New York
Teddy Wilson Orchestra
Bill Coleman (t); Benny Morton (tb); Jimmy Hamilton (cl); George James (bars); Teddy Wilson (p, ldr); Eddie Gibbs (g); Al Hall (db); Yank Porter (d); Helen Ward (v)

29233-1	I never knew	Columbia 35905
29234-1	Embraceable You	
29235-1	But Not for Me	Columbia 36084
29236-1	Lady be good	

1941
Feb 12   New York
Chick Bullock (v) and his All-Star Orchestra
Bill Coleman (t); Benny Morton (tb); Jimmy Hamilton (cl); George James (bars); Teddy Wilson (p); Eddie Gibbs (g); Al Hall (db); J.C. Heard (d)

29703-1	Dolores	Okeh 6123

29704-1	Amapola	Okeh 6100
29705-1	Oh! How I hate to get up in the morning	Okeh 6123
29706-1	There'll be some changes made	Okeh 6100

1943
Dec 8   New York
Coleman Hawkins and his Orchestra
Bill Coleman (t); Coleman Hawkins (ts); Andy Fitzgerald (cl); Ellis Larkins (p); Al Casey (g); Oscar Pettiford (db); Shelly Manne (d)

T 1905	Voodte	Signature 28101
T 1906	How deep is the ocean?	Signature 28102
T 1907	Hawkins Barrelhouse	Signature 28101
T 1908	Stumpy	Signature 28102

1943
Dec 21   New York
Dicky Wells and his Orchestra
Bill Coleman (t); Dicky Wells (tb); Lester Young (ts); Ellis Larkins (p); Freddie Green (g); Al Hall (db); Jo Jones (d)

T 19003-1	I got rhythm	Signature 90002
T 19004-1	I'm fer it too	
T 19004-2	I'm fer it too	*CM 3*
T 1919-1	Hello babe	Signature 28115
T 1919-2	Hello babe	*Be 74*
T 1920-1	Linger awhile	Signature 28115

1944
Mar 1   New York
Sammy Price and his Blusicians
Bill Coleman (t); Joe Eldridge (as); Ike Quebec (ts); Sammy Price (p, ldr); Oscar Pettiford (db); Harold "Doc" West (d)

N 1800-1	That's Kicks	*Circle 73*
N 1800-2	That's Kicks	
N 1800-3	That's Kicks (incomplete)	
N 1800-4	That's Kicks	
N 1801-1	Pluckin' That Thing (incomplete)	
N 1801-2	Pluckin' That Thing	Decca 48097
N 1801-3	Pluckin' That Thing	*Circle 73*
N 1802-1	A Boogie Woogie Notion	
N 1803-1	House Rent Boogie (false start)	
N 1803-2	House Rent Boogie	
N 1804-1	Big Joe (incomplete)	
N 1804-2	Big Joe (false start)	
N 1804-3	Big Joe	
N 1804-4	Big Joe	Decca 48097
N 1805-1	Boogin' A Plenty (false start)	*Circle 73*
N 1805-2	Boogin' A Plenty	
N 1806-1	Sweet Lorraine	
N 1807-1	Honeysuckle Rose (false start)	
N 1807-2	Honeysuckle Rose (incomplete)	
N 1807-3	Honeysuckle Rose (false start)	
N 1807-4	Honeysuckle Rose	

1944
Mar 28   New York
Kansas City Six
Bill Coleman (t); Dicky Wells (tb); Lester Young (ts); Joe Bushkin (p); John Simmons (db); Jo Jones (d)

A 3746	Three Little Words	*Commodore XFL 15352*
A 4746-1	Three Little Words	
A 4746-2'	Three Little Words	
A 4746-3	Three Little Words	Commodore 573
A 4747-1	Jo-Jo	Commodore 555
A 4747-2	Jo-Jo	*Commodore XFL 15352*

A 4747-3	Jo-Jo	
A 4747-4	Jo-Jo	
A 4748-1	I got rhythm	Commodore 555
A 4748-2	I got rhythm	*Commodore XFL 15352*
A 4748-3	I got rhythm	
A 4749-1	Four O'Clock Drag	
A 4749-2	Four O'Clock Drag	Commodore 573
A 4749-1/2	Four O'Clock Drag	
	(composite)	*Commodore XFL 15352*

1944
Aug 10   New York
Mary Lou Williams Trio
Bill Coleman (t); Mary Lou Williams (p); Al Hall (db)

Ma 710	Russian Lullaby	Asch 351-1
Ma 711 (in wax 7111)	Blue Skies	
Ma 712	Persian Rug	Asch 351-2
Ma 713 (in wax 711)	Night and Day	
Ma 714-1-2	You know baby (BC:v)	Asch 351-3
Ma 715	I found a new baby	

1944
Dec 11   New York
Mary Lou Williams and her Orchestra
Bill Coleman (t); Mary Lou Williams (p); Josh White (g, v); Jimmy Butts (db); Eddie Dougherty (d)

Ma 780	Minute Man	Asch 2001
Ma 784	Froggie Bottom	

1944
Dec 15   New York
Mary Lou Williams and her Orchestra
Bill Coleman (t); Coleman Hawkins (ts); Mary Lou Williams (p); Al Lucas (db); Jack Parker (d)

Ma 1237	Lady be good	Asch 552-3
Ma 1259	Carcinoma*	
Ma 1300	Song in my Soul†	Asch 1008
Ma 1301	This and That†	

   * omit Coleman Hawkins and Jack Parker
   † add Claude Green (cl), Joe Evans (as); Denzil Best
   (d) replaces Jack Parker

1945
Mar 30   Hollywood
The Capitol International Jazzmen
Bill Coleman (t); Buster Bailey (cl); Benny Carter (as); Coleman Hawkins (ts); Nat "King" Cole (p); Oscar Moore (g); John Kirby (db); Max Roach (d); Kay Starr (v)

559-3	You can depend on me	Capitol 283
600-1	If I could be with you (KS:v)	Capitol 10031
601-1	Stormy Weather (KS:v)	Capitol 283
602-1	Riffamarole	Capitol 10031

1945
Jun 9   New York
New York Town Hall Concert
Bill Coleman (t); Billy Taylor (p); Matty Chapin (db); Specs Powell (d)

Stardust		Commodore FL 2007

1945
Aug 5   Station WNEW, New York
Bill Coleman with Mary Lou Williams (p)
Bill Coleman (t); Mary Lou Williams (p); Al Hall (db); Specs Powell (d)

Sleep		*Jazz Panorama 11*

1945
Aug 12   Station WNEW, New York
Bill Coleman with Mary Lou Williams (p)
same personnel as session of 5 August 1945

Gjon Milli's Jam Session		*Jazz Panorama 11*

1947
Jan 9   New York
Sy Oliver and his Orchestra
Bill Coleman, Lamar Wright, Lyman Vunk, Skeets Reid (t); Dicky Wells, Henry Wells (tb, v); Gus Chappelle, Bill Granzow (tb); George Dorsey, Eddie Barefield (as); Fred Williams, Gale Curtis (ts); Willard Brown (bars); Billy Kyle (p); Aaron Smith (g); George Duvivier (db); Wallace Bishop (d); Sy Oliver (v, ldr, arr)

A Slow Burn		MGM 10004
Hey Daddy-O (SO, DW:v)		
For Dancers Only		Unissued
If you believe me (HW:v)		MGM 10255

1947
Mar 4   New York
Jimmy Jones Quintet
Bill Coleman (t); Otto Hardwick (as); Jimmy Jones (p); John Levy (db); Denzil Best (d)

105	Five O'Clock Drag	Wax 103

1947
Apr 1   New York
Sy Oliver and his Orchestra
Bill Coleman, Lamar Wright, Wallace Wilson, Frank Galbraith (t); Dicky Wells, Henry Wells (tb, v); Gus Chappelle, Fred Robinson (tb); George Dorsey, Eddie Barefield (as); Ernie Powell (ts); Willard Brown (bars); Buddy Weed (p); Aaron Smith (g); George Duvivier (db); Jimmy Crawford (d); Sy Oliver (v, ldr, arr)

I want to be loved (SO, HW:v)		MGM 10030
Lamar's Boogie		MGM 10133
25 Words or Less (SO:v)		Unissued
Walking the Dog		MGM 11092

1947
Apr 17   New York
Ben Webster Quintet
Bill Coleman (t); Ben Webster (ts); Jimmy Jones (p); Al Hall (db); Denzil Best (d)

112	As Long as I Live	Wax 104
113	All Alone*	
114	Blue Bells of Harlem	Wax 105

   * under the name of Denzil Best and his Orchestra.

1949
Jan 4   Paris
Bill Coleman–Don Byas Quintet
Bill Coleman (t); Don Byas (ts); Bernard Peiffer (p); Jean Bouchety (db); Roger Paraboschi (d)

8001	Just You, Just Me	Jazz Selection (F) 10001
8002	Bill's Brother's Blues	
8003	Idaho	Jazz Selection (F) 10002
8005	Bill Coleman Blues	Jazz Selection (F) 513

1949
Jan 5   Paris
Bill Coleman–Don Byas Quintet
same personnel as session of 4 January 1949

OSW 562-1	What is this thing called love?	Swing (F) 295
OSW 564-1	St Louis Blues	Swing (F) 302
OSW 565-1	Lover Man	

OSW 566-1 Liza Swing (F) 300
OSW 567-1 Blues at Noon Swing (F) 295

1949
May 14 Paris
Jam Session at the International Jazz Festival
Bill Coleman, Kenny Dorham, Aimé Barelli, "Hot Lips"
Page, Miles Davis (t); Russell "Big Chief" Moore (tb);
Hubert Rostaing (cl); Pierre Braslavsky, Sidney Bechet
(ss); Charlie Parker (as); James Moody, Don Byas (ts);
Hazy Osterwald (vib); Al Haig (p); Toots Thielemans
(g); Tommy Potter (db); Max Roach (d)
Farewell Blues *Charlie Parker 3*

1949
Oct 14 1949
Jack Dieval Quintet
Bill Coleman (t); Paul Vernon (ts); Jack Dieval (p);
Emmanuel Soudieux (db); Richie Frost (d)
OSW 603-1 I can't get started (BC:v) Swing (F) 320
OSW 604-1 Jumpin' in C Swing (F) 334
OSW 606-1 Tea for Two (BC:v) Swing (F) 351
OSW 607-1 Blue Skies
OSW 608-1 Don't blame me Swing (F) 320

1949
Oct 20 Paris
Sidney Bechet and his All-Star Band
Bill Coleman (t); Sidney Bechet (as); Frank "Big Boy"
Goudie (ts); Charlie Lewis (p); Pierre Michelot (db);
Kenny Clarke (d)
V 3023-1 Orphan Annie's Blues Vogue (F) 5017
V 3024-1 Happy-go-lucky Blues
V 3025-1 Klook's Blues Vogue (F) 5018

1949
Nov 21 Paris
Buck Clayton and his Orchestra
Bill Coleman, Buck Clayton, Merrill Stepter (t);
George Kennedy (as, bars); Alix Combelle, Armand
Conrad (ts); André Persiany (p); Georges Hadjo (db);
Wallace Bishop (d)
RJS 919 Uncle Buck Royal Jazz (F) 734
RJS 920-2 Buck Special Royal Jazz (F) 731
RJS 921 Night Life
RJS 922-2 Perdido Royal Jazz (F) 734
RJS 923-4 B.C. &•B.C.* Royal Jazz (F) 738
RJS 924 Sweet Georgia Brown†
  *omit Merrill Septer and saxes
  † omit saxes

c1951--2
Paris
Dom Garry et son Orchestre
Bill Coleman (t); Harry Perret (ts); Christian Chevalier
(p); Gabriel Deyrolle (db); Dom Garry (d)
8346 Moi j'ai gardé Lutecia (F) M 557
8347 Le marchand d'oiseaux
8348 Lester Leaps In . Lutecia (F) M 558
8349 Pennies from Heaven
8350 Ça marche Lutecia (F) M 559
8351 Telle que je suis

1951
Nov 9 Paris
Bill Coleman and his Orchestra
Bill Coleman (t, v); Bill Tamper (tb, arr); William
Boucaya (bars); Jay Cameron (as); Art Simmons (p);

Jean-Pierre Sasson (g); Guy de Fatto (db); Gerard
"Dave" Pochonet (d)
ACP 1665-1 Jumpin' at the Pleyel* Philips (F) 7203
ACP 1677-2 Si jolie Philips (F) 72044
ACP 1678-3 The blues jumped up and got me (BC:v)
  Philips (F) 72044
ACP 1679-1 I'm coming Virginia Philips (F) 72045
ACP 1681-1 Tenderly
ACP 1682-1 Come on a'my house Philips (F) 72043
  *omit Bill Tamper, Jay Cameron, William Boucaya,
  Art Simmons

1952
Oct 18 Paris
Bill Coleman and his Swing Stars
Bill Coleman (t, v); Dicky Wells (tb); Guy Lafitte (ts, cl);
Randy Downes (p); Buddy Banks (db); Zutty Singleton
(d)
  One O'Clock Jump Philips (F) N T6006 R
  Black & Blue
  Ghost of a Chance
  St James Infirmary Blues (BC:v)
  Out of Nowhere
  The Sheik of Araby
  Royal Garden Blues
  Knuckle Head Philips (F) N 76008 R
  Baby won't you please come home (BC:v)
  Solitude
  Red Top
  Drum Face
  Perdido (BC:v)
  When the Saints Go Marching in
ACP 2340 St Louis Blues, part 1 (BC:v) Philips (F) N
  72131 H
ACP 2341 St Louis Blues, part 2
ACP 2344 Drum Face Philips (F) N 70900 H
ACP 2346 Muskrat Ramble

1953
Oct 23 Paris
Bill Coleman and his Swing Stars
Bill Coleman (t, v); Bill Tamper (tb); Benny Waters (cl,
as, ss); Jack Starling (p); Edgar de Haas (db); Wallace
Bishop (d)
Royal Garden Blues *Pathé (F) ST 1047*
Mood Indigo
Lover
I surrender dear (BC:v)
Old Maid Blues (BC:v)
St. Louis Blues (BC:v)

1955
Dec 15 Paris
Bill Coleman and his Orchestra
Bill Coleman (t); Michel de Villers (as, bars); Guy
Lafitte (ts); André Persiany (p, arr); Paul Rovere (db);
Teddy Martin (d)
Them There Eyes (EP) Columbia (F) ESDF 1078
I've got my love to keep me warm
Wrap your troubles in dreams
Metro Jazz

1955
Dec 21 Paris
Bill Coleman and his Orchestra
same personnel as session of 15 December 1955, except
Bill Coleman (t, v)
If I had you (EP) Columbia (F) ESDF 1079
Yes sir that's my baby
Confessin' (BC:v)

1956
Mar 13   Paris
Bill Coleman and his Orchestra with Cecily Forde (v)
*Bill Coleman (t, v); Michel de Villers (as, bars); Guy
Lafitte (ts); André Persiany (p, arr); Paul Rovere (db);
Roger Paraboschi (d)*
St. Louis Blues   (EP) Columbia (F) ESDF 1100
Basin Street Blues (BC:v)
Lullaby of Birdland (CF:v)
Ding Dong Boogie (CF:v)

1956
May 24   Paris
Bill Coleman Plays the Blues
*Bill Coleman (t, v); Jean-Claude Pelletier (p); George
Duvivier (db, arr); Roger Paraboschi (d)*
Blues in my Heart   (EP) Columbia (F) ESDF 1119
I've got the right to sing the blues (BC:v)
Tin Roof Blues
Draggie Mama Blues (BC:v)

1956
Sep 12   Paris
Singing and Swinging with Bill Coleman and his Seven
*Bill Coleman (t, v); Fernand Verstraete (t); Charles
Verstraete (tb); Jay Hendrix, Guy Lafitte (ts); Armand
Migiani (bars); Jean-Claude Pelletier (p); George
Duvivier (db, arr); Roger Paraboschi (d)*
Reunion in Paris   *Columbia (F) FP 1093*
My Ideal
Dinah (BC:v)
Just a Gigolo (BC:v)
B & C Bounce
All Too Soon
Walking my Baby Back Home (BC:v)
Jump for Joy (BC:v)

1956
Dec 18   Paris
Album of Cities
*Bill Coleman (t, v); Jean-Claude Pelletier (p); George
Duvivier (db, arr); Christian Garros (d); strings of the
Paris Opéra*
April in Paris   *Columbia (F) FP 1096*
Basel in the Spring
Overheard in Stockholm
Autumn in New York
A Foggy Day in London Town (BC:v)
A Night in Rio
Chicago (BC:v)
The Golden Gate (San Francisco)

1957
Jul 27   Scheveningen
Kurhaus Dixieland Concert
*Bill Coleman (t, v); Jean François (t); Harry Kuypers
(cl); Cees Tanger (tb); Eric Krans (p); Koos van der
Hoeven (g, bj); Hank Wood (db); Louis de Lussanet (d)*
When the Saints Go Marching in
(BB, BBR:v)*   (EP) Columbia (E) SEGH 25
Back Home Again in Indiana
(BC:v)   (EP) Columbia (E) SEGH 29
St. James Infirmary Blues
(BC:v)   (EP) Columbia (E) SEGH 30
* add Albert Nicholas (cl); Beryl Bryden (v, wb);
"Big Bill" Ramsey (v)

1957
Nov 6   Yverdon
Swinging in Switzerland: Bill Coleman and the New
Orleans Wildcats

*Bill Coleman (t, v); Francis Bonjour (t); Fred de Coulon
(tb); Jean-Paul Augsberger (cl); Claude Joly (p); Alain
Dubois (bj); Arnold Hofmänner (db); Pierre Bouru (d)*
Back Home Again in Indiana (BC:v)   *Black & Blue (F)*
                                                  33.182
Blues in my Heart (BC:v)
Basin Street Blues (BC:v)
Limehouse Blues (BC:v)
I'm confessin' (BC:v)
N'embrassez pas ma femme (BC:v)
St. Louis Blues (BC:v)

1957
Nov 13   Zurich
Bill Coleman with the Tremble Kids
*Bill Coleman (t, v); Edi Jegge (tp); Werner Leibundgut
(tb); Werner Keller (cl); Jean-Pierre Bionda (p); Rolf
Cizmek (db); Charlie Antolini (d)*
Sugar (BC:v)   *Columbia (Sz) 102*
Sweet Georgia Brown
Pennies from Heaven (BC:v)
Somebody loves me
Some of these Days
If I had you
Blues for Lily*
Sweet Lorraine (BC:v)*
     * omit Edi Jegge, Werner Keller, Werner
     Leibundgut

1957
Nov 14   Paris
Brother John Sellers (v)
*Bill Coleman (t); Michel de Villers (as, bars); Guy
Lafitte (ts, ldr); Claude Gousset (tb); Georges Arvanitas
(p); Jean-Pierre Sasson (g); Pierre Sim (db); Christian
Garros (d)*
Morning Noon and Night   *Columbia (F) FPX 149*
You've been gone five years
Blue Suede Shoes
Miss Otis Regrets

1957
Nov 21   Paris
Brother John Sellers (v)
*same personnel as session of 14 November 1957, except
Paul Rovère (db) replaces Pierre Sim; add Ffouki Mes-
saoud (congas)*
Baby, How Long?   *Columbia (F) FPX 149*
I cried for you
Outskirts of Town
Let's rock and roll

1957
Nov 29   Paris
Brother John Sellers (v)
same personnel as session of 21 November 1957
Hands Off   *Columbia (F) FPX 149*
Woke up this Morning
I have the blues every day

1958
Bill Coleman Quartet
*Bill Coleman (t, v); Claude Bolling (p); Roland Lob-
ligeois (db); Kansas Fields (d)*
Back Home Again in Indiana (BC:v)   *Giants of Jazz (I)*
                                                  22
I've got rhythm*
     * with uncredited sax and trombone

1959
Jan 23   Paris
Boom Hec 1959: Bill Coleman presents Richard Bennett and his Dixie Cats
Bill Coleman (t, v); Jeff Mariette (tb); Stephane Guerault (cl); Patrick Joubert (p); Nino Ferrer (db); Richard Bennett (d)
Blues for Teddy   (EP) President (F) PRC 133
Jef and Stef
When the Saints Go Marching in
   (BC:v)

1960
Jan 21   Paris
From Boogie to Funk: Bill Coleman and his Orchestra
Bill Coleman (t); Quentin Jackson (tb); Budd Johnson (ts); Patti Bown (p); Les Spann (g); George "Buddy" Catlett (d); Joe Harris (d)
From Boogie to Funk   *Brunswick (F) 87905*
Bill, Budd and Butter
Afromotif in Blue*
Colemanology*
Have blues, will play'em*
   *omit Les Spann

1960
Oct 14   Paris
Bill Coleman
Bill Coleman (t); Maurice Vander (p); Jean Bouchety (db, arr); Roger Paraboschi (d); unknown musicians
Et vous avec ces beaux yeux (Hey you
   with the crazy eyes)   (EP) Polydor (F) 21753
Connais tu?
Ma petite symphonie (The One Finger
   Symphony)
Pardonne moi (I'm sorry)

1961
Jul Antibes Jazz Festival
Jam session with Count Basie Orchestra
Perdido   Broadcast
Sweet Georgia Brown

1966
Paris
Jazz pour Dieu: Bill Coleman
Bill Coleman (t, v); Georges Bence, Louis Laboucarie, Jean Baissat, Tony Russo, Jean Liesse (t); Charles Orieux, André Feraud, André Siot, François Guin (tb); Hubert Fol (as); Claude Lenissois (cl); Jef Gilson (org, arr); Gilbert Rovère, Jack Sewing (db); Gaetan Dupenher, Pierre Alain Dahan (d); Tshura, Jacques Degor (v); choir; Father Rozier (celebrant)
Jericho (BC:v)   *Unidisc (F) 30 145 M (A)*
Pax
Sometimes I feel . . . (T:v)   *Unidisc (F) 30 146 M (A)*
Agnus Dei

1967
Apr 27   London
Swingin' in London: Bill Coleman and Ben Webster
Bill Coleman (t, flh, v); Ben Webster (ts); Fred Hunt (p); Jim Douglas (g); Ron Rae (db); Lennie Hastings (d)
Bill Coleman   *Black Lion (E) 278.086*
But Not for Me*
Pound Horn
Sunday (BC:v)*
Satin Doll (BC:v)*
For Max
   *omit Ben Webster

1968
May 8, 9, 11   Paris
Bill Coleman Sings and Plays 12 Negro Spirituals
Bill Coleman (t, flh, v); Georges Bence, Louis Laboucarie (t); Christian Guizien, François Guin, Raymond Fonsèque, Charles Orieux (tb); Jean Charles Capon (cello); Eddy Louiss (org); Guy Pedersen (db); Lionel Magal (d); Jef Gilson (ldr, arr); vocal trio
Salvation   *Concert Hall (F) SJS 1269*
Swing Low, Sweet Chariot
Go Down Moses
We praise Thee O God
Dark was the night
O When the Saints
Old Time Religion
Sometimes I Feel . . .
Blow Ye the Trumpet
Down by the Riverside
Jericho
Nobody knows the trouble I've seen

1968
Dec 5   1968
Together at Last: Bill Coleman and Buddy Tate
Bill Coleman (t, flh, v); Buddy Tate (ts); Georges Arvanitas (p); Pierre Sim (db); Charles Bellonzi (d)
L 'n L Blues (Lily and
   Liza's Blues)   *EMI Pathé Marconi (F) CPTX 240 863*
Impulsive
Isn't it romantic?
Cute
Together at Last
Metro Jazz
Memories of You (BC:v)
Stompin' at the Savoy

1969
Jan 30–31   Paris
Three Generation Jam: Bill Coleman + Four
Bill Coleman (t); François Guin (tb); Michael Garrett (p); Jean-François Catoire (db); Art Taylor (d)
For Me and My Gal   *77 Records (E) SEU 12/34*
Satin Doll
Don't blame me
How High the Moon
If I had you
I ain't got nobody
I'm in the mood for love
Rosetta
Stairway to the Stars
I believe in miracles

1969
Oct 10   Ronnie Scott's Club, London
Jam session
Bill Coleman (t, flh); Charlie Shavers (t, v); Ruby Braff (t); Buddy Tate (ts); Albert Nicholas (cl); Jay McShann (p); Barney Kessel (g); Spike Heathey (db); Oliver Jackson (d)
Perdido   Broadcast
In a Mellow Tone
Please don't talk about me
Soon or Late Maybe
Indiana (CS:v)
Bye Bye Blackbird (CS:v)
Nature Boy (CS:v)
Body and Soul
Jumping at the Woodside

1971

Mar 7   Zurich
The New Ragtime Band meeting Bill Coleman, Mezz
Mezzrow, Albert Nicholas, Benny Waters
Bill Coleman (t, flh, v); Robert Antenen (t); Jacky Milliet (cl, ldr); Pierre Descoeudre (tb); Vino Montavon (p); Ted Milner (db); Bernard Moritz (bj, g); Peggy Moosman (d)
Summertime (BC:v)   *Evasion (F) EB 100–204*
Diga Diga Doo

1971

Apr 5, 29   Paris
Bill and the Boys: Bill Coleman and Raymond Fonsèque Original Band
Bill Coleman (t, flh); Marcel Bornstein (t); Raymond Fonsèque (tb, ldr, arr); Jacques Caroff (cl); Patrick Deroïde (bs); Philippe Baudoin (p); Jean-Paul Muriel (bj); Claude Pou (wb)
Tenderly Yours   *Concert Hall (F) SJS 1335*
Let me dream
I'm tipsy
Travelin' on a Cloud
Tomorrow is Sunday
Bill and the Boys
Memories of Old Days
Summernight's Dream
Looking Back
Feeling Fine

1971

Jun 4   Montmagny
Bill Coleman and the Original Band of Raymond
Fonsèque
same personnel as sessions of 5 and 29 April 1971, except add Bernard Grenier (bj)
When the Saints Go Marching in (BC:v)   *National (F) 16 169*
Hot Club Blues
Royal Garden Blues
St. James Infirmary Blues (BC:v)

1971

Sep 26   Taverny
Bill Coleman and the Original Band of Raymond
Fonsèque
same personnel as sessions of 5 and 29 April 1971, except Marc Renard (cl) replaces Jacques Caroff
After You've Gone (BC:v)   *National (F) 16 169*
Sweet Georgia Brown

1972

Dec 1, 2   Milan
Bill Coleman in Milan with Lino Patruno and his
Friends
Bill Coleman (t, flh, v); Gianni Acocella (tb); Sergio Rigon (ts, fl); Bruno Longhi (cl); Mario Rusca (p); Lino Patruno (g, ldr); Giancarlo Cinto (db); Giorgio Vanni (d)
Basin Street Blues (BC:v)*   *Durium (I) ms A 77313*
Honeysuckle Rose (BC:v)
I want a little girl (BC:v)*
Pennies from Heaven (BC:v)
I've found a new baby (BC:v)†
Perdido (BC:v)*†
    * add Lino Patruno (db)
    † add Paolo Tomelleri (ts)

1973

Jul 4   Montreux Jazz Festival
Mainstream at Montreux: Bill Coleman and Guy Lafitte
Bill Coleman (t, flh); Guy Lafitte (ts); Marc Hemmeler (p); Jack Sewing (db); Daniel Humair (d)
Blue Lou   *Black Lion (E) Fr-BLP 30.150-278.130*
Idaho
Sur les quais du vieux Paris
L and L Blues (Lily and Liza's Blues)
Tour de force
Montreux Jump

1973

Jul 4   Montreux Jazz Festival
Black Lion at Montreux
same personnel as preceding item
I want a little girl (BC:v) *Black Lion (E) Fr-BLP 30.148*
I know that you know

1973

Nov 15–16   Paris
Paris 1973: Bill Coleman
Bill Coleman (t, flh); Vincent Casino, Louis Vezant, Georges Gay, Pierre Selin (t); François Lussier, Emile Vilain, Benny Vasseur, Charles Verstraete (tb); Pierre Gossez, Georges Grenu, Jean Aldegon, Joseph Hrasko, Georges Bessière (saxes); Guy Boyer, Jacques Lalue, Alain Fougeret (p, vib); François Le Maguer, Pierre Cullaz (g); Alphonse Masselier, Pierre Sim (db); J.M. Hauser, André Arpino (d); strings; Jerry Mengo (ldr, arr)
Blowing for the Cats   *Music For Pleasure (F) 2M056-64822*
One Room Flat
Twenty Turtles on a Tree
Eve's Apple
Serenade for Two
Saucy Suzy
Gentle Storm
Blues is how you feel
Take a trip to the stars
Blow them Sounds
Sweet Lily of Mine
Jumping on the Moon

1973

Dec 3–4   Paris
Stephane Grappelli Quintet featuring Bill Coleman
Bill Coleman (t, flh); Stephane Grappelli (vn); Marc Hemmeler (p); Guy Pedersen (db); Daniel Humair (d)
I got the world on a string *Festival (F) 100.122 A, vol. 155*
St. Louis Blues
Ain't she sweet?
Moonlight in Vermont
It don't mean a thing . . .
Stardust
Where or When
It's Wonderful
Chicago

1974

Jul 15   Nice
Tribute to Louis Armstrong
Bill Coleman, "Wild Bill" Davison, Wallace Davenport (t); Vic Dickenson (tb); Barney Bigard (cl); Budd Johnson (ts); George Wein (p); Arvell Shaw (db); Cozy Cole (d)
Confessin'   *RCA (F) FX 417 159*
All of Me

1975
Jan 26   Paris
Hommage à Hugues Panassié
Bill Coleman (t, flh); Gilbert Rost (t); Raymond Fonsèque (tb); Olivier Franc (ss); Jean Poinsot (cl); Philippe Baudoin (p); Ricardo Galleazzi (db); Claude Alain Du Parquet (d)
Please don't talk to me   *Flamme (F) 1003*
Sugar

1976
Jun 13   Geneva
Bill Coleman and Ed Hubble Meeting the New Ragtime Band
Bill Coleman (t, flh, v); Robert Antenen (t); Jacky Milliet (cl, ldr); Pierre Descoeudres (tb); Vino Mantavon (p); Bernard Moritz (bj); Hans Schläpfer (db); Rolf Sydler (d)
Down by the Riverside (BC:v)   *Evasion (F)*
                                          EB.100.224-A
Blue Turning Grey over You (BC:v)
Sweet Georgia Brown (BC:v)
That's a Plenty

1978
May 7   Paris
Bill Coleman and Raymond Fonsèque Jazz Group
Bill Coleman (t, flh); Raymond Fonsèque (tb); Olivier Franc (ss); Daniel Huck (as); "Dan" Girard (bj); Alain Huguet (db, bs); Claude Pou (wb)
Caravan   Private tape
Petite fleur
Whoopee, you're mine
Don't worry Lily

That's where I left my heart
Sunny Side Up
Mister Bill and Doctor Ray
Bla-Bla
That's all folks

1979
Mar 21–2   Caveau de l'Huchette, Paris
Cave's Blues: Bill Coleman Meets Dany Doriz
Bill Coleman (t, flh, v); Rolf Buhrer (tb); Dany Doriz (vib, ldr); Patrice Authier (p); Henri Tischitz (db); Michel Denis (d)
Goody Goody (BC:v)   *Jazzmosphere (F) 79.03*
Cave's Blues (BC:v)
Bye Bye Blackbird (BC:v)
Cheek to Cheek (BC:v)
Lover Man (BC:v)
In a Mellotone

1980
May 15   Toulouse
Really I Do: Bill Coleman, featuring Guy Lafitte
Bill Coleman (t, flh, v); Guy Lafitte (ts); Red Richards (p); Bill Pemberton (db); Panama Francis (d)
Crazy Rhythm   *Black & Blue (F) 33.162*
You've changed (BC:v)
Tinto Time
On the Trail
Hello Babe
Really I Do
She's Funny that Way (BC:v)
I've got my love to keep me warm
Montreux Jump

The film appearances of Bill Coleman

Bill Coleman – From Boogie to Funk, France, 1961, with Michel Attenoux (as), Raymond Fonsèque (tb), André Persiany (p), Paul Rovère (b), René Thomas (g), Charles Saudrais (drs). Narration by Sim Coppans

Festival de Jazz From Comblain la Tour, Belgium, 1960, The Roman New Orleans Jazz Band with Bill Coleman (tp), Chet Baker (tp), Kenny Clarke (drs)

London, BBC at Ronnie Scott, London, 1969. Film with Bill Coleman, Albert Nicholas, Buddy Tate, Charlie Shavers, Jay McShann, etc.

La Putain Respectueuse (from J. P. Sartre), Paris, 1952, with Aaron Bridgers (p), Jo Benjamin (b), Jim Clark (drs), Bill Coleman (tp), Jimmy "Lover Man" Davis (vo) one number

First European Jazz Festival, France, 1954

Printemps á Paris, Paris, 1956, with Philippe Nicot and Dany Carrel. Some numbers with Bill Coleman with Maxim Saury's band

VIDEOS

Bill Coleman at the Parc Floral in Vincennes, Paris, 1972, with Marc Hemmeler (p), Pierre Sim (b), Jimmy Gourley (g), Michael Silva (drs). Interview with André Francis from France Inter (in French)

Montreux Jazz Festival, Montreux, 1973, with Bill Coleman (tp, fh, vo), Guy Lafitte (ts), Marc Hemmeler (p), Jack Sewing (b), Daniel Humair (drs)

Bienvenue á Duke Ellington (Guy Beart televised programme), Paris, 1973, with Duke Ellington, Bill Coleman (tp, fh, vo), Guy Lafitte (ts), Aaron Bridgers (p), Michel Gaudry (b), Daniel Humair (drs), Cecily Forde (vo) and others

Index